D0150974

SPORT BUSINESS MANAGEMENT

· · ·

Lori K. Miller, EdD, MBA

Director, Sport Administration Program
Wichita State University
Wichita, Kansas

DISCARDED
~~UNIVERSITY OF TULSA LIBRARY~~

AN ASPEN PUBLICATION®
Aspen Publishers, Inc.
Gaithersburg, Maryland
1997

UNIVERSITY OF TULSA-McFARLIN LIBRARY

Library of Congress Cataloging-in-Publication Data

Miller, Lori K.
Sport business management/Lori K. Miller.
p.   cm.
Includes bibliographical references and index.
ISBN 0-8342-0942-X
1. Sports administration.   2. Sports—Finance.   I. Title.
GV713.M55   1997
796´.06´9—dc21
97-7553
CIP

Copyright © 1997 by Aspen Publishers, Inc.
All rights reserved

Aspen Publishers, Inc., grants permission for photocopying for limited personal or internal use.
This consent does not extend to other kinds of copying, such as copying for general distribution,
for advertising or promotional purposes, for creating new collective works, or for resale.
For information, address Aspen Publishers, Inc., Permissions Department,
200 Orchard Ridge Drive, Suite 200, Gaithersburg, Maryland 20878

Orders: (800) 638-8437
Customer Service: (800) 234-1660

About Aspen Publishers ⒈ For more than 35 years, Aspen has been a leading professional
publisher in a variety of disciplines. Aspen's vast information resources are available in both
print and electronic formats. We are committed to providing the highest quality information
available in the most appropriate format for our customers. Visit Aspen's Internet site for more
information resources, directories, articles, and a searchable version of Aspen's full catalog,
including the most recent publications: **http://www.aspenpub.com**
Aspen Publisher, Inc. ⒈The hallmark of quality in publishing
Member of the worldwide Wolters Kluwer group.

Editorial Resources: David A. Uffelman
Library of Congress Catalog Card Number: 97-7553
ISBN: 0-8342-0942-X

DISCARDED

Printed in the United States of America

1   2   3   4   5

ᴺᵛ713
ᴹ55
997

Table of Contents

Foreword

In the past few years, I have participated in several conferences for people seeking careers in the sport industry. Typically about 250 attendees—many of them young account executives, attorneys, and accountants—pay good money to hear speakers like me tell them how difficult it is to break in this field.

What is the best path to a successful career? At one of these conferences a keynote speaker, a well-known National Basketball Association executive, hit the mark when he insisted that sport management was "not rocket science" but *was* a profession requiring an appropriate education. On the other hand, just what kind of education is "appropriate"?

There are many answers to this question; they vary with the individual. At the same time, they all contain certain elements, such as solid grounding in business and legal theory (especially as it applies to sports), excellent communication skills, and practical experience in the industry. This sounds like a simple enough recipe. Simple enough that during the last 20 years, some 200 undergraduate and graduate programs, claiming to offer professional preparation in sport management, have developed in America alone.

Surprisingly, there are not many books on the market that dig into the fundamental questions about managing a business in the sport industry, despite vast public interest and awareness of the staggering growth of the sports marketplace. Phil Knight started Nike with a small investment and lots of hustle; he is now a billionaire. Minor league baseball franchises have appreciated geometrically in the last decade. Ten years ago, few people had ever heard of a Rollerblade. Now, they are everywhere.

Yet still, sport management lacks its own Peter Drucker—someone pulling together evidence into a primer that is at once both academic and practical, accessible and challenging. Lori Miller's *Sport Business Management* fills this void. She skillfully weaves a narrative that will be as valuable in a front office as in a classroom. Her topics cover the most fundamental issues facing any business—planning, organizing, staffing, controlling—but she clearly addresses the special nature of the sport industry with detailed examples. Need to know what the Americans with Disabilities Act means to your new stadium? Miller has it all laid out. What about site selection for a new sporting goods store? Read chapter 9. Customer service for a roller rink? See chapter 12.

Miller and her book combine the very best ingredients for success in the sport professions: solid grounding in business and legal theory, linked with practical experience and magnified by excellent communication skills. We are fortunate to have them both.

Stephen Hardy, PhD
Professor and Coordinator
Sport Studies Program
University of New Hampshire
Durham, New Hampshire

Acknowledgments

There are many people who have contributed to the creation of this text. I would like to recognize those members of the Society for the Study of Sport and Legal Aspects (SSLASPA), including Gary Gray, Sam Adams, Betty van der Smissen, Jim Conn, John Dorowsky, Tom Sawyer, and Doyice Cotten. The support and encouragement that they provided during the early years of my career and that they continue to provide mean more than they will ever realize. I never would have had the confidence necessary to succeed as a researcher and teacher without their continued mentorship.

I would also like to thank my dear friend, Dr. Larry Fielding. Larry is a true scholar. It was from his example that I learned what research is all about and how it should be performed. He taught me to think critically. Larry continues to applaud my efforts and support my endeavors. Thanks, Larry, for always being in my corner.

Additionally, I would like to thank the faculty in the Department of Health and Physical Education (HPE) at Wichita State University (WSU), particularly Dr. Susan Kovar. She is an ideal chairperson and illustrates exemplary management and administrative skills. She is a faculty advocate, encouraging, eager to assist, a good listener, and provides resources necessary for faculty to succeed. Through her efforts and the congenial nature of the rest of the HPE faculty, WSU has provided me with a very comfortable and supportive work environment for which I am grateful. In addition to the HPE faculty, special recognition should go to Mr. Shawn Reed. A graduate teaching and research assistant in the Department of HPE, Shawn is currently completing his MEd in Sport Administration. Shawn designed the tables and graphs contained in this text. He spent many hours assisting me in my efforts to accumulate the needed research. He was always eager and willing to serve and always displayed an amiable and cooperative attitude. Without Shawn's assistance, this book would not have come to fruition in the time span it did. I thank you, Mr. Shawn Reed.

Also, I thank my mom and dad. My dad, a smart and talented dentist and businessman, taught me the importance of a work ethic while my mom, a wonderful person with a soft heart, taught me sensitivity regarding the feelings of other people. Their combined support and encouragement guided me through years of graduate school. Again, thanks!

Last, but not least, I send a warm hug to my precious Brookie, who endured many long days by herself yet was always there when I'd come home, with a happy face, a cold nose, and an unfaltering spirit.

CHAPTER 1

Sport Industry Analysis

Eager entrepreneurs with a love of sport frequently desire to own and manage a sport business. Career opportunities in sport remain very appealing. The economy is in good shape. Low unemployment rates convey that consumers are earning income and likely have discretionary monies to spend in the sport industry. Low interest rates convey that entrepreneurs are more willing to encounter debt needed for sport business investments. Individual health and fitness levels remain a primary concern of most every American. Professional and minor league teams continue both to develop and expand. Flexible work weeks enable consumers to enjoy long weekends of recreational and sporting activities. Further, "Generation Xers" are introducing a whole new realm of sport and recreational pursuits that can be capitalized on by keen sport entrepreneurs. As estimated by Jensen (1995), approximately 21% of an individual's day is "free" and open for the pursuit of sport and recreation. The Department of Commerce reports that spending on leisure and related pursuits will exceed $400 billion annually (Jensen, 1995). It is estimated that by the year 2000, America's Gross National Sport Product (GNSP) will have increased 141% (Parkhouse, 1996). The GNSP represents the amount society has spent on sport and leisure goods and services, which can also be derived by adding together all the incomes "accruing from the production of sport and leisure goods and services" (Berrett, 1996, p. 329). As explained by Jensen (1995, p. 145), " . . . approximately $1 of every $8 earned in this country is spent for leisure activities—a larger share than for housing construction or even national defense." The sport industry clearly is an attractive market.

Entrepreneurial success, however, can be greatly enhanced by conducting thorough analysis of the industry segment in which one plans to compete. Michael Porter's industry analysis model provides much insight into the viability of any particular industry, including the sport industry (Porter, 1980, 1985). An understanding of Porter's model enables the sport business entrepreneur to develop a successful competitive strategy that contends with both internal and external forces. Porter's model highlights five competitive forces: (1) intensity of rivalry among existing firms, (2) threat of entry, (3) buyer's power, (4) supplier's power, and (5) substitutability. This chapter elaborates on each of the competitive forces and how they influence a sport business.

INTENSITY OF RIVALRY AMONG COMPETITORS

Competition can be both good and bad. Good competition can bolster the success and viability of individual firms and the larger sport industry segment. On the other hand, hostile (e.g., bad or "intense") competition can devastate both individual firms and the industry at large.

Benefits of Competition

Sport businesses competing in the same industry benefit stakeholders for four reasons. First, competition assures better product quality. For example, assume that ABC Bowling Alley is the only bowling alley in Small Town, U.S.A. For decades, ABC Bowling Alley captured the market share of Small Town, U.S.A., residents even though the bowling alley was frequently understaffed, had limited ball selection, and had poorly maintained facilities. However, Forbes Manufacturing Company recently located in Small Town, U.S.A., and provided jobs for an additional 10,000 people. The population of Small Town, U.S.A., expanded. Last year, an eager entrepreneur opened up a competing bowling alley. Facilities were new, staff was adequate, ball and shoe selection were superior, and customer service was exceptional. In order to maintain operations, ABC Bowling Alley would have little choice but to renovate the facility, hire additional staff, and order additional inventory. In the end, consumers benefit via a better product. Competition breeds the same product improvement in other sport industries as well. For example, competition within the athletic footwear industry mandates that Nike, Reebok, and Adidas continue investing in research and development as a way continually to offer new and improved products to the consumer.

Second, competition bolsters demand for the entire industry via the marketing and promotional efforts of individual sport businesses. This is seen quite frequently in nonsport-related industries including the meat and dairy industries. For example, one may come across an advertisement for XYZ Health Club. The individual may not be interested in joining XYZ Health Club for a variety of reasons, including location or price structure. However, the promotion may communicate a general "fitness" message to the individual viewer. Although the individual may not join the advertised club, he or she may join another more accessible club. The entire industry benefits from one competitor's message regarding the value associated with a particular sport product. The soccer advertisement appearing in The Wichita Eagle (Figure 1–1) illustrates the way in which a competitor's advertisement can promote an entire industry (i.e., soccer).

Third, competing businesses provide consumers with assurance about a product's viability and, similar to the above, enhance participation in the sport industry segment itself. Let's assume that an individual had a negative experience with sport or physical activity at an early age. Memories of this distasteful experience have remained throughout adult life. Regardless, the individual is contemplating joining a health club. The existence of eight health clubs in the surrounding area may convey to the individual that exercise "can't be all that bad" and may encourage him or her to purchase a membership. Little league football is another illustration of how competition can enhance product demand. Parents, reluctant to enroll a child in football camps due to safety concerns, for example, may find solace in seeing a number of different camp operations. Competition may lead the parent to conclude that the sport must be "okay," as competition would not exist if children-participants were exposed to extreme risk and injuries.

Fourth, competition places a ceiling on prices. From a societal perspective, this is advantageous as it enables the individual consumer to spend more on a variety of discretionary items.

Competition and Related Hostilities

On the other hand, competition can lead to intense rivalry that threatens industry profitability and the survival of individual firms. Industry profitability suffers when competitors engage in unfair trade practices, such as price cutting, false advertising, and contract infringement. Most readers are familiar with frequent price wars among firms in, for example, the airline industry. Most are also familiar with the bankruptcies and financial difficulties resulting from these battles. Sport businesses, engaged in intense rivalry, subject themselves to similar, dismal conditions.

Reference to the sporting goods retail industry illustrates the problem of hostile competition. Let's assume that ABC Sporting Goods Store competes in an area where there are three other sporting goods stores in a 20-minute radius. ABC Sporting Goods decides to lower prices below market value in an attempt to boost market share and profits. ABC's competitors react by lowering their own prices in an attempt to maintain market share. In this "act and react" situation, all stores realize lower profit margins. Each store remains reluctant to raise prices for fear of an even greater loss of profitability and related market share. The hardship placed on each individual store, and the resultant difficulties in paying rent, ordering inventory, servicing the customer, and providing staff benefits are obvious. Often, the cycle can be magnified if ABC Sporting Goods, for example, again lowers

Figure 1–1 Example of How a Competitor's Advertisement Can Promote an Entire Industry.
Source: Reprinted with permission from AYSO, Wichita, Kansas.

prices in an attempt to gain volume sales and generate enough revenues to cover operating expenses. According to Porter (1980, p. 17),

> Rivalry occurs because one or more competitors either feels the pressure or sees the opportunity to improve position. In most industries, competitive moves by one firm have noticeable effects on its competitors and thus may incite retaliation or efforts to counter the move; . . . This pattern of action and reaction may or may not leave the initiating firm and the industry as a whole better off. If moves and countermoves escalate, then all firms in the industry may suffer and be worse off than before.

The same devastating cycle can occur with duplicated service provisions and marketing tactics. For example, once one sport business decides to offer "special" services in an attempt to gain market share, other competitors may quickly follow. The end result is an increased cost structure, lower profitability, and little (if any) gain in market share. The "imitation" by competitors (reflected in pricing, product, marketing, and service offerings) in an attempt to gain market share intensifies rivalry. Porter (1980) explains a number of different factors that precipitate intense competitor rivalry. Six of these factors are described below.

Slow Industry Growth

During periods of slow industry growth, such as the maturity stage of the product life cycle, firms have a more difficult time competing among existing competitors. (See Levitt, 1986, for an excellent review of the product life cycle and its related concepts and importance.) Sales have declined or plateaued while expenses continue to increase (e.g., inflation, increases in minimum wage). Slow industry growth reflects a time period in which demand for the original sport product has matured. In other words, all those willing and able to purchase a particular sport product have probably done so by now. Under these circumstances, revenues and market share are captured by the sport business that can afford needed renovations, product expansions, personnel training, and customer service enhancements. Unfortunately, either due to limited capital, an unwillingness to encounter risk, or a lack of business acumen, sport business managers may resort to price reductions, false advertisements, or competitor disparagement as a way to maintain or build market share.

Sport managers considering entry into a sport business experiencing slow industry growth must differentiate the product offering from existing competitors or offer a "revised" product needed or valued by the consumer. For example, the aerobic dance industry would likely be defunct if entrepreneurs had not introduced step aerobics, slide aerobics, and the like. Similarly, Nike and Reebok would have become stagnant and unprofitable if they had not continued to improve their product, fashion new marketing campaigns, and so forth. Entrepreneurs who "plan for obsolescence" prevent the onset of the product deterioration, lost market share, and hostile competition by continually researching what the consumer might want or need (real or perceived) "next."

Numerous or Equally Balanced Competitors

It is easier to compete in an industry where there are "leaders" and "followers." For example, in the sport marketing industry, major competitors include both International Management Group and Events Marketing Group, International. However, a walk through the yellow pages illustrates the multitude of smaller sport marketing companies. These smaller sport marketing companies are not on the same "playing field" as the larger ones. A large sport marketing company, for example, may focus on the representation of elite athletes (e.g., Tiger Woods, Andre Agassi), whereas a smaller sport marketing company may strive to secure sponsorship monies for local triathalons and fun runs. The sport marketing companies target different markets by providing differentiated services. As a result, competitive practices remain "friendly" because the companies do not attempt to thwart each other's success via contractual interference or other unfair trade practices. In comparison, 10 different local health clubs, each having a market share percentage within 5 to 7 points of each other, continually strive for market leadership. Price cutting, false advertising, and competitor disparagement provide a very difficult competitive environment.

High Fixed or Storage Costs

High fixed costs and/or storage costs intensify competitor rivalry among sport businesses. Golf courses, ski resorts, water parks, and well-equipped health clubs all represent sport businesses with high fixed costs. Sporting goods manufacturing companies and retail establishments represent sport businesses with high storage costs. High fixed costs can devastate a golf course, for example, as a "fixed" amount must be paid on a "fixed," or routine schedule regardless of how many memberships or green fees are sold. Rent, administrative salaries, overhead, maintenance equipment leases, and other notes payable are fixed costs that must be paid regardless of whether a golf club manager, for example, has 1 member or 1,000 members.

Competing in an industry with high fixed costs places pressure on a sport manager to generate a minimum level of sales to cover fixed expenses. Low demand, based on a number of reasons, including bad weather, changing trends, competition, or product inferiority, may force a manager to employ hostile competitive tactics that will boost short-term revenue and provide enough money to cover fixed expenses. Price wars, false advertising, and competitor disparagement are often viewed as ways in which immediate revenues can be generated. Cost monitoring, cost reduction tactics, and maximizing sales efforts during times of peak sales reduce hardships associated with high fixed costs.

Sport businesses with high storage costs are in a similar predicament. Sporting goods retail stores illustrate the difficulties encountered when competing in an industry with high storage costs. Storage generates expense in at least four primary ways. First, the storage space is not being used to generate any income, although rent monies are still expended. Second, stored products create opportunities for pilferage. Third, stored products risk obsolescence. What is in demand in one season may not be in demand the next due to changing consumer trends, changing league standards, and manufactured product alterations or new product developments. Fourth, storage creates additional expense associated with personnel as employees are required to move, maintain, and retrieve stored products. Businesses often find it more cost effective to reduce the price of inventory during "end of season close-outs" or promotions than to pay the price associated with storage. Unfortunately, competing businesses tend to adopt a similar strategy. The ensuing "discount" wars lower product margins for all competing sport businesses and intensify the nature of competition.

Lack of Differentiation

Competing in a homogeneous industry creates challenges for the sport business manager. Porter (1980, p. 19) aptly explains the difficulties sport managers encounter: "Where the product or service is perceived as a commodity or near commodity, choice by the buyer is largely based on price and service, and pressures for intense price and service competition result. These forms of competition are particularly volatile, . . ." The tennis industry could be viewed as a rather homogeneous industry. Each facility has similar product offerings, including indoor and outdoor courts, leagues, clinics, individual lessons, youth programs, a pro shop, professional staff, locker rooms, and day care. Competition can be intense as consumers, possessing limited discretionary income, often choose to patronize that facility offering the lowest prices or perceived as providing the consumer with the "best deal." As mentioned earlier, the ensuing price wars can devastate an entire industry as net income eventually drops below break-even levels. Prudent sport businesses must find some source of differentiation valued by the consumer and effectively market that source of differentiation. Tennis facilities, for example, can gain market share in a rather homogeneous industry via better courts, a safer facility, and/or the employment of superior teaching and coaching professionals.

Economies of Scale

Competition is intensified when a few (or even one) sport businesses realize the benefits associated with economies of scale. Economies of scale refers to the concept that savings per unit are incurred as volume produced or purchased increases. For example, let's assume ABC Athletic Club owns three facilities within a 50-mile radius. Three additional health clubs (separate ownership) compete within the same geographical area as ABC Athletic Club, each with 10,000 members. Each entrepreneur spends $100,000 annually on advertising to the target market residing within that 100-mile area. Let's also assume that each ABC Athletic Club has 10,000 members. The owner/manager of ABC Athletic Club operates with a lower cost structure and spends only one third ($33,000/health club) on marketing as do competitors. Specifically, the owner of ABC Athletic Club spent only $3 on marketing for each membership sold, whereas the individually owned clubs are spending $10 on marketing for each membership sold. The lower cost structure places ABCs at a competitive advantage because the owner can offer lower prices for a similar quality product or price the product comparable to the competition and use the extra margin generated to enhance facility, staff, or product offerings. Economies of scale can be realized in any facet of a sport business, including research and development, manufacturing, marketing, sales, and service.

A 1996 article appearing in *The Wall Street Journal* (Ricklefs) illustrates the devastation that can occur as a result of economies of scale. Ricklefs (1996) elaborates on the declining number of soccer stores. In the Cincinnati area, for example, four soccer stores closed since April 1995. Similarly, Lynn Berling-Manuel, publisher of *Soccer America* magazine, estimates that fewer than 200 soccer stores are operating above break-even levels (Ricklefs, 1996). The bleak future of small soccer stores is attributed to the economies of scale realized by sporting goods "megastore" chains and catalog sales. As explained by one soccer entrepreneur, "At small stores, . . . their mentality is to have every soccer product available" (Ricklefs, 1996, p. B2). Ricklefs (1996, p. B2) further elaborates, "Thus they order each item in such small quantities that they can't get favorable prices—even though the products are essentially the same. . . . The entrepreneur says that larger orders often let the company get merchandise at prices 8% to 12% lower than small operators must pay." Competition is intensified when large-scale competitors, selling homogeneous industry products, are able to pass on cost savings to the end consumer.

High Exit Barriers

The term *exit barriers* refers to the difficulty individual firms encounter when deciding whether or not to sell a business. A sport business experiencing low market share and revenues falling below break-even levels may decide to adopt a harvest strategy, which focuses on the generation of immediate revenues with little consequence for long-term implications; compete; and display little concern regarding how individual firm activities influence the larger sport industry. Although the market share of a sport business may be minimal, the fledgling company represents a concern to competitors, as it still provides capacity in an often saturated industry. As explained by Porter (1980), " . . . companies that lose the competitive battle do not give up. Rather, they grimly hang on and, because of their weakness, have to resort to extreme tactics. The profitability of the entire industry can be persistently low as a result" (p. 21). Companies with high exit barriers tend to intensify rivalry by engaging in often disfavored tactics that can generate immediate revenues (e.g., price fixing, disparaging advertising).

Three different types of exit barriers are (1) financial, (2) emotional, and (3) strategic. *Financial exit barriers* exist when a sport business prolongs exiting the industry due to the inability to recoup its investment in equipment, land, or other fixed or specialized assets. A sport business manager may conclude that it is better to lose $1,000 a month for an indefinite time period versus a $500,000 loss in land that depreciated in value due to urban blight. Rather, a sport business manager may decide to adopt a harvest strategy and hope the land eventually appreciates in value. Other managers may stay in a losing business to lower their tax liabilities by generating negative income, which can be written off against other profitable ventures. *Emotional exit barriers* are more intangible in nature. Sport business managers employing local people may have real reservations about leaving members of their community unemployed. Further, the emotional attachment generated by years of hard work, accompanied by a pride of ownership, may also discourage exit from a particular sport industry. Many professional sport franchise owners exhibit a combination of financial and emotional exit barriers. From an emotional perspective, many professional sport franchise owners find a great deal of stature in ownership and would not forego the associated prestige regardless of bottom-line figures. *Strategic exit barriers* exist when a sport business remains in an industry due to, for example, heritage. For example, Hillerich & Bradsby (H&B) lose a great deal of money from the manufacture of wood baseball bats. However, it would not be prudent for H&B to cease operations in this area, as the wood baseball bat was the first bat manufactured by this company. Further, the wood baseball bat provides great publicity via the minor and major professional baseball leagues. A sport business manager competing in an industry with high exit barriers must match the strengths (if any) of the fledgling company. Maintenance of a quality product may offset inducements offered by the competing company close to extinction.

THREAT OF ENTRY

The ease with which competitors (or new entrants) can enter an industry represents a critical issue to strategic planning and monitoring. New entrants pose problems for the sport business for four primary reasons. First, a new entrant adds another source of competition that can potentially draw market share from existing competitors. Second, new entrants may saturate a market and create a situation where supply exceeds demand. Oversupply is typically a precursor to hostile or aggressive competitive practices such as price cutting, false advertising, and contract interference. Third, new entrants can increase one's cost structure as advertising campaigns may need to be altered in frequency or message, and service offerings may require upgrading. Fourth, new entrants via acquisition or merger often have substantial resources that can considerably alter traditional industry practices. For example, a local amusement park purchased by Walt Disney would have substantial resources needed to upgrade the park facility, enhance service offerings, run extensive advertising campaigns, and continue to price competitively. Existing park competitors failing to adopt a sustainable competitive strategy would likely experience a significant decline in profit margins. Competitors within a sport industry can create barriers to entry. Porter (1980) identifies six major entry barriers that tend to deter the attractiveness of entering a particular industry.

Economies of Scale

As mentioned above, economies of scale can alter the equality of the competitive playing field. Economies of scale can be an effective entry deterrent as new entrants are required to match a competitor's level of advertising, research and development, sale and service offerings, and so forth to launch their product effectively to the consumer. The new entrant may find the scale economies realized by competitors prohibitive. The ability to match the existing competitors' cost structure, without benefits associated with scale, is most difficult as the new entrant's working capital and resource availability is likely being devoted to other start-up expenses.

Existing competitors can further discourage entry by retaliating against new businesses attempting to compete in established industry segments. For example, assume that Roseanne opened a roller-skating rink. She adopted a pricing strategy comparable to her established competitor, Doug from Derby's Roller Rink. Doug simply reduced prices and ran a comprehensive promotional campaign during Roseanne's first 3 months of operation. Roseanne, unable to match Doug's prices or monies spent on promotions, encountered difficulty in meeting the high debt obligation associated with a start-up venture. In the above example, had Doug been an outstanding, established entrepreneur with healthy financial statements, he could have lowered his prices and offered promotional gimmicks for as long as necessary to abort Roseanne's chance of success. Again, economies of scale can be a significant competitive advantage as new businesses would need to secure the capital necessary to match sustained scale economies while also covering start-up expenses.

Product Differentiation

Differentiated products serve as another effective entry barrier. One of the primary advantages of a differentiated product is a loyal customer base. For example, let's look at the bicycle retail market within Stratified Community, U.S.A. Stratified Community is a small community of 50,000 residents. Obviously, not all of the residents are interested in bicycling as a leisure, fitness, or competitive pursuit. However, of the residents that are interested, three stores have been able to service consumer needs effectively. Store A represents a bicycle retail store differentiated by selling specialized bicycles for the experienced, "serious" rider. This store provides detailed training, education, and repair services free of charge. Store B is a name-brand retailer selling the common Swift bicycle. This bicycle is of average quality and moderate price. Middle-class consumers shop at Store B to outfit family cycling needs. Store B frequently hosts bicycle clinics pertaining to sizing, safety, and maintenance concerns. Store C, or C-Mart, is also involved in bicycle retailing. C-Mart sells bicycles at the low end of the price and quality continuum. C-Mart has generated a great deal of community goodwill due to its haggle-free return policy and its role as a corporate citizen within the community itself. Each of the existing retailers has its own loyal following. As explained by Porter (1980, p. 9), "Product differentiation means that established firms have brand identification and customer loyalties, which stem from past advertising, customer service, product differences, or simply being first into the industry."

A new entrant into the bicycle retail industry in Stratified Community, U.S.A., would confront two immediate challenges. First, the new entrant would have to ensure that there was a market for his or her bicycle product offering. It is possible that, in a community with 50,000 people, demand has been tapped, and existing consumers are already loyal to established competitors. Second, if a product demand exists or can be developed, the new entrant needs access to significant monies to develop a loyal customer base (e.g., advertising and promotional monies, money for service offerings). As mentioned earlier, this may not be possible because resource availability may be scarce due to the plethora of additional start-up costs.

The health club industry also illustrates the entry barrier created by differentiation. Let's assume that there are eight health clubs in a town with a population of 80,000. Let's also assume that each club has been in operation for over a decade. Each club has designed its mission and related facility offerings and services to focus on a specified (or differentiated) target market. The specific markets targeted by each club are as follows:

- Club A: targets the 50+ market
- Club B: targets the very affluent
- Club C: targets the "swinging singles" market

- Club D: targets the family
- Club E: targets those looking for a "women's only" environment
- Club F: targets the "hard core" bodybuilder
- Club G: targets those on a minimal income by offering a very "bare" environment
- Club H: targets the disabled constituency

A sport entrepreneur looking to open a health club in the above 80,000-person community should be somewhat cautious and concerned. At face value, it appears that all available markets are being exploited. One could assume that individuals interested, and able, to purchase a health club membership are already frequenting one of the above clubs. A new entrant would have a surmountable battle in attempting to overcome extant customer loyalty.

Capital Requirements

Large capital requirements represent an obvious deterrent to any sport business entrepreneur. For example, the capital requirements to enter the golf club industry are exorbitant. Capital requirements include an approximate 170 acres of land in addition to an estimated $2 million to $10 million investment for golf course construction, maintenance equipment, and maintenance expense (Burgess, 1991). Additional monies must be available for architect and financing fees. The water park industry exemplifies another capital-intensive industry. On the other hand, an aerobic dance studio requires much less capital. Other than the purchase of a good floor, costs are minimal. The ease of entry and the subsequent ability to alter existing industry structure presents a real threat to existing competitors.

Switching Costs

Switching costs refer to the one-time costs incurred when switching from one product supplier to another. The use of switching costs as a deterrent to new entrants is rampant in the sport industry. Season tickets, initiation fees, lifetime memberships, and lengthy contractual agreements are all exemplary of the sport industry's attempt to install switching costs. Health clubs, for example, frequently offer special promotional lifetime memberships. There is an apparent "win-win" relationship established between the consumer and the health club. The consumer benefits via reduced prices. For example, an annual membership might cost a consumer $450. However, this same individual can purchase a *lifetime* membership for $1,000. Eager consumers can deduce that the lifetime membership will be paid for in just over 2 years. If one plans to incorporate exercise into one's daily, long-term regime, the lifetime membership appears very attractive. Management benefits as it gets immediate cash that can be used to provide a better product or pay off necessary debt. However, management also benefits because the consumer is "locked in" to that particular health club. In other words, even though a new health club opens up right across the street, the consumer will feel reluctant about switching clubs due to the $1,000 investment made, and hesitancy to lose that investment, in the original health club. Switching costs represent a successful way for sport managers to eliminate consumer decision making among competing product suppliers.

Lack of Favorable Locations

Within the sport service sector, location represents a critical factor (see Chapter 9, "Site selection," for more detail). Mullin, Hardy, and Sutton (1993) estimate that 90% of potential customers live within 20 minutes from the sport business and that 90% of all fans travel less than an hour to the various sports arenas. Consequently, lack of a good location serves as an obvious impediment to entry.

The practice of franchising provides sport business entrepreneurs with an opportunity to secure the best locations and preempt competitors. Franchisers, unable to generate the capital necessary to expand either locally, regionally, or nationally, benefit from the franchising of their operations. For example, franchising enables the franchiser to generate brand identity and name recognition while preventing the competition from capitalizing on available sites and related target markets. Franchisers can enlist franchisees who are willing to share the expense. Contractual agreements and related clauses can always enable the franchiser an opportunity to retain control of the franchised operation at a later time when franchiser assets and liabilities are stable.

Government Policy

The government has a formidable presence in the sport business industry. Federal and/or state licensing and/or bonding requirements accompany a variety of sport businesses, including ticket distribution, sport agent services, parimutuel racing, and the health club industry. For example, statutes controlling the maximum amount for which a ticket can be sold limit opportunities for ticket distributors of sport events (e.g., Ticketmaster; Miller & Fielding, 1997). Federal legislation was introduced in 1990 and 1992 that attempted to regulate the practices of ticket distribution services. Neither bill passed. However, state statutes do regulate ticket distribution practices. For example, existing statutes in South Carolina and Florida limit the ticket resale price to $1.00 above that paid by the "original seller." Similar statutes exist in North Carolina, Georgia, Connecticut, New Jersey, Michigan, Louisiana, Indiana, Kentucky, and Maryland. Similarly, bonding and licensing requirements present entry barriers for otherwise ethical individuals desiring to represent athletes (Miller, Fielding, & Pitts, 1992). Government policy inundates the parimutuel industry. For example, Kansas's state law requires racetracks to donate a portion of proceeds to charity. Increased competition has decreased consumer demand. Racetracks, consequently, are having difficulty maintaining operations. Financial concerns would be greatly alleviated if the racetracks had access to the money required to be given to charities (approximately $400,000 for the Wichita Greyhound Park in 1997; Hobson, 1996). Government policies toward YMCAs and other nonprofit organizations are good examples of entry barriers established by tax codes. Much debate has been generated over the alleged unfair competitive practices of "commercial YMCAs" (Miller & Fielding, 1995). For-profit health clubs and various other organizations continue to lobby extensively to repeal the exempt status and related subsidies of commercial YMCAs. Sport entrepreneurs contemplating entrance into the health club industry may need to reconsider given the entry barriers created by the lower cost structure of competing "commercial" nonprofits. Conversely, sport entrepreneurs might consider filing for nonprofit status to gain competitive advantages unavailable to other for-profit competitors.

SUBSTITUTE PRODUCTS

Substitute products are those products that perform the same generic function as the original product. Consumers are unable to pursue all desired recreation and entertainment-related activities due to limited discretionary time and monies. Substitute products reflect the competing choices available to the consumer. Looking at sport as part of the "leisure" or "entertainment" industry greatly expands the substitutability of any one product. For example, miniature golf, roller skating, and soap operas are all substitute products for one another. As explained by Mark Andrew, Director of Ticket Sales/Game Operations for the Indiana Pacers, the Indiana Pacers compete with the opera and the movies, among other activities (Andrews, 1992). Andrews stated that the "average" fan attends approximately six games a season. Andrews feels that fans desiring to attend more games are unable to due to competing family commitments and limited discretionary monies.

Sport entrepreneurs must realize that their products are not indispensable, and no sport business operates as a true entertainment monopoly. Inappropriate product pricing and service offerings encourage product substitutability. Product differentiation, real or perceived consumer product value, and switching costs are effective ways to reduce the threat of substitutability.

BUYER POWER

Buyer power refers to the influence, or "power," that the consumer has on the provider of the sport product. The objective of the buyer is to retain the most value while leaving the sport manager with only a modest rate of return. Buyer power represents a concern to sport managers as powerful buyers have more negotiating power regarding prices, delivery, installation, contractual issues, and so forth. Buyers commonly exhibit power in the following four situations.

Buyer Purchases in Volume

Buyers who purchase in volume tend to receive better service and product purchase provisions. It is analogous to buying a 12-pack of soda versus 12 individual bottles. Savings are realized when buying in volume. Corporations negotiating an employee usage contract with health clubs exhibit a great deal of power over the club itself. As explained by West Lewis, owner and manager of the Downtown Athletic Club (DAC) in Louisville, Kentucky, corporate memberships comprise almost 70% of his total membership basis (Lewis, 1995). If Lewis is negotiating with a corporation, for example, he may offer them employee memberships at a significant discount depending on, for example, the size of the club and whether the company will match employee fees. According to Lewis, the volume of memberships and visibility outweighs the discounted price. Corporations in similar situations realize that, if they fail to strike a deal with a particular company, someone else will. Or, even worse, failure to negotiate a "workable" deal could provide a window of opportunity for a particular company to open its own fitness facility for employees.

Products Are Highly Substitutable

Highly substitutable products place the consumer in a position of great power. Prudent sport managers consider the pricing tactics and service provisions of substitute products. Pricing strategies exceeding the consumer's expected price threshold generate little sales. Similarly, if consumers do not, or cannot, receive the services desired, they can give their sale to a competitor better able to meet needs and desires. For example, a consumer buys a treadmill from Retailer A on the contingency that Retailer A delivers and assembles the product. Unless Retailer A complies with the wishes and desires of the consumer, that store is likely to lose the sale. Constant monitoring of consumer needs and values, and the subsequent sincere attempt to meet and serve consumer needs and desires, mitigates the threat of product substitution.

Buyer Possesses Knowledge

Buyers with extensive product knowledge and information tend to possess greater power and can better influence product providers. For example, purchasers of cars vary in their knowledge of the automobile industry. A car buyer is likely to make a purchase decision on more favorable terms after reading and studying trade magazines, like *Consumer Reports*; surveying existing car owners and car dealers;

and obtaining quotes from a variety of competing car dealers. The same is true in the sport industry. The consumer is going to have more negotiating power when he or she is intimately familiar with the product, product usage, product components, and competitor offerings.

Buyer Is Capable of Backward Integration

Backward integration is a concept referring to the buyers' ability to provide for themselves their own desired product. Backward integration usually emerges due to the consumers' dissatisfaction with the original product offering.

The recent debacle between the Indy Racing League (IRL) and the franchise-owned Championship Auto Racing Teams (CART) illustrates the problems that can emanate as a result of backward integration. CART staged its own competing race, allegedly stealing the show from the original Indy 500 race, as a result of actions by IRL. The IRL's indifference to its "buyer" or product user is explained by Paulla Weinberg in a *USA Today* cover story (Ballard, 1996, p. 2E): "It's amazing how the Speedway keeps insulting the teams and drivers, saying that Indy makes the drivers, that the drivers don't make Indy, . . . What do people come to see then? The asphalt?" IRL's apparent indifference to its product user significantly decreased its revenues and the apparent monopoly the IRL had on the race car industry. Backward integration is a concern due to the potential loss of market share, increase in cost incurred, and possible bankruptcy of the original supplier. Again, a constant monitoring of the consumer regarding needs and desires mitigates the likelihood of backward integration.

A similar analogy regarding the issue of buyer power and associated threat of backward integration can be made in reference to a cycling retail and service store. For example, consider an individual who is an elite cyclist. This individual possesses a comprehensive and thorough understanding of the bicycle, its components, and what needs to be done to ensure effective performance. Now let's compare the elite buyer with an average bicyclist consumer, John Doe, with little (if any) knowledge regarding bicycle technology and the like. If John Doe goes to a retail cycling shop requesting his bicycle to be serviced in a certain way, and the cycle shop refuses or explains that the demanded service is unavailable, John Doe is likely to accept the cycling shop's response as definitive with little thought or reaction. On the other hand, the cycle shop that refuses to provide services demanded by the elite cyclist places itself in a different, and perilous, position. Since the elite cyclist possesses great knowledge regarding cycling and what can and cannot be done, poor service may encourage this individual to open his or her own cycle retail and service store. As one can deduce, the new cycling retail and service store would pose direct competition for the existing competitor. Consequently, consumers with a great deal of knowledge, and those actually capable of backward integration, possess great buyer power. In the above cycling illustration, a genuine attempt to buy the existing retail and service store to service the elite cyclist, even if it meant additional staff training and related expenditures, would have proven more fruitful than the bleak result of an additional new entrant (i.e., competitor) possessing extensive product knowledge and a passion for the industry.

SUPPLIER POWER

The term *suppliers* refers to those industries, or companies, that provide the input necessary to offer the sport product. For example, suppliers to the health club would include equipment manufacturers and degree or certification programs that train personnel. Suppliers to a professional athletic team would include organization entities such as National Collegiate Athletic Association (NCAA) Division 1 schools, baseball's minor league system, and little leagues. Because labor is also classified as a supplier, professional athletes are classified as suppliers for the professional franchise teams. The collective bargaining power of labor provides the professional players with a great deal of supplier "power" with which team management must contend. In addition, bats, scoreboards, and the coaching and managerial staff constitute suppliers to the professional sport industry. Suppliers to the water park industry would include manufacturers of the slides, surface contractors, engineers, staff, and insurance availability. Similarly, the suppliers of a boat retail shop would be the boats and related products themselves.

Suppliers are of obvious importance, as without the supplier, one has no product. However, a supplier's fees and service offerings must fit within a sport business manager's budget, needs, and desires. Heightened supplier power can increase the cost structure of a sport business via higher input prices and limited supply provisions (i.e., delivery, installation, favorable credit terms). Suppliers tend to possess the most influence, or power, when operating as either a monopoly or within an oligopoly. In either situation, the sport business has few alternative sources from which to purchase the product, and, consequently, their negotiating power (i.e., buyer power) is reduced.

INDUSTRY ANALYSIS APPLIED

As suggested at the beginning of this chapter, the success of the sport entrepreneur can be greatly enhanced by a thorough analysis of industry structure. A thorough knowledge and understanding of the five competitive forces better enables a sport business manager to capitalize on internal strengths, minimize internal weaknesses, take advantage of external opportunities, and use offensive and defensive tactics to protect against external threats. The following scenario provides an application of the five competitor forces discussed above.

Let's assume a group of sport entrepreneurs express an interest in purchasing the St. Louis Cardinals baseball team placed on the market by Anheuser-Busch in 1995 (Quint, 1995). An analysis of industry structure can help the sport entrepreneurs make an informed decision.

Threat of Entry

As explained earlier, entry barriers represent an important consideration to the individual entrepreneurs as they want to ensure that new or additional competitors do not saturate the market and disrupt current firm profitability. The potential St. Louis Cardinals purchasers desire high, sustainable entry barriers. Significant entry barriers include exclusive franchise assignments, antitrust exemptions, capital requirements, and differentiation (e.g., mascot, facility amenities). The sport entrepreneurs can be fairly confident that they will not have to compete against new baseball teams in the St. Louis area. The high entry barriers suggest that the purchase of the baseball team is a good idea.

Intensity of Rivalry

The sport entrepreneurs want the intensity of rivalry to be low. When rivalry increases, profit margins decrease. The analysis of the intensity of rivalry yields mixed results. MLB represents a slow growth industry in respect to both game attendance and television viewership, the two main revenue sources (Howard & Crompton, 1995; Scully, 1995). The slow growth of the industry is somewhat marginalized, however, due to the MLB cartel, which effectively functions to keep the intensity of rivalry low among competing clubs. However, the rapid introduction and growth of new entertainment alternatives intensify rivalry.

Buyer Power

The prospective purchasers of the St. Louis Cardinals will also want the power of buyers to be low. According to Porter, "The power of buyers determines the extent to which they retain most of the value created for themselves, leaving firms in the industry with only modest returns" (Porter, 1985, p. 9). Baseball games attract two kinds of buyers: (1) the fans and (2) the media.

First, individual spectators purchase tickets to attend select baseball games. Individual spectators have little in the way of bargaining power as they collectively generate less revenue than, for example, season ticket sales. Season ticket packages generate great revenue for ball clubs. Buyer power tends to vary among clubs regarding season ticket packages. Successful, high-demand teams tend to possess more power, whereas less successful teams are more willing to negotiate to fill capacity better. However, all spectators (single ticket game purchasers and season ticket purchasers) can boycott baseball games as they did after the baseball strike in 1995. However, their long-term effect is questionable due to lack of organization. Fans do not act collectively, and, consequently, they do not bargain collectively. As a group, these buyers are weak.

Second, television stations and networks also purchase rights to view baseball games. This second form of buyer is much more powerful than the individual spectator. Networks pay for broadcast rights based on network viewer shares for baseball games. Network audience shares have declined nearly 50% according to Scully (1995). Advertising revenues have realized a direct decrease as well. Consequently, television stations are less willing to pay high amounts for broadcast rights. Networks have high bargaining power and are highly price sensitive. Our baseball entrepreneurs will consider this element of industry structure to be a negative.

Substitutability

The potential franchise purchasers will discover that the threat of substitute products or services is high as the "menu" of entertainment and sport-related products is vast. Switching costs, a quality sport product, and customer service can all effectively reduce product substitutability.

Supplier Power

Supplier power represents a great challenge to the new entrepreneurs. Professional baseball players supply the talent that makes the baseball game marketable. Professional baseball players, organized under the MLBPA, possess great power. For example, collective bargaining resulted in the elimination of the reserve clause, the initiation of free agency, and the adoption of salary arbitration. The prospective buyers of the St. Louis baseball team may view supplier power as the greatest threat to team and industry profitability.

CHAPTER SUMMARY

The five competitive forces described above need to be constantly monitored and, when possible, manipulated, by both individual firms and firms acting collectively to protect an industry's profitability. Industry profitability is maximized when entry barriers are high and the intensity of rivalry, buyer power, threat of substitutes, and supplier power are low. However, just because one of the five elements is disfavorable does not mean the particular sport business is doomed. Rather, it means that the sport business manager must act in ways to insulate and protect the sport business from potentially devastating effects. It is the continual objective of the individual sport business to monitor, react to, and when possible manipulate the five competitive forces in such a way as to protect or enhance a particular company's profitability, competitive position, or market share.

STUDENT ASSIGNMENT

Identify a particular sport industry that you would contemplate entering as a professional or practitioner.

1. What entry barriers would you confront? Elaborate.
2. How would the factors identified in the chapter regarding the intensity of competition influence your success and profitability? Elaborate. How could you reduce the onset of intense rivalry?
3. With what substitute products would you compete? How would you attempt to reduce the threat of substitutability?
4. What type of supplier power, if any, would you encounter? How would you attempt to reduce supplier power?
5. What type of buyer power, if any, would you encounter? How would you attempt to reduce buyer power?

REFERENCES

Andrews, M. (1992). Student interview conducted for a class.

Ballard, S. (1996, May 24). NASCAR's stock rises as Indy-cars split. *USA Today,* pp. E1–E2.

Berrett, T. (1996). Economics and sport management. In B. Parkhouse (Ed.), *The management of sport.* New York: Mosby.

Burgess, D.H. (1991). Lending to golf course communities. *Journal of Commercial Bank Lending, 73*(7), 19–30.

Hobson, G. (1996, June 15). Racetracks take hits to stay afloat. *The Wichita Eagle,* pp. 9A, 12A.

Howard, D.R., & Crompton, J.L. (1995). *Financing sport.* Morgantown, WV: Fitness Information Technology, Inc.

Jensen, C.R. (1995). *Outdoor recreation in America* (5th ed.). Champaign, IL: Human Kinetics.

Levitt, T. (1986). Exploiting the product life cycle. In *The Marketing Imagination.* New York: Free Press.

Lewis, W. (1995). Management practices in the health club industry. Presented to class at University of Louisville Sport Administration Program, Louisville, KY.

Miller, L.K., & Fielding L.W. (1995). The battle between the for-profit health club and the "commercial" YMCA. *Journal of Sport & Social Issues, 19*(1), 76–107.

Miller, L.K., Fielding, L.W., & Pitts, B.G. (1992). A uniform code to regulate athlete agents. *Journal of Sport & Social Issues, 16*(2), 93–102.

Miller, L.K., & Fielding, L.W. (1997). Ticket distribution agencies and professional sport franchises. *Sport Marketing Quarterly, 6*(1).

Mullin, B.J., Hardy, S., & Sutton, W.A. (1993). *Sport marketing.* Champaign, IL: Human Kinetics.

Parkhouse, B.L., ed. *The management of sport.* St. Louis, MO: Mosby.

Porter, M.E. (1980). *Competitive strategy.* New York: Macmillan.

Porter, M.E. (1985). *Competitive advantage.* New York: Macmillan.

Quint, M. (1995, October 26). Cardinals and snack unit are out on block by Busch. *New York Times.* p. D2.

Ricklefs, R. (1996, August 13). Small soccer stores stumble as megastores join the game. *The Wall Street Journal,* pp. B1–B2.

Scully, G.W. (1995). *The market structure of sports.* Chicago, IL: The University of Chicago Press.

CHAPTER 2

A Generic Competitive Strategy and the Value Chain

Strategy represents a proactive look at where an organization wants to be and how it plans to get there. As explained by Thompson and Strickland (1992, p. 32), "Strategy-making is all about *how*—how to reach performance targets, how to out-compete rivals, how to seek and maintain competitive advantage, how to strengthen the enterprise's long-term business position." A strategy is "management's game plan" for a sport business. Strategy includes a synergetic, collective plan incorporating all the traditional business functions (e.g., marketing, management, finance, risk management). The chosen strategic plan should provide guidance to all stakeholders and be reflected in, and permeate throughout, every business operation, resource allocation, and decision-making process.

A strategic plan, and its implementation and execution, is one of the most telling signs of good management. As explained by Thompson and Strickland (1992, p. 3), "The better conceived an organization's strategy and the more flawless its execution, the greater the chance that the organization will be a peak performer in its industry." A survey of 966 companies with 500 or fewer employees reported in *USA Today* highlighted the benefits associated with strategic planning. As reported in the survey, the companies with strategic plans realized "100% higher profits, on average" (Rogoszynski, 1996, p. 6B). An additional reported benefit of strategic planning included better access to capital from banks (Rogoszynski, 1996). Banks, concerned about lending to companies who cannot survive, view strategic planning as a rudimentary task of good management.

A GENERIC COMPETITIVE STRATEGY

Unfortunately, a strategic planning "blueprint" does not exist for the immediate adoption by any business, including a sport business. However, the adoption of a

I thank Lawrence W. Fielding (Indiana University) for his contributions to this chapter.

generic competitive strategy facilitates a sport business's ability to maintain consistency throughout its functional areas as it strives to achieve, and maintain, profitability. Porter (1980) identifies three generic strategies sport businesses can adopt in an effort to maintain competitiveness and successfully contend with the five competitive forces (Chapter 1). Sport business managers can design and adopt a strategic plan built around one of the three generic strategies. The three generic strategies include: (1) differentiation, (2) overall cost leadership, and (3) focus or niche. The strategies are not mutually exclusive. For example, adoption of the differentiation strategy does not mean the sport manager views costs indifferently. Similarly, a low-cost producer does not mean that no facet of the sport business can be unique or of a valued quality. However, decision making and resource allocation should consistently be made with the adopted strategy in mind.

Differentiation

Differentiation refers to the unique value created by management that differs from other industry segment competitors. Sport businesses can differentiate in a number of different ways (e.g., marketing, product quality, services). For example, Nike products are differentiated via the acquisition of particular endorsees (e.g., Michael Jordan, Andre Agassi) and the related image. A health club may be differentiated via superior equipment, facilities, trainers, locker rooms, parking, social activities, hours of operation, or other amenities. Similarly, a sport franchise may be differentiated due to its quality of play, half-time entertainment, customer service, interactive scoreboard, and facility amenities (e.g., arcade, lounge). Any sport product can adopt a differentiation strategy.

Benefits of a Differentiated Strategy

A differentiated strategy helps protect and insulate a sport business against the five competitive forces (discussed in Chapter 1) in the following ways.

Entry barriers. As mentioned in Chapter 1, a highly differentiated sport business creates an entry barrier. Newcomers encounter difficulty in trying to lure loyal customers from a differentiated existing sport business offering a unique and valued sport product. However, ample resource availability facilitates the success of a new entrant (i.e., sport business) as monies needed for extensive promotional campaigns exist. Of course, product demand, real or perceived, remains a prerequisite for success in any market.

Buyer power. Differentiation also provides partial protection against the power of the buyer as sport businesses are better able to demand premium prices due to the uniqueness of the particular sport product offered. Buyers are less likely to haggle over prices when receiving a valued, heterogeneous product. A differentiated strategy, however, does not mean that price is irrelevant. Rather, price is not a primary feature in the marketing of that particular product.

Substitutability. The source of differentiation deters the likelihood of substitutability. Consumers substitute sport products less frequently when competitors remain unable or unwilling to provide the same valued source of differentiation.

Intensity of rivalry. A differentiated product insulates a company from attack. Competition is not likely to be as hostile when competitors have their own market following and do not directly compete for market share.

Supplier power. Differentiation can also reduce the negative effects of supplier power. A supplier may give a differentiated sport producer better buying terms (e.g., credit terms, delivery, installation) to be associated with the differentiated product. Similar to product sponsorship, supplying inputs used in the production of the sport product provides the supplier with excellent visibility and image enhancement opportunities. For example, cities supply potential sport franchises with stadiums and arenas. Cities routinely supply, or offer, multimillion dollar stadiums to franchises in hopes of securing economic activity, improving the city's quality of life, and improving the status and perception of the city itself. Similarly, an equipment manufacturer may provide a high-profile health club serving a very elite market with equipment on favorable terms (e.g., service, delivery, credit). The reason for providing the equipment and related terms focuses on the supplier's desire to maintain visibility and to have a "token," successful club it can list as a reference when marketing and promoting equipment to other possible purchasers. The same equipment analogy can be applied to National Collegiate Athletic Association (NCAA) Division I athletic programs with large weight rooms. Equipment manufacturers may again choose to provide equipment at very favorable terms as a marketing tool, knowing that the success of a football program, for example, may be attributed in part to superior weight-training programs using superior equipment.

Risks of a Differentiated Strategy

The effectiveness of a differentiated strategy remains contingent on a number of factors. Sport businesses adopting a differentiated strategy need to be cognizant of *two primary risks* associated with a differentiated strategy.

Imitation by competitors. A chosen generic strategy needs to be sustainable and built upon core competencies that cannot be easily imitated. Imitation dissolves the *unique* qualities associated with a particular product while simultaneously eroding the competitive positioning in relation to the five competitive forces. Contractual clauses and restrictive covenants ensuring confidentiality, coupled with patent securement and trademark and copyright registration enhance the likelihood that a sport business will be able to sustain a proprietary source of differentiation.

Uniqueness not valued by competitors. Sport businesses need to be sure they are providing a source of differentiation valued by the customer. Sport entrepreneurs can lose large sums of monies when consumers do not value the differentiated product. No competitive advantage can be gained when sport businesses present consumers with products they do not value. "Overuniqueness," coupled with a pricing strategy above the consumer's expected price threshold, represents a combination sure to decrease market share and resultant profitability. Market research and continual interaction with the consumer decrease the likelihood of producing a sport product not valued by the consumer.

Low-Cost Producer

Adopting a *low-cost producer* strategy conveys that the sport business is attempting to perform all business functions (e.g., input acquisition, sport product production, marketing, sales, and service) in a low-cost manner. Low-cost producers tend to resemble "bare bones" operations. For example, a sporting goods retail store selling standardized products in volume, providing little customer service (e.g., fitting, customization) and employing only minimal (if any) marketing could classify as a low-cost producer. A health club that offers only free-weight equipment in a very barren environment (no neon lights, wallpaper, carpet, etc.) with limited locker room facilities and no day care also exemplifies a low-cost producer. Similarly, a golf course with less than perfect fairways, sparse locker rooms, and a limited-item snack bar would exemplify a sport business adopting low-cost producer strategy. Sport managers must remember, however, that serving as a low-cost producer still requires a degree of quality. For example, the greens and fairways would need to be playable, and restrooms would need to be hygienic and appropriate in number. The adoption of a generic strategy can be viewed as one of degree.

The adoption of a low-cost producer strategy places the sport entrepreneur in an enviable position for two reasons. First, a sport business adopting a price strategy comparable to competitors realizes a higher profit margin (Figure 2–1). A higher rate of return provides a sport entrepreneur with monies needed to maintain premises, improve facilities, enhance customer service provisions, and extend product offerings. In the end, the low-cost producer offers consumers a high-quality product at the same price as the competitor. Second, adopting a low-cost producer strategy enables a sport business to price below the competitor, maintain a comparable profit margin, and increase market share (Figure 2–1). When two products are homogeneous, each containing similar sport products and sport product offerings, consumers tend to patronize that sport business offering the product at the lowest price.

Figure 2–1 The Low-Cost Producer.

(a) Price similar to competitor, receive greater profit margin.

(b) Price below competitor, greater market share, profits the same.

Benefits of a Low-Cost Producer Strategy

Similar to the differentiation strategy, adopting a low-cost producer strategy insulates a sport business against the five competitive forces.

Entry barrier. Serving as a low-cost producer establishes a significant entry barrier. New entrants often possess limited capital. Due to exorbitant start-up expenses, a sport business can rarely afford to adopt a penetration pricing strategy for a sustained time period. (A *penetration pricing strategy* refers to a new entrant entering an industry and pricing products below the price offered by existing competitors. In comparison, a *skimming pricing strategy* refers to a new entrant entering the industry and pricing products above the price offered by existing competitors.) The low-cost producer, in an effort to thwart the success of the new entrant, can simply lower its own product prices indefinitely while maintaining above–break-even level profits. Product similarities attract consumers to the lower price alternative. New entrants find the advertising expenses, coupled with the other start-up expenses and maturing debt obligations, prohibit their ability to match their competitor on price. Limited revenues and mounting debt create a tenable position for the new sport business. The acquisition of enough capital to cover

3 to 5 years of operations mitigates the problems associated when competing against a low-cost producer.

Buyer power. Low-cost producers are able to offer the customer a comparable (or often improved) product at comparable and often lower prices than the competitor. Consequently, adoption of the low-cost producer strategy reduces the power of the buyer to negotiate for lower prices.

Substitutability. Consumers receiving a good product at a reduced price, or a good product priced within the customer's expected price threshold, have less incentive to defect to a competitor's product. (The *expected price threshold* refers to that price that the consumer is mentally able and willing to spend for a particular product. The price tends to fall within the middle of a price continuum—not excessively high and yet not excessively "cheap.") Constant consumer surveillance enables a sport business adopting the low-cost production strategy to keep a pulse on consumer demands and needs. The ability continually to provide the consumer with a valued product further reduces the threat of substitutability.

Intensity of rivalry. As a low-cost producer, the sport business occupies an enviable position when, and if, a price war ensues among competitors. In a price war, competitors possessing a higher cost structure will see margins diminish to a greater degree than will the low-cost producer. This creates a positive situation for the low-cost producer as the sport business remains less likely to fall below break-even figures regardless of intense or hostile competition.

Supplier power. The low-cost producer (e.g., large sporting goods retail stores) often purchases in volume. Most suppliers prefer volume purchasing as it reduces their own costs associated with administration and distribution. Consequently, low-cost producers may be in an advantageous bargaining position when dealing with the supplier for favorable credit terms, delivery, and installation, for example.

Risks of a Low-Cost Producer Strategy

The effectiveness of a low-cost producer strategy remains contingent upon a number of factors. Sport businesses adopting a low-cost production strategy need to be cognizant of three primary risks associated with a low-cost strategy.

Imitation by competitors. The competitive advantages achieved via a low-cost producer strategy can be lost by competitor imitation. Competitor intelligence, now a common practice in all industries, is used to discover competitor advantages that can be imitated or defensively destroyed (competitor intelligence is discussed more thoroughly later). Other competitive "secrets" can be discovered by asking questions of a competitor's equipment suppliers, sales force, and customers. Valuable competitor information can also be accessed via computer databases. Staying abreast of current literature constitutes another excellent method of learning new ways to provide a better service at a lower cost. As mentioned earlier, the registration of patents, trademarks, and copyrights and the use of restrictive covenants represent offensive actions sport businesses can employ to reduce the risk of imitation.

Fixation on costs at the expense of consumer demands. Often, low-cost producers become fixated on ways to lower costs, and maintain low costs, at the expense of the customer. Providing a sport product with a low-cost structure provides marginal, if any, benefits if the sport product is not desired by the consumer. Low-cost production and customer monitoring need to exist simultaneously.

Fixation on costs at the expense of litigation. Low-cost producers may be tempted to cut corners in order to keep prices low. For example, eliminating storage space, decreasing lighting intensity, or reducing security would lower cost structure without directly affecting a particular activity area. Similar expenses could be saved by foregoing various personnel practices (e.g., checking references, creating job analysis). Unfortunately, the cost reductions could prompt expensive litigation, consumer harm, and negative media attention.

Niche or Focus Strategy

The third generic strategy represents the "niche" or "focus" strategy. As the terms connotate, this strategy reflects a sport business choosing to focus on a particular target market, product line, or geographic market. In comparison to the two other generic strategies, the niche or focus strategy serves a narrow market, while the others tend to serve much larger and broad target markets. A niche producer is providing a specific sport product to a specific target market that the market leaders are not interested in serving. Focus strategies, for example, would be employed by retailers selling used sporting goods or a tennis facility serving the wheelchair-bound constituency only. Dennis Rodman successfully employed the niche strategy to his National Basketball Association (NBA) career. As explained by Rodman in his book, he does what no one else wants to do: *rebound* (Rodman, 1996). Similar to the above generic strategies, a focus or niche strategy offers protection against the five competitive forces.

Benefits of a Niche or Focus Strategy

Barriers to entry. A sport business focusing on a particular market segment gains a monopoly on the market share if it serves this segment effectively and is able to secure a solid and loyal customer following. The limited market focus deters competitors wishing to serve a larger market and profit from volume business.

Buyer power. As mentioned above, the sport business adopting a niche strategy serves a limited target market with a specialized product not provided by other mass producers. Consequently, consumers who value the sport product provided have few, if any, competing providers from which to purchase the particular product. Limited product availability reduces buyer power.

Intensity of rivalry. The sport business adopting the niche or focus strategy is often viewed as a friendly competitor. The niche sport business rarely tries to usurp market share from the sport business serving the larger market. Similarly, the business serving the larger market is typically not interested in catering to the particular niche targeted by the particular sport business. Consequently, intense competition remains minimal.

Substitutability. Again, the uniqueness of the particular sport product tailored to such a specific market mitigates the threat of product substitution. Consumers served by a niche provider typically are unable to purchase a similar sport product from another provider.

Supplier power. The sport business adopting the niche or focus strategy creates an ideal situation for the supplier and sport business to interact as a partnership. The established camaraderie and loyalty can create a positive situation for the sport business negotiating with suppliers as both parties strive to create a "win-win" situation.

Risks of a Niche or Focus Strategy

As with the other strategies, the sport business adopting a niche or focus strategy encounters risks. The dominant risk associated with the niche or focus strategy is described below.

Competitors serving the larger market will become interested in the niche segment. As competition intensifies and products enter the maturity stage of the product life cycle, larger sport businesses may find the niche market a viable way to gain additional market share. The available resources and shared linkages of the larger company places the smaller, niche company in a perilous position. A service orientation and genuine concern for the consumer may generate customer loyalty and preclude market intervention and disruption by a larger sport business.

Communication of the Strategy to Stakeholders

The adoption of a generic strategy is not in and of itself a recipe for success. Effective communication of the strategy remains essential.

Involvement of Front Line Personnel

Contrary to past managerial practices, strategy is not something that is written in a policy manual and never discussed or a document hidden in the archives of a boardroom. Nor is the strategy of a sport business something read by a new employee only during orientation. Rather, the strategy of any sport business must permeate throughout the entire business. It must guide and direct every decision being made by all personnel. Involvement of front-line personnel generates a sense of ownership and pride in the sport business itself. Rewards and incentives should also be provided based on adherence to the chosen strategy. Only when the entire organization remains actively committed to a chosen strategy can it effectively take an offensive position, and effectively defend, against the five competitive forces.

Total Commitment by Top Management

It is not uncommon for top management to be oblivious to their own chosen generic strategy. The adoption of any strategy will be meaningless unless top management understands, adheres to, and supports the chosen strategy through both actions and words.

THE VALUE CHAIN: A VALUABLE MANAGEMENT TOOL

The Value Chain Defined

Sport businesses, as mentioned above, adopt generic competitive strategies to maintain consistency throughout functional areas, to ensure that all functional efforts have a common foundation, and to position the sport business favorably in comparison to other rival firms. Sport businesses achieve favorable competitive positions, or competitive advantages, when able to generate value for the consumer. Value can be delivered to the consumer via a lower cost structure or a differentiated product. The value chain, popularized by Michael Porter, enables a sport business to visualize where value (i.e., differentiation or a lower cost structure) can be passed on to the consumer. As explained by Porter (1985, p. 33), "The value chain disaggregates a firm into its strategically relevant activities in order to understand the behavior of costs and the existing and potential sources of differentiation." Every sport business resembles an assimilation of activities that collectively produce an end product for intended consumers. A value chain represents a pictorial representation in sequential fashion of those activities involved in the deliverance of the end product.

Value chains can either be "generic" or "personalized." Generic value chains represent a sport industry segment at large, depicting functions performed by the majority of competing sport businesses. Personalized value chains represent individual sport businesses, highlighting those activities that provide a particular sport business with a competitive edge over competitors.

The value chain reflects two primary component areas: primary activities and secondary activities. Primary activities represent the sequence of activities necessary to produce the end product (Figure 2–2). The following list itemizes and defines primary activities.

- *Input:* Refers to the generic or unique activities, supplies, and/or materials needed to produce the sport product.
- *Input logistics:* Refers to the generic or unique ways in which the inputs are actually delivered to the site of operations or sport product production/consumption.
- *Operations (a.k.a., throughput):* Refers to the generic or unique characteristics associated with the actual manufacture or production of a sport product.
- *Distribution:* Refers to the generic or unique characteristics associated with the distribution of the sport product.
- *Marketing and sales:* Refers to the generic or unique marketing and sales tactics used to create the exchange between the buyer and seller.
- *Service:* Refers to the generic or unique service provisions available to the sport consumer.

A generic value chain representing the above primary activity areas addresses each of the above facets in generalities. A personalized value chain adopted by an indi-

Primary Activities >	Input	Input Logistics	Operations	Distribution	Marketing & Sales	Services
	Itemizes the generic or unique activities, supplies, and/or materials needed to produce the sport product.	Itemizes the generic or unique ways in which the inputs are actually delivered to the site of operations or sport product production/consumption.	Itemizes the generic or unique characteristics associated with the actual manufacture or production of a sport product.	Itemizes the generic or unique characteristics associated with the distribution of the sport product.	Itemizes the generic or unique marketing and sales tactics used to create the exchange between the buyer and seller.	Itemizes the generic or unique service provisions available to the sport consumer.

Secondary Activities >	Procurement	Technology Dev.	Firm Infrastructure	Human Resource Mgmt.
	Means and process associated with the purchase of inputs (e.g. credit terms, computer systems).	Research and development, layout and design, "how to" procedures (e.g. paperwork, routine documents), etc.	"General management, planning, finance accounting, legal, government affairs, and quality management" (Porter, 1985 p.43)	Hiring, training, promoting, terminations, pension management, benefits, compensation, etc.

Figure 2–2 A Pictorial Representation of a Sport Business's Chosen Generic Strategy.

Source: Adopted from Porter, M.E. (1985). *Competitive Advantage.* New York, NY: The Free Press.

vidual sport business, however, finds particular areas within some or each of the above areas where differentiation can be created or costs can be lowered. Only those areas that are somehow different or unique in comparison to industry competitors are identified.

Secondary activities include support services, such as human resource management, procurement, technology development, legal services, and general administrative staff. The type of tasks or activities involved in secondary activities are identified below:

- *Human resource management:* Hiring, training, promoting, terminations, pension management, benefits, compensation, etc.
- *Technology development:* Research and development, layout and design, "how to" procedures (e.g., paperwork, routing documents), etc.
- *Firm infrastructure:* "General management, planning, finance, accounting, legal, government affairs, and quality management" (Porter, 1985, p. 43)
- *Procurement:* Means and process associated with the purchase of inputs (e.g., credit terms, computer systems)

Secondary activities exist to varying degrees within all sport businesses and serve to facilitate the functioning of primary activities.

Application #1: The Value Chain of a Sporting Goods Company Manufacturing a Baseball Bat

A generic value chain represents both primary and secondary activities. The primary activities, as identified above, can be described in the following manner. The *input* phase refers to those activities, supplies, and/or materials needed to produce the particular sport product. The *input logistics* phase refers to the actual manipulation or delivery of the input to the location where production occurs. The *throughput* phase, or the *operational* phase, of the value chain represents the actual manufacturing of a sporting good or the delivery of a sport product. *Output,* as the term implies, refers to the actual product or service itself. *Marketing and sales* are rather obvious functions, including promotions, distribution considerations, and price considerations. *Service,* the final section of the value chain, remains an increasingly important competitive advantage for many sport businesses and could include provisions regarding delivery and employee training, for example.

A value chain representing the primary activities for Hillerich & Bradsby (H&B), however, would detail areas of differentiation based on quality manufacturing and prudent marketing strategies. For example, the *inputs* might reflect H&B's use of top-grade white ash wood. The limited supply of this white ash wood, and H&B's unlimited access to the wood via ownership of timber yards, places H&B in a position to differentiate successfully its wooden baseball bats via quality of timber. The *operations* phase of H&B's value chain emphasizes their cellular layout; use of a laser lathe; and refined sanding, finishing, and branding activities. H&B's unique *marketing and sales* tactics include the select use of, for example, influential endorsees and credit and sales policies. H&B's unique *services,* adding to their source of differentiation, include product demonstrations and retailer assistance programs. Again, H&B's value chain (primary activities) reflect product differentiation tactics. The importance of supportive, secondary activities is illustrated by H&B's adoption of just-in-time (JIT) manufacturing in 1988 (*firm infrastructure*). For example, H&B's inventory turnover ratio climbed from 2.7 in 1985 to 15.4 in 1989, 1 year after JIT implementation. H&B's fixed asset turnover ratio improved from 1.44 in 1989 to 1.63 in 1991. Similar benefits were realized in total asset turnover (Miller, Fielding, Gupta, & Pitts, 1995). Although cost remains important, it remains secondary to areas of differentiation.

Application #2: The Generic Value Chain of a Professional Baseball Team

The value chain of a sport service product differs only slightly from the value chain of a manufacturing company. For example, items included in the value chain of a professional baseball team would include the following.

The *input* includes access to primary players, recruitment policies, and negotiation strategies. Additional inputs would include the stadium, playing fields, seating, and related amenities as these all represent items needed to produce the actual product (i.e., the game). Again, the purpose of the value chain is to dissect and scrutinize these individual activities to ascertain if value can be created for the consumer via differentiation or a low-cost structure. As with the manufacturing example above, the quality of the inputs (e.g., players, stadium) directly influences the quality of the product.

Input logistics represent the development or manipulation of the inputs into a form that contributes to the actual development of the particular product. Grading players and assigning them to the appropriate minor or major leagues and player development and training are critical in the actual delivery of the baseball game itself. In addition, transporting fans from the parking lots to their seats is an input logistics concern. An appropriate infrastructure, stadium access roads, parking lots, convenient entrance gates, and ushers enable fans to find their seats so the game can be consumed.

Throughput and output are combined for the sport service product as the game is produced and consumed simultaneously (Mullin, Hardy, & Sutton, 1993). As players perform the various activities associated with game production, spectators consume the product.

Marketing and sales again connotate a wide variety of tasks in which a franchise can create consumer value. Ticket distribution, promotional strategies, and pricing tactics represent a few of the critical areas.

Service, the final phase of the value chain, also provides sport franchises with a plethora of ways to generate consumer value as well. Scoreboards, interactive networking, concession offerings, arcade rooms, and program sales are a few of the many service offerings a professional baseball team can offer to its consumer.

Application #3: The Generic Value Chain for a Golf Course

Factors represented within a generic value chain for a golf course would include the following. *Input* components include those things necessary to produce the product. Consequently, the inputs for a golf club include the land and its related characteristics (water hazards, rolling hills, sand traps, etc.). The irrigation system and maintenance represent significant input components as well. *Input logistics,* similar to the professional sport franchise, pertain to the manipulation of the inputs so that the consumer is able to consume the product. Greens maintenance, adequate parking, and usable infrastructure represent a few input logistics applicable to a golf course. The *throughput and output* phases are again combined as the game is produced and consumed in the same location. *Marketing and sales and service* phases of the value chain resemble generic marketing functions and considerations.

The Value Chain: A Competitive Intelligence Tool

Managers of sport businesses gain a great deal of competitive intelligence by comparing individual value chains with those of competitors. Acquired knowledge enables a sport business to exploit a competitor's weaknesses while capitalizing on individual firm or industry opportunities. Analysis of competitors' value chains can convey to a sport manager both offensive and defensive competitive opportunities (Herring, 1988). Vella and McGonagle (1987, p. 37) suggest that a sport business "become the competitor" and learn "to think and react just the way the competitor does." The following list identifies 10 ways in which a sport business can become intimately familiar with the competitor (Hendrick, 1996):

1. Monitor personnel changes.
2. Review press releases and newspaper articles.
3. Attend trade shows.
4. Communicate and network with competitor suppliers and buyers.
5. Learn about the background of key decision makers.
6. Purchase and scrutinize the competitor's product.
7. Scrutinize advertising and other promotional campaigns.
8. Maintain intimate familiarity with financial statements and competitor literature.
9. Monitor and review computer databases containing valuable information (e.g., LEXIS-NEXIS, PACER, the internet, etc.).
10. Attend and listen to speeches made by competitor executives or managers.

An intimate knowledge about a competitor and its competitive strategy can be used to identify and react to new markets, new products, future promotional campaigns and more. Prudent use of this information facilitates a sport business's ability to maintain and further develop market share.

CHAPTER SUMMARY

All sport businesses tend to represent one of the three generic strategies. Cognizance of which strategy a sport business manager has adopted for a sport business can provide lasting benefits, including the ability to stay focused, enhanced decision making, maintained profitability, and, in the end, the deliverance of a sport product valued by the customer. Similarly, a sustained study of the value chains of both the individual firm and the competitor provides great benefit to the sport business manager.

STUDENT ASSIGNMENT

1. Identify a sport business entity.
   a. Elaborate on its perceived generic strategy.
   b. Design the value chain for the identified sport business entity.
   c. Design the value chain for *two* of the sport business entity's competitors.
2. Read the brief application and answer the questions listed in Appendix 2–A.

REFERENCES

Burgess, D.H. (1991). Lending to golf course communities. *Journal of Commercial Bank Lending, 73*(7), 19–30.

Gimmy, E.A., & Benson, M. (1992). *Golf courses and country clubs: A Guide to appraisal, market analysis, development, and financing.* Chicago: Appraisal Institute.

Golf consumer profile. (1989). Jupiter, FL: National Golf Foundation.

Hendrick, L.G. (1996, July). Is competitive intelligence getting the proper attention? *Security Management,* p. 150.

Herring, J.P. (1988, May/June). Building a business intelligence system. *The Journal of Business Strategy,* pp. 4–9.

Miller, L.K., Fielding, L.W., Gupta, M., & Pitts, B.G. (1995). Case study: Hillerich & Bradsby Company, Inc.: Implementation of just in time manufacturing. *Journal of Sport Management, 9*(3), 349–362.

Mullin, B.J., Hardy, S., & Sutton, W.A. (1993). *Sport marketing.* Champaign, IL: Human Kinetics.

Porter, M.J. (1980). *Competitive strategy.* New York: Macmillan.

Porter, M.J. (1985). *Competitive advantage.* New York: Macmillan.

Rodman, D. (1996). *Bad as I wanna be.* New York: Delacorte Press.

Rogoszynski, N. (1996, June 28). Strategic plan helps small business shine, survey finds. *USA Today,* p. 6B.

Thompson, A.A., Jr., & Strickland, A.J. III. (1992). *Strategic management.* Boston, MA: Irwin Publishers.

Vella, C.M., & McGonagle, J.J. Jr. (1987, September/October). Shadowing markets: A new competitive intelligence technique. *Planning Review,* pp. 36–38.

Appendix 2–A
Application

A golf course could choose to compete in the competitive golf industry in a variety of ways. For the purpose of analysis, we will refer to two golf courses that have adopted different generic strategies. As mentioned in Chapter 1, an analysis of the five competitive forces provides managers an understanding of the playing field on which they are to compete.

The STAR Course, Sunbelt, USA

The STAR Course is a championship, 18-hole golf course with beautiful, carpet-like fairways; finely cut, expansive greens; challenging water hazards; difficult sand traps; and interesting bunkers. Golf carts are equipped with computerized "coaches." The STAR Course is located in a major metropolitan area of 4.3 million and occupies 50 acres of high-rent property. It is obvious to even the novice eye that the layout of the STAR Course was strategically and meticulously planned and designed. The $25 million invested in the STAR Course far exceeds the $11.7 million investment required to build an "average" golf course (Burgess, 1991). The view of the course itself remains secluded and is visible only to those making the long drive down the two-lane, winding, yet eloquent club entrance. The club's pro shop carries a small, select assortment of the finest in clothes, clubs, and related equipment. The club's dining area is majestic in appearance, and the food is exquisite. Average green fees amount to $75 during the week and $225 during the weekends. Pro shop purchases and dining expenses are affordable only to the most affluent. The target market of the STAR Course is limited by both the expense and the level of difficulty. There is only one other golf course similar to the STAR Course within the metropolitan area. There are 25 other private golf courses located in the competitive area and 35 public golf courses, both of lesser quality.

The Economical Course, Meager, USA

The Economic Course ("E-C" as referred to by locals) is a spartan-like course in comparison to the STAR Course. E-C is a 9-hole golf course located off the interstate on 30 acres in a remote, noncommercialized area. The population of this metropolitan area is 1.2 million. The level of course difficulty is minimal, and the challenge for the advanced player is absent. The greens are not manicured, and the fairways are rough. There are no sand traps or water hazards. The pro shop selection includes tired-looking t-shirts with various golf caricatures that appear to be designed for the "Generation X" population. E-C has no restaurant. The concession area includes a carnival-like soft drink dispenser and a varied selection of chips and candies. Within the competitive area, there are 17 private clubs and 25 public golf courses; 18 courses are 18-hole courses, and 7 courses are 9-hole courses.

I. QUESTIONS RE: THE INDUSTRY ANALYSIS

A. Entry Barriers

1. How did E-C golf course reduce entry barriers for itself when entering a competitive industry?
2. What is a problem, or threat, associated with low entry barriers?
3. What could E-C course do to try to mitigate the threat of additional entrants?
4. What benefits does STAR Course enjoy from its established entry barriers? Elaborate.
5. What benefits does a differentiated product have regarding the concept of entry barriers? Elaborate.

B. Intensity of Rivalry

1. As indicated by Burgess (1991), golf course maintenance averages $1 million annually. Why would this intensify rivalry among homogeneous competitors? Explain.
2. Since the golf course industry has such high fixed costs, what types of revenue-generating activities should course managers focus on to cover expenses?
3. Regarding Question 2, what type of research would you want to look at to see where you should focus your efforts?
4. The golf course industry has high exit barriers. How would you explain the high exit barriers of the golf industry? Elaborate.
5. Do high exit barriers intensify or relax competition within a particular industry? Elaborate.

6. What dangers are associated with high exit barriers? Elaborate.
7. It is estimated that it takes a population of approximately 25,000 to support one golf course (Burgess, 1991). Further, industry experts report that the popularity of golf is increasing between 2% to 8% each year. From a conservative perspective, Burgess (1991) estimates that a new golf course will have to be built each day until the year 2000 in order for supply (e.g., golf course availability) to meet demand (e.g., consumer interest). In reference to the above course histories, what does this information infer about the intensity of rivalry?

C. Buyer Power

1. Gimmy and Benson (1992) state that high-frequency players (251 rounds per year) account for only 20% of all golf consumers. However, this 20% of the market provides approximately 75% of golf green-fee revenues. What does this communicate to the golf course manager? Specifically, how important are the needs and wants of the high-frequency player?
2. The above data are likely to send a stronger message to which of the courses (E-C or STAR Course)? Elaborate on your reasoning.
3. It is estimated that beginners make up 55% of the golf market in the 1990s (Gimmy & Benson, 1992). What message does this communicate to E-C? STAR Course? If you were E-C, what marketing and promotional efforts would you pursue? Elaborate.
4. With which golf course(s) (if any) would the buyer possess power? Elaborate.
5. How could the use of switching costs influence buyer power?
6. In what ways could switching costs be developed?

D. Substitutability

1. Golf Consumer Profile (1989) lists the following as the top five reasons people choose to participate in golf:
   • recreational enjoyment (78%)
   • because friends play (63%)
   • for relaxation (59%)
   • for exercise (56%)
   • to get o39tdoors (54%)
   (The percentages do not add up to 100% because of multiple responses. We have listed the top five response categories out of a total 11 categories.) Based on the above five reasons, what inferences can be made regarding the substitutability of golf?

2. What threats are associated with a product that is highly substitutable?
3. In what ways has the STAR Course attempted to mitigate the threat of substitutability? In what ways has E-C attempted to mitigate the threat of substitutability?

E. Supplier Power

1. One supplier to the golf course industry is the course designer or architect. Renowned designers like Jack Nicklaus and Arnold Palmer, for example, charge in excess of $1 million for their services (Burgess, 1991). Less sophisticated courses can be designed at a fraction of that cost. With this insight, which of the courses (E-C or STAR Course) will be subject to more extensive supplier power and why?
2. In addition to the golf course designer or architect, who else would be considered a "supplier" to the golf course industry, and is their "power" likely to be high or low? Does your answer differ among the two types of clubs addressed above (i.e., E-C and STAR Course)? Elaborate.

II. QUESTIONS RE: THE GENERIC STRATEGY

As mentioned in the chapter, the choice of competitive strategy depends on how a sport business manager chooses to compete, or position itself, among the five industry forces.

1. What generic strategy has STAR Course adopted? Elaborate.
2. What generic strategy has E-C adopted? Elaborate.

III. QUESTIONS RE: THE VALUE CHAIN

1. Design the value chain for STAR Course including only those activities or functions that reflect the generic strategy identified in II (1) above.
2. Design the value chain for E-C Course including only those activities or functions that reflect the generic strategy identified in II(2) above.

IV. CONCLUSION

1. Elaborate on the interaction between industry structure, the adopted generic strategy, and the value chain.

CHAPTER 3

The Mission Statement, Objectives, and Organizational Issues

THE MISSION STATEMENT

A mission statement, although somewhat of an intangible, nebulous array of sentences, remains integral to optimal business success. As stated by Krohe (1995, p. 18), "no one can prove they *don't* work." A survey conducted by a Boston consulting group revealed that 90% of the 500 companies surveyed used a mission statement at some time within the past 5 years (Krohe, 1995). The mission statement and its related benefits can be better understood when one has a clear picture of what components comprise a mission statement.

As explained by Thompson and Strickland (1992), a mission statement includes the following three components: (1) the *what,* (2) the *how,* and (3) the *who.* The *what* refers to that need or value that is being provided by the particular sport business. The *how* refers to the manner in which the particular product is being provided. The *who* refers to the consumer being targeted by the particular sport business. Review the following mission statements and identify the inclusion of the three necessary criteria (i.e., *who, what, and how*).

The ABC professional baseball team
To provide the finest quality of baseball entertainment to the family and fan at an affordable price in a clean, healthy, and happy environment.

The ABC professional ice hockey team
The ABC professional ice hockey team is a professional organization providing unique hockey entertainment through a successful blend of excellence, creativity, and affordability.

As evidenced from the above examples, mission statements should be written in clear and concise language that will be understood by all stakeholders. The use of jargon and technological terms should be avoided. Although new and eager entrepreneurs may want their mission statement to reflect a profit orientation, it is important to remember that without the customer and customer satisfaction, there can be no profit.

Benefits of a Mission Statement

Mission statements provide four primary advantages. First, mission statements provide all stakeholders with a conceptual understanding of what the business is, who the target market is, and how the target market is to be serviced. The mission statement is a quick and abrupt way to convey the fundamental business to all concerned.

Second, a mission statement represents a great public relations tool and can be used effectively in marketing efforts as well. For example, the YMCA mission statement communicates to all stakeholders that the organization is a non-profit, charitable organization based on Judeo-Christian principles. This statement has proven most beneficial in defending lawsuits alleging that the YMCA operates as a for-profit, commercial organization (Miller & Fielding, 1995).

Third, stakeholders can infer that a sport business with a mission statement is proactive and engages in prudent managerial practices. In essence, communication of the mission statement to stakeholders is telling the stakeholder that the particular sport business pledges adherence to the mission statement, which usually is focused on providing customer value and excellent customer service.

Fourth, the mission statement facilitates decision making and resource allocation. For example, the mission statement of the Louisville Motor Speedway (LMS) is to provide family entertainment via exciting and stimulating motor-car racing. Hooters offered to sponsor a night at the race track, scantily clad women included. Management at LMS found it much easier to turn down Hooters' offer by referring back to the LMS mission (Atlas, 1996). Similarly, a bare-bones weight club for the hard-core weightlifters would not be as likely to veer off into tertiary product offerings (e.g., body massages, aqua-swim classes) with a solid mission statement for guidance. The California Country Club (CCC) provides another illustration of how the mission statement enabled the organization to refocus at a time of financial and operational peril (Pellissier, 1994). As explained by Pellissier (1994), the CCC was losing $350 a day from their fine dining operations. The formal dining room was open to the public and targeted primarily non-CCC members. Eventually, CCC management realized they had strayed from their mission statement of providing a "golf" environment to their club constituency. As a result, the fine dining room was changed to a more casual, golf-motif restaurant. Although the restaurant continues to lose money, the amount lost each day has reduced to $50 to $100. Most importantly, member satisfaction has increased.

One caveat, however, is that to be believable, the mission statement must have 100% backing by top management. As stated by Bell and Zemke (1992, p. 163), "Live the mission by making sure your daily actions are consistent with the purpose you've set for your people. Examine how you spend your time, what you show excitement about, what you worry about. Your actions telegraph your true priorities to those around you." Top management can endorse the intent of the mission statement by ensuring that the mission statement is adequately communicated.

Communication of the Mission Statement

Similar to possessing a generic strategy, the possession of a mission statement is useless unless the mission statement is communicated and adhered to by the sport business itself. There are a number of ways in which a mission statement can be communicated to its stakeholders. The following list provides a sampling of different ways in which sport businesses communicate their mission:

- Post (via signage) the mission statement in visible locations, such as the registration desk or entry ways.
- Print the mission statement on employee paychecks or paycheck envelopes.
- Post the mission statement in the employee lounge or break room.
- Print the mission statement on the letterhead of the sport business.
- Print the mission statement on newsletters, brochures, ticket stubs, portfolios, and so forth.
- Print the mission statement in all operating and policy manuals.

OBJECTIVES

Objectives are a much more tailored extension and reflection of the generic strategy and the mission statement. As explained by Thompson and Strickland (1992, p. 27), "Unless an organization's mission and direction are translated into *measurable* performance targets, and managers are pressured to show progress in reaching these targets, an organization's mission statement is just window-dressing." Sport businesses need to establish both financial and strategic objectives. The following paragraphs elaborate on the distinction between financial and strategic objectives.

Financial Objectives

Most organizations are familiar with financial objectives. Financial objectives pertain to information contained on the financial statements. For example, a financial objective might address the need to increase or decrease advertising monies, labor costs, workers' compensation rates, or membership fees. Thompson and Strickland (1992) indicate that financial objectives tend to be more short term in nature. As stated in their text, "Achieving acceptable financial performance is a must; otherwise the organization's survival ends up at risk" (Thompson & Strickland, 1992, p. 27). Two financial objectives of a major league ball club might include the following:

1. to sell 2.2 million tickets in 1998
2. to generate an operating profit in excess of $3 million in 1998

Two financial objectives of a conference fitness program might include the following:

1. to decrease workers' compensation costs by 3% in 1998
2. to decrease insurance premium by 1% in 1998

Strategic Objectives

Strategic objectives are integral to long-term business success. They focus on things like product extension, product expansion, customer service, and customer turnover. Strategic objectives of a major-league ball club might include the following:

- Answer in excess of 95% of all incoming telephone calls by the fourth ring (20 seconds maximum) by December 1998.
- Fill all mail and phone orders within 2 working days of receipt of order in 1998.
- Process 2.2 million tickets with less than 1% errors in 1998.
- Provide excellent customer service to guests such that the ticket operation receives in excess of 80% excellent and/or good ratings on efficiency, courtesy, and accuracy as measured by in-stadium guest satisfaction surveys.

Two strategic objectives of a corporate fitness program might include the following:

1. to increase employee participation by 2% in 1998
2. to increase the hours of operation (open 2 hours earlier and stay open 2 hours later) in 1998

Strategic objectives on average are more long-term oriented. In other words, it is not likely that one can decide to open a second facility on the opposite side of town within a 6-month time period. Site selection and zoning approval in itself may take 6 months. However, the long-term classification of strategic objectives and the short-term classification of financial objectives are not absolutes. In actuality, sport businesses always will have both short- and long-term strategic financial objectives. For example, a sport business should immediately strive to improve a strategic objective regarding customer satisfaction. Similarly, financial objectives will deal with long-term acquisitions and other plans for disposing of long-term debt in addition to more short-term goals regarding, for example, expense reduction.

Components of a "Good" Objective

Objectives, like anything else, can be either "good" or "bad." A good objective is composed of four vital components.

First, the objective must be realistic. One objective of all sport business entrepreneurs might be to make $1 million. However, unless this is realistic, this is a very poor objective that has little (if any) merit. L.A. Gear's lofty objective of generating $1 billion in sales is attributed to its decline in the early 1990s. As explained by Almaney and colleagues (1996, p. 401), "Employees had to push hard to attain the new growth objective. As a result, the company's internal controls got out of hand."

Second, objectives must be understandable. Similar to the mission statement, objectives should be clear and concise and free of jargon and technical terms unfamiliar to the user.

Third, objectives must be measurable. The term *measurable* refers to a time definition. For example, the following objective is of little merit: "To increase membership sales by $500,000." One's immediate question would be, "by when?" Have I met my objective as a salesperson if I am able to generate $500,000 of membership fees in 5 years? Or is this objective conveying that I need to generate $500,000 of membership sales in 1 year?

Fourth, objectives need to be quantifiable. In the above example, a nonquantifiable objective would state, "To increase membership sales." As a performance objective, this conveys little. A good objective would quantify the exact amount by which an employee is expected to increase membership sales.

Benefits of Established Objectives

Objectives are critical to a sport business for a variety of reasons. Two primary benefits of objectives are identified below.

Objectives Clarify Job Expectations

As indicated in the above quote, objectives clarify for employees the expectations of management. A familiar sentiment among employees is summarized in the following statement, "I don't mind the game so long as I know the rules." Objectives communicate the rules of the game or, rather, job expectations. Employees, knowing what they need to do to meet performance objectives, are less frustrated and better able to deliver optimal customer service. The sport organization benefits as satisfied employees are more productive and investments made in the hiring and recruitment process are better retained.

Objectives Help Defend Managerial Practices When Legally Challenged

Objectives can be a significant asset to any company forced to build a legal defense against questionable employment practices. Establishing performance objectives that are communicated to employees provides a sport business manager with a viable performance evaluation tool. Subsequent decisions regarding bonuses, terminations, opportunities to attend workshops, and the like can be defended by showing the court that objectives were communicated and known to be used as standards for performance.

ORGANIZATIONAL STRUCTURE

The organizational structure reflects the "skeleton" of a particular sport business. The organizational chart is the pictorial representation of an organization's formal structure (Figure 3–1). The adoption and implementation of an appropriate organizational structure is integral to carrying out a sport business's strategic intent, fulfilling the business's mission, and achieving stated objectives. The type of structure adopted is dependent on a variety of factors, including available monies, product complexity, management's philosophy, and staff expertise. Key organizational structure concepts are described below.

Tall versus Flat Organizational Structures and the Related Span of Management

Organizations with significant resources will be able to have a *taller* structure if so desired. A *tall* organizational structure refers to a structure that has a number of different layers (i.e., middle management) and usually smaller spans of management (number of employees per supervisor). Tall and narrow structures are good when the task is complex and varied (Figure 3–1). For example, more managerial "layers" may be needed in a sport entity that prescribes exercise programs for the disabled and elderly. One can easily deduce that one person would not want to supervise 50 disabled and/or elderly individuals. Similarly, an organization that employs novice staff is not likely to allow them to supervise a large number of employees due to their inexperience. Consequently, this particular sport business may choose a tall and narrow organizational structure. Tall structures are criticized, however, for the propensity of an employee to lose focus on the larger organization while simultaneously developing a "that's not my job" attitude. On the other

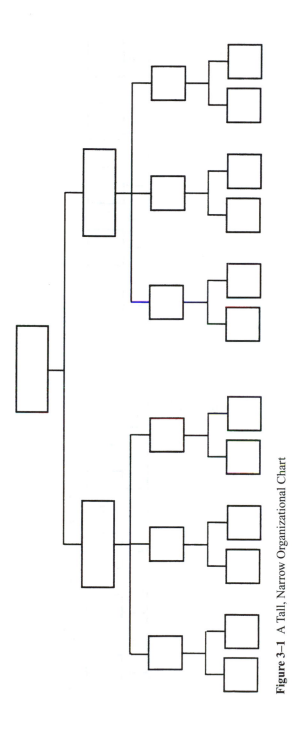

Figure 3–1 A Tall, Narrow Organizational Chart

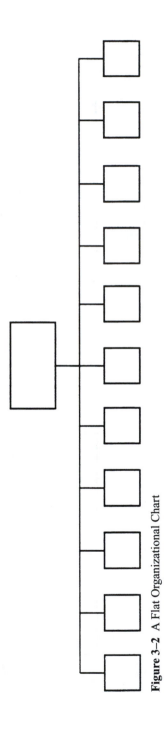

Figure 3-2 A Flat Organizational Chart

hand, a flat structure with very few layers of management (Figure 3–2) may be preferred in a bowling alley, for example. Proponents of flat organizational structures suggest that employees are not as likely to develop tunnel vision at the expense of the "whole" organization.

Centralized versus Decentralized Management

Centralized management is often associated with a very bureaucratic, dogmatic type of leadership looked down upon in the 1990s. Organizations employing centralized management keep all decision making in the hands of select individuals or departments. Employee advocates argue that centralized management dehumanizes employees and precludes opportunities for employee empowerment. Slow decision making resulting in cumbersome operations illustrates another disadvantage of centralized management. Horine (1996) suggests that sport managers prefer centralized management because many are "workaholics" and overachievers hesitant to delegate. Consequently, these individuals prefer to do things themselves as a way to ensure that "things will be done right." Managers may also choose to retain all managerial control in fear that delegation will promote the subordinates at the expense of their own status and power. Unfortunately, total centralization provides little employment motivation or intrinsic satisfaction. Discontent employees, in turn, directly affect bottom-line figures via an increase in turnover, absenteeism, injuries, and poor customer service.

Decentralized management reflects an organization where decisions are passed down to employees within a particular sport business. In a decentralized organization, employees are allowed to make decisions that affect individual employment responsibilities. For example, the general manager of Aero-Club would delegate all aerobic class scheduling, employee hiring and firing, program monitoring, and class scheduling to the aerobics coordinator. Decentralization advocates argue that delegation enhances efficiency as better decisions are made more quickly. For example, one could easily deduce that the aerobics coordinator, not the club's general manager who may know very little (if anything) about aerobics, is best qualified to hire, train, orient, and monitor aerobic instructors and their performance. Further, the aerobics coordinator is in a better position to monitor the aerobic industry and decide what class offerings would best meet the needs and desires of the people. In exchange, the general manager is free to pursue other opportunities that contribute to the growth and financial success of Aero-Club. Lengthy time spans between idea generation and implementation simply provide the competitor with an opportunity to offer the product first and secure market share. Decentralization is only effective if managers support the decisions of the subordinates (including failures) while giving them credit for successes.

Regardless of a sport manager's enthusiasm for the decentralized management structure, it is important to remember that all organizations reflect fragmentations of centralization. Some centralization is necessary to maintain a degree of order and organization. Owners and managers continue to retain ultimate decision-making power for how their sport business operates in the larger industry segment.

Unity of Management

Behavioral scientists have long recognized the individual frustrations associated with role conflict. Requiring employees to report to two different "superiors" violates Henry Fayol's concept of unity of control (i.e., management). For example, an individual employed by a school district as both a teacher and a coach violates the unity of management principle. Role conflict, in this example, may emanate as the individual tries to please both the athletic director (the "superior" regarding coaching responsibilities and expectations) and the school principal (the "superior" regarding teaching responsibilities). The unity of management concept is not as sacred as it was in the early 1900s. Many businesses, including sport businesses, are moving away from the hierarchical structure and advocating a "bossless" workplace where empowered employees routinely make strategic decisions and/or provide necessary input.

Employee Specialization versus the Multifunctional Worker

Early management theory advocated, and related business structures reflected, the specialized worker. During early industrialization, workers performing the same task over and over were thought to be specialized "experts." Advocates of this theory (e.g., Henry Fayol, Frederick Taylor) believed that the daily repetition decreased employee confusion while enhancing efficiency and productivity. The pure specialized worker is somewhat archaic in the 1990s. Today's organizational policies (oftentimes not reflected in a pictorial representation of the organization itself) tend to favor the multifunctional worker for three reasons.

1. *Employees have a better conceptual understanding of the entire business.* Employees who are exposed to many different facets of the business have a better understanding of how their work contributes to the "whole." In other words, it gives them a greater sense of pride in the production of the product itself. This mental enhancement translates into a happier, more productive employee. Further, a better understanding of the product and its intricacies enables the employee to better address product concerns and questions both on and off the job.

2. *Employees are more marketable.* Corporate responsibility has become a big issue. In an era of downsizing, it has become business's responsibility to provide the employee with as many skills as possible. Employees are more likely to be loyal to an organization if they feel they have been treated fairly by it.

3. *Repetitive injury problems are reduced.* Both manufacturing and service jobs frequently required the worker to perform the same task over and over. As statistics reveal, repetitive injuries create hardships for both the injured employee and the respective business. Injured employees are subject to the obvious hardships and change of lifestyle precipitated by the injury itself. Management is affected in a number of ways, including employee absenteeism and/or turnover, workers' compensation costs, and interrupted operations. Multifunctional jobs, in comparison, can eliminate the repetition associated with specialized labor.

Organizational Departmentalization

There are four primary ways in which the organization's structure may be departmentalized. Each structure benefits via specialization of perspective areas, and each results in the duplication of some business functions. The best structure to adopt depends on the type of business, its size, and the experience of the employees. Each of these four types of departmentalization will be briefly discussed below.

Functional Structure

The term *functions* refers to the traditional business functions. A professional sport franchise, for example, could be segmented according to the following departments: marketing and community relations, ticket operations, finance, sales, stadium operations, and media and public relations (see the organizational chart of the Detroit Tigers, Figure 3–3). Other sport business entities organized according to function would also be segmented in accordance with the traditional business functions (e.g., marketing, finance, accounting, risk management, human resources).

Product Structure

This structure is departmentalized by product offerings and commonly employed in midsize sport organizations. For example, a health club may be structured with an aquatics manager, a fitness manager, a racquet sport manager, and an outdoor specialist manager. Similarly, an athletic department may be structured by teams offered (i.e., football, basketball, swimming, tennis, track and field). See the Example Organizational Chart for Anywhere, U.S.A., Parks Department (Figure 3–4).

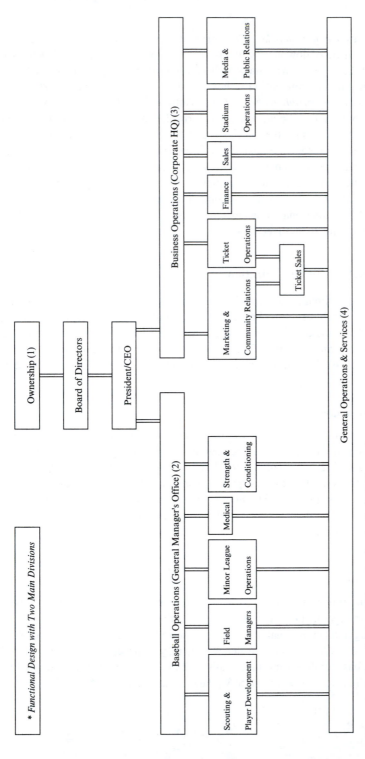

Figure 3–3 Organizational Blueprint for the Detroit Tigers, Inc.

Notes: (1) Ownership is private. (2) Baseball Operations is a term used within Major League Baseball to describe business issues and deals that pertain to the day-to-day and long range functions of the team. (3) Business Operations is a term used within Major League Baseball to describe all business performed in the production and promotion of the team and its games. (4) General Operations & Services is a combination of building maintenance, building security, and receptionists.

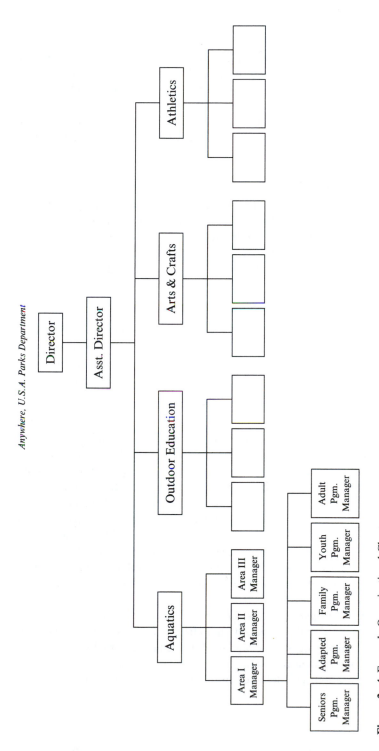

Figure 3–4 Example Organizational Chart

Geographic Structure

Very large sport businesses may departmentalize according to geographic regions. Common departmentalization titles would include managers for the Eastern, Western, Northern, Southern, or Central regions of the country. On a smaller scale, organizations with multiple facilities may departmentalize according to various sections of the local town. Large city park and recreation departments typically employ some type of geographical structure within their larger organizational chart (Figure 3–4).

Client or Customer Structure

This is another common form of departmentalization adopted by sport businesses. For example, a health club could be segmented with managers for toddlers, infants, adolescents, young adults, single adults, married couples, and older adults. The third tier of the Anywhere, U.S.A., Parks Department represents departmentalization by client (e.g., seniors, adapted, family, youth, and adult, Figure 3–4).

Benefits Derived from an Organizational Chart

As mentioned above, an organizational chart is a pictorial representation of an organization's formal structure. The adjective *formal* is used as a way to recognize that all organizations have informal as well as formal structures. Although somewhat of a vague and shallow pictorial, the organization chart does offer three primary benefits:

1. *Provides employees with a conceptual, "wholistic" picture of the sport business.* Persons employed in large organizations are often only familiar with those business facets influencing their individual job descriptions. The pictorial organizational chart provides employees with a greater understanding of product offerings and their position as it fits in the larger organization. For example, a tennis pro at a country club may be exposed only to the tennis operations on a routine basis. However, it would be most beneficial to all stakeholders if that tennis pro was familiar with other club operations and offerings. Similarly, a marketing executive at Nike would need to be familiar with all departments of the company (e.g., manufacturing, distribution, research and development). The people and departments are conveyed through the organizational chart.

2. *Communicates to employees the "chain of management."* New employees are typically exposed to the organizational chart at some time during the orientation or training process. The organizational chart lets employees better understand not only their role within the larger organization but also the chain of communication. The defined communication patterns reduce the likeli-

hood that employees will bother high-ranking sport managers with questions that can be better addressed by subordinate employees.

3. *Provides employees with a visual representation of promotional opportunities.* The organizational chart can serve as a source of motivation for employees wishing to ascend into higher ranking positions. For example, a director of a single recreation center might be able to see promotional opportunities available as managers of park district or regional area managers.

Criticisms Alleged Against the Organizational Chart

Three primary criticisms have surfaced regarding the organizational chart. First, critics state that the organizational chart is archaic and perpetuates the dogmatic,

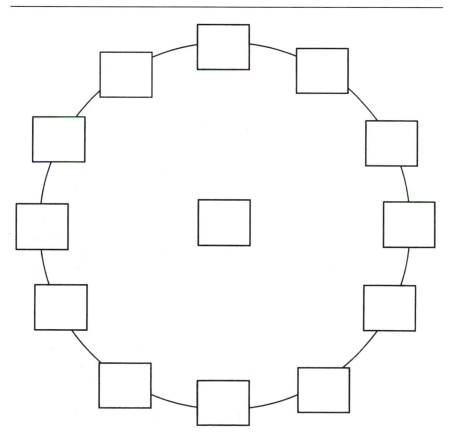

Figure 3–5 The Circular Organizational Chart

autocratic management style of the preindustrial era. According to critics, the organizational chart stigmatizes some employees as "superior," while other employees are relegated to an "inferior" status. Management in the 1990s has tried hard to diminish status demarcations. In an attempt to eliminate the "we" versus "they" connotation, many businesses have flattened the organizational chart. Organizations, instead, are depicted via a circular format (Figure 3–5). Other organizations have attempted to eliminate the hierarchical concept by avoiding the use of the word *employee* in exchange for terms such as *team player* or associate. Second, critics suggest that the organizational chart promotes inflexibility. In other words, individuals view their jobs and related responsibilities as existing only within the parameters of their pictorial box. Requests to perform tasks in other areas are often rejected by employees at the expense of the larger sport business and related operations. Third, the organizational chart only represents the formal organizational structure. It is well recognized that established lines of communication are frequently bypassed as certain individuals, regardless of formal titles, possess some form of influential power (e.g., referent, expert, etc.).

CHAPTER SUMMARY

The internal strengths of a sport business entity stem, in part, from the ability to define a mission that appropriately identifies who the sport business is attempting to serve, what the sport product is, and how the sport product will be provided. The mission guides many other facets of the sport business. Failure to define a mission, and then adhere to the identified mission, makes other managerial functions difficult and less than efficient. Similarly, objectives provide a sport business entity with structure. They serve as important planning tools that further convey the direction the sport business entity is pursuing and plans to pursue in the future. The organizational chart is another planning tool of essence to a sport business and its stakeholders. A sport business with a good, well-defined, organizational chart is more likely to maintain its course while minimizing redundancy and waste.

STUDENT ASSIGNMENT

1. Identify a sport business entity.
   a. What is the mission statement of the particular sport business entity?
   b. What would you do to improve the mission statement (if anything)?
   c. How does this sport business entity communicate the mission statement to its stakeholders?
   d. Do the employees, as well as managers, appear to be familiar with the sport business's mission statement?
2. Regarding the sport business entity identified in #1, identify two financial objectives and two strategic objectives of the sport business entity. If you are

unable to access two objectives (strategic and financial), develop your own based on your knowledge of the sport business and its related industry. If objectives are provided by the sport business entity, critique these objectives.

3. Regarding the sport business entity identified above, respond to the following.
   a. Obtain an organizational chart for the particular sport business entity.
   b. What, if anything, would you do to improve this organizational chart?
4. Interview a sport business manager of the chosen sport business entity.
   a. How does this sport business manager feel about delegation?
   b. What decisions (if any) remain centralized within this sport business entity?
   c. Do employees tend to be more multifunctional or specialized? Elaborate.
5. Develop the following for a hypothetical sport business:
   a. a mission statement
   b. two financial objectives and two strategic objectives
   c. an organizational chart

REFERENCES

Almaney, A.J., et al. (1996). L.A. Gear, Inc. In *Strategic management: Concepts and cases* (3rd ed.). Englewood Cliffs, NJ: Prentice Hall.

Atlas, E. (1996, February 20). [Interview with Mr. Ed Atlas, Marketing, Louisville Motor Speedway].

Bell, C.R., & Zemke, R. (1992). *Managing knock your socks off service.* New York: American Management Association.

Horine, L. (1996, June/July). Deciding to delegate. *Athletic management,* p. 13.

Krohe, J. Jr. (1995, July/August). Need a mission statement? *Across the Board,* p. 17–20.

Miller, L.K., & Fielding, L.W. (1995). The battle between the for-profit health club and the "commercial" YMCA. *Journal of Sport & Social Issues, 19*(1), 76–107.

Pellissier, J.L. (1994). Adapting to a changing market: The 10th tee grill. *The Cornell H.R.A. Quarterly, 35*(6), 90–95.

Thompson, A.A. Jr., & Strickland, A.J. III. (1992). *Strategic management.* Boston, MA: Irwin Publishers.

CHAPTER 4

Sport Business Structure Formations

Sport managers interested in opening up sport-related businesses, such as bowling alleys, roller-skating rinks, miniature golf courses, and health clubs, must decide on the business structure providing optimal benefits and minimal hardships. Liability, tax treatment, access to capital, managerial input and control, and ease of formation all vary among the different business structures. The type of business structure a sport business adopts greatly influences short- and long-term operations. The purpose of this chapter is to examine the various business structure alternatives available to sport entrepreneurs. Although sport business entrepreneurs should consult an attorney in deciding the optimal structure, this chapter summarizes key facets associated with each business structure alternative and provides the sport manager with a rudimentary understanding of related concepts.

Traditional business formations include the sole proprietorship, the general partnership, the limited partnership, the S corporation, and the C corporation. States, in an effort to attract new businesses (interstate and global) and enhance the retention rates of existing businesses, pass legislation to make business structure choices more favorable. Two recent examples of this process are the limited liability corporation (LLC) and the limited liability partnership (LLP). The first part of this chapter briefly reviews advantages and disadvantages commonly associated with the sole proprietorship, general partnership, limited partnership, S corporation, and corporation (Exhibits 4–1 through 4–5). The second part elaborates on the LLC, including its advantages and disadvantages (Exhibit 4–6). The third part discusses the LLP as well as its advantages and disadvantages (Exhibit 4–7). The fourth part analyzes the criteria used to ascertain whether an entity should be taxed as a corporation or a partnership. The fifth part analyzes the criteria used to ascertain whether the veil of limited liability should be pierced. Last, some concluding comments are offered.

Exhibit 4–1 Advantages and Disadvantages of the Sole Proprietor

---

Primary advantages
Total control over all decision making
Revenues subject to single taxation
Ease of formation
Great flexibility
Reduced government and legislative restrictions
Individual retention of profits
Better ability to maintain confidentiality

Primary disadvantages
Limited access to capital
Limited managerial expertise
Unlimited liability
Limited longevity

Source: Adapted with permission from L.K. Miller and L.W. Fielding, The Appropriate Business Structure: A Decision For Sport Managers, *Journal of Legal Aspects of Sport*, Vol. 6, No. 2, pp. 101-116, © 1996, Society for the Study of Legal Aspects of Sport and Physical Activity.

Exhibit 4–2 Advantages and Disadvantages of the General Partnership

---

Primary advantages
Greater access to capital than the sole proprietor
More enhanced managerial talent than the sole proprietor
Pass-through taxation benefits

Primary disadvantages
Limited longevity
Joint and several liability
Limited capital in comparison to the corporation
Limited managerial talent in comparison to the corporation

Source: Adapted with permission from L.K. Miller and L.W. Fielding, The Appropriate Business Structure: A Decision For Sport Managers, *Journal of Legal Aspects of Sport*, Vol. 6, No. 2, pp. 101-116, © 1996, Society for the Study of Legal Aspects of Sport and Physical Activity.

Exhibit 4–3 Advantages and Disadvantages of the Limited Partnership

---

Primary advantages
Limited partners retain limited liability
Ability to generate needed capital
Limited partners provided with a diversified portfolio
Retained "pass-through" tax benefits for limited partners

Primary disadvantage
Inability of the limited partner to participate in management

Source: Adapted with permission from L.K. Miller and L.W. Fielding, The Appropriate
Business Structure: A Decision For Sport Managers, *Journal of Legal Aspects of Sport*, Vol. 6,
No. 2, pp. 101-116, © 1996, Society for the Study of Legal Aspects of Sport and Physical
Activity.

Exhibit 4–4 Primary Advantages and Disadvantages of the S Corporation

---

Primary advantages
Limited liability
Single taxation
Ease of raising capital
Ability to secure better talent
Avoidance of the alternative minimum tax
Lower tax liabilities incurred by personal service corporations

Primary disadvantages
Size limited to 75 shareholders
Only one type of stock issued by entity
Prohibition of employee-shareholders from borrowing money from pension plans
Limited employee benefit deductions if employee-shareholder owns less than 2% of
the corporate stock

Source: Adapted with permission from L.K. Miller and L.W. Fielding, The Appropriate
Business Structure: A Decision For Sport Managers, *Journal of Legal Aspects of Sport*, Vol. 6,
No. 2, pp. 101-116, © 1996, Society for the Study of Legal Aspects of Sport and Physical
Activity.

Exhibit 4–5 Primary Advantages and Disadvantages of the Corporation

Primary advantages
Access to capital
Limited liability
Ability to secure the best managerial talent
Decreased tax liabilities for small or one-person entities
70% tax-free dividends paid to a corporation
Benefit as some favor corporate accounts

Primary disadvantages
Double taxation
Shareholders' inactive role in management of the firm
Extensive corporate formalities
Extensive government scrutiny

Source: Adapted with permission from L.K. Miller and L.W. Fielding, The Appropriate Business Structure: A Decision For Sport Managers, *Journal of Legal Aspects of Sport*, Vol. 6, No. 2, pp. 101-116, © 1996, Society for the Study of Legal Aspects of Sport and Physical Activity.

Exhibit 4–6 Primary Advantages and Disadvantages of the LLC

Primary advantages
Limited liability
Pass-through taxation benefits
LLC members can include corporations and partnerships
Unlimited number of members
Ease of parent-subsidiary structures

Primary disadvantages
Limited precedent established due to newness
Conversion expense

Source: Adapted with permission from L.K. Miller and L.W. Fielding, The Appropriate Business Structure: A Decision For Sport Managers, *Journal of Legal Aspects of Sport*, Vol. 6, No. 2, pp. 101-116, © 1996, Society for the Study of Legal Aspects of Sport and Physical Activity.

Exhibit 4–7 Primary Advantages and Disadvantages of the LLP

Primary advantages
Pass-through tax benefits
Easy formation in comparison to corporation
Limited liability

Primary disadvantages
Limited precedent established due to newness
Conversion expense

Source: Adapted with permission from L.K. Miller and L.W. Fielding, The Appropriate Business Structure: A Decision For Sport Managers, *Journal of Legal Aspects of Sport*, Vol. 6, No. 2, pp. 101-116, © 1996, Society for the Study of Legal Aspects of Sport and Physical Activity.

THE SOLE PROPRIETORSHIP

Artisans and entrepreneurs adopted the sole proprietorship business structure during the preindustrial era. The sole proprietorship remains a popular business structure for many sport business owners. For example, sole proprietorships accounted for 19% of all public golf courses, 14% of all membership sports and recreation clubs, 32% of all sporting goods and bicycle shops, and 20% of all physical fitness facilities in 1992 (Figures 4–1 through 4–4). Sport business proprietors own the particular business assets and assume all financial responsibilities. Adoption of the sole proprietorship business structure includes seven significant advantages.

Advantages

First, a sport entrepreneur retains total control over all business issues including competitive strategy, budgeting, and marketing tactics. Lengthy consultation, persuasion, and negotiation among individual partners or a board of directors are eliminated. A sport business entrepreneur seeking to circumvent the need for, and time devoted to, consensus building finds the sole proprietorship very appealing.

Second, the sole proprietorship benefits from single taxation. Individual tax rates apply to generated business income. The sport business, as a separate entity, escapes payment of corporate taxes on generated income.

Third, the ease of formation appeals to individuals eager to establish a sport business in an efficient and effective manner. Typically, minimum requirements

Figure 4–1 Business Structure Choices: Public Golf Course Membership

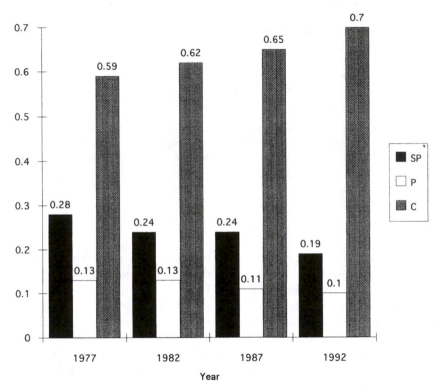

Source: Reprinted from the Census of Service Industries, Department of Commerce.

include only a "business license obtained from the city and a tax permit obtained from the state" (Ellis & Norton, 1988, p. 42).

Fourth, the flexibility inherent in the sole proprietorship attracts potential sport business managers. It enables a sport entrepreneur to implement ideas rapidly and secure first-mover advantages. First-mover advantages are important when the following apply:

1. Brand identity is important to the buyer.
2. Gains via the learning curve can be realized.
3. Entry barriers can be established.

Figure 4–2 Business Structure Choices: Membership Sports and Recreation Clubs

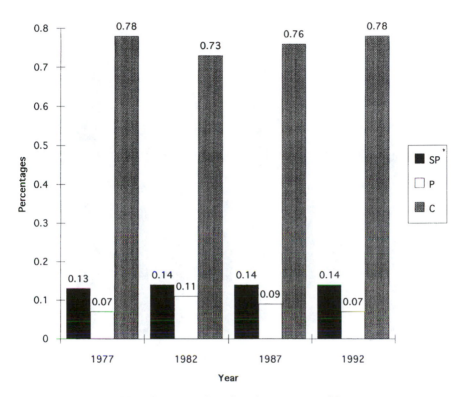

Membership Sports & Recreation Clubs

Source: Reprinted from the Census of Retail Trade, Department of Commerce.

4. Switching costs can be secured.
5. Cost advantages can be gained via first access to raw materials, distribution channels, and so forth (Porter, 1980).

For example, a sole proprietor in the business of manufacturing ski equipment, seeing an opportunity in ski retail, avoids the often cumbersome process of changing the articles of incorporation in order to sell skis. In comparison, a corporation must change its articles of incorporation in such instances. Consequently, a sole proprietor can implement and adjust to opportunities much more rapidly. This flexibility allows a health club, for example, owned by a sole proprietor to expand to

Figure 4–3 Business Structure Choices: Sporting Goods and Bicycle Shops

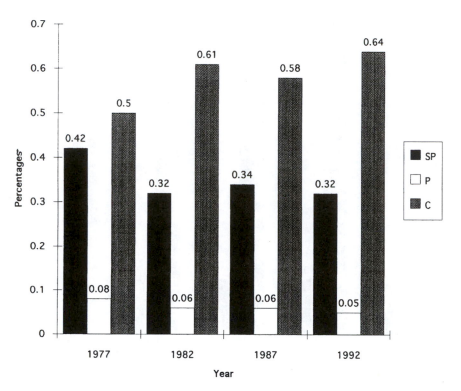

Sporting Goods & Bicycle Shops

Source: Reprinted from the Census of Service Industries, Department of Commerce.

another ideal site without having to secure partnership consensus. Further, the sole proprietorship can be easily converted to another business structure (e.g., corporation, partnership) as desired.

Fifth, a sport business operated as a sole proprietorship, partly due to the entity's smaller size, avoids numerous government and legislative restrictions imposed on other types of business formations. For example, sole proprietors typically avoid antitrust scrutiny. Antitrust laws attempt to protect the small business against the unfair trade practices and other monopolistic ploys of big business. Further, some legislation (e.g., Title VII, Family Medical Leave Act, and the Americans with Disabilities Act [ADA]) qualifies the number of employees an entity must have prior

Figure 4–4 Business Structure Choices: Physical Fitness Facilities

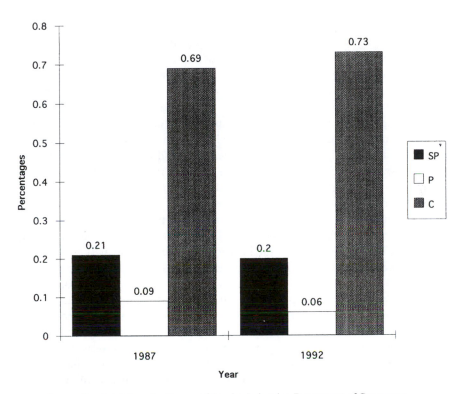

Source: Reprinted from the Census of Service Industries, Department of Commerce.

to the mandate of legal compliance. A sport business operating as a sole proprietorship with few employees spares the expense of compliance.

A sixth attraction, total profit retention, benefits the sole proprietor as well. A
sport entrepreneur, working long hours to provide the consumer with a quality,
high-demand product, often faces significant frustration when forced to share profits with those contributing far less in managerial expertise, time, or idea generation.

Seventh, a sole proprietor maintains confidential operations better than an
owner of an alternative business structure. Consequently, the adoption of a sole
proprietorship business structure provides protection against a competitor's ability to imitate or sabotage product introductions, marketing campaigns, and other

competitive strategies. A sport business entrepreneur, cognizant of the substitutability of any one product, views the confidentiality feature favorably.

Disadvantages

The following section elaborates on five significant disadvantages a sport business may incur when organized as a sole proprietor. First, access to capital presents a formidable limitation. Launching a new sport business requires adequate capital to cover start-up expenses as well as to fund growth via new equipment, expanded personnel (in-house or outsourced), geographic expansion, program expansion, or target market expansion. Unfortunately, a sport business proprietor, due to a number of factors, including limited capital, lack of experience, and/or unproven business capabilities may find borrowing unavailable or too expensive. Unavailable or inaccessible capital forces a sport business entrepreneur to pass opportunities and market share on to other competitors possessing greater capital resources.

Second, limited managerial expertise stagnates the profitability and viability of a sole proprietor operating a sport business. Few sole proprietors possess highly specialized knowledge in *all* of their business's functional areas (e.g., management, marketing, budgeting). Even if a sport business entrepreneur possesses expertise in all functional areas, time restrictions make the optimal development of each area unlikely. The sole proprietorship business structure hinders the attainment of premier employees as well. The scarcity of promotion opportunities forces job candidates possessing functional expertise to look at larger, competing organizations better equipped to provide more autonomy, empowerment, responsibility, status (e.g., office, job title), remuneration, benefits, and deferred compensation plans (e.g., stock bonus, profit sharing, 401K). This lack of managerial expertise places the sport business at a competitive disadvantage in comparison to competitors operating with other business structures.

Third, unlimited liability often constitutes the dominant disadvantage associated with the sole proprietorship business structure. The risk inherent to sport, coupled with a litigious society, magnifies concerns regarding unlimited liability. Unlimited liability provides creditors and tort claimants access to personal investments and properties (e.g., car, home) when a sport business cannot cover debt or the claims against the assets. Further, a person may work for years to pay off incurred debts if losses do exceed personal wealth.

Fourth, the life of an individual sole proprietor defines the longevity of a particular sport business. The death or incapacity of the sport proprietor brings about the dissolution of the particular sport business. Disadvantages accrue even when the sport business is rejuvenated. For example, creditors may question the financial and managerial integrity of the new owner, customers may defect during the "reorganization" period, personnel changes may influence existing consumers to switch from one sport product provider to another, and monies and time are lost as a result of paperwork.

THE GENERAL PARTNERSHIP

A general partnership consists of two or more persons organized to engage in a business (or businesses) for profit. The partners exist as co-owners "and share equally in the operation, management, and liability of the business" (Ellis & Norton, 1988, p. 44). In 1992, the partnership business formation was adopted by 10% of all public golf courses, 7% of all membership sports and recreation clubs, 5% of all sporting goods and bicycle shops, and 6% of physical fitness facilities (Figures 4–1 through 4–4). (The census data report partnerships at large and do not distinguish between general and limited partnerships. See U.S. Department of Commerce, 1977a, 1977b, 1982a, 1982b, 1987a, 1987b, 1992a, 1992b.)

Advantages

The general partnership presents sport businesses with three primary advantages unavailable to the sole proprietor. First, a sport business formed as a general partnership provides greater access to capital resources than that available to a sport business proprietor. Although an advantage in comparison to the sole proprietorship, the capital available to the general partnership is limited in contrast to other business structure alternatives (i.e., the corporation). Similarly, the limited capital and promotion/ownership opportunities of a partnership hinders securement of the best managerial talent in comparison to the corporation. Access to capital enables the partnership to take better advantage of opportunities and trends resulting in greater revenue generation, increased market share, and enhanced customer satisfaction. As mentioned above, capital availability provides a sport business with needed monies for new distribution outlets, geographic expansion, the additional hiring of personnel, and/or the provision of product extensions.

Second, a sport business formed as a partnership enhances the internal degree of managerial talent. "Multiple minds," or pooled intelligence, is likely to produce better sport business decisions in comparison to a single entity or a "single mind." Further, individual partners possessing distinct qualities and expertise are better able to address diverse market demands and company needs. Banks and other lenders look favorably on the pooled collateral and the pooled managerial expertise, as both of these factors reduce creditor risk.

The benefits of capital access and managerial talent reflect, in part, revenues generated. As illustrated in Figures 4–1 through 4–4, sport businesses formed as partnerships generated more revenue per establishment than the sport businesses operating as a sole proprietor in the years 1977, 1982, 1987, and 1992 in the following industries: public golf courses (Figure 4–1), membership sports and recreation clubs (Figure 4–2), sporting goods and bicycle shops (Figure 4–3), and physical fitness facilities (Figure 4–4; 1987 and 1992 data available only; U.S. Department of Commerce, 1977a, 1977b, 1982a, 1982b, 1987a, 1987b, 1992a, 1992b).

Third, similar to a sport business proprietorship, yet deserving of more comment, the general partnership as an entity avoids paying corporate taxes on generated revenues. Rather, this income is "passed through" and added (profits) or subtracted (losses) from other generated income. As explained by Booth (1995, p. 550), "The primary purpose of a tax shelter is to generate losses (at least in the early years of operation), thus generating gains—in the form of tax savings—that have little to do with the success or failure of the business." A particular sport business may not worry if it produces a loss. Instead, a sport business may favor generated losses as a way to reduce tax payables. For example, if an individual's income amounted to $150,000, the accompanying tax liability would amount to $43,370.50 (single filing status, 1995 tax rate schedule). If, however, that individual had a $75,000 loss associated with Health Club ABC, the individual partner's tax liability would be reduced to $18,518. On the other hand, profits earned by the partnership increase individual tax liabilities. According to the Internal Revenue Service (IRS), an average of 56% of all partnerships reported a loss between 1985 and 1993 (Internal Revenue Service [IRS], 1995).

Disadvantages

Two primary disadvantages incurred by the sport business operating as a general partnership are (1) the limited longevity of the entity itself and (2) joint and several liability. The partnership lacks continuity of life because the firm "is necessarily dissolved by withdrawal, bankruptcy, or death of a partner" (Bromberg & Ribstein, 1995, p. 196). The rationale associated with dissolution of the partnership by the withdrawal of any one member is explained by McGuire (1989, pp. 302–303):

> A partnership is a combination of persons, each bringing unique abilities and credit ratings to the business. Parties dealing with the firm may rely on the joint abilities and credit of the firm's members, and each partner relies on the abilities and credit of his or her partners as well. If a partner leaves the firm, that combination of abilities and credit has been changed. As a result, the creditors and remaining partners should be given the opportunity to reassess their relationships with the firm in light of the changed circumstances.

Limited longevity jeopardizes established relationships with creditors and consumers while interrupting the general cash flow of the sport business.

Second, similar to the sole proprietorship, the individual partners in a sport business partnership possess unlimited liability and consequently endanger personal assets. Further, the general liability of a general partner includes liability for individual errors and omissions, in addition to joint and several liability for the acts of other individual partners. Partners are individually liable for the acts of another partner regardless of consent, actual, or constructive notice. Individuals within a partnership attempt to prevent errors and omissions by "monitoring" or looking into each other's activities. However, the act of monitoring presents a limitation as it restricts the size, and resultant economies of scale, of any one partnership. Further, resources (both time and money) spent in monitoring each other's activities detract from productivity and efficiency. The unlimited liability of individual partners discourages passive investors and thwarts opportunities dependent on access to additional capital. The era of litigation and the risk-prone nature of sport magnify this limitation. However, legislation in the 1980s curbed many problems associated with the joint and several liability of general partners. As reported by the American Tort Reform Association (Middleton, 1995), 41 states modified or abolished joint and several liability since 1986.

THE LIMITED PARTNERSHIP

A limited partnership consists of one or more general partners who retain full liability for the business and "limited" or "special" partners who invest monies, and, in turn, receive a proceed of generated income proportionate to their investment. Sport business managers typically manager the operation (e.g., serve as the general partners), while individuals often unfamiliar with the sport product itself serve as removed investors (i.e., limited partners).

Advantages

A sport business operating as a limited partnership realizes four primary advantages. First, a limited partner retains no liability for the claims against the organization's assets. Rather, a limited partner's loss mirrors the amount invested.

Second, the limited partnership provides attractive investment opportunities for individual investors. Investors, realizing the liability risks encountered with sport and fearful of the joint and several liability associated with the general partnership, find the limited partnership a viable investment. The sport business, on the other hand, benefits from the capital infusion.

Third, a limited partnership provides the investor with an opportunity to strengthen individual earnings while simultaneously obtaining a diversified portfolio. Investors often find sport businesses attractive investments as demand for sport-related products continues to increase. Serving as a limited partner allows individuals to spread wealth without inordinately expanding liability risks.

Fourth, the limited partnership provides individuals with a tax shelter as limited partners retain pass-through tax benefits associated with the general partnership. The ability to deduct generated passive losses (those losses incurred from businesses in which the individual does not materially participate) from passive income (e.g., dividends, interest, annuities, and gains from the sale or exchange of stock and securities) lowers tax liabilities.

Disadvantage

The inability of a limited partner to provide input regarding management-related issues constitutes a primary disadvantage of a sport business considering the limited partnership business structure alternative. Limited partnerships jeopardize classification by the IRS and the courts when limited partners participate in the management of the sport business itself. Unfortunately, individuals investing large sums of money may prefer to have input when strategic decisions directly influence the profitability of their investment. Consequently, potential investors wanting to exercise some control over business operations often choose to invest in sport businesses with alternative business structures.

THE S CORPORATION

Congress created the S corporation in 1958 as a vehicle to foster small business success by recognizing a business structure that combined the best of the partnership and the corporation into one entity. S corporations grew in number after President Reagan's Tax Reform Act (TRA) of 1986. As stated by the IRS, S corporation filings increased an average 14.1% per year between 1986 to 1992 (IRS, 1995). The TRA lowered both corporate and individual tax rates, but, more importantly, the corporate tax rate now exceeded tax rates (34% versus 28%). A sport business formed as an S corporation avoids paying the higher corporate tax rate. Individuals pay lower taxes on pass-through income versus paying both the higher corporate tax rate plus taxes on distributed income.

Advantages

The S corporation has six primary advantages. First, a sport business formed as an S corporation eliminates the joint and several liability of the general partner. All S corporation member-shareholders, similar to the traditional corporate entity, bear limited liability, and personal assets cannot be accessed to pay claims against the entity itself. Similar to the corporation and the limited partner, an individual shareholder can lose only the amount invested.

Second, similar to the partnership, the S corporation eliminates the financial hardship associated with double taxation. The generated income passes through to individual shareholders. A sport business formed as an S corporation pays no federal corporate income tax.

Third, a sport business formed as an S corporation increases access to capital via stock distribution opportunities. Sole proprietors and partnerships recognizing this advantage often change to an S corporation as a sport business grows and needs capital.

Fourth, a sport business formed as an S corporation secures managerial talent better than either the sole proprietorship or the partnership. The wisdom of prudent employees enhances the competitive strength and positioning strategies of any sport business.

Fifth, the S corporation avoids the alternative minimum tax (AMT). The AMT taxes items such as tax-exempt interest, passive losses, and deductions claimed for charitable contributions in an effort to ensure that wealthy individuals and corporations pay income tax (IRS, 1995). In comparison to the C corporation, AMT tax avoidance lowers a sport business's cost structure and enhances competitive positioning.

Sixth, sport medicine personnel find the S corporation attractive for another reason. Personal service corporations (PSCs) can form an S corporation and escape the flat tax rate while retaining limited liability. As a C corporation, personal service organizations incur a flat tax of 34%. In other words, a PSC generating $60,000 would be taxed at 34%. In comparison, an S corporation would be taxed at lower individual rates. To quantify, let's assume a PSC generates $50,000 of net income. A single individual, assuming no other income, would incur a tax liability of $10,964.50 (1995 tax filing schedules). As a C corporation, the tax liability amounts to $17,000.

Disadvantages

Prior to December 1996, sport businesses formed as S corporations encountered three restrictions yielding substantial disadvantages. First, the qualifying restrictions listed below limited the ability of the sport business formed as an S corporation to expand and acquire needed capital:

1. The S corporation is limited to 35 shareholders.
2. The S corporation can issue only one class of stock.
3. The S corporation may not own 80% or more of the stock of another corporation.

However, effective December 1996, a tax law revision (Code Sec. 1361) provides greater flexibility for a sport business formed as an S corporation. For example, the number of allowed shareholders increases to 75. Similarly, S corporations may hold 80% or more of the stock of another corporation.

Second, the S corporation prohibits employee-shareholders from borrowing money from pension plans (allowed in C corporations). Consequently, the S corporation alternative can hinder access to needed or valued employees desiring this benefit.

Third, an employee's benefits can be deducted as a business expense only when the employee-shareholder owns less than 2% of the corporate stock. An employee owning in excess of 2% of the stock "must declare 75% of those premiums as income and pay income, Social Security, and Medicare payroll taxes on the amount" (McQuown, 1992, p. 124). Consequently, a sport business formed as an S corporation may lose tax-favored fringe benefits including medical and insurance plan write-offs.

THE CORPORATION

Chief Justice John Marshall defined the corporation in 1819 (*Dartmouth College v. Woodard*) as follows: "A corporation is an artificial being, invisible, intangible and existing only in the contemplation of the law." The evolution of the corporation is a direct result of business growth. Demands for capital, liability protection for owners, order, and accountability prompted the recognition and growth of corporate formations. In 1992, corporations accounted for 70% of all public golf courses, 78% of membership sports and recreation clubs, 64% of sporting goods and bicycle shops, and 73% of physical fitness facilities (U.S. Department of Commerce, 1977, 1982, 1987, 1992). (The census data does not demarcate between S corporations and C corporations. However, the inclusion of S corporations with C corporations explains why revenue per establishment is often below that of the partnership as the majority (83%) of S corporations have 1 to 2 members [see the *Statistics of Income Bulletin* published by the IRS, 1992].)

Advantages

A corporation offers a sport business six primary advantages. First, due to the corporation's ability to issue shares in accordance with its articles of incorporation, a sport business can access needed capital. This access to capital places the sport business formed as a corporation at a strategic advantage in comparison to other business formation alternatives, as capital availability provides for market or product expansion.

Second, the liability of each shareholder/owner reflects only that amount invested by the individual shareholder. Recognized by the IRS and the courts as an individual, the corporate sport business maintains liability for its own debts, while the personal wealth of the shareholder remains protected. (Although a rarity, the courts have recognized situations that dictate the piercing of the "corporate veil," and liability is transferred to the shareholders.)

Third, available and/or accessible resources enable the corporation to secure the best sport management personnel. A sport business formed as a corporation can attract premium employees via stock ownership, promotional opportunities, large salaries, and deferred compensation plans.

Fourth, the corporation can decrease tax liabilities for small or one-person entities. For example, assume a sport business generated a net income of $75,000. As an individual sport business proprietor, this $75,000 would incur a tax of $18,518 (individual filing, 1995 tax schedule). However, if the individual splits net income 1:2 ($25,000 salary and $50,000 retained corporate earnings), the total tax liability amounts to $12,652 ($7,500 corporate tax + $5,152 individual income tax), or a savings of almost $6,000.

Fifth, dividends received from corporate investments remain 70% tax-free (i.e., corporate income tax is not paid on these revenues). This constitutes a significant tax advantage for a large sport business with prudent investment strategies. A sport business can use the tax savings to produce a better, more diversified product line or otherwise improve competitive advantage.

Sixth, as a corporation, individual executives often find greater ease in doing business (McQuown, 1992). A sport business formed as a corporation often experiences less resistance and scrutiny in accessing credit, ordering inventory, and so forth due to established corporate accounts.

Disadvantages

Four primary disadvantages a sport business encounters when formed as a corporation include: (1) double taxation, (2) the separation of management and ownership, (3) the extensive corporate formalities requirement, and (4) government scrutiny. First, the corporation, as an entity separate from its managers and owners, pays corporate income taxes. Viewed as an individual person, the sport business formed as a corporation must pay taxes as do individual taxpayers. In addition to the corporate tax, individual shareholders pay taxes on distributed dividends at their respective tax rates. As a result of this double taxation, shareholders receive only a diluted portion of original earnings. The accumulated earnings tax, a tax on retained earnings above a specified amount, discourages companies from retaining monies to avoid the double taxation. The accumulated earnings tax enables the IRS to tax the retained earnings by as much as 75% (McQuown, 1992).

Consequently, a sport business may find it most economically advantageous to pay dividends regardless of the double taxation.

Second, owners (i.e., shareholders) typically play an inactive role in the management of a larger sport business formed as a corporation. Management scholars have criticized this separation of ownership and management (Drucker, 1992). Critics argue that the separation of management and ownership results in goal conflict as managers of a sport business focus on short-term results at the expense of long-term objectives. For example, sport managers may emphasize those activities that enable them to meet quarterly financial quotas (selling a certain volume of product regardless of quality or defect rates). From the perspective of the sport managers, acquisition of short-term goals provides job security while enhancing bonus or merit opportunities. On the other hand, maintaining company image or product quality becomes secondary. Corporate downsizing further reinforces the need for sport managers to meet or exceed short-term objectives.

Third, in comparison to other business structures, the sport business operating as a corporation subjects itself to more intricacies regarding corporate organization, structure, voting, and other shareholder rights. The required formalities increase expenses and delay the implementation of competitive strategies while jeopardizing strategic opportunities.

Fourth, a large sport business formed as a corporation undergoes more extensive government scrutiny than does a sport business adopting an alternative business structure. Government, in an attempt to protect innocent consumers against the power of corporate monopolies and oligopolies, enacts laws restraining operations. For example, the Sherman Act, the Clayton Act, the Hart-Scott-Rodino Antitrust Improvement Act, and the Federal Trade Commission all attempt to regulate business in the best interests of free trade and the consumer. Compliance with the various laws can be an onerous, expensive task for a sport business formed as a corporation.

THE LLC

The LLC, although an entity long recognized and popular in foreign countries (principally Central and South America), did not reach the United States until introduced by Wyoming in 1977 (Goforth, 1995; Horwood & Hechtman, 1994). Regardless of the other long-standing business structures mentioned above, both legal commentators and IRS officials view the LLC as the business structure of the future (Fox, 1994). Some commentators go so far as to argue that the LLC may eventually bring about the demise of the general partnership, limited partnership, and S corporation (Gazur, 1995; Johnson, 1983). As explained by Macey (1995, p. 437), "If this prediction proves correct, a business environment may emerge in which all firms except sole proprietorships would enjoy the benefits of limited liability, and all firms except publicly traded corporations could enjoy the benefits of pass-through tax treatment."

The real revolution in LLC business formation emerged in 1988 when the IRS formally recognized the LLC as a partnership for federal income tax purposes (Rev. Rul. 88-76). By January 1, 1995, every state had LLC statutes except Hawaii, Massachusetts, and Vermont (Bamberger & Jacobson, 1995; Gazur, 1995). The rapid adoption of the LLC is attributed to state legislatures' interest in attracting business (both domestic and foreign) and related revenues (Goforth, 1995; Johnson, 1983). States, although forfeiting franchise taxes from entities formed as C corporations, recognize that the increased economic vitality produced by the LLC alternative outweighs the loss in tax dollars. Although, as explained by Macey (1995), some states and local ordinances require LLCs to pay business taxes. For example, New York City requires that LLCs pay a 4% partnership tax (similar to the required tax payment for partnerships). Booth (1995) expects every state to recognize the LLC by late 1995 or 1996.

Advantages

The LLC presents three primary advantages. Previously addressed were two advantages common to other business structures: limited liability and partnership tax status. A third benefit focuses on the flexibility allowed within the LLC, especially when compared to the S corporation. Unlike the S corporation, which prohibits other corporations or partnerships from becoming shareholders, the LLC extends membership opportunities to these entities. In addition, the LLC permits an unlimited number of members. Arkansas, Colorado, Georgia, Idaho, Indiana, Missouri, Montana, New Mexico, New York, and Texas recognize one-person LLCs (Gazur, 1995). Further, the LLC business structure encourages parent-subsidiary structures. In comparison to the S corporation, there are no qualifications limiting the percentage of stock an LLC can hold in another corporation. The establishment of parent-subsidiary relationships serves as a competitive advantage due to common linkages and shared functions (e.g., marketing, distributions). Some states permit the perpetual existence of an LLC, a benefit not available to the partnership or sole proprietorship.

Disadvantages

The time and expense required to convert from a partnership to an LLC constitutes a disadvantage of the LLC. As explained by Hester (1995, p. LLP-7), "Difficulties relating to negotiating and drafting the agreements and documents required to convert an existing partnership to an LLC or other form of entity are often cited as major obstacles to such a conversion." Sport business managers may find that other established business structure alternatives that meet existing needs present a lower cost to the particular organization.

The newness of the LLC business formation and its lack of established precedent constitutes a second disadvantage associated with this business structure alternative. As explained by Gazur (1995, p. 138), "The LLC's future will be marked by legislative, judicial, regulatory, and practitioner experimentations with the new entity, revisiting issues already settled in other contexts." Sport businesses may find that the uncertainties and possible resultant litigation outweigh benefits associated with the LLC.

The lack of uniformity and predictability among the various LLC statutes represents a third disadvantage of the LLC business formation. The National Conference of Commissioners on Uniform State Laws adopted the Uniform Limited Liability Company Act in 1994 as a way to eliminate the jurisdictional confusion presented by the differing language within the various LLC statutes (Brayer, 1995). As noted above, the possible confusion and resultant litigation emanating for sport businesses engaged in interstate commerce may represent a significant deterrent to LLC adoption.

THE LLP

LLP represents the newest type of business structure alternative. Texas introduced the first LLP in 1991. (Texas adopted the statute primarily as a means of protection for law and accounting firms who were being sued by the numerous savings and loan and thrift associations that failed in the 1980s [Bromberg & Ribstein, 1995].) The primary intent of the LLP was to provide professional service partnerships (e.g., accounting, medical, and legal practices) the opportunity to retain the traditional partnership structure while eliminating risk due to joint and several liability. Most service organizations preferred the partnership structure, as the personal holding corporations do not have the same tax benefits as general business and professional corporations. Only New York currently restricts the LLP to professional service organizations. As explained by Hester (1995, p. LLP-4),

> A common approach is to shield a partner from partnership debts, liabilities or obligations incurred while the partnership is an LLP and arising from the negligence, malpractice, wrongful act or misconduct committed by another partner, employee or agent of the partnership, unless the negligence, malpractice, wrongful act or misconduct was committed by someone under his direct supervision and control.

By 1994, 18 states had adopted LLP legislation, while three other states had legislation pending. By 1995, 34 states had adopted LLP legislation.

Advantages

The LLP provides three significant advantages, all of which have been discussed above. First, an LLP retains the pass-through tax benefits associated with the traditional partnership. Second, an LLP can be easily formed in comparison, for example, to the complexities associated with a corporation. Third, an LLP provides limited liability. The first two elements should be familiar to the reader. The limited liability associated with the LLP, however, has its own interesting evolution. The earliest LLP statutes protected partners from acts of negligence only. Individual LLP members retained liability for contractual wrongs. Other statutes provided immunity for tort claims with the exception that individual partners would be liable for the acts of those they supervised. As revealed by Hester (1995), 14 of the existing 18 LLP statutes in 1994 contained partner liability for those supervised and/or when a partner had actual knowledge of another's errors and omissions. Later statutory amendments and newly enacted LLP statutes more closely resemble corporations or LLCs that offered protection from virtually all partnership obligations, including both tort and contract. Further, statutory language may provide partners with both contribution and indemnification rights.

Disadvantages

Similar to the LLP, the conversion expense and the lack of established precedent constitute the primary disadvantages associated with this type of business structure.

PARTNERSHIP VERSUS CORPORATE STATUS: A "TAXING" ISSUE

The Corporation Defined

As noted throughout the above analysis, pass-through tax benefits can decrease tax liabilities. An understanding of the analysis used by the IRS and the courts in distinguishing whether a particular entity qualifies as a partnership or corporation for taxation purposes protects a sport business from erroneously acting in ways that jeopardize or eliminate this benefit. The Supreme Court defined a corporation by the following six attributes in *Morrissey v. Commissioner* (1935);

1. Associates;
2. An objective to carry on a business and divide the gains therefrom;
3. Continuity of life;
4. Centralization of management;
5. Liability for corporate debts limited to corporate property; and
6. Free transferability of interests. (Booth, 1995, p. 546)

The Supreme Court, the IRS, and subsequent legal literature agree that the first two attributes—having associates and an objective to carry on a business and generate revenues—characterize most businesses. For example, associates (e.g., individuals) collectively represent both a partnership and a corporation. Further, the objective to generate profits and divide according to predetermined agreements also characterizes both the partnership and corporation. Supreme Court analyses focus on whether a particular entity possesses one or more of the remaining four characteristics (Numbers 3 through 6 above). The IRS views businesses possessing three or more of the four characteristics as a corporation. The IRS treats businesses with only one or two of the four characteristics as a partnership. Again, a familiarity with the analysis benefits a sport manager wanting to retain the pass-through taxation benefits associated with the traditional partnership. The following paragraph briefly elaborates on the meaning associated with Items 3 through 6 listed above.

The third element, continuity of life, refers to the perpetual existence of the corporate entity regardless of the "death, retirement, resignation, incapacity, bankruptcy or insolvency of one or more of its members" (Goforth, 1995, p. 1,211). The fourth element, centralization of management, refers to the vested authority of the Board of Directors to set corporate policy and appoint management responsible for the daily operations. The fifth element, limited liability, refers to the shareholders' immunity for claims against the corporation. The sixth element, free transferability of interests, refers to the ability of all owners to transfer ownership interests, both managerial and financial, without the consent of any other owner.

To summarize, LLCs and LLPs must lack any two of the following: continuity of life, centralized management, limited liability, and free transferability of interests. The subsequent paragraphs analyze each of the four characteristics in more detail as they pertain to the LLC and LLP.

Free Transferability of Interests

Both LLCs and LLPs tend to lack free transferability of interests. Free transferability of interests exists when members can transfer both financial and management or governing rights to another nonmember without the consent of the other LLC or LLP members. As explained by Booth (1995, p. 597), "Typically, with minor and unimportant variations, the statutes forbid the LLC members from transferring an interest in both the economic and the governance rights to a nonmember unless either all or a majority of the nontransferring members consent to the transfer." Although some statutes allow the LLC members to transfer economic rights, very few allow the transfer of both economic and governing rights. LLPs tend to lack free transferability of interests as well. LLCs and LLPs prefer to limit the transferability of individual interests for three reasons. First, partners, due to joint and several liability, remain very selective regarding partnership admissions.

Although most LLPs limit tort liability, some statutes retain liability for contractual claims. Consequently, partners or entity members want input regarding the transfer of memberships due to possible contractual liability as a result of another's actions. Second, continuing the tradition of nontransferable partnership rights clarifies to interested parties (e.g., the IRS and the Supreme Court) that the entity operates as a partnership. Third, although a rarity, the "corporate veil" of an entity may be pierced in certain circumstances as a result of individual member activities (e.g., fraudulent behavior). Member scrutiny via limited transferability of rights helps protect individuals against the unforeseeable acts of partners.

Continuity of Life

Similar to the lack of free transferability of rights, LLCs and LLPs both tend to lack continuity of life as well. As defined by Wirtz and Harris (1995, p. 55), an organization lacks continuity of life when the "death, insanity, bankruptcy, retirement, resignation, or expulsion of *any* member will cause a dissolution of the organization." However, the IRS allows continued existence if either "all or a majority of the members agree to continue the business" (Booth, 1995, p. 592). Since the continuation of the business requires member approval, and thus is not assured, the IRS rationalizes that an entity lacks continuity of life. LLPs tend to adopt the Uniform Partnership Act, Section 29, characteristic of dissolution upon the disassociation of any one partner. As mentioned above, retention of traditional partnership characteristics ease classification efforts by the IRS and the courts.

Centralized Management

LLCs can be either managed by members where each member has equal management rights (aka "member-managed") or managed by managers hired or appointed exclusively to manage the business and conduct related business affairs (aka "manager-managed" or "centralized management"). In other words, centralized management exists when a particular individual or group of individuals have total authority to manage and direct entity operations. Managers may not necessarily be LLC members. Evidence that managers resemble corporate board members tends to characterize the entity as an association subject to corporate taxation. Wirtz and Harris (1992, p. 383) state, "An organization has centralized management if any person (or any group of persons not including all of the members) has continuing, exclusive authority to make the management decisions necessary to the conduct of the organization's business and such authority does not require ratification by members of the organization." Most LLC members, however, prefer the member-management option (Fox, 1994). LLC members prefer direct involvement in the LLC affairs as a means of protecting their investment (Fox, 1994). As explained by Fox (1994, p. 1,152), "participation in management is the rule rather than the exception." However, some LLCs engage in centralized management to attract passive investors seeking a steady return on investment while retaining limited liability.

Similar to the LLCs, most LLPs are directly managed by members in the partnership. As summarized by Bromberg and Ribstein (1995, p. 121), "Management decisions have important consequences for partners who have invested their human capital even if they are not personally liable for the firm's debts." The LLP statutes providing liability for supervisory activities create an additional concern regarding participatory management. Again, the potential for injury in the realm of sport magnifies the need of a sport business manager to scrutinize closely subordinate activities.

Limited Liability

Limited liability indicates that sport business individuals remain free from liability for the debts and obligations of the LLC. The limited liability provision contains one of the most attractive characteristics to sport businesses operating as either an LLC or an LLP, as the amount of personal loss reflects only the amount of individual investment. As stated by Macey (1995, p. 447), "LLCs are not liable, directly or indirectly (or by way of indemnification, contribution, or otherwise), for the debts, obligations or liabilities of the firm. Similarly, unlike in the partnership context, members are not liable for the tort or contractual obligations of other members of the firm, even when those obligations have been incurred in the conduct of the firm's business." A sport business entrepreneur often views limited liability as a prerequisite to engaging in business due to liability concerns. One caveat, however, is that some LLC and LLP statutes retain member liability for acts held to be either intentional, grossly negligent, or reckless conduct (Gazur, 1995).

PIERCING THE CORPORATE VEIL: PROTECTION FOR THE LLC AND LLP

As explained above, LLCs and LLPs provide significant advantages for sport business shareholders by curbing the extent of taxation and limiting personal liability. However, the veil of limited liability, although a fundamental tenant of corporate law, faces continued challenge in the courts because of perceived social injustice. As explained by Black (1990, p. 1,148), piercing the corporate veil is "The doctrine which holds that the corporate structure with its attendant limited liability of stockholders may be disregarded and personal liability imposed on stockholders, officers, and directors in the case of fraud or other wrongful acts done in name of corporation." A sport business manager can protect individual shareholder wealth by understanding the analysis undertaken by the courts when ascertaining if a business's actions necessitate the imposition of individual liability. Case law precedent establishes the analyses used by the courts when considering corporate veil piercing. Piercing the corporate veil appears to be of little threat to LLP partners, LLC members, and corporate shareholders. As revealed by Thompson's research (1991), only 14% of all cases challenging an entity's limited liability were tort related. A total of 1,572 veil-piercing cases were analyzed. Of the 226 tort-related cases analyzed, only 31% were actually successful in piercing the corporate veil.

The newness of the LLC and LLP and the resultant lack of precedent provides nominal situations in which the piercing of the corporate veil doctrine has been applied to these new business formations. However, legal experts predict that the same analysis applied to a corporation will also be used to ascertain when, and if, the veil of an LLC's or LLP's limited liability protection should be discarded (Fox, 1994; Gazur, 1995; Thompson, 1991). LLP statutes, for example, in Colorado, Minnesota, and North Dakota specifically make provisions within their state statutes that apply corporate law standards to veil piercing.

The four commonly cited reasons justifying judiciary intervention into the otherwise sanctity of limited liability are (1) fraud, (2) improper adherence to corporate formalities, (3) inadequate capitalization, and (4) the issue of separateness. The following paragraphs elaborate on each of these four reasons.

Fraud

As explained by Easterbrook and Fischel (1985, p. 112), fraud may occur "When a corporation misrepresents the nature of its activities, its ability to perform, or its financial condition. Less obvious situations crop up when a firm misleads a creditor into believing that it would have recourse to the assets of other corporations in the event of nonperformance." The commission of fraud and the resultant liability incurred by corporate shareholders appears harsh. Shareholders, not involved in the management of the business itself, lack knowledge about (or involvement in) the fraudulent behavior itself. The social justice of imposing liability on noninvolved shareholders remains questionable. However, the imposition of liability on individual LLC and LLP members appear more plausible due to the individual's direct involvement in the management of the business. One can deduce that LLCs and LLPs involved in fraudulent acts will not be able to hide behind the veil of limited liability.

Adherence to Corporate Formalities

Corporate formalities refer to items such as the election of directors or officers, issuance of stock certificates, maintenance of corporate records, and meetings (Fox, 1994). For example, a typical formality for the majority of LLCs includes filing of articles of organization. Articles of organization typically contain the entity's name, purpose, and address. The filing notifies creditors of the shareholder's limited liability. Creditors then enter into contractual agreements with knowledge regarding recourse possibilities. However, state statutes minimally define required LLC and LLP formalities. For example, as of 1995, LLP statutes include at minimum a filing requirement and application identifying factors such as the name, number of partners, and a brief business statement (Hester, 1995). Adherence to such corporate formalities can be accomplished with little effort and expense. There is little to suggest that LLCs and LLPs jeopardize limited liability protection by failing to follow such innocuous requirements.

Inadequate Capitalization

Veil piercing due to inadequate capitalization poses the biggest threat to LLCs and LLPs, as it has drawn the most scrutiny by the courts (Fox, 1994). Consumer advocates view access to capital (either the firm's or an individual's personal assets) as critical to satisfy a plaintiff-claimant wrongly injured by an entity. LLC and LLP statutes try to pacify such societal concerns by either imposing capital requirements or mandatory insurance. For example, a number of statutes prohibit distributions to the LLC members unless LLC assets exceed debt (e.g., Arizona, Iowa, Kansas, Louisiana, Maryland, Minnesota, Nevada, Oklahoma, Texas, Utah, Virginia, West Virginia, and Wyoming). LLP statutes attempt to do the same thing via mandatory insurance requirements (e.g., Delaware; Washington, D.C.; Utah). As explained by Hester (1995, p. LLP-11), early LLP statutes required LLPs to carry a minimum amount of insurance "For the purpose of satisfying judgments against the partnership or its partners based on the kind of conduct for which liability of partners is limited by statute." However, LLP statutes requiring insurance only "if reasonably available" present interpreters with uncertainties. Further, 15 of the 18 LLP statutes existing in 1994 omit the insurance requirement in its entirety. Inadequate capitalization, alone, rarely constitutes an immediate withdrawal of limited liability as the courts require the prevalence of one or more of the above factors as well (Fox, 1994; Kapusta & Nichols, 1994).

The Issue of "Separateness"

The state recognizes a corporation as a legal entity separate and apart from its shareholders. The corporation, as a legal entity, can sue and be sued. The issue of separation exists when the courts determine that there is "substantial similarity in interest that the corporation no longer has a personality separate from its owners" (Fox, 1994, p. 1,164). Both the LLC and the LLP are likely to fail the separate entity analysis since LLC members and LLP partners typically remain substantially involved in the intricacies of the entity. As noted above, failure to satisfy the test of separateness does not result in an automatic removal of limited liability protection.

Rather, LLPs or LLCs should spend time ensuring that they meet or comply with other listed factors of analyses (i.e., fraud, formalization, and capitalization).

CHAPTER SUMMARY

The business structure adopted by a sport business influences potential liability, cost structure, and managerial efficiencies. Each business structure alternative has advantages and disadvantages influencing sport business decision making. LLCs and LLPs are two recent business structure alternatives combining the flexibility and tax benefits associated with partnerships with the fundraising ability and liability protection offered to the corporation. Most sport business entrepreneurs favor the pass-through benefits associated with a partnership and limited liability. However, there is no "best" business structure for a sport entrepreneur. The size of a sport business, competition, and inherent risk of a particular product all influence the business structure alternative decision.

STUDENT ASSIGNMENT

1. Identify a sport business entity.
   a. Identify its chosen business structure.
   b. Elaborate on why the particular sport business owner chose this business structure alternative.
   c. Elaborate on the perceived strengths and weaknesses (as perceived by the sport business owner) of the chosen structure.
   d. Elaborate on the owner's plans (if any) to alter the chosen sport business structure.
2. Pick a segment of the sport industry within a local area (e.g., major or minor league sport teams, health and fitness clubs, or bowling alleys). Interview the owners (or knowlegeable managers) of the various sport businesses. Specific questions should focus on why the particular sport business structure was chosen.
   a. Outline the reasons why each sport business chose the particular structure.
   b. Perform a competitive analysis and identify which sport business, as a result of the chosen business structure, has the greatest competitive advantage.
3. Obtain local data regarding the number of different businesses operating as either a sole proprietor, general partnership limited partnership, S corporation, C corporation, LLC, or LLP. Compare this data with sport industry–specific data.

REFERENCES

Bamberger, M.A., & Jacobson, A.J. (Eds.). (1995). State limited liability company and partnership law. Gaithersburg, MD: Aspen Publishers.

Black, H.C. (1990). *Black's law dictionary* (6th ed.). St. Paul, MN: West Publishing Company.

Booth, R.A. (1995). Profit-seeking, individual liability, and the idea of the firm. *Washington University Law Quarterly, 73,* 539–563.

Brayer, J.S. (1995, July). Comprehending the uniform limited liability company act. *The Practical Real Estate Lawyer,* pp. 75–84.

Bromberg, A.R., & Ribstein, L.E. (1995). *Limited liability partnerships and the revised Uniform Partnership Act.* New York: Little, Brown.

Census of Retail Trade, U.S. Dept. of Commerce, 1977, 1982, 1987, 1992.

Census of Service Industries, U.S. Dept. of Commerce, 1977, 1982, 1987, 1992.

Dartmouth College v. Woodward, 17 U.S. (4 Wheat.) 518 (1819).

Drucker, P.F. (1992). *Managing for the future.* New York: Penguin Books.

Easterbrook, F.H., & Fischel, D.R. (1985). Limited liability and the corporation. *The University of Chicago Law Review, 52*(1), 89–117.

Ellis, T., & Norton, R.L. (1988). *Commercial recreation.* St. Louis, MO: Times Mirror Mosby.

Fox, E. (1994). Piercing the veil of limited liability companies. *The George Washington Law Review, 62*(6), 1,143–1,177.

Gazur, W.M. (1995). The limited liability company experiment: Unlimited flexibility, uncertain role. *Law and Contemporary Problems, 58*(2), 135–185.

Goforth, C.R. (1995). The rise of the limited liability company: Evidence of a race between the states, but heading where? *Syracuse Law Review, 45*(4), 1,193–1,289.

Hester, E.G. (1995). Practical guide to registered limited liability partnerships. In M.A. Bamberger & A.J. Jacobson (Eds.), *State limited liability company and partnership law.* Gaithersburg, MD: Aspen Publishers.

Horwood, R.M., & Hechtman, J.A. (1994). The ABCs of LLCs. *The Practical Lawyer, 40*(6), 65–82.

Internal Revenue Service. (1995). *Statistics of income bulletin (1987–1995).* Washington, DC: Author.

Johnson, R. (1983). The Limited Liability Company Act. *Florida State University Law Review, 11*(2), 387–405.

Kapusta, S., & Nichols, B. (1994). Limited liability companies: The optimal business organization for the twenty-first century? *St. John's Journal of Legal Commentary, 9*(2), 803–834.

Macey, J.R. (1995). The limited liability company: Lessons for corporate law. *Washington University Law Quarterly, 73,* 433–454.

McGuire, C.R. (1989). *The legal environment of business.* Columbus, OH: Merrill.

Middleton, M. (1995, August). A changing landscape. *ABA Journal,* pp. 56–61.

Morrissey v. Commissioner, 296 U.S. 344 (1935).

Rev. Rul. 88-76, 1988-2 C.B. 360 (1988).

Thompson, R.B. (1991). Piercing the corporate veil: An empirical study. *Cornell Law Review, 76*(5), 1,036–1,074.

U.S. Department of Commerce. (1977a). Census of retail trade. Washington, DC: Author.

U.S. Department of Commerce. (1982a). Census of retail trade. Washington, DC: Author.

U.S. Department of Commerce. (1987a). Census of retail trade. Washington, DC: Author.

U.S. Department of Commerce. (1992a). Census of retail trade. Washington, DC: Author.

U.S. Department of Commerce. (1977b). Census of service industries. Washington, DC: Author.

U.S. Department of Commerce. (1982b). Census of service industries. Washington, DC: Author.

U.S. Department of Commerce. (1987b). Census of service industries. Washington, DC: Author.

U.S. Department of Commerce. (1992b). Census of service industries. Washington, DC: Author.

Wirtz, F.J., & Harris, K.L. (1992, June). The emerging use of the limited liability company. *Taxes,* pp. 377–397.

Wirtz, F.J., & Harris, K.L. (1995, February). Assessing the long-awaited LLC classification guidelines. *Taxes,* pp. 51–62.

CHAPTER 5

Federal Legislation Influencing the Sport Business

Prior to the 1960s, employers had great leeway in how they recruited, hired, compensated, promoted, treated, and terminated employees. Today, employment litigation is "the fastest growing area of civil litigation in the federal system" and viewed by David C. Belt as being in a "state of crisis" ("Developments," 1996, p. 1,571). Equal opportunity legislation and litigation have greatly altered employment practices, and there is no sign that this trend will abate. The following legislation, described very briefly below, greatly influences management's interactions with job applicants and existing employees. In addition to employment-related legislation, sport business operations are further influenced by legislation regulating, for example, minimum wage and work place health and safety. This chapter reviews various pieces of legislation influencing the management of personnel and operations in general. This chapter strives only to introduce the student to legislation influencing sport business management. Sport business managers are encouraged to delve further into each piece of legislation to obtain a better and more thorough understanding.

TITLE VII OF THE CIVIL RIGHTS ACT OF 1964

Many legal scholars and academicians refer to Title VII as "the single most important piece of legislation that has helped to shape and define employment law rights in this country" (Bennett-Alexander & Pincus, 1995, p. 62). The Civil Rights Act of 1964 prohibits discrimination in employment as well as in housing, education, public accommodations, and federally assisted programs. Employment litigation quickly became the most common area of litigation as other areas of the law, such as access to hotels and public accommodations, became a moot point if minorities could not earn the income to frequent these places.

Title VII prohibits discrimination in any facet of employment (e.g., hiring, promotions, compensation, terminations, opportunities for training) based on race, sex, national origin, religion, or color. Sex discrimination does not include affinity orientation or transsexuals, although protective legislation may be provided by individual state laws. For example, 8 states and over 125 municipalities have legislation extending employment protection and benefits to gays and lesbians (Bennett-Alexander & Pincus, 1995). *Color* refers to one's skin pigmentation [e.g., dark or light]. For example, black complexions run a continuum from being very light to very dark. Research and case law allegations, for example, suggest that black individuals with lighter complexions receive higher income and better employment opportunities than blacks with darker complexions. (Bennett-Alexander & Pincus, 1995; *Walker v. Secretary of the Treasury, IRS,* 1990). The Equal Employment Opportunity Commission (EEOC), created in 1978, is responsible for enforcement and interpretation of the law. The legislation pertains to only those businesses affecting commerce and employing 15 or more employees for each working day in each of 20 or more weeks in the current or preceding calendar year. Bona fide private clubs (e.g., country clubs) are not required to comply with Title VII (Sawyer, 1993). As of 1991, Title VII also covers individuals employed by American firms outside the United States.

Disparate treatment and disparate impact represent two types of discrimination that can take place in violation of Title VII. Sport managers may argue that discrimination was necessary because of a "business necessity" or a required "bona fide occupational qualification" (BFOQ). Proof of a business necessity or a BFOQ qualifies as a viable defense against claims of discrimination. Disparate treatment, disparate impact, business necessity, and BFOQs are addressed in the following paragraphs.

Disparate Treatment

Disparate treatment refers to the *intentional,* differential treatment of employees based on race, color, religion, national origin, or sex. Disparate treatment represents overt discrimination. For example, a sport business adopting a policy prohibiting the employment of minorities illustrates a form of disparate treatment. If direct evidence of intentional discrimination is unavailable, an *inference* of discrimination can be deduced by the following four-prong analysis defined by the Supreme Court in *McDonnell Douglas Corp. v. Green* (1973). According to the Supreme Court, the plaintiff may successfully prove a prima facie case of discrimination by showing

1. classification in a protected class
2. that plaintiff applied and was qualified for a job for which plaintiff was seeking applicants

3. that, despite qualifications, plaintiff was rejected
4. that, after the rejection, the position remained open and the employer continued to seek applicants from persons of complainant's qualifications

Upon proof of the above by the plaintiff, burden then shifts to the defendant. A defendant employer can avoid liability by proving there was some legitimate, nondiscriminatory reason for the employee's rejection. The burden of proof then shifts back to the plaintiff, where the plaintiff must prove the defendant's justification represents "pre-text" only. The term *pre-text* mean that the justification provided is not "good" or sufficient but, rather, represents a nonmeritorious and lame attempt to disguise discriminatory employment practices. As explained by the Supreme Court in the 1981 case, *Texas Department of Community Affairs v. Burdine* (p. 256).

> The plaintiff retains the burden of persuasion. She now must have the opportunity to demonstrate that the (defendant's) proffered reason was not the true reason for the employment decision. This burden now *merges* with the ultimate burden of persuading the court that she has been the victim of intentional discrimination. She may succeed in this either directly, by persuading the court that a discriminatory reason more likely motivated the employer or indirectly by showing that the employer's proffered explanation is unworthy of credence.

Unfortunately, the uniformity among the courts regarding the significance of pre-text material or the degree of weight given to pre-text material differs among circuits ("Developments," 1996).

For example, a closely watched case was that of *Postema v. National League of Professional Baseball Clubs* (1992). Postema, a female professional baseball umpire, sued a number of defendants alleging discrimination in violation of Title VII. Postema argued (*Postema v. National League,* 1992, p. 1,479),

> She was fully qualified to be a major league umpire, and she had repeatedly made known to Defendants her desire for employment in the major leagues. While she was not promoted to or hired by the National League or American League, male umpires having inferior experience, qualifications, and abilities were repeatedly and frequently promoted and hired by the National and American Leagues.

In accordance with the above *McDonnell* (1973) criteria, Postema met the first requirement of belonging to a protected class. The second prong of the *McDonnell* (1973) analysis required Postema to prove that she was qualified to umpire in the major leagues yet was rejected based on her sex. Lastly, Postema was required to show that after her denial, the defendant baseball leagues continued to seek employment from males with similar qualifications. Unfortunately for Postema, she was not able to prove that the defendant league hired or promoted an individual (male or female) to the position she sought.

Disparate Impact

Disparate impact deals with the *consequences* of a particular employment policy. Policies, for example, that appear to be neutral may in fact have a disparate or adverse impact on an otherwise protected group (*Griggs v. Duke Power Co.,* 1971). As explained by the Supreme Court (*Griggs,* 1971, p. 424), "What is required by Congress (under Title VII) is the removal of artificial, arbitrary, and unnecessary barriers to employment when the barriers operate invidiously to discriminate on the basis of racial or other impermissible classifications." Courts have held that educational requirements, arrest records, credit status, and height and weight requirements are screening devices with a disparate impact on protected groups of individuals. Height and weight requirements, for example, are not discriminatory at face value. However, the *consequences* of a height and weight requirement may serve to eliminate women or people of Asian descent who are smaller than male, American counterparts. For example, baseball league policies requiring umpires to be a certain height and weight were argued necessary to ensure that umpires would be able to endure the physical aspects of the game and would be respected by the players. Unfortunately, these requirements are discriminatory, as they tend to discriminate against women and other minorities who are capable of withstanding the physical element of the game while commanding the respect of the players. Similarly, imposing height and weight standards for lifeguards due to a misperception "that strong, large men" make better lifeguards is problematic as well. All testing and measuring procedures, however, are not prohibitive. Employers making employment-related decisions based on testing or measuring procedures must ensure that the particular skill or trait tested or measured represents the ability to perform an essential, required job function.

In 1978, the EEOC provided quantifiable guidelines to help clarify what constitutes a disparate impact. The 1993 edition of the Uniform Guidelines on Employee Selection Procedures ("Uniform Guidelines," 1993) describes a test commonly referred to as the *four-fifths rule.* The burden of proof is on the employer to show how the particular criterion is job related. Bennett-Alexander and Pincus (1995, p. 77) explain how the four-fifths rule operates:

> 100 women and 100 men take a promotion examination. One hundred percent of the women and 50 percent of the men pass the exam. The men have only performed 50 percent as well as the women. Since the men did not pass at a rate of at least 80 percent of the women's passage rate, the exam has a disparate impact on the men. The employer would now be

required to show that the exam is job related. If this can be shown to the satisfaction of the court, then the job requirement, though it has a disparate impact, will be permitted.

To summarize, any test or measuring device administered should never have greater than a 20% discrepancy among the protected classes identified in Title VII.

Business Necessity

A defense against a claim of disparate impact is that the particular policy or screening device is "necessary" to ensure effective business operations. For example, a credit history performed on all individuals applying for the position of ticket manager at Professional Team, Inc., could be defensible even though a potential female or minority employee could challenge this policy as discriminatory since statistics validate that women and minorities have less stable credit histories.

BFOQ

A BFOQ legalizes discrimination against an individual based on only sex, religion, and national origin only when such ascribed characteristics can be considered essential for job success. For example, Southwest Airlines argued that its female-only hiring policy was a BFOQ (*Wilson v. Southwest Airlines Company,* 1981). The court concluded that Southwest's business operations (and resultant revenues) would not be reduced if male employees were hired because the primary concern of the customer was safely reaching his or her destination at an affordable price. In a sport-related case, *U.S. Equal Employment Opportunity Commission (EEOC) v. Sedita* (1991), the defendants argued that their policy of hiring only female managers, assistant managers, and instructors in the health club for female patrons was a BFOQ. The court held in favor of the plaintiff. Religion may also constitute a BFOQ. For example, educational institutions may employ those of a particular religion "if they are owned in whole or in substantial part by a particular religion." (See *Pime v. Loyola University of Chicago,* 1986; *U.S. EEOC v. Kamehameha Schools/Bishop Estate,* 1993). National origin has been used as a BFOQ when the employer deems it necessary to preserve the authenticity or ambience of a particular business (e.g., hiring only Chinese employees for a Chinese restaurant).

Defendants could argue, although very narrowly applied, that a discriminatory policy was a genuine business necessity for privacy reasons. Defendants arguing the business necessity defense must prove the following three elements (*Dothard v. Rawlinson,* 1977):

1. There is a factual basis for assuming that hiring members of one particular sex (or protected classification) would hurt business.
2. The customer's privacy deserves protection.
3. There is no reasonable alternative to protect the rights of the customer other than to engage in discriminatory hiring.

In *U.S. EEOC v. Sedita* (1991), for example, the U.S. District Court held that the defendant manager of Women's Workout World failed to prove that the employment of male managers would result in member attrition. Today's sport business managers will find BFOQs very narrowly construed and rarely applicable in defending Title VII cases.

Harassment

Sport business managers should be cognizant that "discrimination" in employment encompasses harassment. The manager's best defense against claims of harassment is a good offense. In other words, sport managers should make it clear that racial harassment, sexual harassment, and harassment based on national origin is not tolerated or condoned. Further, all allegations of harassment should be taken seriously and quickly investigated, and corrective action should be implemented when necessary.

Sexual Harassment

Sexual harassment is a growing area of litigation of great importance to sport business managers. Employees and customers of for-profit sport business have access to recourse under Title VII. Sexual harassment complaints increased in number by 53% between 1991 and 1992 (Bennett-Alexander & Pincus, 1995). The costs associated with sexual harassment are alarming. As explained by Bennett-Alexander & Pincus (1995, p. 194), "Sexual harassment cost the federal government $267 million from May 1985 to May 1987 for losses in productivity, sick leave costs, and employee replacement costs." More important, however, are the costs incurred by victims, including emotional stress, trauma, humiliation, embarrassment, anxiety, and guilt.

Claims of sexual harassment may allege discrimination via quid pro quo or a hostile environment. *Quid pro quo,* defined by Black (1990) as "something for something," refers to the exchange of a sexual favor in return for a job-related benefit or retention of a current job. A *hostile work environment,* as recognized by the Supreme Court in *Meritor Savings Bank v. Vinson* in 1986, represents a much more nebulous concept. The sport business manager should watch and listen for the following types of conducts contributing to a hostile work environment (Wolohan, 1995, p. 342):

1. Unwelcome sexual propositions, invitations, solicitations or flirtations.
2. Unwelcome verbal (or written) expressions of a sexual nature, including graphic sexual commentaries about a person's body, dress, appearance, or sexual activities.
3. Unwelcome use of sexually degrading language, jokes or innuendoes.
4. Unwelcome suggestive or insulting sounds or whistles, obscene phone calls.
5. Sexually suggestive objects, pictures, videotapes, audio recordings or literature, placed in the work or practice area, that may embarrass or offend individuals.
6. Unwelcome and inappropriate touching, patting, or pinching or other obscene gestures.
7. Consensual sexual relationships where such relationships lead to favoritism . . . where such favoritism adversely affects others.

The EEOC and recent Supreme Court decisions have favored the plaintiff in cases alleging sexual harassment. For example, in 1990, the EEOC issued a policy statement that altered the use of the "reasonable person" standard routinely applied in common law cases. Rather, the EEOC and subsequent courts recognized the "reasonable victim" standard (i.e., the reasonable woman standard). As explained by the Supreme Court in *Ellison v. Brady* (1991, p. 879), "We adopt the perspective of a reasonable woman primarily because we believe that a gender-blind reasonable person standard tends to be male biased and tends to systematically ignore the experiences of women." Critics argue that the reasonable woman standard significantly hinders communication in the workplace and resultant efficiency and productivity. For example, it is argued that males, unsure of what a "reasonable woman" would interpret as offensive, may tend to avoid dealing and interacting with women and, in the process, jeopardize sport business operations. Subsequent court cases have not addressed the reasonable woman standard.

In *Harris v. Forklift Systems, Inc.* (1993), regarded as a landmark opinion, the Supreme Court held that plaintiffs are not required to show severe psychological injury so long as they can show that the offensive behavior was unwelcome and interfered with the work environment. As stated by the Court (1993, p. 114), "Title VII comes into play *before* the harassing conduct leads to a nervous breakdown (emphasis added)." The *Harris* Court (1993) adopted the reasonable person standard. Again, no comment was made regarding the *Ellison* Court's (1991) usage of the "reasonable woman" standard.

Some suggest that sport business managers need to be especially concerned about sexual harassment due to the historical "culture" of sport. Sport is replete with "locker-room talk," slapping each other on the rear for purposes of inspiration or acknowledgment, hanging posters of scantily clad women/men in locker rooms and on office walls, and a basic overt concern with the body. Further, the manner in which professional relations are cultivated or employees become bonded with one another may need reevaluation. Drinking after hours in dimly lighted taverns with colleagues, third-party vendors, or potential sport sponsors may not be a good idea. Similarly, Loyle (1995, p. 20) states that "certain unique aspects of the fitness industry make it vulnerable to sexual-harassment charges by employees." Health clubs filled with attractive, physically fit people, emphasizing movement and the body create a ripe environment for sexual harassment problems. To compound the issue, employees (typically young and single) working long hours tend to build social relationships within the work environment. As explained by Geater, vice president of human resources for TCA (Loyle, 1995, p. 22), "Relationships that inevitably start among employees under this scenario . . . can end bitterly, and behaviors that used to be welcomed are now deemed unwelcome and offensive." Employers and employees, both cognizant of what constitutes sexual harassment, can better recognize behaviors among others and within themselves that could be construed as harassing.

As sport business managers, it is important to remember that you can be liable for the harassing acts of supervisors, subordinates, and vendors (e.g., nonemployee third parties, such as ticket, equipment, or concessionaire vendors) upon the showing of actual or constructive notice. As explained by McNerney (1996, p. 4), "Companies face a new set of liabilities. Not only do they have to protect employees from unwelcome sexual advances from coworkers, but they also have to protect them from unwelcome advances from third parties—customers, clients, vendors, contingent workers, members of the general public and the like."

A plaintiff has recourse against sexual harassment via Title VII as well as tort and criminal liability. For example, allegations in tort could include assault, battery, intentional infliction of emotional distress, false imprisonment, and intentional interference with contractual relations. Criminal prosecution could include allegations of criminal assault, battery, and rape.

Management Precautions

The doctrine of respondeat superior places sport managers, who obviously do not condone sexual harassment, in a precarious position. There are a variety of practices sport managers can employ as a way to prevent sexual harassment allegations. Courts tend to look favorably on a business's implementation or adoption of the following:

- total commitment by top management that sexual harassment will not be tolerated
- adoption and communication of an antisexual-harassment policy. Johannes and Lublin (1996, p. B4) reported on the sexual harassment claims against Astra and Mitsubishi in the *Wall Street Journal* on May 9, 1996. As they stated,

"Both companies lack one of the most basic requirements consultants insist on: a clear and strong written policy on harassment." It is difficult to believe that two large, successful companies had poorly performed such a seemingly rudimentary task.

- education regarding the two types of sexual harassment and what types of actions constitute each
- a grievance system in place for sexual harassment complaints. System should include two avenues for one to complain, as it is illogical to expect a plaintiff-employee to file a complaint with the harasser-supervisor.
- immediate and appropriate corrective action taken for all sexual harassment complaints. (See Nobile 1996 for insights regarding the investigation of a sexual harassment claim.)

The responsibility of the sport manager is overwhelming, as sport business managers routinely deal with concession vendors, the public, independent contractors, and potential sponsors. Implementation of the above management precautions reduces the likelihood of sexual harassment practices.

As explained by Wolohan (1995), the statute of limitations on both Title IX (discussed later) and Title VII sexual harassment claims is 180 days. Sport business managers can deter the filing of Office of Civil Rights (OCR) or EEOC complaints by grieved plaintiffs if an efficient and thorough internal grievance system is established.

Discrimination Based on Religion

Sport managers are typically familiar with the constitutional problems associated with prayer or other religious activities in public institutions or on the playing fields of public property (Fried & Bradley, 1994; Palomo, 1996). However, sport managers also need to use caution when conducting prayer before meetings or on company property. Discrimination based on religion is predicted to be an increasingly common cause of action in our litigious society. In 1993, 5% of all claims filed with the EEOC alleged discrimination based on religious beliefs (Schaner & Erlemeier, 1995). The EEOC also reported a 30% increase in religious discrimination claims filed against employers since 1990 (Kurtz, Davis, & Asquith, 1996). As society continues to diversify, and the workplace becomes more and more occupied with people of various religions, the potential conflict is likely to accelerate. As explained by Schaner and Erlemeier (1995, p. 17), "If an employer sponsors or creates religious-based activities in the workplace, whether it be a required prayer meeting, Bible study, or reading of the Torah, the employer risks Title VII liability." Similarly, an employer can also be responsible for the religious practices of employees when behaviors create an uncomfortable work environment.

Relevant Cases

Plaintiffs alleging a prima facie case of discrimination based on religion must prove the following:

1. The plaintiff has a bona fide religious belief that conflicts with an employment requirement.
2. The plaintiff informed the employer of this belief and the resultant employment conflict.
3. The plaintiff was disciplined for failure to comply with the conflicting employment requirement.

Employers must attempt to reasonably accommodate an employee's religious requests unless the accommodation would impose an undue hardship. In *Wilson v. U.S. West Communications, Inc.* (1994), the plaintiff was terminated for her refusal to remove or cover an antiabortion button depicting a color photograph of an 18 to 20-week fetus. The plaintiff argued that she could not remove the button for religious purposes. However, coworkers found the button offensive, disturbing, and stressful. As a result of the tension, the workplace environment became very uncomfortable. The court in this case ruled in favor of the employer-defendant who had attempted to accommodate the plaintiff reasonably by providing her with alternatives, such as wearing the button with the fetus covered.

Further, it is *not* necessary that a plaintiff-employee's religious belief replicate an established religious faith (e.g., Presbyterian, Catholic, Jewish). Court precedent indicates that employers will be required to accommodate an employee who merely has a *sincere* religious conviction (*U.S. EEOC v. J.C. Penney Co., Inc.,* 1990). Further, it is *not* necessary that a plaintiff-employee prove religious association. For example, in *Compston v. Borden, Inc.* (1976, p. 158), the plaintiff sued under Title VII alleging religious discrimination because his supervisor routinely referred to him as "the Jew-boy," "the kike," "the Christ-killer," "the damn Jew," and "the goddamn Jew." At trial, the defendants attempted to prove that the plaintiff-employee was dismissed for reasons related to poor performance, not for discriminatory reasons based on religion. In support of their argument, the defendants argued that the plaintiff "Testified that he is not now, nor has he ever been, a practicing member of the Jewish faith. His grasp of the fundamental tenets of Judaism is a rather poor one" (*Compston v. Borden, Inc.,* 1976, p. 161). The U.S. District Court, in holding for the plaintiff, provided in part, "When a person vested with managerial responsibilities embarks upon a course of conduct calculated to demean an employee before his fellows because of the employee's professed religious views, such activity will necessarily have the effect of altering the conditions of his employment" (*Compston v. Borden, Inc.,* 1976, p. 160–161).

Similar to other protected classes identified in Title VII, the law prohibits harassment based on religious beliefs. The most common allegation made by plaintiffs in religious harassment cases is that they are the target of derogatory comments because of individual religious preferences. As noted above in *Compston v. Borden, Inc.* (1976), the court found the defendant supervisor's continued litany of verbal abuse constituted religious discrimination in violation of Title VII. Another format of harassment includes continued proselytizing to employee(s) who are not interested or receptive to the message being delivered. For example, in *Ground Transport Corp. v. Pennsylvania* (1990), the court held that the printing of Bible verses on employee paychecks and printing of religious articles in the company newspaper constituted the harassment of non-Christian employees.

Schaner and Erlemeier (1995) suggest that religious harassment be judged according to the factors defining a hostile work environment adopted in the *Harris* case (1993). In fact, most court decisions regarding the issue of religious harassment have mirrored the analysis defined by both the *Meritor* (1986) and *Harris* (1993) courts. The following factors could guide a court's analysis regarding the legitimate existence of the alleged religious harassment and its contribution to a hostile work environment.

- frequency of the conduct
- severity of the conduct
- whether the conduct is physically threatening or humiliating
- whether the conduct is merely an offensive utterance
- whether the conduct unreasonably interferes with work performance

Quid pro quo religious discrimination, similar to quid pro quo sexual harassment cases, would prohibit employers from providing or denying employment or employment-related benefits to certain individuals based on religious beliefs.

In 1993, the EEOC issued guidelines governing all forms of harassment, including that based on age, race, color, gender, national origin, disability, and religion. The guidelines adopted a similar analysis as that provided by the *Meritor* (1986) and *Harris* (1993) courts. The EEOC later withdrew the guidelines amidst great controversy. Opponents vehemently protested the guidelines. As explained by Brierton (1996, p. 734), "The concern was that harassment could be defined under the guidelines as affirmative expressions of religion. In addition, religious pieces of clothing or religious objects could be considered as creating a hostile workplace." Opponents also argued that the guidelines would violate the Religious Freedoms Restoration Act (1993) and interfere with the sanctity of the constitutionally protected freedom of religious expression. Regardless of the EEOC's withdrawal of the guidelines mentioned above, court decisions will continue to apply the analysis established by the *Meritor* (1986) and *Harris* (1993) courts regarding sexual harassment to cases of religious harassment.

Management Precautions

Sport managers can best protect against claims of religious harassment by adopting a policy prohibiting *all* forms of harassment, including religious. Further, employee training is essential, and the concept of reasonable accommodation should be fully explained to all stakeholders. Training practices should include the broad definition of religion. As explained by Kurtz, Davis, and Asquith (1996, p. 12), "The definition of religion includes the well-recognized faiths, but also goes much further to encompass sincerely held, unorthodox beliefs as well. Even atheism is considered a religion. . . . In addition, a religious practice, observance or belief does not have to be mandated by a religion to receive protection." This quote was reinforced in *Wilson v. U.S. West Communications, Inc.* (1994), where the plaintiff insistent on wearing the abortion button felt compelled to wear the button as a devout Roman Catholic even though the Roman Catholic religion does not mandate that all believers wear similar buttons.

The Civil Rights Act of 1991: Implications

Title VII was not intended to be punitive in nature. Rather, the law intended to restore plaintiffs to preinjury position. Back pay was commonly awarded to successful Title VII plaintiffs. The Civil Rights Act of 1991 revolutionized the way Title VII is interpreted by all stakeholders in two dominant ways. First, plaintiffs alleging intentional employment discrimination can now sue for both compensatory and punitive damages. (Employers with greater than 14 and fewer than 101 employees can be subject to liability not greater than $50,000. Employers with greater than 100 and fewer than 201 can be subject to liability not greater than $100,000. Employers with greater than 200 and fewer than 501 employees can be subject to liability not greater than $200,000. Employers with greater than 500 employees can be subject to liability not greater than $300,000.) Second, plaintiffs alleging intentional discrimination now have the right to a trial by jury. As evident, the Civil Rights Act of 1991 intensified the consequences of Title VII violations.

THE AGE DISCRIMINATION IN EMPLOYMENT ACT, 1967, 1978, 1986

The Age Discrimination in Employment Act (ADEA) was passed in 1967; later amendments were made in 1978 and 1986. The 1986 amendment prohibits any form of mandatory retirement previously stipulated in the earlier acts. The ADEA prohibits employers from discriminating against individuals over 40 years of age. Similar to the Title VII analysis set forth by *McDonnell Douglas* (1973), employees have a prima facie case of age discrimination if the following apply:

1. The individual is a member of the protected class.
2. The individual was terminated or demoted.
3. The individual was doing the job well enough to meet his or her employer's legitimate expectations.
4. Others were treated more fairly.

A 1996 decision by the Supreme Court broadened the number of potential ADEA plaintiffs by allowing an individual to file a suit against an employer if he or she was "replaced by someone younger—even if that younger replacement falls within the ADEA protected class" (Piskorski, 1996, p. 98). In other words, the individual receiving the preferred treatment can be over 40 years old. The employer may use the BFOQ as a defense if substantially all of the individuals in a particular age category are unable to perform the job adequately. For example, a sport business manager may discriminate against an older individual when seeking an employee to transport children to and from camp grounds since statistics exist to document the diminished driving ability of elderly individuals. A careful consideration of the job relatedness of selection requirements mitigates the likelihood that a sport manager will unlawfully discriminate based on age.

Sport managers need to be cautious of comments that could be construed as discriminatory. For example, Westinghouse encountered discriminatory age allegations resulting from a memo that quoted an employee as saying, "We . . . need to get younger individuals who think well and who think differently involved in the process as well." Another person was quoted as saying, in reference to the older employees, "We need to get the blockers out of the way" (Thomas, 1996, p. 81). Similarly, comments such as "seeking recent college graduates" and "we need to promote a younger image" can prove problematic for sport businesses when attempting to defend an age discrimination lawsuit (Coleman, 1985, p. 25).

Regardless of company downsizing and related attempts to decrease costs, a 1996 *USA Today* article reported that age discrimination complaints received by the EEOC had *decreased* annually between 1992 and 1995 (Jones, 1996b). Further, interviews conducted by the article's author, Del Jones (1996b, p. 1B), revealed this:

(a) Unemployed managers and executives are finding jobs faster than at any time in 16 years. . . . ;
(b) The typical 50-plus job hunter takes about 3 1/2 months to find a job; only about 3 weeks longer than it takes their younger counterparts; . . .
(c) Laid-off executives in their 60s take 5 1/2 months to find jobs. . . . That's two weeks faster than executives between 41 and 45.

The low employment rate is attributed to the improved employment opportunities available to the 40+ age group.

THE FAMILY MEDICAL LEAVE ACT OF 1993

The Family Medical Leave Act (FMLA; 1993) represents one of the most recent pieces of legislation passed by the Clinton administration. The FMLA pertains to employers with 50 or more employees, although legislation was introduced in June 1996 by Rep. Patricia Schroeder (D. Colorado) to expand the coverage to employers with 25 or more employees. As defined by the law, all eligible employees must be given 12 weeks of unpaid leave for individual medical reasons; the birth or adoption of a child; or the care of a child, spouse, or parent with a serious health condition. Employee benefits must remain throughout the entire leave. The caveat is that the employer, after the 12 weeks has expired, must "reemploy" the individual in the same or a similar position with equivalent pay, benefits, and other terms and conditions of employment. Exemptions are only allowed if the employer is able to show that the employee's absence would result in substantial economic hardship to the business. In addition, the employer may prohibit the leave if the employee ranks in the top 10% of the highest paid employees. Advocates of the law view it as a reflection of the changing demographics and family structure. The Act excludes a "pro-family" sentiment, enabling employees with dual responsibilities (e.g., family and work) to fulfill family obligations and demands better and in a more "friendly" environment.

Critics of the law view the FMLA as another form of government intrusion into business operations, resulting in economic hardship. For example, sport businesses must incur the costs (recruiting, hiring, training, or job reallocation expenses) of finding a replacement during the employee's absence. Further, business flow may become interrupted as suppliers and buyers, accustomed to doing business with the particular employee now on leave, contemplate their own expense of learning to do business with another employee. Sport businesses incur additional costs in reorienting the employee to current operations upon his or her return. The cost of administration is overtly burdensome, argue employers, for a piece of legislation that is used by only 5% of all eligible employees ("The FMLA: Benefit or Burden?," 1996). As explained in the February 1996 issue of *HR Focus* regarding a survey of 300 members of the Society for Human Resources Management, 75% of survey respondents indicated that "the FMLA caused *daily* administrative headaches" (emphasis added). "About 64 percent also said the FMLA created little or no benefit" ("The FMLA: Benefit or Burden?", 1996, p. 11). Employees may bring civil action against employers alleging violation of the law for a period of 2 years after the date of the last event constituting the alleged violation.

President Clinton proposed an extension of the FMLA to make the workplace more "family friendly" in June 1996. As reported in *The Wall Street Journal*, President Clinton advocates legislation requiring employers to provide all employees with 24 unpaid hours per year to "handle such obligations as taking an elderly parent to a doctor's appointment or meeting with a child's teacher" (Stout, 1996, p. A2). Critics of this legislation argue that President Clinton's proposal is for political reasons only as most companies already agree to let employees off work to tend to family emergencies or responsibilities.

THE OCCUPATIONAL SAFETY AND HEALTH ACT, 1970

The Occupational Safety and Health Act (OSHA) was established by Congress due to a concern of the following 1970 facts and figures (Occupational Safety, 1970)

- Job-related accidents accounted for more than 14,000 worker deaths.
- Nearly 2.5 million workers were disabled.
- Ten times as many person-days were lost from job-related disabilities as from strikes.
- Estimated new cases of occupational diseases totaled 300,000 (U.S. Department of Labor, 1991).

Congress, in an attempt to mitigate the expense and loss of productivity, passed OSHA to ensure "healthful working conditions and to preserve our human resources" (U.S. Department of Labor, 1991, p. 1). Specifically, OSHA seeks to "furnish a place of employment which is free from recognized hazards that are causing or are likely to cause death or serious physical harm to his employees" (U.S. Department of Labor, 1991, p. 5). OSHA is one of the most inclusive pieces of legislation, as it extends to all businesses with one or more employees (Appendix 5–A). The assertive and often aggressive nature of sport, which frequently results in blood, vomit, or injury, makes OSHA very relevant to the sport business manager. However, even sport businesses that are more passive in nature must meet OSHA stipulations. For example, a bowling alley is not likely to have patrons hurt or exhausted to the point of an upset stomach. However, the law states that material safety data sheets (MSDS) (Appendix 5–C) be available to all employees for all chemically based products. The MSDS must describe the product, its chemical composition, and appropriate emergency response actions if the product should be swallowed, inhaled, or the like. The need for sport managers to maintain MSDS is rather encompassing for the entire industry since all sport businesses likely maintain cleaning fluids.

Unfortunately, OSHA represents one of the most complex, confusing, and burdensome acts passed by Congress. OSHA imposes record-keeping requirements on businesses with 11 or more employees. Injuries resulting in medical treatment, loss of consciousness, restriction of work or motion, or transfer to a different position must be reported and documented. Injuries involving fatalities or hospitalization of 5 or more employees must be reported to OSHA administration within 48 hours. All records regarding injuries must be posted for employees to view between February 1 to March 1 on an annual basis. OSHA's required paper work presents both positives and negatives. From the positive perspective, OSHA's recording requirements can augment a sport business's risk management plan and facilitate risk identification. From a negative perspective, OSHA recording requirements cost a sport business significant time and money.

A concern for occupational exposures, specifically exposure to blood-borne pathogens, has generated much anxiety. In its attempt to maintain a safe work environment, OSHA has a variety of requirements regarding exposure to blood-borne pathogens. For example, all job classifications and respective employees who have occupational exposure to blood-borne pathogens must be notified. Blood-borne pathogen exposure may occur, for example, through the cleaning up of vomit at an amusement park or through injuries occurring during sport or physical activity. The Federal Register provides extensive OSHA requirements ("Occupational Exposure," 1991). The following represents only a sampling of those requirements.

- Hand-washing facilities or appropriate alternatives must be provided.
- Containers for the handling of potential infectious materials must be appropriately labeled or color-coded prior to being stored, shipped, or transported.
- Personal protective equipment must also be provided to employees at no cost (e.g., gloves, gowns, face shield or masks and eye protection, etc.).
- Situations in which employees fail or choose not to use the equipment must be documented.
- Garments with blood on them must be immediately removed.
- Contaminated work surfaces must be decontaminated with appropriate disinfectants.
- Contaminated laundry should be handled with gloves and when shipped off-site for cleaning, should be labeled accordingly.
- Employers must make available the hepatitis B vaccine and vaccination series to all employees who have occupational exposure, and also conduct a post-exposure evaluation and follow-up to all employees who have had an exposure incident.
- Employers must have employees declining vaccination to sign an OSHA-prepared statement.
- Employers must provide employee training for those employees exposed to occupational exposures on an annual basis.
- Adopt and employ a Hazard Communication Plan including container labeling, other warnings, material safety data sheets and employee training.

Izumi's (1991) research provides alarming insights into the need to communicate OSHA standards and demand compliance among athletic trainers. As reported by Claussen (1993, p. 26), 73% of surveyed student trainers had direct contact with blood/body fluid at least once a year. Sixty-one percent of the surveyed student trainers had contact with blood/body fluid two to five times per year. Regardless, only 42.5% of those surveyed indicated the use of gloves at least once during the year. An alarming 79% indicated they would perform unshielded cardiopulmonary resuscitation on an athlete bleeding in the mouth. As elaborated on by Claussen (1995, p. 26), "In the most recent and most comprehensive study yet done, the NCAA [National Collegiate Athletic Association] surveyed 540 universities, and found that only 40% of head athletic trainers regularly followed the universal precautions, as did 29% of assistant trainers and 35% of student trainers."

OSHA greatly affects a sport business due to the often aggressive and physical nature of sport and the use of sport implements (e.g., golf clubs, bats), which invite injury. OSHA requirements are broad, elaborative, and comprehensive. This section of the text provides only a rudimentary introduction to OSHA and its requirements. Sport business managers should contact their state office for a copy of the legislation and related information. Safety specialists (e.g., firefighters, police officers), workers' compensation insurance carriers, professional consultants, and the staff enforcing the OSHA law can provide excellent advice (often gratuitously) regarding OSHA compliance. OSHA compliance, although tedious and cumbersome, provides great benefits to a sport business. Primary benefits resulting from OSHA compliance include a more risk-free environment, enhanced customer satisfaction, lower insurance premiums, and more positive publicity (i.e., fewer crises). Further, sport businesses with qualified health and safety programs can reduce OSHA penalties by 15 to 80% ("It pays to own up," 1996).

THE FAIR LABOR STANDARDS ACT OF 1938

The Fair Labor Standards Act of 1938 (FLSA) covers three primary areas: minimum wages, overtime pay, and child labor laws. As explained by Dixon (1994, pp. 5–6), "Private employers are subject to the FLSA if they are engaged in interstate commerce *and either* exceed specified dollar volumes of business *or* are engaged in certain industries . . . Effective April 1, 1990, enterprises are subject to the Act if their annual dollar volume of business exceeds $500,000 per year, exclusive of excise taxes."

Many sport businesses exceed the $500,000 volume of business, and most every sport business engages in interstate commerce. The following illustration demonstrates the inclusiveness of the FLSA. Assume a health club generated the minimum $500,000 annually. This would equate to an average of 1,000 memberships sold at $500 each per year, a realistic sales volume. The following sections address concerns associated with the FLSA, specifically minimum wage laws, and child labor laws.

Minimum Wage Laws

Minimum wage laws, although frequently abused and circumvented, remain a contentious issue. As explained by Zachary (1996b), minimum wage violations almost encourage noncompliance, as violators are only required to pay due back wages. Consequently, many adopt the philosophy that they will pay below minimum wage until they are "caught." This gives employers more working capital for today and, again, little problems unless investigated. As stated by Zachary (1996b, p. A1), "Indeed, minimum-wage laws at both the federal and state levels are among the country's most frequently flouted statutes, making the congressional battle irrelevant for many intended beneficiaries." The FLSA originally sought to protect women and children who were often forced to work 60+ hours per week yet remained powerless to protect themselves. Further, OSHA intended to assist those in low-paying jobs to maintain an adequate standard of living. In 1938, the minimum wage was 25 cents per hour. Until August 1996, the minimum wage was $4.25 per hour. President Clinton signed legislation in August 1996, which increased the minimum wage to $4.75 (effective October 1, 1996) and to $5.15 in 1997 (effective September 1, 1997). Various states, however, advocate much more stringent minimum wage laws. For example, Montana voters are considering an increase in minimum wage to $6.25. Oregon is considering an increase in minimum wage to $6.50. Missouri is considering an initiative that will increase the minimum wage to $6.75 by 1999. Denver, however, has advocated increasing the minimum wage to $7.15 by 1999 ("Minimum wage battles," 1996, p. A1). Advocates of minimum wage laws continue to argue the need to assist those at the low end of the pay scale. Opponents, on the other hand, argue that minimum wage laws only increase unemployment (and related poverty) because businesses refuse to pay more for low-skilled, low-productivity workers.

FLSA regulations enable employers to pay lower wages for apprentices, learners, or disabled workers. Sport business managers wishing to fulfill ethical responsibilities within the community may find the employment of these individuals to be a "win-win" situation. Employees exempt from both overtime (1.5 times the base pay) and minimum wage laws include the following:

1. outside salespeople, executive, administrative, and professional employees, including teachers and academic administrative employees in elementary and secondary schools (Bennett-Alexander & Pincus, 1995)

2. any physically separate business establishment that only employs the parents, spouse, children, or other immediate family members of the owner (Dixon, 1994)
3. employees of certain seasonal amusement or recreational establishments and organized camps that do not operate more than 7 months in any calendar year and during the preceding calendar year, "average receipts for any six months of the year were not more than one-third of its receipts for the other six months of the year" (Dixon, 1994, p. 45)
4. employees of interstate, state, and local public agencies who volunteer to perform services without any compensation, or in exchange for the receipt of an expense reimbursement, reasonable benefits or a nominal fee, are considered to be volunteers and not employees while performing such services (*e.g., park and recreation volunteers*; Dixon, 1994, emphasis added)
5. volunteers who provide services to private employers are also not considered to be employees (Dixon, 1994)

A large number of sport businesses fall into the above exempt categories. The benefit, of course, to the sport business exempt from FLSA includes a reduced cost structure via lower wages and unnecessary overtime pay compliance requirements.

However, those sport businesses that must comply with the FLSA should be cognizant of important FLSA tenets. The following nine items provide sport managers with additional insights regarding the FLSA:

1. Compensable work time includes all ancillary activities associated with a particular job (e.g., equipment maintenance, loading or fueling a vehicle).
2. Travel time to and from work is generally noncompensable.
3. Travel that is compensable by contract, custom, or practice must be counted as work time.
4. Meal periods are noncompensable if they are 30 minutes or longer, if the employee is relieved of all duties, and if the employee is free to leave his or her work station.
5. Sleep time can be excluded from work time only if an employee is on duty for 24 hours, the employee can usually enjoy an uninterrupted night's sleep, the employee has reasonable sleeping facilities, not more than 8 hours of sleep are excluded from any 24-hour period, and the employee has agreed to exclude sleep time from compensable hours of work.
6. On-call time is not compensable if the employee can use the time spent on call primarily for his or her own benefit.
7. Brief breaks up to 15 minutes are considered to be work time.
8. An employee's attendance at training programs will not be considered to be work time where attendance is outside of regular work hours, attendance is

in fact voluntary, no productive work is performed during the training, *and* the training is not directed toward making the employee more proficient in the individual's present job.

9. Time spent in a meeting pertaining to an employee's job is compensable.

Child Labor Laws

The FLSA regulates all labor of individuals under 18 years of age. Federal and state laws typically categorize children and related restrictions in three categories: (1) 16- and 17-year-olds, (2) 14- and 15-year olds, and (3) those under 14 years. (See Appendix 5–B.) The employment of child labor remains a genuine concern to society and greatly influences employment practices of both sporting goods manufacturing companies and sport business companies involved in the service sector.

Labor activists and the media continue to scrutinize U.S. manufacturing companies employing children in foreign countries to manufacture products for American companies (Jones, 1996a). As explained by Joel Joseph, Chairman of the Made in the USA Foundation (Joseph, 1996),

> Fully half of the soccer balls sold in the United States are made in Pakistan, and every one of those soccer balls had an assist from a child under 14 who toils 10 hours a day in subhuman sweatshops, stitching the ball or cutting material used to make it. . . . Nike similarly bases its operations on finding the lowest-cost labor to make its athletic shoes. Twelve-year-old girls work in Indonesian sweatshops 70 hours a week making Nikes in unhealthy plants that reek of glue.

A school board member in Portland, Oregon, was so disturbed by Nike's exploitation of children that he actually advocated *rejecting* a large donation from Nike as a symbol of protest regardless of the plight of decreasing federal funds (Zachary, 1996a). The problem, as explained by Joseph, not only revolves around the inhumane treatment and exploitation of children, but around the loss of American jobs as well. India, Pakistan, Nepal, Bangladesh, Malaysia, and Indonesia allegedly employ children at a young age to work for minimal, if any, pay in dismal conditions (Joseph, 1996). In other words, jobs that could be filled by Americans are being filled by those living and working in foreign countries.

The sport business service sector (e.g., YMCAs, swimming pools, parks and recreation, ball parks, and amusement parks) also employs people under the age of 18 on a routine basis. In 1993, for example, the U.S. Department of Labor prohibited a 14-year-old batboy from working during the summer with the South Atlantic League ball club due to the violation of teenage work rules. As explained by

The Atlanta Journal in a 1993 article (Bennett-Alexander & Pincus, 1995, p. 564), "It's hard to imagine how the time-honored tradition of being a batboy—or batgirl, for that matter—could adversely affect a youngster's health or education. Baseball is a summer game with minimal conflicts with school nights, and there's hardly a more wholesome environment left in our jaded society than the old ballpark." Regardless of the overinclusiveness of the law, the issue of child labor remains very serious. Lack of compliance exposes sport businesses to fines of up to $10,000, possible imprisonment for second convictions, and product boycotts. Sport business managers operating in a particular state(s) will need to know the details of respective state labor laws and should remember that documentation represents a key method of demonstrating compliance.

THE EQUAL PAY ACT OF 1963

The Equal Pay Act of 1963 (EPA) is an extension of the above FLSA. The EPA prohibits pay discrimination based on gender for jobs that require similar "skill, effort, and responsibility and which are performed under similar working conditions." The law permits pay differentials if based on one or more of the following: seniority, merit, quality or quantity of work produced, and/or any other factor besides gender.

The EPA has been an avenue of litigation used by females employed in athletic departments. For example, plaintiffs in *Tyler v. Howard University* (1993), *Pitts v. Oklahoma* (1994), and *Stanley v. USC* (1994) alleged violations of the EPA when they were paid less than the men basketball coaches. However, the use of the EPA by a female plaintiff coaching a women's basketball team is limited for two primary reasons. First, the fourth prong of EPA's affirmative defenses overlooks discrimination in pay if based on *other factors besides gender.* Other factors recognized by the courts include the maintenance of media relations, revenue-generating pressures, market forces, and background experiences (Fitzgerald, 1995). Second, both men and women coaching women's teams tend to receive less money than men coaching men's team. As explained by Claussen (1995, p. 151), "If both men and women are performing the same job (coaching women's sports) for the same low pay, it is difficult to argue that women are being discriminated against simply because of their sex." Similarly, women alleging Title VII (discussed above) violations encounter the same difficulty when men coaching women's sports receive less pay than men coaching men's sports.

TITLE IX, 1972

Title IX has received increased attention since the passage of the Civil Rights Restoration Act in 1987. Title IX states (Title IX of the Education Amendments of

1972), "No person in the United States shall, on the basis of sex, be excluded from participation in, be denied the benefits of, or be subjected to discrimination under any education program or activity receiving Federal financial assistance." Title IX has great influence on interscholastic and intercollegiate physical education, athletics, and intramural programs. Similar to Title VII, the term *discrimination* encompasses sexual harassment allegations in addition to terms of employment, student-athlete participation opportunities and so forth. Common Title IX allegations include pay disparities among coaches as well as program offering inequities for student-athletes. The OCR publication, *Title IX Athletics Investigator's Manual* (1990), provides guidelines regarding Title IX enforcement and investigative analysis (Bonnette, 1990). The remainder of this section elaborates on the analyses for compliance undertaken by the OCR. Refer to Exhibit 5–1 for an abbreviated analysis of Title IX.

OCR's three-prong analysis is defined below.

1. Financial assistance must be allocated in proportion to the numbers of male and female participants in intercollegiate athletics.
2. All other benefits, opportunities, and treatment afforded participants of each sex must be equivalent. Factors to consider include the following:
   - provision of equipment and supplies (quality, amount, suitability, maintenance and replacement, availability of)
   - scheduling of games and practice times (number of competitive events, number and length of practice opportunities, time of day of competitive events, time of day of practices, opportunities to engage in available pre- and postseason competition)
   - travel and per diem allowances (type of transportation, type of housing during trip, length of stay before/after event, per diem allowances, dining arrangements)

Exhibit 5–1 Title IX: The Legislation at a Glance

1. Financial assistance
2. "Other" benefits, opportunities, and treatment
3. Accommodation of interests
   a. General student population percentage versus student-athlete population percentage (based on gender)
   b. History of improvement
   c. Interests and abilities have been fully and effectively accommodated

- opportunity to receive coaching and academic tutoring
- assignment and compensation of coaches and tutors (tutor availability; tutor qualifications and experience, rates of pay)
- provision of locker rooms, practice and competitive facilities (exclusivity of use, quality, availability, maintenance, size, age, condition, special features)
- provision of medical and training facilities and services (availability of medical personnel assistance, qualifications of athletic trainers, availability and quality of training and conditioning facilities, access, exclusivity of use, proximity to locker rooms and facilities, insurance coverage)
- provision of housing and dining facilities and services
- publicity (availability and quality of sports information personnel, access to other publicity resources, quantity and quality of publications and other promotional devices featuring the men's and women's programs)
- other: support services (amount of administrative, secretarial, and clerical assistance provided to men's and women's programs)
- recruitment (equal opportunities provided for recruitment; financial sources for recruiting are equivalent to meet needs in programs; benefits, opportunities, and treatment afforded prospective student-athletes of each sex

3. Accommodation of athletic interests and abilities must be equivalent with respect to the number of participation opportunities, team competitive levels, and selection of sports offered:
   - provision of participation opportunities to male and female students in numbers substantially proportionate to their respective enrollments
   - a proven history and continuing practice of program expansion responsive to the developing interests and abilities of the "underrepresented sex"
   - evidence that the athletic interests and abilities of students of the "underrepresented sex" have been equivalently, fully, and effectively accommodated

The OCR elaborates on the requirements associated with athletic financial assistance. As explained by the OCR, "Athletic financial assistance generally is the only aspect of an institution's intercollegiate athletics program that is evaluated separately for compliance with Title IX. In addition, it is the only aspect for which an expenditure test is the standard of compliance." The "expenditure test" interpretation is as follows. Assume ABC University allocated $600,000 for student-athlete scholarships. The men's athletic program received $400,000, and the women's athletic program received $200,000. ABC University has 200 male athletes and 100 female athletes. Mathematically, $2,000 should be awarded to each individual athlete regardless of gender. The OCR defines two situations allowing a disproportionality among financial assistance. First, scholarship monies per athlete may differ among the sexes when costs are escalated for one program as a result of higher out-of-state tuition costs. Second, scholarship monies per athlete may differ among the sexes based on the professional discretion necessary to serve the programs best.

The second criterion, "all other benefits, opportunities, and treatment," is to be considered in totality. For example, assume that, at ABC University, the men's basketball team has better quality locker rooms than the women's team. This in itself does not equate to noncompliance so long as some aspect of the women's athletic program exceeds the quality of the men's program from a comparative perspective (e.g., tutor availability). Monies spent on each criterion do not need to be equal. For example, athletic programs with football as a sport will have a much higher equipment budget than the women's athletic team. However, a school can still fall into compliance so long as the quality of the equipment used by the various programs remains equitable or of similar kind and quality. In other words, a practice of handing down the men's cross-country team uniforms to the women while the men wore newly purchased uniforms would be very questionable.

The OCR ruled that the *source* of funding used to provide the 10 above provisions remains irrelevant. In other words, men's athletic programs cannot argue that booster monies or revenue production justifies more spending for the men's athletic program. Title IX focuses on how the money is spent regardless of its source. Wilde (1994, p. 223) identifies other examples of situations where disparate treatment would be viewed as nondiscriminatory:

> The unique aspects of particular sports, such as football, where the rules of play, equipment requirements, rates of participation injury, and facilities requirement for competition may result in an imbalance in favor of men; special circumstances of a temporary nature; spectator management requirements at more popular athletic events; and, differences that have not been remedied but which an institution is voluntarily working to correct.

The above represents the sport-specific clause referred to by the OCR.

Title IX, as a cause of action in a pay disparity among male and female coaches, can be considered under 2(d) and (e) of the above three-prong analysis prescribed by the OCR. In *Cohen v. Brown University* (1993), men's sports received 72% of salary expenditures in contrast to the 28% devoted to women's sports salaries. The court concluded that this could be a factor contributing to Brown's Title IX violations (Claussen, 1995).

Most litigation has concentrated on the third prong of OCR's analysis: effectively accommodating the athletic interests and abilities of all students. Schools, in order to comply, must meet any one of the three criteria under this third prong.

The first criterion is very difficult to meet, especially for those schools with a football program. In order to comply, a school with a general student population composed of 50% men and 50% women would need to have student-athletes in "substantially proportionate" numbers (i.e., 50% women athletes and 50% men athletes). Unfortunately, the OCR has no clear and definitive definition of what constitutes "substantially proportionate." In *Roberts v. Colorado State* (1993), the 10th Circuit Court of Appeals held that a 10.5% disparity between the enrollment of the general student population and athletic participation was not substantially proportionate. Similarly, in *Cohen* (1993), an 11% disparity was deemed insufficient for compliance purposes.

Schools with football programs will have exceptional difficulty complying with this tenet. In excess of 80 student-athletes may participate on a football team. There is no equivalent sport for women that generates that many participant opportunities. Schools attempting compliance with this first prong would need to drop football, to reduce the number of football players allowed on a team, to drop a significant number of other sports for male athletes, or to increase significantly the number of athletic opportunities for women. Limited money availability often curtails the opportunity to add sport opportunities for women. Consequently, many administrators, boosters, and politicians associated with or following various athletic programs argue vehemently that football should be excluded from Title IX compliance analysis. Congressional amendments attempting to absolve football from Title IX analysis include the Tower Amendments in 1974 and 1975, the Helms Amendment in 1975, and the McClure Amendment in 1976.

The second criterion on a history and continuing practice of program expansion, provides administrators with an easier mode of compliance. This criterion, similar to an affirmative action plan, requires schools to adopt plans that, for example, detail when and how new programs will be added, additional coaches hired, or facilities improved. *Adherence* to the plan, however, remains critical for compliance purposes. As stated by the U.S. District Court in *Favia v. Indiana University of Pennsylvania* (1993), p. 585), "You can't replace programs with promises."

The third criterion argues that different percentages between male and female athletic participation rates exist because women (or the "underrepresented sex") simply are not interested in sport and would not pursue additional athletic opportunities regardless of their availability. Surveys of the general student population are commonly used as a way to ascertain whether the desires of a student population are being met. However, the survey design used by a particular defendant is subject to intense scrutiny. Further, as explained by the U.S. Court of Appeals (1st Cir.) in *Cohen v. Brown University* (1993, p. 898), "The fact that there are some female students interested in a sport does not *ipso facto* require the school to provide a varsity team in order to comply . . ." Rather, the interest must be substantial enough to sustain a team and compete with other institutions within a reasonable destination.

AFFIRMATIVE ACTION

Affirmative action has many interpretations and generates diverse emotional responses. As it was first introduced by President Kennedy in 1961, the term represented a dedicated effort to end discrimination (Executive Order No. 10925, 1961). The intent of this Executive Order was to encourage employers to eagerly recruit minority employees and suppliers. Executive Order 11246, signed by President Johnson in September 1965, was more definitive. This Executive Order states that employers who receive federal funding or who contract to furnish the federal government with goods and services exceeding $10,000 in value cannot discriminate against employees on the basis of race, color, religion, gender, or national origin. The spirit of the Executive Order was remedial in nature. Specifically, as stated by the Supreme Court, affirmative action sought to "ameliorate the effects of past discrimination on the opportunities enjoyed by members of minority groups in our society" (*City of Richmond v. J. A. Croson Co.,* 1989, p. 713). Regulatory powers were also transferred from the EEOC to the Secretary of Labor who created the Office of Federal Contract Compliance Program (OFCCP). The Executive Order was amended in 1967 to include women. In 1968, organizations with 50 or more employees who had federal contracts exceeding $50,000 were *required* to adopt written affirmative action plans in addition to seeking out qualified minority applicants, training for qualified minority groups, hiring preferentially from minority groups if the applicants are substantially equal in qualifications, and establishing a timetable delineating goals for correcting minority employment deficiencies. Further, the Supreme Court recognized in *United Steelworkers v. Weber* (1979) that private-sector affirmative action plans voluntarily adopted were legal so long as the plan did not unnecessarily violate the interests of non-minorities, did not preclude advancement opportunities for nonminorities, and remained temporary.

An important distinction exists between the term *goal* and the term *quota*. No Executive Order requires organizations to adopt or achieve quotas. Quotas, however, may be imposed by the courts if an organization is found to have a history of discrimination. In establishing goals, federal contractors should consider the availability of qualified minorities within the area of recruitment. As explained by Robinson, Fink, and Allen (1995, p. 667), "If 10% of all contract/subcontracts are to be set-aside for minority contractors, then it must first be established that 10% of the pool of potential *qualified* contractors are minority." Opponents argue that its time has expired. As explained by Eastland (1996, p. 14), "In the late 1960s and during the 1970s, advocates of affirmative action often said that it was only a temporary measure whose success would render it unnecessary in the future. But these temporary measures often seem to go on and on and on—well beyond the point at which they were supposed to end."

The assault on affirmative action appears to have reached epic proportions in Congress, the Executive Office, and the Supreme Court. In 1995, Senator Dole and Representative Canady (R-Fla) introduced the Equal Opportunity Act (EOA) to Congress. As explained by Glaser and Cooke (1996, p. 5), "This legislation would prohibit government programs from giving preferential treatment on the basis of race, color, national origin or gender and essentially would eliminate the Office of Federal Contract Compliance Programs (OFCCP), which enforces the laws creating affirmative action obligations." The initial sentiment expressed by Senator Dole and Representative Canady has been echoed in state legislatures as well. For example, California, Colorado, Illinois, Louisiana, South Dakota, and Washington have all introduced legislation that would end affirmative action programs based on sex, race, religion, or national origin (Glaser & Cooke, 1996). In July 1995, President Clinton ordered an intense urgent review of affirmative action programs. Likewise, presidential nominee Bob Dole also urged an end to affirmative action programs. Even federal judges have begun to challenge the statistics and surveys used to justify affirmative action programs used by municipalities (Barrett, 1996). The leery sentiment of affirmative action programs was recently echoed by the Supreme Court in *Adarand Constructors, Inc. v. Pena* (1995).

In the *Adarand* case (1995, p. 2100), the Supreme Court held that any racial classification "must be analyzed by a reviewing court under strict scrutiny." In other words, such classifications are constitutional only if they are narrowly tailored measures that further compelling government interest. Justice O'Connor, in writing the *Adarand* opinion, quoted Justice Powell's statement in *Regents of the University of California v. Bakke* (1978, pp. 273, 289–290), "The level of scrutiny does not change merely because the challenged classification operates against a group that historically has not been subject to government discrimination . . . The guarantee of equal protection cannot mean one thing when applied to one individual and something else when applied to a person of another color." The *Adarand* case did not conclude whether the federal agency's compensation clause was "compelling" and "narrowly tailored." However, the Adarand case is significant as it overrules an earlier 1990 case, *Metro Broadcasting, Inc. v. FCC,* in which the Supreme Court adopted the more relaxed, intermediate test requiring that the racial classification "serve *important* government objectives within the power of Congress and are *substantially related* to achievement of those objectives" (*Metro Broadcasting, Inc. v. Federal Communications Commission,* 1990, pp. 564–565).

In *Hopwood v. State of Texas* (1996), the Fifth U.S. Circuit Court of Appeals, struck down an admissions-preference policy for black and Mexican American applicants on constitutional grounds. The Fifth Circuit Court of Appeals echoed the strict scrutiny analysis advocated by Justice Powell in *Regents of University of*

California v. Bakke (1978) and the opinion delivered by Justice O'Connor in the *Adarand* case. Although the Court of Appeals decision affects only Texas, Mississippi, and Louisiana, the decision has contributed to the uncertainty regarding the future of affirmative action programs. In a cynical editorial, Murray Sperber, Indiana University associate professor and author, questions the irony of eliminating admissions-preference policies yet retaining the "special action" admittance category for students with "special talents" in, for example, athletics. As explained by Sperber (1995, p. A52),

> Why trumpet academic merit as vital for the admission of most minority-group students and at the same time retain a huge loophole for athletes with glaringly substandard grades and G.P.A.'s? Only if one is indifferent to the academic progress of minority youngsters in general— and if one views college athletes simply as sources of entertainment— can one justify being anti-affirmative action for most admissions but pro-special admissions for athletes.

In a unique case, Spartanburg Methodist (South Carolina) lost two coaches and generated public debate when announcing that its athletic teams should reflect the same racial composition as its general student population. Carolyn White, writing for *USA Today,* questions whether this policy would be maintained under judicial scrutiny. The men's basketball program would appear to be the most affected, as 73% of the general population at this 2-year private college is white, 24% black, and 3% is Hispanic and Asian. As opined by Alex Johnson, a University of Virginia law professor (White, 1996, p. 6C), "It may be possible to integrate the basketball team. But for them to do so this blatantly is bound to be problematic."

Executive Order 11246 does not influence private business not engaging in contracts with the federal government. However, courts may impose affirmative action mandates on businesses to remedy past discrimination.

Affirmative Action in the Sport Organization

Although the *Adarand* (1995) Supreme Court decision only influences *federal* affirmative action programs, the recent upsurge regarding affirmative action and its merit infers that private sector affirmative action programs will also be strictly scrutinized. Assume, for example, that affirmative action advocates vehemently voice outrage by the alleged discrimination existent in the administrative ranks of college and professional sport. Research conducted during the 1995 College Football National Championships revealed that 100% of those participating who were employed as presidents, athletic directors, head coaches, associate athletic directors, sport information directors, or members of the medical staff were white, while

64% of all players were minorities (Lapchick, 1996). Only 6% of the NCAA's Division 1-A coaches are black (Wieberg, 1996). Sports represent a domain abundant with racial discrimination. Shropshire (1996) argues that the lack of minorities in administrative positions results from an intentional maintenance of the status quo in comparison to a lack of qualified minority applicants. Shropshire encourages governmental intervention. Robinson and colleagues conclude (1995, p. 668), "Federal courts still retain the authority to order race and gender-based preferential treatment in instances where employers have been shown to have engaged in unlawful discrimination." Regardless of a potential for government involvement in the employment practices of professional sport, there are six primary reasons why Shropshire and others appalled by the lack of minorities in the administrative ranks of sport are not likely to see government intervention.

First, recent court decisions resoundly conclude that remedial or benign race-based preferential programs are not proper avenues of remedying past discrimination inbred with greater society. As explained by the Fourth Circuit Court of Appeals in *Podberesky v. Kirwin* (1994, p. 952), "Mere knowledge of historical fact is not the kind of present effect that can justify a race-exclusive remedy." As decided in prior court decisions, plaintiff allegations that an entity had a poor reputation within a local community or an entity perceived as being a hostile environment for people of race exemplify types of societal discrimination versus the discrimination caused by the specific entity. Research clearly supports the historical discrimination of minorities in the American society. However, as noted by court precedent, often this has not been enough to justify race-based preferences.

Second, a plaintiff would likely fail even if we narrow the perspective from discrimination in "society" to discrimination in the "sport industry." For example, the Fifth Court of Appeals in the *Hopwood v. State of Texas* case (1996) refuted the argument that the minority preference admission policy at the University of Texas Law School was needed as a means to remedy, in part, the discrimination within higher education. The *Hopwood v. State of Texas* court responded (1996, p. 944), "The vast majority of the faculty, staff, and students at the law school had absolutely nothing to do with any discrimination that the law school practiced in the past." As applied to the sport industry, one can deduce that the history of discrimination in the administrative ranks of sport is not enough, in itself, to justify minority-based hiring practices in a particular sport organization.

Third, there would have to be some proof that the dearth of minorities in the ranks of sport administration was directly attributable to discrimination. In the case *City of Richmond v. J. A. Croson Co.* (1989), the Supreme Court referred to quotas attempting to replicate the percentage of minorities in the surrounding population to the percentage of minorities employed at a business as "sheer speculation" (*City of Richmond v. J. A. Croson Co.,* 1989, p. 724). In that case, the Supreme Court argues that there are a variety of factors that could account for the scant number of minorities employed in any one industry. As explained by the Court (1989, p. 727), "There are numerous explanations for this dearth of minority participation, including past societal discrimination in education and economic opportunities as well *as both black and white career and entrepreneurial choices* (emphasis added)." Similarly, one could argue based on court precedent that the absence of minority sport administrators is *not* due to discrimination but rather to the fact that minorities would rather pursue alternative career opportunities.

Fourth, to defend a claim of disparate treatment under the Fourteenth Amendment, the defendant must show that the racial classification serves a compelling government interest, and it is narrowly tailored to achieve that goal (*Adarand Constructors, Inc. v. Pena,* 1995; *Hopwood v. State of Texas,* 1996). Based on court precedent, one could find difficulty in convincing the appropriate people that a mandatory affirmative action program for the college and professional sport industry constituted a *compelling* state interest. One could argue that better hiring practices, improved recruitment efforts, and sensitivity training, for example, meet similar objectives in a less restrictive environment.

Fifth, often argue that affirmative action programs negatively stigmatize minorities who are hired or promoted (*City of Richmond v. J. A. Croson Co.,* 1989). This argument suggests that individuals may be subject to "more scrutiny and skepticism regarding their qualifications" (Terpstra, 1995, p. 311). As stated by Eastland (1996, p. 198), "Wherever affirmative action operates, the very existence of such a program will lead some people to think that every minority student or every minority employee would not have won opportunity without preferential treatment, a judgment that strips people of the respect due them as individuals." Sport is a world of earned recognition. Athletes earn gold medals, for example, through years and years of arduous training, pain, and perseverance. To award someone additional "merit" or an employment preference based on race offends the very sanctity of sport.

A sixth argument justifying the difficulty with imposing affirmative action plans on the world of sport, although not a strong constitutional argument, is worth mentioning. Professional sports operate as a collusive organization serving individual interests. A prime individual interest, of course, is money. Affirmative action opponents suggest that mandated affirmative action programs impose a costly burden on organizations as they are forced to alter employment practices. For example, research documents that employees hired via employee referrals or through word-of-mouth recruitment are more efficient, are more productive, are happier, and have a longer tenure with the organization (Wiley, 1992). Managers naturally favor this recruitment avenue, as costs associated with turnover, absenteeism, poor morale, and so forth are mitigated. Hiring in accordance to an affirmative action plan would require organizational change and expense via recruitment (e.g., application dissemination, air travel, lodging, meals). The resultant organizational costs, coupled with a fear of recruiting and employing individuals with subpar standards, would place a sport business at a competitive disadvantage (Terpstra, 1995).

The Future of Affirmative Action

Legislative and judicial activity in 1995 and 1996 signal an end to affirmative action based on preferential treatment and quantitative measurement. Further, polls indicate that 61% of all adults and 68% of white males favor the elimination of affirmative action (Shropshire, 1996). However, many other happenings indicate that affirmative action will remain a tenant of managerial and societal responsibility. For example, a reflection on the Rodney King beating in 1991 and the alleged racially motivated church burnings in the South throughout the summer of 1996 represent racism that remains embedded in American society. A recent study by sociologist David Maume, Jr., attributes the widening wage gap between white and black males to the effects of discrimination (Cancio, Evans, & Maume, 1996; "Race Still Plays Role," 1996). Further, the passage of the welfare reform bill and related allegations of the hardship it will place on the disadvantaged minority population encourages politicians and other elected officials to support some degree of affirmative action programs. As stated by Citrin (1996, p. 48), if affirmative action continues the path toward abolition, politicians will need to ensure that "tax, welfare, and education policies . . . genuinely improve the circumstances of blacks and other minorities within a framework of individual rights."

Opponents of affirmative action argue that government should not intervene into the affairs of business. Rather, the marketplace will necessitate the integration of the work force as businesses continue to globalize and society becomes more racially integrated. Based on history, however, it appears that the "freedom to employ" concept is doomed to failure. For example, Supreme Court cases throughout the 1960s clearly indicate that when parents were given an option through a school board's adopted "freedom to choose" plan, school integration rarely occurred for a variety of reasons (*Green v. County School Board,* 1968).

The combined efforts of the Rainbow Coalition for Fairness in Athletics, the National Football League (NFL) Coaches Fellowship Program, the Professional Golf Association (PGA) Tour Internship program, and involvement with minority professional associations can help curb the discrimination in sport regardless of legal intervention (Shropshire, 1996). Sport organizations are apt to continue voluntary affirmative action efforts, although the intensity of those efforts will likely vary. For example, some sport organizations will favor interviewing a broad number of people regardless of race, gender, national origin, or ethnicity and will place job descriptions in minority-oriented publications, whereas other sport organizations will adhere to a rigid affirmative action plan complete with quantitative goals and timetables. However, there is a little possibility that the government will intervene and require professional sport organizations or other sport businesses to hire minorities in accordance to prescribed numerical quotas.

Regardless of the apparent apathy by those in sport to integrate minorities into the ranks of administration, other businesses have concluded that the voluntary adoption of an affirmative action plan better fulfills their corporate or community responsibilities of a diversified workplace while bolstering their bottom line. As society continues to diversify, a multicultural and multiracial work force will provide a sport business with a better understanding of competitive forces, including competition, the buyer or end-consumer, and the supplier.

THE IMMIGRATION REFORM AND CONTROL ACT OF 1986

As explained by Bennett-Alexander and Pincus (1995, p. 526), the purpose of the Immigration Reform and Control Act (IRCA) is to "Protect employment of American citizens by reducing the number of illegal aliens, as well as to allow entry by aliens in areas where the nation's economy would be helped." All employers are subject to IRCA requirements. IRCA prohibits employers from hiring undocumented workers. Appropriate documentation requires the possession of either a U.S. passport, a driver's license, or a birth certificate. Most sport businesses comply with the IRCA by asking on job applications whether the applicant is eligible to work in the United States. Questions that query an individual's national origin or citizenship should be avoided due to Title VII legislation prohibiting discrimination against national origin.

EMPLOYMENT-RELATED LITIGATION ABSENT VIOLATION OF LEGISLATION

Employers may be sued by an employee for *unjust dismissal* even though the employee is not alleging violation of existing legislation. Unjust dismissal cases have involved alleged dismissal resulting from acts including the following:

> . . . signing a union card, filing workers' compensation claims, refusing to assist the employer in committing a crime, refusing to commit a crime on the employer's behalf, refusing to forego suit against the employer for a valid legal claim against the employer, refusal to not serve jury duty, refusal to falsify records, refusal to lie in testifying in a case involving the employer, reporting wrongdoing or illegal activity by the employer, and termination at a time when the employee was about to receive a substantial bonus from the employer. (Bennett-Alexander & Pincus, 1995, p. 10).

Sport business managers must pay special attention to the management of their human resources. However, in addition to the above legislation that may foster litigation by a grieved employee, allegations of unjust discrimination can be brought by *any* individual with or without a discriminatory complaint. Claimants pursuing an unjust dismissal case have the right to a jury trial as well as unlimited compensatory and punitive damages.

Federal regulation passed after 1960 intervenes in the operations of the sport business manager. Sport managers can best protect themselves from violating one of the above pieces of legislation via knowledge, understanding, communication, documentation, and evaluation of current practices and exposed compliance weaknesses.

CHAPTER SUMMARY

Extant legislation greatly influences sport business operations. As mentioned so many times before, a sport business manager cannot simply open up the doors and have patrons come in and "play." Efforts must be taken to ensure that discrimination is avoided, employee rights are respected, pay is equitable, and the workplace remains safe. Continual in-service training, the availability of videotapes regarding discriminatory practices for employees to view, guest speakers, posted information regarding employee rights, and a constant familiarity with Supreme Court interpretations and legislative enactments can assist a sport business manager in his or her efforts to maintain a legally defensible workplace.

STUDENT ASSIGNMENT

Identify a sport business you would like to study. Attach all relevant documents to your paper to be turned in to your professor.

1. Elaborate on which legislation discussed above pertains to the particular sport business.
2. Identify the types of activities, programs, or policies the sport business employs in an attempt to ensure compliance (e.g., in-service training, stated policies described in policy manuals).
3. What would you do differently, or in addition to, the efforts and/or tactics identified in 2 above?
4. Interview the sport business manager, and inquire about how this person feels the legislation influences sport business operations.
5. Pick five cases identified in this chapter. Retrieve and read the cases and prepare a legal brief of the case (as defined by your instructor).

REFERENCES

Adarand Constructors, Inc. v. Pena, 115 S.Ct. 2097 (1995).

Barrett, P. M. (1996, September 26). Courts attack studies used for set-asides. *The Wall Street Journal,* pp. B1, B7.

Bennett-Alexander, D. D., & Pincus, L. B. (1995). *Employment law for business.* Chicago, IL: Irwin.

Black, H. C. (1990). *Black's law dictionary* (6th ed.). St. Paul, MN: West Publishing Company.

Bonnette, V. M. (1990). *Title IX athletics investigator's manual.* Washington, DC: U.S. Department of Education.

Brierton, T. D. (1996). Religious harassment under Title VII. *Labor Law Journal, 46*(12), 732–740.

Brierton, T. D. (1996). Religious harassment under Title VII. *Labor Law Journal, 46*(12), 732–740.

Cancio, A. S., Evans, T. D., & Maume, D. J., Jr. (1996). Reconsidering the declining significance of race: Racial differences in early career wages. *American Sociological Review, 61,* 541–556.

Citrin, J. (1996, Winter). Affirmative action in the people's court. *The Public Interest, 122,* 39–48.

City of Richmond v. J. A. Croson Co., 488 U.S. 478 (1989).

Claussen, C. L. (1993). HIV positive athletes and the disclosure dilemma for athletic trainers. *Journal of Legal Aspects of Sport, 3*(2), 25–34.

Claussen, C. L. (1995). Title IX and employment discrimination in coaching intercollegiate athletics. *Entertainment & Sports Law Review, 12*(1,2), 149–168.

Cohen v. Brown University, 809 F. Supp. 978 (D. R. I. 1992), aff'd, 991 F.2d 888 (1st Cir. 1993).

Coleman, J. J. III (1985). Age-conscious remarks: What you say can be used against you. *Personnel, 62*(9), 22–29.

Compston v. Borden, Inc., 424 F. Supp. 157 (1976).

Developments in the law: Employment discrimination. (1996). *Harvard Law Review, 109*(7), 1,568–1,692.

Dixon, R. B. (1994). *The federal wage and hour laws.* San Francisco, CA: Society for Human Resource Management.

Dothard v. Rawlinson, 433 U.S. 321 (1977).

Eastland, T. (1996, July 24). The other side of Atlanta's affirmative action story. *The Wall Street Journal,* p. A19.

Ellison v. Brady, 924 F.2d 872 (9th Cir. 1991).

Equal Pay Act of 1963, 29 U.S.C. § 206(d)(1)(1982).

Executive Order No. 10925 (1961).

Fair Labor Standards Act of 1938, 52 Stat. 1060, 29 U.S.C. § 201.

Family Medical Leave Act of 1993, Pub. L. No. 103-3, 107 Stat. 6 (1993).

Favia v. Indiana University of Pennsylvania, 812 F. Supp. 578 (W.D. Pa. 1993).

Fried, G., & Bradley, L. (1994). Applying the First Amendment to prayer in a public university locker room: An athlete's and coach's perspective. Marquette Sports Law Journal, 4(2), 301–321.

Glaser, G., & Cooke, E. (1996, April). The scrutiny intensifies. *HRFocus,* p. 5.

Green v. County School Board, 391 U.S. 430 (1968).

Griggs v. Duke Power Company, 401 U.S. 424 (1971).

Ground Transport Corp. v. Pennsylvania, 578 A.2d 555 (Pa. 1990).

Harris v. Forklift Systems, Inc., 114 S.Ct. 367 (1993).

Hopewood v. State of Texas, 78 F.3d 932 (1996).

Immigration Reform and Control Act of 1986, 8 U.S.C. 1101.

It pays to own up. (1996, April). *HRFocus,* p. 16.

Izumi, H. (1991). AIDS and athletic trainers: Recommendations for athletic training programs. *Athletic Training, Journal of the National Trainers Association, 26,* 358–363.

Johannes, L., & Lublin, J. S. (1996, May 9). Sexual-harassment cases trip up foreign companies. *The Wall Street Journal,* p. B4.

Jones, D. (1996a, June 6). Critics tie sweatshop sneakers to 'Air' Jordan. *USA Today,* p. 1B.

Jones, D. (1996b, September 9). Job hunters over 50 do well. *USA Today,* p. 1B.

Joseph, J. D. (1996, May 31). Abetting child slavery. *The Wichita Eagle,* p. 8A.

Kurtz, J., Davis, E., & Asquith, J. A. (1996, July). Religious beliefs get new attention. *HRFocus,* pp. 12–13.

Lapchick, R. E. (1996). *Sport in society.* Thousand Oaks, CA: Sage Publications.

Loyle, D. (1995, January). The employer minefield: Harassment. *Club Industry,* 19–25.

McDonnell Douglas Corp. v. Green, 411 U.S. 792 (1973).

McNerney, D. J. (1996, July). New legal worry: Third-party sexual harassment. *HRFocus,* p. 4–6.

Metro Broadcasting, Inc. v. Federal Communications Commission, 497 U.S. 547 (1990).

Meritor Savings Bank v. Vinson, 447 U.S. 57 (1986).

Minimum-wage battles continue as drives for local ballot initiatives escalate. (1996, August 27). *The Wall Street Journal,* p. A1.

Nobile, R. J. (1996, January). Sexual harassment: Do you know how to respond? *HRFocus,* pp. 13–14.

Pime v. Loyola University of Chicago, 803 F. 2d 351 (7th Cir. 1986).

Piskorski, T. J. (1996). O'Connor v. Consolidated Coin Caterers Corp.—Supreme Court establishes new prima facie burden for ADEA plaintiff to satisfy. *Employee Relations Law Journal, 22*(2), 95–101.

Postema v. National League of Professional Baseball Clubs, 799 F. Supp. 1475 (S.D.N.Y. 1992).

Robinson, R. K., Fink, R. L., & Allen, B. M. (1995). Adarand Constructors, Inc. v. Pena: New standards governing the permissibility of federal contract set-asides and affirmative action. *Labor Law Journal, 46*(11), 661–668.

Occupational Exposure to Bloodborne Pathogens; Final Rule, 56 *Fed. Reg.* 64175 (1991) (to be codified at 29 C.F.R. § 1910.1030).

Occupational Safety and Health Act of 1970, 29 C.F.R. 1910.1030.

Pitts v. Oklahoma, No. CIV-93-1341-A (W.D. Okla. 1994).

Podberesky v. Kirwan, 38 F.3d 147 (4th Cir. 1994).

Polomo, J. R. (1996, March 13). Students, parents sue Elgin district; federal suit alleges coaches pushed Christianity during school events. *Austin American-Statesman,* p. B1.

Race still plays role in wages, study says. (1996, September 7). *The Wall Street Journal,* p. B1.

Regents of the University of California v. Bakke, 438 U.S. 265 (1978).

Roberts v. Colorado State, 814 F. Supp. 1507 (D. Colo. 1993), aff'd in part, rev'd in part sub nom. *Colorado State Board of Ag. v. Roberts,* 998 F.2d 824 (10th Cir. 1993), cert. denied, 126 L.Ed. 2d 478 (1993).

Sawyer, T. H. (1993). Private golf clubs: Freedom of expression and the right to privacy. *Marquette Sports Law Journal, 3*(2), 187–212.

Schaner, D. J., & Erlemeier, M. M. (1995). When faith and work collide: Defining standards for religious harassment in the workplace. *Employee Relations Law Journal, 21*(1), 1995.

Shropshire, K. L. (1996). *In black and white: Race and sports in America.* New York: New York University Press.

Sperber, M. (1995, October 13). Affirmative action for athletes. *The Chronicle of Higher Education,* p. A52.

Stanley v. USC, 13 F3d 1313 (9th Cir. 1994).

Stout, H. (1996, June 25). Clinton to seek wider family-leave law. *The Wall Street Journal,* p. A2.

Terpstra, D. K. (1995). Affirmative action: A focus on the issues. *Labor Law Journal, 46*(5), 307–313.

Texas Department of Community Affairs v. Burdine, 450 U.S. 248 (1981).

The FMLA: Benefit or burden? (1996, February). *HRFocus,* p. 11.

Thomas, P. (1996, August 29). Restructurings generate rash of age-bias suits. *The Wall Street Journal,* pp. B1, B14.

Title VII of the Civil Rights Act of 1964, 42 U.S.C. § 2000(e).

Title VII of the Civil Rights Act of 1991, 42 U.S.C. § 1981.

Title IX of the Education Amendments of 1972, 86 Stat. 235 (codified at 20 U.S.C. §§ 1681–1688 (1990)).

Title IX Athletics Investigator's Manual (1990). Washington, D.C.: U.S. Department of Education.

Tyler v. Howard University, No. 91-CA11239 (D.C. Super. Ct. 1993).

Uniform guidelines on employee selection procedures. (1993 edition). 29 C.F.R. Ch. XIV-7.

United Steelworkers, Etc. v. Weber, 443 U.S. 189 (1979).

U.S. Department of Labor. (1991). *All about OSHA* (OSHA 2056). Washington, DC: U.S. Government Printing Office.

U.S. Equal Employment Opportunity Commission v. J.C. Penney Co., Inc., 753 F. Supp. 192 (N.D. Miss. 1990).

U.S. Equal Employment Opportunity Commission v. Sedita, 755 F. Supp. 808 (N.D. III. 1991).

Walker v. Secretary of the Treasury, IRS, 742 F.Supp. 670 (N.D. Ga., Atlanta Div. 1990).

White, C. (1996, July 22). Spartanburg Methodist's diversity plan raises concern. *USA Today,* p. 6C.

Wieberg, S. (1996, August 22). Black coaches make mark at major schools. *USA Today,* p. 10C.

Wilde, T. J. (1994). Gender equity in athletics: Coming of age in the 90's. *Marquette Sports Law Journal, 4*(2), 217–258.

Wiley, C. (1992). Recruitment research revisited: Effective recruiting methods according to employment outcomes. *Journal of Applied Business Research, 8*(2), 74–79.

Wilson v. Southwest Airlines Company, 880 F.2d 807 (1981).

Wilson v. U.S. West Communications, Inc., 860 F. Supp. 665 (D. Neb. 1994).

Wolohan, J. T. (1995). Sexual harassment of student athletes and the law: A review of the rights afforded students. *Seton Hall Journal of Sport Law, 5*(1), 339–357.

Zachary, G. P. (1996a, June 28). Nike comes under increasing attack over Asian wages. *The Wall Street Journal,* p. B4.

Zachary, G. P. (1996b, May 20). While Congress jousts over minimum wage, some people ignore it. *The Wall Street Journal,* p. A1.

APPENDIX 5–A
U.S. DEPARTMENT OF LABOR JOB SAFETY AND HEALTH PROTECTION NOTICE

JOB SAFETY & HEALTH PROTECTION

The Occupational Safety and Health Act of 1970 provides job safety and health protection for workers by promoting safe and healthful working conditions throughout the Nation. Provisions of the Act include the following:

Employers

All employers must furnish to employees employment and a place of employment free from recognized hazards that are causing or are likely to cause death or serious harm to employees. Employers must comply with occupational safety and health standards issued under the Act.

Employees

Employees must comply with all occupational safety and health standards, rules, regulations and orders issued under the Act that apply to their own actions and conduct on the job.

The Occupational Safety and Health Administration (OSHA) of the U.S. Department of Labor has the primary responsibility for administering the Act. OSHA issues occupational safety and health standards, and its Compliance Safety and Health Officers conduct jobsite inspections to help ensure compliance with the Act.

Inspection

The Act requires that a representative of the employer and a representative authorized by the employees be given an opportunity to accompany the OSHA inspector for the purpose of aiding the inspection.

Where there is no authorized employee representative, the OSHA Compliance Officer must consult with a reasonable number of employees concerning safety and health conditions in the workplace.

Complaint

Employees or their representatives have the right to file a complaint with the nearest OSHA office requesting an inspection if they believe unsafe or unhealthful conditions exist in their workplace. OSHA will withhold, on request, names of employees complaining.

The Act provides that employees may not be discharged or discriminated against in any way for filing safety and health complaints or for otherwise exercising their rights under the Act.

Employees who believe they have been discriminated against may file a complaint with their nearest OSHA office within 30 days of the alleged discriminatory action.

Citation

If upon inspection OSHA believes an employer has violated the Act, a citation alleging such violations will be issued to the employer. Each citation will specify a time period within which the alleged violation must be corrected.

The OSHA citation must be prominently displayed at or near the place of alleged violation for three days, or until it is corrected, whichever is later, to warn employees of dangers that may exist there.

Proposed Penalty

The Act provides for mandatory civil penalties against employers of up to $7,000 for each serious violation and for optional penalties of up to $7,000 for each nonserious violation. Penalties of up to $7,000 per day may be proposed for failure to correct violations within the proposed time period and for each day the violation continues beyond the prescribed abatement date. Also, any employer who wilfully or repeatedly violates the Act may be assessed penalties of up to $70,000 for each such violation. A minimum penalty of $5,000 may be imposed for each wilful violation. A violation of posting requirements can bring a penalty of up to $7,000.

There are also provisions for criminal penalties. Any wilful violation resulting in the death of any employee, upon conviction, is punishable by a fine of up to $250,000 (or $500,000 if the employer is a corporation), or by imprisonment for up to six months, or both. A second conviction of an employer doubles the possible term of imprisonment. Falsifying records, reports, or applications is punishable by a fine of $10,000 or up to six months in jail or both.

Voluntary Activity

While providing penalties for violations, the Act also encourages efforts by labor and management, before an OSHA inspection, to reduce workplace hazards voluntarily and to develop and improve safety and health programs in all workplaces and industries. OSHA's Voluntary Protection Programs recognize outstanding efforts of this nature.

OSHA has published Safety and Health Program Management Guidelines to assist employers in establishing or perfecting programs to prevent or control employee exposure to workplace hazards. There are many public and private organizations that can provide information and assistance in this effort, if requested. Also, your local OSHA office can provide considerable help and advice on solving safety and health problems or can refer you to other sources for help such as training.

Consultation

Free assistance in identifying and correcting hazards and in improving safety and health management is available to employers, without citation or penalty, through OSHA-supported programs in each State. These programs are usually administered by the State Labor or Health department or a State university.

Posting Instructions

Employers in States operating OSHA approved State Plans should obtain and post the State's equivalent poster.

Under provisions of Title 29, Code of Federal Regulations, Part 1903.2(a)(1) employers must post this notice (or facsimile) in a conspicuous place where notices to employees are customarily posted.

Source: Reprinted from the U.S. Department of Labor, Occupational Safety and Health Administration.

APPENDIX 5–B
KENTUCKY CHILD LABOR LAW NOTICE

KENTUCKY CHILD LABOR LAW

HOURS OF WORK PERMITTED FOR MINORS 14 BUT NOT YET 18 YEARS OF AGE

AGE	MAY NOT WORK BEFORE	MAY NOT WORK AFTER	MAXIMUM HOURS WHEN SCHOOL IS IN SESSION	MAXIMUM HOURS WHEN SCHOOL IS NOT IN SESSION
14 and 15 Yrs.	7:00 A.M.	7:00 P.M. (9:00 P.M. June 1 through Labor Day)	3 Hours per day 18 Hours per week	8 Hours per Day 40 Hours per Week
16 and 17 Yrs.	6:00 A.M.	11:30 P.M. Sunday through Thursday; 1:00 A.M. Friday and Saturday When School is in Session	6 Hours per day Monday through Friday 8 Hours per Day Saturday and Sunday 40 Hours per week	NO RESTRICTIONS

Minors under 14 years of age shall not be permitted to work at any gainful occupation at any time, except for employment in connection with an employment program supervised and sponsored by the school and approved by the Department of Education.

* * * * * * * * * *

Minors under 18 years of age shall not be permitted to work more than five (5) hours continuously without an interval of at least thirty (30) minutes for a lunch period.

* * * * * * * * * *

Definitions:
Section 1. (1) "School in session" means that time which an individual student is required to be in school as established by local school district authorities.
(2) "School not in session" means period of time not included in subsection (1) of this section.

Minors 14 but not yet 16 years of age may NOT be employed in:
Any manufacturing, mining, or processing occupations, including occupations requiring the performance of any duties in work rooms or work places where goods are manufactured, mined, or otherwise processed; occupations which involve the operation or tending of hoisting apparatus or any power-driven machinery other than office machines; operation of motor vehicles or service as helpers on such vehicles; public messenger service; occupations in connection with: transportation of persons or property by rail, highway, air, water, pipeline, or other means, warehousing and storage, communications and public utilities, construction (including demolition and repair).

OCCUPATIONS PROHIBITED FOR ALL MINORS UNDER 18 YEARS OF AGE

1. Occupations in or about Plants or Establishments Manufacturing or Storing Explosives or Articles containing Explosive Components
2. Motor Vehicle Driver and Outside Helper
3. Coal Mine Occupations
4. Logging or Sawmill Operations
5. Operation of Power-Driven Woodworking Machines
6. Exposure to Radioactive Substances
7. Operation of Power-Driven Hoisting Apparatus
8. Operation of Power-Driven Metal Forming, Punching, and Shearing Machines
9. Mining, other than coal
10. Slaughtering, Meat Packing or Processing, or Rendering
11. Operation of Bakery Machines
12. Operation of Paper Products Machines
13. Manufacture of Brick, Tile and Kindred Products
14. Operation of Circular Saws, Band Saws, and Guillotine Shears
15. Wrecking, Demolition and Shipbreaking Operations
16. Roofing Operations
17. Excavating Operations
18. In, about or in connection with any establishment where alcoholic liquors are distilled, rectified, compounded, brewed, manufactured, bottled, sold for consumption or dispensed.
19. Pool or billiard room

PROOF OF AGE REQUIRED FOR MINORS 14 BUT NOT 18 YEARS OF AGE

For Further Information Contact:
DIVISION OF EMPLOYMENT STANDARDS AND MEDIATION
1049 U.S. 127 South
Frankfort, Kentucky 40601
Phone: (502) 564-2784

POST THIS ORDER WHERE ALL EMPLOYEES MAY READ
Paid for by State Funds

Source: Reprinted with permission from the Division of Employment Standards and Mediation, Kentucky.

APPENDIX 5–C
U.S. DEPARTMENT OF LABOR MATERIAL
SAFETY DATA SHEET

Material Safety Data Sheet May be used to comply with OSHA's Hazard Communication Standard, 9 CFR 1910.1200. Standard must be consulted for specific requirements.	U.S. Department of Labor Occupational Safety and Health Administration (Non-Mandatory Form) Form Approved OMB No. 1218-0072	
IDENTITY *(As Used on Label and List)* CARBON DIOXIDE - CO2	Note: *Blank spaces are not permitted. If any item is not applicable, or no information is available, the space must be marked to indicate that.*	

Section I

Manufacturer's Name Airco Industrial Gases	Emergency Telephone Number CHEMTREC	800 424-9300
Address *(Number, Street, City, State, and ZIP Code)* 1856 Lumber ST.	Telephone Number for Information	800 424-9300
	Date Prepared June 1987	
Chicago, IL 60616	Signature of Preparer *(optional)*	

Section II — Hazardous Ingredients/Identity Information

Hazardous Components (Specific Chemical Identity; Common Name(s))	OSHA PEL	ACGIH TLV	Other Limits Recommended	% *(optional)*
N/A				

Section III — Physical/Chemical Characteristics

Boiling Point
      Sublimation point
	-109.3° F
	-78.5° C
		Specific Gravity (H₂O = 1)
		              @ 70°F (21.1°C)
			1.53

Vapor Pressure (mm Hg.) @70°F. (21.1°C)	856 psia (5900 kPa)	Melting Point	N/A
Vapor Density (AIR = 1) @70°F (21.1°C)	.1144# ft³	Evaporation Rate (Butyl Acetate = 1)	N/A
Solubility in Water Very soluble			
Appearance and Odor Colorless, odorless gas — white solid			

Section IV — Fire and Explosion Hazard Data

Flash Point (Method Used)
              N/A
	Flammable Limits
	                  N/A
		LEL
		      N/A
			UEL
			      N/A

Extinguishing Media Nonflammable. Inert gas			
Special Fire Fighting Procedures N/A			

Unusual Fire and Explosion Hazards   N/A

continues

Section V — Reactivity Data

Stability	Unstable		Conditions to Avoid CO_2 is stable under ordinary conditions of use & storage. It does not polymerize. It decomposes to CO when heated above $1700^{\circ}C$.
	Stable	XX	

Incompatibility (Materials to Avoid) Dry Ice can form shock sensitive mixtures with sodium, potassium or sodium-potassium alloy.

Hazardous Decomposition or Byproducts
Carbon Monoxide

Hazardous Polymerization	May Occur		Conditions to Avoid
	Will Not Occur	XX	N/A

Section VI — Health Hazard Data

Route(s) of Entry:	Inhalation? XXX	Skin?	Ingestion?

Health Hazards (Acute and Chronic)
Low concentrations cause increased respiration & headache.

8 - 15% concentrations cause headache, nausea & vomiting which may lead to unconsciousness if not moved to open air or given oxygen.

Carcinogenicity: N/A	NTP? N/A	IARC Monographs? N/A	OSHA Regulated? no

Signs and Symptoms of Exposure Nervous control system of body is dependent on CO_2 level breathed in air, if CO_2 level in air is increased O_2 is decreased causing headache & shortness of breath, dizziness, drowsiness, muscular weakness and ringing in ears.

Medical Conditions Generally Aggravated by Exposure N/A

Emergency and First Aid Procedures Conscious person should be assisted to an uncontaminated area & inhale fresh air. Unconscious person should be moved to an uncontaminated area, given mouth-to-mouth resuscitation and supplemental oxygen and seek medical assistance immediately.

Section VII — Precautions for Safe Handling and Use

Steps to Be Taken in Case Material Is Released or Spilled
Evacuate area of major spill or release of CO_2. Notify safety personnel. Provide ventilation. Clean-up personnel needs special training and protection against contact with very cold materials or excessive inhalation of gaseous CO_2.

Waste Disposal Method
Allow gas to bleed off at a moderate rate or solid to sublime to a well ventilated area.

Precautions to Be Taken in Handling and Storing The insulated storage container should be located in an area where there is adequate ventilation. DO NOT PUT DRY ICE IN CLOSED CONTAINER WHERE EVOLVED GAS CANNOT ESCAPE! Allow solid to sublime to a well ventilated area.

Other Precautions Compressed gas cylinders should not be refilled except by qualified producers of compressed gases. Shipment of a compressed gas cylinder which has not been filled by the owner or with his WRITTEN consent is a violation of Federal Law (49CFR)

Section VIII — Control Measures

Respiratory Protection (Specify Type) Positive pressure air line with mask or self-contained breathing apparatus should be available for emergency use.

Ventilation	Local Exhaust To prevent accumulation above the TWA	Special N/A
	Mechanical (General) N/A	Other N/A

Protective Gloves Insulated, loose fitting	Eye Protection Safety goggles or glasses

Other Protective Clothing or Equipment Safety shoes; Handling of Solid CO_2 — "Tongs"

Work/Hygienic Practices Avoid direct contact with skin to prevent frost bite if more than momentary contact is possible

Source: Reprinted from the U.S. Department of Labor, Occupational Safety and Health Administration.

CHAPTER 6

The Americans with Disabilities Act

Sport business managers tend to be familiar with legislation passed during the 1960s prohibiting discrimination based on ascribed characteristics such as race, color, sex, national origin, and age (see Chapter 5). The Americans with Disabilities Act (ADA) of 1990 mandates that sport businesses also eliminate policies, procedures, and practices that discriminate against the 49 million disabled individuals living in America.

A principal element in understanding the ADA legislation is to understand how the ADA defines a "disabled individual." The ADA (1990) defines a disabled individual as one whom

1. has a physical or mental impairment that substantially limits one or more of his/her major life activities;
2. has a record of such impairment; or
3. is regarded as having such an impairment.

The first category represents the type of disability most lay people presume the ADA protects. This category prohibits discrimination against qualified individuals with a particular disease or condition (e.g., cancer, acquired immunodeficiency syndrome [AIDS], epilepsy, depression, mental retardation). The second category, having a "record of such impairment," prohibits discrimination against qualified individuals who, for example, have a *history* of cancer or mental illness. Medical records and related documentation facilitate a plaintiff's ability to prove he or she is a "disabled individual" subject to coverage under the ADA. The third category of defined disability, "regarded as having such an impairment," prohibits discrimination based on preconceived, subjective stereotypes. Facial burns and other physical deformities qualify as discrimination under this third category and are covered by the ADA legislation. For example, a health club could not deny a person access to services on the basis of a feared "negative reaction" from other paying members. The law also identifies conditions, behaviors, and impairments that do not qualify as disabilities, including compulsive gambling, kleptomania, pyromania, pedophilia, homosexuality, bisexuality, transsexualism, voyeurism, and transvestites (ADA, 1990; "Nondiscrimination," 1994). Many criticize the act for not including the above as "disabilities," while others argue that the definition of what constitutes a disability is too nebulous and creates confusion for well-intended employers attempting to comply with the ADA mandates (Barnard, 1990).

In the area of sport litigation, the question regarding the validity of a plaintiff's alleged physical disability raises little debate. Mental injuries, on the other hand, present a more perplexing dilemma. Mental injuries represent the second most common complaint filed with the Equal Employment Opportunity Commission (EEOC) between July 1992 and September 1995. Unfortunately, emotional problems present complicated issues for both sport businesses and the courts because mental diseases consist of symptoms often difficult to measure. Remedies for mental impairments are not as clear as remedies for physical impairments. The installation of a wheelchair, for example, is obvious. Further, psychiatric impairments present sport business employers with perilous dilemmas as they attempt to balance ADA compliance with the maintenance of a safe, violence-free work environment.

Possession of a physical disability as defined in any one of the above three categories, however, does not automatically qualify someone as disabled under the ADA. The particular disability "substantially limits one or more" major life activities. The ADA does not cover a disabled individual *unless* the disability limits a major life activity (*Jasany v. U.S. Postal Service*, 1985; *Taylor v. U.S. Postal Service*, 1991). "Major life activities" are defined as "caring for one's self, performing manual tasks, walking, seeing, hearing, speaking, breathing, *learning* and working" (U.S. Equal Employment Opportunity Commission [EEOC] and the U.S. Department of Justice [DOJ], 1991, p. I-27). *Temporary* impairments, such as a broken leg, or the common cold, are not qualified as disabilities impairing a major life activity ("Nondiscrimination," 1994). Courts differ on their interpretation regarding what qualifies as a major lie activity (e.g., learning). Plaintiffs, for example, routinely argue that sport participation represents a "major life activity" (*Doe v. Dolton*, 1988; *Pahulu v. University of Kansas*, 1995; *Taylor v. U.S. Postal Service*, 1990). Relying on the educational and learned benefits derived from athletics (e.g., improved social skills, better grades, self-concept), a number of courts have concluded that participation in athletics constitutes a "major life activity" (*Doe v. Dolton Elementary School District No. 148*, 1988; *Pahulu v. University of Kansas*, 1995). As explained by the U.S. District Court in *Sandison v. Michigan High School Athletic Association* (1994, p. 489), "Defendant downgrades the importance of interscholastic sports in plaintiffs' learning programs . . . Participation on the cross-country and track team is an important and integral part of the education of plaintiffs, it is to them a major life activity as contemplated by ADA and the Rehabilitation Act." Consequently, disabled individuals prohibited from participation due to existing interscholastic or intercollegiate rules, for example, may have legal recourse through the ADA.

The determination of whether the plaintiff's disability in *Anderson v. Little League Baseball, Inc.* (1992) limited one or more of his major life activities is less subjective. In the Anderson case, the plaintiff-coach sought to enjoin the defendants from enforcing a rule that would prohibit him from coaching from the on-field coach's box in a wheelchair. The plaintiff-coach using a wheelchair was disabled and could not stand or walk. As defined by the federal regulations, walking represents a "major life activity." Consequently, the plaintiff in this case had little trouble qualifying as a disabled individual as defined by the ADA. Courts agree that the question regarding whether a plaintiff qualifies as a disabled person whose disability substantially limits one or more major life activities must be done on a case-by-case basis. ADA critics argue that the time and resultant cost required to conduct the analyses is extremely burdensome and potentially debilitating to small businesses.

The ADA has five titles, or sections, that define the law. Title I addresses discrimination in employment. Title II addresses discrimination by state and local governments. Title III addresses discrimination in places of public accommodation. Title IV addresses discrimination in telecommunications. Title V addresses miscellaneous areas, including federal wilderness areas and dispute resolution. Titles I, II, and III are of great relevance to sport business managers and will be elaborated on in the remainder of this chapter.

TITLE I: DISCRIMINATION IN EMPLOYMENT

As of July 26, 1992, the ADA prohibited businesses employing 25 or more employees from discriminating against a qualified individual based solely on the individual's disability. As of July 26, 1994, the ADA applies to all sport businesses with 15 or more employees. No individual liability exists under the ADA (see *U.S. EEOC v. AIC Security Investigations, Ltd.,* 1995). Title I seeks to better employ the 13 million unemployed, disabled people between the ages of 21 and 64 (Epstein, 1995). As reported by a Lou Harris poll conducted in 1994, 79% of the disabled constituency said they would exchange their government benefits for a full-time job (Epstein, 1995). The employment of the disabled undoubtedly would enhance the self-esteem and self-worth of the disabled individual. However, society also would benefit, as tax monies needed to support this constituency would be reduced, and the disabled's earned discretionary income could increase the sales of local businesses.

The ADA defines a *qualified individual with a disability* as one who "Satisfies the requisite skill, experience, education and other job-related requirements of the employment position such individual holds or desires, and who, *with or without reasonable accommodation,* can perform the *essential functions* of such positions" (ADA, 1990; emphasis added). The ADA does not require employers to hire disabled individuals who are not qualified for the particular job. However, the law presents confusion for employers attempting to comply with its mandates (Andrews, 1991; Jeffries, 1991; Lindsay, 1989/1990). The following seven areas will be discussed in an attempt to clarify related ambiguities: (1) essential versus nonessential job functions, (2) selection criteria, (3) application accessibility, (4) job interview and application inquiries, (5) confidentiality, (6) reasonable accommodations, and (7) the direct threat defense.

Essential versus Nonessential Job Functions

The ADA prohibits sport businesses from excluding the disabled from job opportunities because a disabled individual who meets job prerequisites (e.g., education, work experience, training, licenses) cannot perform nonessential (i.e., marginal) job functions. For example, assume Hypothetical University's (HU's) Athletic Department is housed in a two-story building. Also assume HU is hiring a person to work at the first-floor ticket window on the campus of HU. HU's Athletic Department would not be able to eliminate a candidate who was unable to deliver mail to the upstairs office, as it is unlikely that this task represents an *essential* job function. The EEOC suggests that the employer handle nonessential job functions by one of the following modes:

1. Provide an accommodation that will enable the individual to perform the function.
2. Transfer the function to another position.
3. Exchange the function for one the applicant is able to perform.

The EEOC classifies job functions as essential or nonessential on a case-by-case basis. The EEOC guidelines (1992) identify various factors that can facilitate a sport entrepreneur in defining those tasks defined as "essential" versus "nonessential." This list includes the employer's judgment, job descriptions, time spent performing particular functions, the impact or consequences of not performing a function, a collective bargaining agreement, the work experience of people who have either in the past or are presently performing the job, and the organizational structure. Completed job analyses are critical to a sport business manager attempting to defend why a particular task was deemed "essential."

Regardless of the assistance provided by the EEOC, debate continues over what constitutes an "essential" job function. Job attendance, for example, has been viewed as an essential job function when work cannot be performed at home (*Tyndall v. National Education Centers,* 1994; *Wimbley v. Bolger,* 1986). In the *Tyndall* case, the employee-plaintiff was a teacher who had lupus and frequently needed to remain at home on account of her own illness or to care for her disabled son. The Fourth Circuit Court concluded that attendance was an essential job requirement. Further entrenchment of the virtual office on employment practices could foreseeably alter this "essential" nature of attendance. To illustrate, the continued interest in, and attractiveness of, telecourses and course lectures provided by computer may alter the ability of a defendant school or sport business to argue successfully that job attendance constitutes an essential job function.

Selection Criteria

Sport business managers can establish job selection criteria based on a variety of physical and mental qualifications. Job selection criteria can reflect both essential and nonessential job functions, as noted by the EEOC technical manual (1992). Selection criteria may relate to the following:

- education
- skills
- work experience
- licenses or certification
- physical and mental abilities
- health and safety
- other job-related requirements, such as judgment, ability to work under pressure, or interpersonal skills (p. IV-5)
- physical agility tests (p. IV-8)

Only when the criteria have a disproportionate impact on the disabled individual(s) does the ADA require sport business employers to show how selection criteria are both job-related and consistent with a business necessity. Reference to the job analysis facilitates ambiguity by providing the employer with specific information regarding selection criteria directly related to the adequate performance of a particular job.

Application Accessibility

Employment opportunities for the disabled exist only if the disabled have access to employment related information. The ADA requires sport businesses to make application procedures accessible to disabled individuals (EEOC, 1992). For example, facilities posting job information must provide access to the mobility impaired. Wheelchair ramps and first-floor postings illustrate two simple ways employers can better assist the disabled population. Job applications listing tele-phone numbers also must list a telecommunication device for deaf persons (TDD; the new preferred term is *text telephone*) number when no established telephone relay service exists. Further, the ADA requires sport businesses to help disabled applicants who need assistance in completing the application form (e.g., writing assistance, reading assistance). Posting job descriptions in trade magazines, at con-ferences, and at training facilities targeting the disabled constituency represent ad-ditional ways sport business managers can comply with the spirit of the ADA.

Interview and Application Inquiries

The ADA greatly alters the manner in which sport business employers design job applications and conduct employment interviews. Questions regarding work-ers' compensation claims, medical histories, and illegal drug addictions, for example, were common. The frequency and routine practice of hiring and inter-viewing individuals makes this area of the ADA of primary importance to the sport employer.

The issue regarding medical exams and inquiries is best categorized into three different stages: (1) preoffer, preemployment; (2) postoffer, preemployment; and (3) postemployment. The following paragraphs address the distinctions and privi-leges associated with each phase of the employment process.

Preoffer, Preemployment Questioning Practices

Prior employment practices allowed sport business employers to question ex-tensively a candidate about his or her medical history and to require a medical exam in the preemployment stage. Disability-related questions and medical exams revealing "hidden" disabilities (e.g., epilepsy, diabetes) often posed a barrier to employment. For example, sport managers harboring biases about epilepsy or fear-ful of escalating insurance costs associated with victims of cancer could previously refuse to hire an otherwise qualified individual.

Disability-related questions. Sport businesses are no longer able to ask "disability-related questions" or require medical examinations during the preoffer, preemployment stage. The EEOC provides assistance in ascertaining what con-stitutes "disability-related questions" and a "medical exam." As defined by the EEOC (1995, p. 4), a "disability-related question" means a "question that is *likely to elicit* information about a disability." Exhibit 6–1 represents disability-related questions identified by the EEOC (1992) that cannot be asked on application forms or in job interviews.

Job-related questioning. Sport managers interviewing job candidates *can* ask an array of questions about the individual's ability to carry out various job re-

Exhibit 6–1 Examples of Questions that Cannot Be Asked on Application Forms or in Job Interviews

1. Have you ever had or been treated for any of the following conditions or diseases? (Followed by a checklist of various conditions and diseases)
2. Please list any conditions or diseases for which you have been treated in the past 3 years.
3. Have you ever been hospitalized? If so, for what condition?
4. Have you ever been treated by a psychiatrist or psychologist? If so, for what condition?
5. Have you ever been treated for any mental condition?
6. Is there any health-related reason why you may not be able to perform the job for which you are applying?
7. Have you had a major illness in the last 5 years?
8. How many days were you absent from work because of illness last year?
9. Do you have any physical defects that preclude you from performing certain kinds of work? If yes, describe such defects and specific work limitations.
10. Do you have any disabilities or impairments that may affect your performance in the position for which you are applying?
11. Are you taking any prescribed drugs?
12. Have you ever been treated for drug addiction or alcoholism?
13. Have you ever filed for workers' compensation insurance?

Source: Reprinted from the Equal Employment Opportunities Commission, p. V6–8. 1992.

sponsibilities. Sport managers can freely inquire about the applicant's ability to perform specific job functions. For example, a sport business manager hiring a fitness program director can ask about a candidate's ability to use the fitness equipment and knowledge of related benefits. Further, sport managers are free to inquire about nonmedical qualifications and skills, including the applicant's education, work history, and certifications and licenses (EEOC, 1995). The employer also can ask the applicant to "describe or demonstrate how he or she will perform specific job functions," *provided the employer makes this same request of every applicant regardless of disability* (EEOC, 1992, p. V-13).

Discriminatory questioning among job candidates. The law defines two situations in which a sport business may discriminate among candidates during a job interview. First, sport business managers may divert from a uniform list of questions asked of all candidates when an applicant's disability is overt (e.g., a missing limb). For example, a health club manager could ask a potential candidate having only one leg to demonstrate how he or she would teach swimming lessons. In this situation, the law does not require the sport business to ask every applicant to make the same demonstration. In a rather "gray" area, the EEOC (1995) states that it is legal to ask about temporary physical impairments that *do not* limit a major life activity. In other words, a sport business employer may ask an applicant with a leg in a cast how the leg was broken. However, further questioning such as, "Do you expect the leg to heal normally?" or "Have you had many broken bones?" would constitute illegal disability-related questions (EEOC, 1995, p. 9). Second, a sport manager may ask additional questions of a particular applicant that are not asked of other applicants when a particular candidate has volunteered information about a disability.

Questions regarding past and/or present drug or alcohol use, addictions. Past drug and/or alcohol addictions qualify as disabilities under the ADA. Questions regarding past drug or alcohol addictions are illegal. Questions regarding current *legal* drug use are also illegal, as use of the drug azidothymidine (AZT) provides information about a qualified disability that could result in the refusal to hire an otherwise qualified individual.

In another "gray" area, sport business employers may ask "innocuous questions about lawful drug use" that "are not likely to elicit information about disability" (EEOC, 1995, p. 10). As explained by the EEOC (1995, p. 10),

> During her interview, an applicant volunteers to the interviewer that she is coughing and wheezing because her allergies are acting up as a result of pollen in the air. The interviewer, who also has allergies, tells the applicant that he finds "Lemebreathe" (an over-the-counter antihistamine) to be effective, and asks the applicant if she has tried it. There are many reasons why someone might have tried "Lemebreathe" which have nothing to do with disability. Therefore this question is not likely to elicit information about a disability.

Again, the sport business manager's ability to interpret these seemingly "fine lines" between legal and illegal questions on a daily basis is troublesome. Sport business employers can best protect themselves against claims of discrimination by avoiding all questions and comments regarding the applicant's usage of any legal drug or over-the-counter medicine.

Questions regarding job attendance, sick days. Employers can ask applicants about their attendance record at their prior job. As explained by the EEOC (1995, p. 8), "There may be many reasons unrelated to disability why someone cannot meet attendance requirements or was frequently absent from a previous job (for example, an applicant may have had day-care problems)." However, a sport business employer could not ask the candidate the number of *sick* days taken, as this represents a prohibited disability-related question.

Questions regarding the need for a reasonable accommodation. During the preoffer, preemployment stage, unfounded questions regarding the applicant's need for a reasonable accommodation are also prohibited. Sport business employers can legally inquire about the candidate's need for a reasonable accommodation when the candidate displays an obvious disability, the candidate voluntarily discloses a disability, or the candidate voluntarily discloses the need for a reasonable accommodation. Two examples provided by the EEOC illustrate legal queries (1995, p. 7):

(a) An individual with diabetes applying for a receptionist position voluntarily discloses that she will need periodic breaks to take medication. The employer may ask the applicant questions about the reasonable accommodation such as how often she will need breaks, and how long the breaks must be. Of course, the employer may not ask any questions about the underlying physical condition.

(b) An applicant with a severe visual impairment applies for a job involving computer work. The employer may ask whether he will need reasonable accommodation to perform the functions of the job. If the applicant answers "no," the employer may not ask additional questions about reasonable accommodation (although, of course, the employer could ask the applicant to describe or demonstrate performance). If the applicant says that he *will* need accommodation, the employer may ask questions about the type of required accommodation such as, "What will you need?" If the applicant says he needs software that increases the size of text on the computer screen, the employer may ask questions such as, "Who makes the software?" "Do you need a particular brand?" or "Is that software compatible with our computers?" However, the employer may not ask questions about the applicant's underlying condition. In addition, the employer may not ask reasonable accommodation questions that are unrelated to job functions such as, "Will you need reasonable accommodation to get to the cafeteria?"

Reasonable accommodations needed now or in the immediate future are legal, whereas inquiries regarding reasonable accommodations in the distant future are prohibited.

A sport business's inquiries regarding a reasonable accommodation may be viewed as discriminatory by a disabled plaintiff who failed to get a particular job. Clear documentation regarding individual job deficiencies and assets should be clearly documented and maintained for all candidates to best defend against potential claims of discrimination.

The medical exam. The ADA prohibits sport businesses from administering or requiring medical exams at the preemployment, preoffer stage. The EEOC also provides a sport business with assistance regarding the definition of a "medical exam." As explained by the EEOC (1995, p. 14), the following factors tend to infer that a particular exam represents a "medical exam":

1. Test is administered by a health care professional or someone trained by a health care professional.
2. Test results are interpreted by a health care professional or someone trained by a health care professional.
3. Test is designed to reveal a physical or mental impairment.
4. The employer is attempting to determine the applicant's physical or mental health or impairments.
5. The test is invasive (e.g., blood test, urinalysis).
6. Test measures the applicant's physiological responses to performing the task.
7. Test is normally given in a medical setting (e.g., a health care professional's office).
8. Test administration involves the use of medical equipment.

The above eight factors may be viewed individually or collectively based on the particular situation.

Sport business employers often question whether their use of physical agility tests, physical fitness tests, or psychological exams constitute medical exams in violation of the ADA. Again, the EEOC provides employers with interpretive assistance. According to the EEOC, the above-mentioned tests can be legally administered. Although not required, physical agility and fitness tests should simulate actual job requirements. Sport managers denying employment to a disabled candidate based on the applicant's performance on a physical agility or fitness test must be prepared to show how the test results are job-related and consistent with business necessity.

Physical agility or fitness tasks can turn into medical exams, however, if the test measures or monitors physiological or biological responses. As explained by the EEOC (1995, p. 16), "A messenger service tests applicants' ability to run one mile in 15 minutes. At the end of the run, the employer takes the applicants' blood pressure and heart rate. Measuring the applicant's physiological responses makes this a medical examination." Similarly, employers may give psychological exams that measure traits including "honesty, tastes, and habits" (EEOC, 1995, p. 16). Psychological exams disclosing mental disorders or impairments, however, represent medical exams. Further, personality tests asking questions about sexual practices or religious beliefs are often discouraged, as information revealed may later be used by a plaintiff in an invasion of privacy claim against the employer (Schuster, 1996). The EEOC supports using waivers, obtaining the candidate's prior written consent to the exam, and requiring the applicant to provide medical approval regarding his or her ability to safely perform an agility or physical exam.

Postoffer, Preemployment Questioning Practices

This second phase of the employment process represents a situation when a sport business, for example, has offered the job to a candidate conditional on the passing of a medical exam and related inquiries. This situation might transpire when, for example, hiring an exercise prescriptionist to work with the older clientele. A sport business employer might want to ensure that the individual did not have any disabilities that would pose a direct threat to, for example, the potential employees or other patrons. Questions regarding "workers' compensation history, prior sick leave usage, illnesses/diseases/impairments, and general physical and mental health" are appropriate at this time (EEOC, 1995, p. 18). A sport business employer, however, cannot arbitrarily require only certain "suspect" candidates to take a medical exam or answer medical inquiries. If an employer requires one candidate to take a medical exam or answer medical inquiries, the employer must require all other candidates applying for that same job to do the same.

During the postoffer, preemployment stage, medical exams and inquiries regarding medical conditions do not have to be job-related or consistent with business necessity. However, sport business employers who revoke a job offer based on the outcome of the medical exam or inquiry must show that the disclosed medical information precluded the candidate from meeting existing, essential job criteria. Further, the employer must show that no reasonable accommodation was possible without subjecting the employer to an undue burden (ADA, 1990).

Postoffer, Postemployment Questioning Practices

The postoffer, postemployment stage refers to established employees. Sport business employers can only require current employees to take medical exams or answer medical inquiries when an individual's mental or physical condition detrimentally affects job performance (ADA, 1990). For example, a sport business employer could require an employee who is continually falling asleep on the job to take a medical exam (EEOC, 1992).

The ADA recognizes two exceptions to the above that permit an employer to subject a current employee to medical exams or inquiries that are not job related and consistent with business necessity. First, current employees can volunteer to take a test or answer inquiries as "part of an employee health program (such as medical screening for high blood pressure, weight control, and cancer detection)" (EEOC, 1992, p. VI-15). Second, federal legislation mandates medical testing for employees working in certain occupations. For example, the U.S. Department of Transportation requires medical examinations of personnel employed as air traffic controllers, airline pilots, and interstate truck and bus drivers (EEOC, 1992).

Drug testing is not a medical examination as defined by the ADA. Consequently, sport businesses can drug test job applicants and current employees at any stage in the hiring or employment relationship (ADA, 1990). However, sport business managers who require a drug test at the initial preemployment, preoffer stage cannot demand follow-up medical exams or inquiries. Consequently, sport managers should wait until after the job offer has been made before requiring a drug test (EEOC, 1992).

Reasonable Accommodations and the Undue Hardship Exception

The issue of what constitutes a "reasonable accommodation" has generated extensive and heated debate. Critics of the ADA argue that the law's failure to define quantitatively what constitutes a reasonable accommodation and an undue hardship "promises to be both a source of new litigation worries and a potential compliance nightmare for large and small businesses alike" (Holtzman, Jennings, & Schenk, 1992, p. 279). As of 1992, less than 2 years after the passage of the ADA, 25% of all ADA claims allege the employer's failure to provide a reasonable accommodation (Epstein, 1995).

The ADA requires employers to make reasonable accommodations for disabled individuals who are otherwise capable of performing essential job functions. Approximately 26% of the employable disabled population require some type of reasonable accommodation (Epstein, 1995). The ADA required employers to make reasonable accommodations only at the request of the disabled job candidate or current employee. The ADA *does* require the employer to look at each case independently to ascertain whether a reasonable accommodation can be made (*Anderson v. Little League*, 1992; *Bombrys v. City of Toledo*, 1993). The *EEOC Technical Assistance Manual* (EEOC, 1992) provides the following examples of reasonable accommodations:

a) making facilities accessible;
b) job restructuring;
c) modifying existing work schedules;
d) acquiring or modifying equipment;
e) providing qualified readers or interpreters;
f) reassignment to a vacant position;
g) permitting use of accrued paid leave or unpaid leave for necessary treatment;
h) providing reserved parking for a person with a mobility impairment.
(p. III-6)

Reasonable accommodations resulting in a significant loss of efficiency or requiring a seemingly impossible task (i.e., the elimination of job stress) are not required ("Developments," 1996).

An individual's request and need for an accommodation cannot diminish a job candidate's employment opportunities. However, the ADA does not require accommodations that "would impose an undue hardship" on the employer or establishment (ADA, 1990). Again, a concise definition of "undue hardship" is unavailable and remains subjective. For example, in *Arneson v. Heckler* (1989), the Eighth Circuit remanded the case back to the lower court requiring further consideration as to whether the hiring of a part-time assistant and possible employee relocation constitute "reasonable" accommodations. In a dissenting opinion (*Arneson v. Heckler,* 1989, p. 400), the district judge stated, "The Government (defendant) should bend over backwards to accommodate the handicapped. However, this does not mean the Government should be a floor mat to be walked on by individuals intent on taking advantage of the Government's perceived inability to discharge non-productive or unqualified employees . . ."

The EEOC (1992) classifies an undue hardship as any accommodation that is financially excessive, is disruptive, or fundamentally alters the nature of the business. Again, the interpretation of terms, including *financially excessive, disruptive,* and *fundamental alteration* is likely to create some confusion for sport business managers. The following paragraphs attempt to clarify ambiguities.

Financially Excessive

Critics of the ADA argue that the law's mandated reasonable accommodation requirement represents an overintrusive attempt by the government to regulate business while increasing a business's cost structure. The Bush Administration's Council of Economic Advisors estimated it would cost employers between $1.7 billion and $10.2 billion annually to reasonably accommodate disabled employees (Epstein, 1995). As explained in "Developments" (1996, p. 1,619), "One can view the ADA as simply an extension of the social decision that employers should bear all or part of certain social welfare costs (for example, pension plans, health plans, and minimum wage laws)." Research has provided a variety of estimates on the costs incurred by business as a result of the ADA's reasonable accommodation provision. The President's Committee on Employment of People with Disabilities' Job Accommodation Network revealed data indicating that the mean cost of accommodation between 1992 and 1994 was $992 (Epstein, 1995). Other studies indicate that the average cost to "reasonably accommodate" a disabled individual remains minimal (Tannenbaum, 1994). As indicated by Schwadel (1996, p. B6), a 1995 Harris Poll of 400 executives indicated that the median cost of providing accommodations was $233 per employee. Similarly, in another study, the EEOC indicated the average cost of a reasonable accommodation amounted to $263. As reported by McGraw (1993, p. 535), 1992 figures compiled from the Job Accommodation Network revealed the following:

- 31% of all accommodations cost nothing.
- 50% cost less than $50.00.
- 69% cost less than $500.
- 88% cost less than $1,000.

Data compiled in 1996 by Peter Blanck's study of Sears revealed that the average cost to accommodate a disabled employee amounted to $45 (Schwadel, 1996). As indicated by Blanck, approximately 75% of the accommodations "were made at no cost, with many involving changes in scheduling or job duties" (Schwadel, 1996, p. B6). Sears determined that accommodating the disabled equated to financial prudence, as the company spends between $1,800 and $2,400 to terminate and replace the average employee.

As indicated by the above studies, it would be difficult for most employers to argue successfully that a $500 accommodation is "unreasonable." Unfortunately, the intangible costs associated with providing reasonable accommodations are not figured into any quantifiable definition or average expense. For example, as explained by McGraw (1993, p. 535), "Other costs, such as lost production time and training time for a new device, although intangible, are nonetheless real and must also be borne by the employer." Business opponents view the intangible costs as yet another facet of the ADA that drafters of the legislation failed to consider. This absence, opponents argue, only further complicates and confuses compliance efforts.

The ADA does not mandate that employers make accommodations that are financially excessive, although large, profitable businesses are expected to incur more expensive accommodations than the small, meager businesses. However, even wealthy employers will not be required to accommodate the every whim of a disabled individual. As explained by the U.S. Court of Appeals (7th Cir.) in *Vande Zande v. State of Wisconsin Department of Administration* (1995, pp. 542–543),

> Even if an employer is so large or wealthy . . . that it may not be able to plead "undue *hardship*," it would not be required to expend enormous sums in order to bring about a trivial improvement in the life of a disabled employee. If the nation's employers have potentially unlimited financial obligations to 43 million disabled persons, the Americans with Disabilities Act will have imposed an indirect tax potentially greater than the national debt.

Four states (Delaware, Louisiana, North Carolina, and Virginia) have quantitatively defined *financially excessive*. Delaware and North Carolina, for example, cap the amount an employer must spend to reasonably accommodate a disabled employee to 5% of the individual's annual salary. Virginia takes a more conservative approach and limits the amount required by the employer to $500. Louisiana, however, states that employers are not required to spend any money on accommodations.

A quantitative definition of *financially excessive* would benefit sport business managers in three ways. First, interactions between management and disabled employees would improve. Management unable to provide a reasonable accommodation could rely on objective data when denying someone a reasonable accommodation and deter the perception of bias, discrimination, or inadequate treatment. Second, the litigation that could ensue from disparate opinions regarding undefined legislative terms presents a loss to all stakeholders. As explained in "Developments" (1996, p. 1,616), "This potentially excessive litigation would waste the time and resources of employers, employees, courts, and agencies . . . that frequently litigate such claims." Third, an unfair playing field among competing sport businesses is foreseeable, as some sport businesses would be forced to make more extensive, and expensive, reasonable accommodations. The resultant increase in cost structure may hurt the small sport business as well as the sport business competing in a global environment. In the end, all stakeholders suffer as unemployment increases, tax contributions decrease, and consumer product alternatives decline.

The cost of an accommodation becomes irrelevant when the disabled employee is willing to pay for and provide the needed accommodation. Disabled individuals may also mitigate otherwise financially excessive accommodations by splitting the cost of the accommodation with the sport business. State vocational rehabilitation agencies also provide money for the funding of reasonable accommodations. Tax benefits are included in the legislation for those employers spending monies to provide reasonable accommodations. As reported by Epstein (1995, p. 404), tax benefits include a "tax deduction of up to $15,000 a year for removal of qualified architectural or transportation barriers, a tax credit of up to $5,125 a year for the provision of reasonable accommodations by small businesses, and a tax credit of up to $2,400 a year for the employment of individuals with "targeted" disabilities.

Disruptive

The ADA does not require employers to make accommodations that disrupt the work environment. For example, the law would not expect a health club to accommodate an aerobic dance instructor who was hard of hearing by maintaining the intercom system at an excessively high decibel level that would be disruptive to the surrounding health club activities.

Fundamentally Alters the Nature of the Business

Furthermore, the ADA does not require employers to make accommodations that would fundamentally alter the nature of a business. For example, the law would not require a night club, operating with dim lights, to increase lighting for an employee who had difficulty seeing in dim lighting ("Equal Employment Opportunity," 1991). Further, the law would not require a country club hosting a swim party to have a dance instead due to a disabled person's inability to partake in swimming.

Confidentiality

Employers have a legal obligation to keep confidential all information regarding medical exams (including drug test results and exams taken on a voluntary basis) and inquiries in confidential files that are separate from personnel files. This information is only available to the following persons:

1. appropriate supervisors and managers
2. first aid and safety personnel
3. government officials
4. insurance companies
5. state workers' compensation offices or second injury funds (ADA, 1990)

Regardless of the latitude provided above, sport business employers should ensure that medical information is shared *only* with those individuals who need to know the related information.

The Direct Threat Defense

The direct threat defense is available to employers when the hiring or continued employment of a disabled individual would pose a significant risk or a direct threat to the individual and surrounding others (e.g., employees, patrons). However, before barring employment, a sport business manager must search for reasonable accommodations that would eliminate or reduce the associated risk. A sport business can legally refuse to hire the individual only if a reasonable accommodation that lowers the severity of risk would impose an undue hardship (ADA, 1990).

As mentioned above, the employee with a mental disorder or psychiatric impairment presents a sport manager with a perplexing problem. Psychological and mental disorders are often difficult to detect and document. As explained in a 1996 *HRFocus* article ("Caught Between Violence," p. 19),

> Employers cannot discriminate against such employees unless they pose a "direct threat" to someone's health and safety that cannot be solved with a reasonable accommodation. But if the company does not dismiss the worker because the actual or threatened misconduct does not amount to a direct threat, coworkers or other injured parties may charge the employer with negligence.

According to Coil and Shapiro (1996), the EEOC does not view the threatening comment(s) of a disabled person as a "direct threat." Rather, the EEOC suggests management gather additional information to ascertain the degree of risk presented by the individual. On the other hand, overt acts of violence, such as a mentally disabled employee who assaults his supervisor, for example, have been held to create a direct threat (*Marino v. U.S. Postal Service,* 1994). Professional evaluations provide protection for sport managers deciding to dismiss employees opined as a direct threat to the individual and surrounding others. Sport business managers may find solace by imitating the policy taken by Wells-Fargo Bank, which immediately dismisses employees engaging in "bodily harm, physical intimidation or threats of violence" ("Caught Between Violence," 1996).

TITLE II: DISCRIMINATION BY PUBLIC SERVICES

Title II prohibits discrimination on the basis of disability in state and local government services. Application and interpretation of Title II mirror the application and interpretation of the Rehabilitation Act of 1973. As explained by the *Pottgen v. Missouri Senior High School Activities Association (MHSAA)* court (1994, p. 930), "Congress intended Title II to be consistent with section 504 of the Rehabilitation Act. This desire for consistency is evident from the ADA statutory scheme itself. Enforcement remedies, procedures and rights under Title II are the same as under section 504." Consequently, the following Title II discussion will focus on how the law applies to the age restriction laws imposed on disabled individuals by governing athletic associations.

Numerous plaintiffs have alleged that age restrictions preventing participation in interscholastic sports because of age (typically 19-year-olds are prohibited from playing) represent discrimination in violation of the ADA, Title II, and the Rehabilitation Act. The facts in *Pottgen v. MHSAA* (1994) resemble the facts in a variety of cases tried in the courts alleging ADA violations (*Dennin v. Connecticut Interscholastic Athletic Conference,* 1996; *J.M., Jr. v. Montana High School Association,* 1994; *Johnson v. Florida High School Activities Association, Inc.,* 1995; *Reaves v. Mills,* 1995; *Sandison v. Michigan High School Athletic Association,* 1994; *UIL v. Buchanan,* 1993). In the *Pottgen* case, the learning disabled plaintiff repeated two grades in elementary school. As explained by the court, "Pottgen was active in sports throughout junior high and high school. . . . However, because he had repeated two grades, Pottgen turned nineteen shortly before July 1 of his senior year. Consequently MHSAA By-Laws rendered Pottgen ineligible to play." The plaintiff challenged the MHSAA's age limit as violating Title II of the ADA, the Rehabilitation Act, and section 1983 of the federal constitution. The plaintiff in the *Pottgen* (1994) case as in other similar cases initiated action for injunctive relief prohibiting the governing athletic associations from enforcing age restriction rules. The familiar test determining injunctive relief includes the following four factors (*Pottgen,* 1994):

1. the plaintiff's likelihood of success on its merits
2. the possibility of irreparable harm to the plaintiff if injunction is not granted
3. the harm incurred by the defendant if the injunction is granted
4. the public interest

The success of the injunction request hinges on how the court interprets the plaintiff's likelihood of success on its merits (factor 1 above). Plaintiffs alleging Title II violations must prove:

1. the athletic association represents a "public entity;"
2. the plaintiff is a "qualified individual with a disability;"
3. the plaintiff has been excluded from participation or denied the benefits of the activities of the public entity. (*Johnson v. Florida High School,* 1995, p. 582).

Courts consistently conclude that the athletic associations are public entities (*Johnson v. Florida High School,* 1995; *Sandison v. Michigan High School,* 1994; *Hoot by Hoot v. Milan Area Schools,* 1994). Title II of the ADA defines a public entity as follows:

1. any state or local government
2. any department, agency, special purpose district, or other instrumentality of a state or local government
3. the National Railroad Passenger Corporation, and any commuter authority (ADA, 1990)

As emphasized by the U.S. District Court in *Sandison* (1994, p. 487), athletic associations represent an *instrumentality of a state* or local government. Factors considered by the courts in concluding that athletic associations represent public entities include their regulatory authority over public schools, the use of public employees (i.e., coaches) to administer and organize the various competitions and tournaments, and the use of public facilities in which the activities are conducted.

The second prong of the Title II analysis, whether the plaintiff represents a "qualified individual with a disability," produces a more difficult analysis. Often, the question of fact regarding the validity of the plaintiff's alleged disability is not an issue. The primary focus of the analysis tends to hinge on whether a disabled plaintiff exceeding the age limit for participation represents a "qualified individual." The ADA (EEOC and the DOJ, 1991, p. II-26) defines a *qualified individual* as "An individual with a disability who, with or without reasonable modifications to rules, policies, or practices, . . . meets the essential eligibility requirements for the receipt of services or the participation in programs or activities provided by a public entity." Plaintiffs argue that they represent qualified individuals as defined by the law and that the athletic association should waive the age restriction policy as a reasonable accommodation. Defendants, on the other hand, present three primary reasons to refute the "reasonableness" of modifying or waiving the age restriction rules (*Pottgen,* 1994; *Cavallaro by Cavallaro v. Ambach,* 1983; *Reaves,* 1995; *Mahan v. Agee,* 1982; *Sandison v. Michigan High School Athletic Association,* 1995).

One, the ADA does not require an entity to make reasonable accommodations that require "fundamental" program alterations or changes resulting in an "undue financial or administrative burden." In 1995, the U.S. Court of Appeals (6th Circuit) concluded that a waiver of the age restriction rule would fundamentally alter necessary program requirements (*Sandison,* 1995). A similar conclusion was drawn in subsequent cases, including *Pottgen* (1994) and *Reaves* (1995). As espoused by the *Sandison* court and others, age restriction rules provide essential benefits, including the following:

1. eliminates competitive advantage flowing from the use of older athletes;
2. protects younger athletes from harm;
3. discourages student athletes from delaying their education to gain athletic maturity; and
4. prevents overzealous coaches from engaging in repeated red-shirting to gain a competitive advantage (*Pottgen,* 1994, p. 929).

Courts have concluded that the waiver of the age restriction rule would fundamentally alter interscholastic athletic competition.

Two, in *Sandison* (1995), the U.S. Court of Appeals argued that it would be an undue administrative burden to expect athletic administrators to determine on an individual basis whether particular athletes possessed or presented an unfair competitive advantage. As explained by the court,

> The MHSAA's expert explained that five factors weight in deciding whether an athlete possessed an unfair competitive advantage due to age: chronological age, physical maturity, athletic experience, athletic skill level, and mental ability to process sports strategy. It is plainly an undue burden to require high school coaches and hired physicians to determine whether these factors render a student's age an unfair competitive advantage. The determination would have to be made relative to the skill level of each participating member of opposing teams and the team as a unit. And of course each team member and the team as a unit would present a different skill level. Indeed, the determination would also have to be made relative to the skill level of the would-be athlete whom the

> older student displaced from the team. It is unreasonable to call upon coaches and physicians to make these near-impossible determinations. (*Sandison,* 1995, p. 1,035)

The burden associated with an individual assessment, argues the *Sandison* court (1995), is not a required element of the ADA.

Three, the age restriction does not discriminate against disabled individuals. Rather, the rule prohibits *any student* from participating in interscholastic athletics whose age exceeds the prescribed restriction. As explained by the *Sandison* court (1995, p. 1,034), "The age restriction disqualifies an overage nondisabled student just as it disqualifies the overage disabled plaintiffs." The uniform application of the rule regardless of a person's ascribed characteristics nullifies the merit of discriminatory allegations.

Unfortunately, courts are not identical in their interpretation and application of Title II to the age restriction rules of various athletic associations. The dispositive issue regarding whether age restriction policies violate a plaintiff's rights under Title II of the ADA focuses on whether the waiver of the age restriction rule, presented as a reasonable accommodation, *fundamentally* alters the operations of the athletic association (i.e., the public entity) or imposes undue hardships (*Johnson v. Florida High School,* 1995). As explained in *Johnson v. Florida High School* (1995) and in *Crocker v. Tennessee Secondary School Athletic Association* (1990), a waiver of the rule does not harm or fundamentally alter the athletic association operations or present an undue hardship for the following reasons:

1. The waiver would not require excessive, if any at all, expenditures by the athletic association.
2. The waiver would not diminish the authority or power of the athletic association.
3. The waiver would not conflict with the spirit of the rule as most disabled plaintiffs are not blue-chip players attempting to exploit athletic opportunities.

Future court decisions will further determine the rights given to disabled individuals under Title II of the ADA.

No question of fact exists regarding the meaning or intent of the challenged age restriction rules: the rules clearly prohibit participation based on age. Further, the above analysis clearly indicates that athletic associations do qualify as a "public entity" as interpreted by the courts. Consequently, no further analysis is necessary under this prong of the three-factor test.

Plaintiffs argue that the failure to grant the injunction imposes great harm. As explained by the court in *Crocker* (1990, p. 759), "Money damages simply cannot make up for the lost chance to play with one's classmates and experience the thrill and excitement of competitive sport. Money is not an adequate substitute for memories." Plaintiffs encounter additional harm via diminished self-esteem, self-concept, self-confidence, and social skills.

Defendants, as the plaintiffs argue, encounter little harm, as their operational policies and procedures remain intact. Further, what little imposition the defendant does encounter in ascertaining whether an individual poses a direct threat to surrounding others is clearly supported by the U.S. District Court in *Anderson v. Little League* (1992).

The public interest represents a final factor in ascertaining the plaintiff's likelihood of succeeding on its merits. Plaintiffs argue that accommodating disabled employees remains in the best interest of society, as participation better prepares employees with disabilities for life in mainstreamed society. As summarized in *Wright v. Columbia University* (1981, p. 794), "The public interest is enhanced by plaintiff's "dramatic example" that 'hard work and dedication to purpose can overcome enormous odds.'"

As noted in the above analysis, case law regarding eligibility issues of the student-athlete with disabilities and the ADA remain undecided. Sport business managers employed in the athletic industry (e.g., interscholastic and intercollegiate athletics) should check with respective athletic associations and stay abreast of case law in order to make the best decisions regarding similar issues.

TITLE III: DISCRIMINATION BY PUBLIC ACCOMMODATIONS AND SERVICES OPERATED BY PRIVATE ENTITIES

Title III extends the provisions of the Rehabilitation Act, which prohibits public entities from discriminating against the disabled individual, to include *private* entities operating places of public accommodations and services. The ADA lists 12 categories of public accommodations (ADA, 1990). The breadth of the public accommodation definition has a direct impact on the sport industry. Public accommodations must be operated by a private entity, must affect interstate commerce, and must fall within 1 of the 12 categories used to define a *public accommodation*. As noted in Table 6–1, each of the 12 areas contains an area of application within the sport industry.

The ability for disabled persons to access places of public accommodations benefits all stakeholders. Those with disabilities benefit via increased opportunities to network with others in a social and/or business environment, enjoyment of greater recreational opportunities, and the enhancement of individual self-concept and self-worth. Sport businesses benefit via the greater revenue potential available from an untapped, 49 million-person market segment. Society and local communities benefit from tax dollars contributed from various social security, sales, and excise taxes generated by increased economic activity.

Table 6–1 Categories Defining a Public Accommodation

Category	Example of areas applicable within the sport industry
Places of lodging	Ski resorts; vacation hotels, motels renting 6 or more rooms
Establishments serving food, drink	Sport bars; lounges in health clubs
Places of exhibition or entertainment	Athletic stadiums
Places of public gathering	Auditoriums, convention centers, lecture halls
Sales or rental establishments	Athletic equipment stores
Service establishments	Sport medicine clinics, sport masseuse, professional sport agent businesses, insurance offices
Public transportation terminals, depots, or stations (not including facilities related to air transportation)	Arenas, stadiums providing transportation from parking lot to area of event
Places of public display or collection	The Baseball Hall of Fame
Places of recreation	Parks, zoos, amusement parks
Places of education	Nursery schools, elementary, secondary, undergraduate, or postgraduate private schools
Social service center establishments	Day-care centers
Places of exercise, recreation	Gymnasiums, health clubs, bowling alleys, golf courses

Source: Reprinted with permission from L.K. Miller and L.W. Fielding, *Clinical Kinesiology*, Vol. 47, No. 3, pp. 63–70, © 1993, The American Kinesiotherapy Association.

Title III poses a new legal challenge to managers and administrators of private entities. Title III requires managers and administrators to examine, for example, traditional admission, participation, and integration policies; channels of communication; structural barriers; new construction plans; and plans for facility alterations. The following paragraphs address the impact of the ADA on the above five areas, among other issues.

Admission, Participation, and Integration Policies

Title III prohibits policies, procedures, and stereotypes that deny access or participation to the disabled population. Further, the law clearly states that admission cannot be denied on the basis of *association*. In other words, a youth soccer camp could not deny participation to a young child whose sibling or friend has the human immunodeficiency virus (HIV). As explained by the U.S. District Court in

Anderson v. Little League Baseball, Inc. (1992, p. 344), "Many disabled people lead isolated lives and do not frequent places of public accommodation . . . The U.S. Attorney General has stated that we must bring Americans with disabilities into the mainstream of society . . ." For example, a health club cannot arbitrarily deny an individual using a wheelchair the opportunity to participate in an aerobic dance class. Nor could a health club require the disabled individual to participate in aerobic classes designed only for those using a wheelchair. However, eligibility criteria that screened out certain individuals would be appropriate if necessary for safety purposes. For example, it would be appropriate for an amusement park to impose height requirements for particular amusement rides. Similarly, it would be appropriate for park and recreation departments to impose swimming proficiencies on individuals going on white water rafting trips. Sport businesses do not need to forego all safety requirements so long as they are based on actual, versus perceived or stereotyped, risks.

The ADA mandates that sport businesses modify existing admission policies and procedures to provide disabled individuals with an equal opportunity to participate in programs, services, or activities (ADA, 1990). For example, it would be in violation of the ADA if sporting goods retail stores required a driver's license as a prerequisite to allowing a patron to write a check for purchases. Since the blind or other individuals with severe disabilities, for example, are not able to drive a car, policy modification allowing the use of an alternative means of identification (e.g., another photo ID) should be allowed ("Nondiscrimination," 1994).

Further, no place of public accommodation can impose a surcharge on a disabled individual or group to recover costs associated with the provision of nondiscriminatory access and participation. However, deposits that are totally refundable are allowed to ensure that an entity is able to provide equipment as needed without incurring great expenses resulting from lost, damaged, or misused equipment. Plaintiffs alleging a violation of Title III must prove the following:

1. The individual is disabled;
2. The sport business represents a "private entity" operating a "place of public accommodation;" and
3. The person was denied the opportunity to "participate in or benefit from services or accommodations on the basis of his disability," and that reasonable accommodations could be made which do not fundamentally alter operations of the sport business. (*Johnson,* 1995, p. 582)

Unfounded Segregation Policies and the Direct Threat Defense

The ADA prohibits unfounded segregation policies. Although eligibility criteria based on safety factors are legal, the eligibility criteria must be based on actual risk. Similar to Title I, criteria based on stereotypes that have a disparate impact on the disabled population are prohibited. As noted by the U.S. Department of

Justice (DOJ, 1992), the ADA strives to provide opportunities for the disabled in an inclusive, integrated environment. An entity can deny participation only if the individual's participation would pose a direct threat to other patrons or employees in close proximity. The *Federal Register* ("Nondiscrimination," 1991) defines a direct threat as "A significant risk to the health or safety of others that cannot be eliminated by a modification of policies, practices, or procedures, or by the provision of auxiliary aids or services" (p. 87). The *Federal Register* cites three factors analyzed to determine whether a direct threat actually exists:

1. The nature, duration, and severity of the risk;
2. The probability that the potential injury will actually occur; and
3. Whether reasonable modifications of policies, practices, or procedures will mitigate the risk. ("Nondiscrimination," 1991, p. 87)

For example, allowing racquetball players using wheelchairs to play racquetball doubles with nonwheelchair users may constitute a direct threat. Although consultation with a physician is generally not required, the U.S. Department of Justice does encourage the public accommodation to consult with public health authorities (e.g., U.S. Public Health Service, Centers for Disease Control and Prevention) prior to making a determination.

The Individualized Assessment and the Direct Threat Continued

The ADA mandates that the private entity perform an individualized assessment before denying participation. In *Anderson v. Little League* (1992), for example, the defendant Little League Baseball, Inc., adopted a policy prohibiting coaches using wheelchairs from coaching from the on-field coaches' box. The policy, argued the defendants, was adopted because individuals coaching in wheelchairs presented a direct threat to youth playing the game. The contested policy stated, "Little League must consider the safety of the youth playing the game, and they should not have the added concern of avoiding a collision with a wheelchair during their participation in the game." (*Anderson*, 1992, p. 343) The plaintiff sought declaratory and injunctive relief, which would enjoin defendants from "preventing plaintiff from participating fully . . . or otherwise being involved to the full extent of his responsibilities as coach" (*Anderson*, 1992, p. 344). A key facet within the court's decision favoring the plaintiff was the defendant's failure to perform an *individualized* inquiry regarding the nature, severity, or frequency of the potential risk. As explained by the U.S. District Court (*Anderson*, 1992, p. 345), "In determining whether an individual, such as plaintiff, poses a direct threat to the health or safety of others, a public accommodation must make an individualized assessment, based on reasonable adjustment that relies on current medical knowledge or on the best available objective evidence . . ." Conclusions regarding a direct threat drawn upon subjective generalizations or stereotypes represent the discriminatory behavior the ADA intended to eliminate.

Special Services for the Disabled

The ADA does not require sport businesses to extend special services to the disabled when other members do not receive the same services (DOJ, 1992). For example, the law would not require a health club to assist members with a shower and changing of clothes when other members do not receive this same assistance. However, an athletic retail store that regularly assists individuals with fittings cannot refuse to do so because of an individual's disability.

Channels of Communication

Communication difficulties often impair an individual's ability to enjoy services and benefits provided by a sport business. The ADA mandates that employers provide auxiliary aids "to ensure that no individual with a disability is excluded, denied services, segregated or otherwise treated differently" due to communication difficulties or impairments (ADA, 1990, p. III-78). Auxiliary aids and services include "qualified interpreters, notetakers, computer-aided transcription services, written materials, telephone handset amplifiers, assistive listening devices, . . . video text displays, . . . qualified readers, taped texts,. . . . Brailled materials. . . ." (EEOC and the DOJ, 1991, p. III-78, 79). The law does not mandate that sport businesses provide auxiliary aids that would either fundamentally alter the nature of the business or result in an undue burden (ADA, 1990). An undue burden represents a significant difficulty or expense (DOJ, 1992). The U.S. Department of Justice *Technical Assistance Manual* (1992, pp. 12–13) identifies five items to consider when ascertaining the definition of a significant difficulty or expense:

1. The nature and cost of the action;
2. The overall financial resources of the site or sites involved; the number of persons employed at the site; the effect on expenses and resources; legitimate safety requirements necessary for safe operation, including crime prevention measures; or any other impact of the action on the operation of the site;
3. The geographic separateness, and the administrative or fiscal relationship of the site or sites in question to any parent corporation or entity;
4. If applicable, the overall financial resources of any parent corporation or entity; the overall size of the parent corporation or entity with respect to the number of its employees; the number, type, and location of its facilities; and

5. If applicable, the type of operation or operations of any parent corporation or entity, including the composition, structure, and functions
of the work force of the parent corporation or entity. (p. 258)

Consequently, a financially unstable franchise or subsidiary cannot plead the "excessive expense" defense when affiliated with a lucrative parent company.

Many communication barriers hindering or prohibiting participation can be
eliminated at minimal cost. For example, sport service businesses (e.g., health
clubs, retail sporting goods stores, and ball parks) can facilitate communication
with deaf individuals by the exchange of written notes, the use of interpreters, or
computer terminals. Likewise, sport service providers can facilitate communication with vision- or speech-impaired individuals via auxiliary aids (e.g., taped
texts, Braille materials, speech synthesizers, TDDs).

Structural Barriers

As noted by the U.S. Department of Justice (DOJ, 1992, p. 258), the ADA requires private entities to remove "architectural and communication barriers that
are structural in nature, when it is readily achievable to do so." Clarification is provided by defining key terms, including *architectural barriers, communication barriers, facilities,* and *readily achievable.*

An *architectural barrier* is "any physical element that impedes access" (DOJ,
1996, p. 258). For example, steps, curbs, drinking fountains, mirrors, paper towel
dispensers, deep-pile carpeting, equipment, and conventional door knobs constitute architectural barriers.

The U.S. Department of Justice (DOJ, 1992, p. 258) defines a *communication
barrier* as something "structural in nature," "an integral part of the physical structure of a facility." For example, an audible alarm system may prevent effective
communication with hearing-impaired persons. Similarly, visual signage may prevent effective communication with vision-impaired persons. Communication barriers may also include the presence, or the lack of, partitions. For example, a health
club that has a 4-ft partition may not allow an individual using a wheelchair to
communicate effectively with individuals on the opposite side of the partition.

The U.S. Department of Justice (DOJ, 1992) defines a *facility* as "Any part of a
building, structure, equipment, vehicle, site (including roads, walks, passageways,
and parking lots), or other real or personal property" (p. 259). The removal of barriers is required in both permanent and temporary facilities.

Readily achievable modifications refer to modifications "easily accomplishable
and able to be carried out without much difficulty or expense" (DOJ, 1992, p. 259).
For example, schools may stack mats, chairs, and other equipment in hallways due
to a lack of storage. The equipment, however, may impede the ability of an indi-

Exhibit 6–2 Examples of Readily Achievable Barrier Removal

1. Installing ramps;
2. Making curb cuts in sidewalks and entrances;
3. Repositioning shelves;
4. Rearranging tables, chairs, vending machines, display racks, and other furniture;
5. Repositioning telephones;
6. Adding raised markings on elevator control buttons;
7. Installing flashing alarm lights;
8. Widening doors;
9. Installing offset hinges to widen doorways;
10. Eliminating a turnstile or providing an alternative accessible path;
11. Installing accessible door hardware;
12. Installing grab bars in toilet stalls;
13. Rearranging toilet partitions to increase maneuvering space;
14. Insulating lavatory pipes under sinks to prevent burns;
15. Installing a raised toilet seat;
16. Installing a full-length bathroom mirror;
17. Repositioning the paper towel dispenser in a bathroom;
18. Creating designated accessible parking spaces;
19. Installing an accessible paper cup dispenser at an existing inaccessible water fountain;
20. Removing high pile, low density carpeting; or
21. Installing vehicle hand controls

Source: Department of Justice (1992), BNA's Americans with Disabilities Act Manual, "ADA Highlights: Title III: Public Accommodations and Commercial Facilities," pp. 13–14.

vidual using a wheelchair to travel through the hallways. Eliminating the barrier presented by the equipment stacked in the hallway is readily achievable. The U.S. Department of Justice (DOJ, 1992, p. 259) provides other examples of readily achievable modification (Exhibit 6–2). The five considerations used to determine what is a "readily achievable" modification are the same considerations listed above that are used to determine a significant difficulty or expense, or an undue burden. However, the readily achievable standard presents a less demanding level of exertion than does the undue burden associated with auxiliary aids.

It is important that sports managers remember that accessibility must be continually maintained and serviced. For example, sport business managers should continually watch for hallways that are obstructed by storage or plants as well as elevators that are inoperable. Further, the U.S. Department of Justice recognizes that an implementation plan serves as evidence of managerial diligence and good faith compliance efforts that can serve to mitigate the effects of litigation.

New Construction Plans

The ADA requires total accessibility to newly constructed buildings for places of public accommodation occupied after January 16, 1993 (DOJ, 1992). Although Title I of the ADA applies only to those businesses with 15 or more employees, Title III requires that all newly constructed sport businesses comply with the ADA. The ADA Accessibility Guidelines (ADAAG) are to be "applied during the design, construction, and alteration" phases of building or renovating (EEOC & DOJ, 1991). Deviations from the ADAAG are allowed if adherence would be "structurally impractical." For example, it may not be possible for a boat club to build an adjacent, accessible parking lot on marshland. However, the U.S. Department of Justice (DOJ, 1992) warns that the structurally impracticable characteristic defense is narrowly defined and will be considered only in rare circumstances.

The ADAAG also contains scoping requirements, which specify exactly the specific number of items or required space configurations (DOJ, 1992). The following two examples illustrate the ADAAG's scoping requirements. First, the ADAAG requires that new buildings install an elevator only when each floor has more than 3,000 sq ft *and* when the building has more than three stories. In other words, a five-story building with only 2,800 sq ft per story would not be required to have an elevator. Similarly, buildings with two floors do not need to have an elevator, even though each floor has 20,000 sq ft. Second, drinking fountains must also be accessible to disabled persons when a building has only one drinking fountain per floor. Fifty percent of all drinking fountains must be accessible when there is more than one drinking fountain per floor.

The ADAAG are not all-inclusive. For example, the ADAAG do not cover bowling alleys, golf courses, or exercise equipment. The U.S. Department of Justice (DOJ, 1992) states that professional technical standards should apply when the ADAAG does not cover the activity. When no professional standards exist, the ADAAG mandates that at least one area be accessible. For example, the law requires a bowling alley to have at least one lane accessible to the disabled.

Facility Alterations

All facility alterations begun after January 26, 1992, must also comply with the ADAAG (DOJ, 1992). Alterations include any change that affects usability. For example, changing the layout of exercise equipment or replacing worn out carpeting or floor surfaces affects usability and, therefore, must comply with ADAAG. Minor alterations must also meet accessibility guidelines. For example, the law requires private entities to build all new doors in compliance with ADAAG, equip all doors with lever handles, and relocate electrical outlets reachable at wheelchair height.

The ADA distinguishes between alterations made within a primary function area (e.g., weight room, bowling alley lanes) versus a nonprimary function area (e.g., mechanical rooms, supply rooms). An alteration to a primary function area triggers what the ADA refers to as the "path of travel" requirement (ADA, 1990). This requirement mandates that alterations include an accessible route from the altered primary function area to the entrance. Phones, restrooms, and drinking fountains within the route would also need to meet ADAAG. The law does not require private entities to make accommodations that exceed 20% of the original expense incurred by the primary function area alteration (DOJ, 1992). For example, if it cost $10,000 to replace the carpet in an exercise room, the law requires the entity to spend a minimum of $2,000 on path of travel requirements. The U.S. Department of Justice suggests that the entity prioritize changes, and spend the $2,000 accordingly when the path of travel requirements exceed $2,000. For example, the U.S. Department of Justice has prioritized the following alterations (in the following order):

1. An accessible entrance;
2. An accessible route to the altered area;
3. At least one accessible restroom for each sex or a single unisex restroom;
4. Accessible telephones;
5. Accessible drinking fountains. ("Nondiscrimination," 1994, p. 631)

Alterations to windows, hardware, controls, electrical outlets, and signs within a primary function area do not trigger the path of travel requirements. However, alterations must still comply with ADAAG requirements.

Seating and Phone Provisions in Assembly Areas

The area of the law dealing with seating in assembly areas is of great concern to many sport practitioners. According to the law, individuals with disabilities can no longer be relegated to isolated seating arrangements separate from family or friends. Many assembly areas (e.g., movie theaters) have removed permanent seats in an effort to allow segregated seating. If the removal of seats and other segregated seating accommodations cannot be "readily achieved," the U.S. Department of Justice suggests that a reasonable number of seats have removable aisle-side armrests so that those individuals wishing to transfer from a wheelchair to an existing seat are able to do so. In newly constructed arenas and stadiums exceeding a 300-person capacity, the law requires wheelchair seating to be available in more than one location. Six accessible wheelchair seating locations are required in stadiums or arenas with 300 to 500 seats. Further, sport business managers should realize that the law requires one interior "text telephone" (i.e., TDD) where four or more public pay phones exist.

Title III Exemptions

Private clubs are exempt from ADA compliance. As noted by Sawyer (1993), managers should use caution before presuming private club status. Factors indicative of a truly private club include exclusivity of memberships, the lack of advertising on public media, and substantial membership fees. Private clubs frequently lose private club status when engaged in advertising or when hosting tournaments that bring nonmembers onto private club property. In addition, certain programs or activities associated with, or linked to, an exclusive club may constitute a public accommodation. For example, a restaurant open to the public would be considered a public accommodation even though it is located on property owned by an exclusive golf club. Also, according to the ADA, a minimum of 5% (but not less than 1) of the tables at a newly constructed restaurant must be accessible. Similarly, a pro shop open to the public would require accessible counters or check-out areas.

The ADA also exempts religious organizations from Title III compliance (ADA, 1990). However, a public accommodation that leases space at a religious facility must meet ADA requirements. For example, a private health club is subject to Title III regulations when leasing property owned by a religious entity. However, the religious entity leasing the space remains exempt from ADA compliance (DOJ, 1992).

The ADA holds both the landlord and tenant responsible for compliance with Title III when leasing property not owned by a religious entity. However, the two parties may allocate particular responsibilities via contract. The party who had to pay could then sue for a breach of contract. Indemnification clauses may be helpful in recouping expenses associated with legal fees and required facility modifications.

CHAPTER SUMMARY

The effectiveness of the ADA on employment practices remains undecided. According to research by Peter Blanck (1995), the ADA has proved the most benefit to *employed* disabled individuals. In excess of 50% of all claims allege wrongful discharge (Blanck, 1995). The ADA has had little, if any, effect on the unemployed disabled constituency. In fact, survey results revealed by Louis Harris & Associates indicate that only 40% of disabled adults have even heard of or are familiar with the ADA ("Developments," 1996). On the other hand, the percentage of disability-related claims filed with the EEOC did increase from 1.4% in 1992 to 49.3% in 1995 (Rupe & Holt, 1996).

The Civil Rights Act of 1991 provides further impetus to sport managers to bring business practices into compliance. As mentioned in the previous chapter, the Civil Rights Act of 1991 provides plaintiffs with money awards for "future pecuniary losses, pain and suffering, inconvenience, mental anguish, loss of enjoyment of life, other nonpecuniary losses and punitive damages" (Rupe & Holt, 1996, p. 273).

The ADA provides opportunities previously not available to the disabled population. Compliance with the ADA requires sport business managers to evaluate existing practices and policies. As noted by earlier case law, ADA issues will be decided on a case-by-case basis. Although the opportunity for abuse is apparent, individual sport managers need to review each potential disability case thoroughly (Barnard, 1990). As explained by Barnard (1990, p. 252),

> Employers and employees will have to resort to the courts continuously to answer even the most rudimentary inquiries. . . . While motions for summary judgment have been a useful procedure to weed out the other types of frivolous Title VII actions, the "individualized, case-by-case" approach to disability claims will not lend itself very well to such notions. . . . Each "individualized inquiry" will be a jury question. The jury will sit virtually as a court of equity without meaningful legal guidance.

Consultation with disabled individuals and professional organizations can provide entities with insight regarding necessary modifications and cost-efficient means of accessibility. The U.S. Department of Justice suggests that entities outline an ADA implementation plan (DOJ, 1992). An implementation plan provides an organized approach to the provision of equal opportunities for the disabled population. Further, thorough job analyses should be performed for each job and essential job functions identified. Appropriate personnel should be educated regarding legalities associated with the personnel process, while all personnel should be educated regarding how they can make the particular place of business more user friendly and accessible to the disabled. The U.S. Department of Justice notes that the courts could perceive the implementation plan as a "good faith effort" and possibly mitigate or eliminate related litigation.

STUDENT ASSIGNMENT

Identify a sport business entity to study. Attach all related documents necessary to support your responses to the following.

1. Elaborate on how it has altered employment practices as a result of the ADA.
2. Elaborate on the accessibility provisions undertaken as a result of the ADA.
3. Elaborate on the sport business's future plans (if any) for better accessibility and employment representation for the disabled.

REFERENCES

Americans with Disabilities Act of 1990, 42 U.S.C. 12101.

Ambiguities in disabilities law cause frivolous suits. (1995, September 7). *Labor Relations Reporter,* pp. 476–478.

Anderson v. Little League Baseball, Inc., 794 F. Supp. 342 (D. Ariz. 1992).

Andrews, R. (1991). The Americans with Disabilities Act of 1990: New legislation creates expansive rights for the disabled and uncertainties for employers. *Cumberland Law Review, 21*(3), 629–646.

Arneson v. Heckler, 879 F.2d 393 (8th Cir. 1989).

Barnard, T. H. (1990). The ADA: Nightmare for employers and dream for lawyers? *St. John's Law Review, 64*(2), 229–252.

Blanck, P. D. (1995). Accessing five years of employment integration and economic opportunity under the Americans with Disabilities Act. Mental and Physical Disability Law Reporter, *19*(3), 384–392.

Bombrys v. City of Toledo, 849 F. Supp. 1210 (N.D. Ohio 1993).

Caught between violence and ADA compliance. (1996, March). *HRFocus,* p. 19.

Cavallaro by Cavallaro v. Ambach, 575 F. Supp. 171 (1983).

Coil, J. H. III, & Shapiro, L. J. (1996). The ADA at three years: A statute in flux. *Employee Relations Law Journal, 21*(4), 5–38.

Committee studies federal learning-disability response. (1996, August 19). *The NCAA News,* p. 7.

Crocker v. Tennessee Secondary School Athletic Association, 735 F. Supp. 753 (M.D. Tenn. 1990).

Dennin v. Connecticut Interscholastic Athletic Conference, 913 F. Supp. 663 (D. Conn. 1996).

Developments in the law: Employment discrimination. (1996). *Harvard Law Review, 109*(7), 1,568–1,692.

Doe v. Dolton Elementary School District No. 148, 694 F. Supp. 440 (N.D. Ill. 1988).

Epstein, S. B. (1995). In search of a bright line: Determining when an employer's financial hardship becomes "undue" under the Americans with Disabilities Act. *Vanderbilt Law Review, 48*(2), 391–478.

Equal Employment Opportunity for Individuals with Disabilities. 29 C.F.R. 1630 (1991).

Holtzman, G. T., Jennings, K. L., & Schenk, D. J. (1992). Reasonable accommodation of the disabled worker—A job for the man or a man for the job. *Baylor Law Review, 44,* 279.

Hoot by Hoot v. Milan Area Schools, 853 F. Supp. 243 (E.D. Mich. 1994).

Jasany v. U.S. Postal Service, 755 F.2d 1244 (6th Cir. 1985).

Jeffries, F. (1991, March 10). Firms getting new rules on rights of disabled. *The Louisville Courier-Journal,* pp. E1–E2.

J.M., Jr. v. Montana High School Association, 875 P.2d 1026 (Mont. 1994).

Johnson v. Florida High School Activities Association, Inc., 899 F. Supp. 579 (M.D. Fla. 1995).

Lindsay, R. A. (1989/1990). Discrimination against the disabled: The impact of the new federal legislation. *Employee Relations Law Journal, 15*(3), 333–345.

Mahan v. Agee, 652 P.2d 765 (Okl., 1982).

Marino v. U.S. Postal Service, 25 F.2d 1037 (1st Cir. 1994).

McGraw, E. J. (1993). Compliance costs of the Americans with Disabilities Act. *Delaware Journal of Corporate Law, 18,* 521–542.

NCAA could meet swimmer in court. (1996, August 13). *USA Today,* p. 3C.

Nondiscrimination on the basis of disability by public accommodations and in commercial facilities. (1991; 1994). 28 C.F.R. 36.

Pahulu v. University of Kansas, 897 F. Supp. 1387 (D. Kan. 1995).

Pottgen v. Missouri Senior High School Activities Association, 40 F.3d 926 (8th Cir. 1994).

Reaves v. Mills, 904 F. Supp. 120 (W.D.N.Y. 1995).

Rupe, A. L., & Holt, J. (1996). Who is disabled in Kansas. *Washburn Law Journal, 35,* 272–293.

Sandison v. Michigan High School Athletic Association, 863 F. Supp. 483 (E.D. Mich. 1994).

Sandison v. Michigan High School Athletic Association, 64 F.3d 1026 (6th Cir. 1995).

Sawyer, T. (1993). Tee'd off women golfers! *Journal of Legal Aspects of Sport, 3*(1), 1–14.

Schuster, R. (1996, March). Personality tests and privacy rights. *HR Focus,* p. 22.

Schwadel, F. (1996, March 4). Sears sets model for employing disabled. *The Wall Street Journal,* p. B6.

Tannenbaum, J. A. (1994, July 25). More small employers must adhere to disabilities act. *The Wall Street Journal,* p. B2.

Taylor v. U.S. Postal Service, 771 F. Supp. 882 (S.D. Ohio 1990).

Taylor v. U.S. Postal Service, 946 F.2d 1214 (6th Cir. 1991).

Tyndall v. National Education Centers, 31 F.3d 209 (4th Cir. 1994).

UIL v. Buchanan, 848 S.W.2d 298 (Tex. App. Austin 1993).

U.S. Department of Justice. (1992). *Title III of the ADA: Department of Justice technical assistance manual.* Washington, DC: Bureau of National Affairs.

U.S. Equal Employment Opportunity Commission & U.S. Department of Justice. (1991). *Americans with Disabilities Act handbook.* Washington, DC: U.S. Government Printing Office.

U.S. Equal Employment Opportunity Commission. (1992). *Title 1 of the ADA: EEOC technical assistance manual.* Chicago: Commerce Clearing House, Inc.

U.S. Equal Employment Opportunity Commission. (1995). *ADA enforcement guidance: Preemployment disability-related questions and medical examinations.* Washington, DC: Author.

U.S. Equal Employment Opportunity Commission v. AIC Security Investigations, Ltd., 55 F.3d 1276 (7th Cir. 1995).

Vande Zande v. State of Wisconsin Department of Administration, 44 F.3d 538 (7th Cir. 1995).

Welsh v. City of Tulsa, Oklahoma, 977 F.d 1415 (10th Cir. 1992).

Wieberg, S. (1996, August 14). Michigan state hopeful fights eligibility ruling. *USA Today,* p. C1.

Wimbley v. Bolger, 642 F. Supp. 481 (W.D. Tenn. 1986).

Wright v. Columbia University, 520 F. Supp. 789 (1981).

CHAPTER 7

Employment-Related Issues

THE EMPLOYEE: A VALUED ASSET

Employment decisions are critical to a sport business. The management literature repetitively states that employees are the greatest asset of any business, and businesses have begun renewed efforts to rebuild a loyal work force (Bell & Zempke, 1992; "Continuous Employment," 1996; White & Lublin, 1996). Benefits associated with a stable work force, include, for example, retained investment made in the employee, enhanced customer service and customer satisfaction, and managerial ease. Each benefit will be elaborated on briefly in subsequent paragraphs.

First, loyal employees directly influence a sport business's cost structure. For example, the entire employee recruiting, interviewing, training, and retaining costs can be exorbitant. Mercer (1988) estimated that employee turnover costs for one computer programmer amounted to $20,080. Included in the costs of turnover were the following:

- the exit interview (time in salary for both interviewer and departing employee): $60
- administrative and record-keeping actions: $30
- advertising for replacement person: $2,500
- preemployment administrative and record-keeping requirements: $100
- selection interview: $250
- employment tests: $40
- meetings to discuss potential candidates (time in salary for committee members): $250
- training booklets, manuals, and reports: $50
- education (salary and benefits of new employee for 10 days of training courses, workshops, and seminars): $2,400

- coaching of new employee (estimated by combining salary of new employee and current employee for 20-day period): $9,600
- salary and benefits of new employee until he or she gets "up to par": $4,800

Hiring and retaining quality, professional employees is much more cost effective than subjecting the sport business expense report to the above turnover costs and related lost productivity.

Second, employee loyalty directly influences customer satisfaction and represents a form of switching costs on which a sport business can capitalize. Customers appreciate employees who are able to deliver that "personal touch." For example, assume a patron frequents a health club on a routine basis and enjoys the congenial atmosphere of the health club, in part, because of the employees who have worked for the club for a number of years. Employees address the patron by name and are familiar with exercise objectives. High employee turnover, in comparison, interrupts this congenial environment and provides an opportunity for patrons to defect to competing clubs. The employee influences the satisfaction of the end-consumer in addition to the satisfaction of vendor relationships. For example, a particular vendor may be unable to establish the same working relationship he or she had with a previous employee. The tangible and intangible costs associated with this broken relationship can include lost accounts and time spent reestablishing vendor relationships.

Third, loyal employees facilitate the job of a sport business manager. Sport business managers who have worked with employees tend to develop their own style of communication in which each party can intuitively decipher the expectations of the other party. Similarly, sport business managers learn, over time, how best to motivate different individuals and what capabilities individual employees possess.

Proper and prudent employee or personnel practices can facilitate the ability of a sport manager to retain employees. Reichheld (1993) summarizes the value of the employee and proper employee selection:

> The fact is that employee retention is key to customer retention, and customer retention can quickly offset higher salaries and other incentives designed to keep employees from leaving. The longer employees stay with the company, the more familiar they become with the business, the more they learn, and the more valuable they can be. Those employees who deal directly with customers day after day have a powerful effect on customer loyalty. Long-term employees can serve customers better than newcomers can; after all, a customer's contact with a company is through employees, not the top executives. It is with employees that the customer builds a bond of trust and expectations, and when those people leave, the bond is broken. (p. 68)

Prudent employment practices can help protect the sport business's investment in any one individual while defending itself against future legal action. This chapter will look at various employee-related issues, including negligent hiring and retention, the criminal check, the job description, job analysis, and job application.

NEGLIGENT HIRING, NEGLIGENT RETENTION, AND THE CRIMINAL CHECK

As mentioned above, employee turnover can hurt the competitive abilities of a sport business manager. Consequently, it is critical that a sport business manager employ prudent employment policies and practices that facilitate proper hiring and employee retention. Obtaining appropriate background information is required to ensure the hiring of appropriately trained, competent, and nondangerous employees. The 1990s has witnessed an explosion in work environment criminal activity. Workplace violence is at an all-time high. The act of terminating an employee has become one of the riskiest tasks that any manager can face. Besides potential harm that can confront other employees, a dangerous employee also presents significant risks to customers or program users. Assault, theft, sexual abuse, and other criminal acts now represent a growing litigation problem for employers. These employee actions are typically considered outside the scope of the employment agreement, and do not subject the employer to vicarious liability. However, individuals injured by employee criminal acts are now aggressively suing employers under the theory of negligent hiring.

Acts of violence and other illegal behaviors continue to permeate the work environment in alarming numbers. For example, as reported by Schaner (1996, p. 84),

1. In 1993, for example, homicide was the third leading cause of death in the workplace and the leading cause of occupational death for women.
2. The National Institute for Occupational Safety and Health reports that on average 15 workers are victims of work-related homicides every week.
3. The Northwestern National Life Insurance study found that more than 2 million people were physically attacked in the workplace from July 1992 to July 1993.

The tort of negligent hiring is recognized as a cause of action in most states (Silver, 1987). Negligent hiring places liability on the employer when the doctrine of respondeat superior cannot apply. The doctrine of respondeat superior places liability on an employer for acts of the employee performing duties within the defined job description. However, the employer retains no liability for *ultra vires* acts, or acts falling outside the scope of authority. For example, in *D.T. by M.T. v. Independent School District No. 16* (1990), the plaintiff sued the Oklahoma School

District alleging the negligent hiring of a 30-year-old male teacher-coach who sexually molested three elementary school students. Similarly, the plaintiffs in *Doe v. British Universities North American Club* (1992) argued that the defendant should be liable for the negligent hiring of a camp counselor who sexually assaulted a camper. Plaintiffs demand recourse when an employer's investigation could have revealed information that would put the employer on notice, hence the tort of negligent hiring. As explained by Levin (1995, p. 420), "Negligent hiring occurs when the employer knows, or should have known, of an applicant's dangerous or violent propensities, hires the individual, and gives the employee the opportunity to repeat such violent behavior." This tort has gained rapid prominence in the area of employment law, as violence and other adverse behaviors infiltrate the work environment. Further, society is questioning whether greater employer prudence could have prevented the injury-related behavior. A survey conducted by the Society for Human Resource Management, for example, revealed that "Two out of three respondents believed that they could have identified the aggressors in advance as possible perpetrators of violent acts" (Schaner, 1996, p. 85). Society feels that it is negligent conduct for an employer to have the capabilities to spot possible aggressors and reduce their contact with the public yet fail to do so. Plaintiffs seeking recovery must prove the four elements of negligence. A breach of duty is determined by looking to the employer's hiring practices to ascertain if the employer had either actual or constructive notice regarding the employee's abusive or criminal propensity. A key determinant lies in whether the employer was acting as a reasonable professional when relying on the information provided by the job application, resume, and/or references.

Employers who rely solely on job applications and resumes, while making no additional inquiries, risk litigation. Research states that one out of every three resumes and applications are fabricated or contain misrepresentations (Jones, 1996). Supporting research by Broussard and Brannen (1986) states that 25% of all applications and resumes are misleading. More alarming statistics are reported by Davidson (1984, p. 147): "Nearly 80% of all resumes contain some misleading information." The courts agree that reasonable, prudent employers have a responsibility to "read between the lines" when screening prospective employees' applications and resumes in order to detect employees with problematic tendencies. Two contentious areas include the performance of a criminal history investigation and the employee reference.

The Criminal History Investigation: Considerations

Unfortunately for employers, there are no prescribed standards stipulating when to undertake a criminal history investigation for an applicant (Silver, 1987). In fact, a criminal investigation is not necessary in all cases. For example, the Supreme

Court of Minnesota said in *Ponticas v. K.M.S. Investments* (1983, p. 913) that criminal record investigations are not required for every prospective employee. Specifically, the court concluded in part, "If the employer has made the adequate inquiry or otherwise has a reasonable sufficient basis to conclude the employee is reliable and fit for the job, no affirmative duty rests on him to investigate the possibility that the applicant has a criminal record" (p. 913). A careful analysis of an individual's job application and resume can alert the reasonable, prudent employer to an individual's possible criminal history and the need to undertake a more thorough investigation.

Literature emphasizes the need to question employment gaps and claims of self-employment (Broussard & Brannen, 1986; Vecchio, 1984). Employment gaps and claims of self-employment are often used when individuals want to conceal activity during a particular time period(s). For example, an individual working at ABC Athletics for only 2 months, from December 1998 through January 1999, is able to extend 2 months of employment into 2 entire years by reporting tenure as 1998–1999.

Employers who investigate an individual's criminal history should not prohibit employment based solely on a criminal record. An automatic bar would be counterproductive to the penal system's objective of rehabilitating individuals so that one day they can return to society as contributing, productive citizens. Further, the lack of employment opportunities could actually encourage criminal behavior (e.g., stealing, committing fraud, burglarizing). As noted by the court in *Garcia v. Duffy* (1986, p. 441), "actual knowledge of an employee's criminal record does not establish as a matter of law the employer's negligence in hiring him." However, there are certain situations when an individual with a criminal background should not be hired. The following five considerations can assist the employer deciding whether or not to hire an ex-criminal.

The Degree of Public Contact and Nature of Employment

Employers have a greater obligation to investigate prospective employees working directly with the public than to investigate potential employees needed to work in remote, desolate environments (Miller & Fenton, 1991). For example, an employer would have a greater obligation to investigate a youth program director than to investigate a groundskeeper (*Garcia v. Duffy*, 1986). All states, for example, require all potential public school teachers to be screened. If employment is in a "sensitive" area, then a criminal investigation should be performed. For example, the Georgia court of appeals concluded in *C.K. Security Systems v. Hartford Accident & Indemnity Company et al.* (1976) that the contacting of past employers, the passing of a course in criminology, and the passing of a personnel test did not constitute a reasonable investigation when hiring a security guard. As noted by Gregory (1988, p. 34), "The greater the risk of harm, the higher will be the level of care demanded of the employer." The reasonableness of the investigation will be decided by the jury.

The Nature of the Crime

Ample consideration should be given to the crime and its relationship to particular job responsibilities (Gregory, 1988). For example, a prior marijuana conviction may not be indicative of a person's ability to be a good youth program director, whereas a rape conviction should immediately alarm an employer seeking an individual to serve as a youth program director. A general rule is that anyone convicted of a crime(s) against people (rather than property or traffic) should not be hired to work with children.

Time Lapsed since Prison Release

Consideration should be given to the time lapsed since serving a prison sentence (Gregory, 1988). For example, a person released from prison 15 years ago, and who has since been employed, may be less "suspect" than a person released from prison within the last 12 months.

Statutory Legislation

Statutory enactments and amendments regarding criminal investigation procedures will continue throughout the 1990s. States are actively upgrading information within state repositories in addition to identifying who has access to the information. However, there remains a great deal of variance among state statutes. For example, states vary about who can access information, who must be screened, and what access fees are required. Sport business managers should become intimately familiar with their own local legislation regarding this issue.

Federal Legislation

Two significant pieces of federal legislation were passed in 1990 that restrict hiring practices when job responsibilities include working with children. The Victims of Child Abuse Act mandates that federal government agencies involved in child care services need to perform a criminal history investigation on all existing and potential employees. The Act's definition of a child-care service includes "education (whether or not directly involved in teaching) . . . and recreational" programs. This federal mandate has broad implications for sport industry employers. For example, employers hiring physical education teachers, secondary or postsecondary coaches, or park and recreation employees must perform a criminal history investigation. All applications must ask whether the prospective employee "has ever been arrested for or charged with a crime involving a child." Furthermore, the Act stipulates that all candidates sign an investigation consent form and that the employer provide a copy of the completed investigation to the applicant (Crime Control Act). Employers may deny employment when convictions are for a sex crime, a child offense, or a drug felony. The Act encourages, but does not mandate, that criminal histories be obtained for volunteers.

The second act, the Indian Child Protection and Family Violence Prevention Act (1990) is designed to protect Indian children. This act prohibits the employment of individuals who "Have been found guilty of, or entered a plea of nolo contendere or guilty to, any offense under Federal, state, or tribal law involving crimes of violence; sexual assault, molestation, exploitation, contact or prostitution; or crimes against persons" (Sec. 8 [b]).

The utilization of extant information technology represents an efficient and effective way for prudent sport managers to perform criminal checks on employees. However, the key to accessing any information about an individual is a signed release providing consent to have individual records investigated. Investigation without a signed consent can otherwise represent an invasion of privacy.

The responsibility of performing a criminal check on potential employees is well accepted. However, the frequent use of volunteers in sport-related businesses (e.g., schools, YMCAs, sport camps) presents additional concerns for the sport business industry. Some states have legislated provisions for checking the criminal backgrounds of volunteers (e.g., Washington). Others, however, have found this practice cost-prohibitive. For example, the expense of performing criminal checks is not financially feasible when the volunteer may be working with the organization for only a limited time period. The same financial concerns affect large organizations with thousands of volunteers. Regardless of the costs, sport managers should become intimately familiar with laws providing volunteer immunity and legislation either requiring or supporting the practice of criminal inquiries for volunteers.

Hypothetical Illustration

Consider the following scenario in which a Chicago health club is seeking a youth program director. The ex-program director quit 2 weeks before the scheduled programs were to begin, and the employer is pressured to employ a new director as soon as possible. One particular candidate looks very promising due to his apparent experience with youth programs. His application states that he worked from 1978 to 1984 as a program director for a YMCA in Colorado. No employment history has been identified between 1985 and 1989. Since 1990, the candidate has worked for two different child-care centers, each for approximately 3 months. The applicant had received his cardiopulmonary resuscitation (CPR) and first aid certification in the fall of 1992. The application asked candidates to explain the nature of any criminal convictions. The only convictions reported were for traffic violations. The employer considered this a trivial point since the job of program director entailed no driving responsibilities. The candidate listed the names of two references, although no phone numbers or street addresses were provided. No inquiry was made as to the relationship of these people to the candidate. The individual was hired in May 1993. Two months later, the employee was convicted of abusing a 7-year-old girl enrolled in the club's youth programs. The parents of the child are now suing the club for negligently hiring the employee.

The tort of negligent hiring, like any other negligence action, requires that a plaintiff prove all four elements of negligence. In the illustration above, the Chicago health club undoubtedly has a duty to the club's patrons. The question for the jury will be to decide whether the employer breached this duty by hiring an employee who the reasonable, prudent professional would have found to be unfit.

In reflecting back over the scenario, the jury will likely take into consideration the following six issues.

1. The Chicago health club did not verify the candidate's alleged YMCA employment record. The candidate did work at the YMCA between 1978 and 1984. However, a simple phone call would have informed the employer that the individual had been fired and convicted of child molestation.
2. The employer made little inquiry into what the candidate was doing between 1985 and 1989. The candidate told the employer he was self-employed during that time period. The employer made no further inquiry.
3. The short duration of recent employment was not questioned. Again, had past employers been contacted, the employer would have been alerted to blatant abusive problems.
4. The employer never asked to see the CPR and first aid certification cards.
5. The references provided were the candidate's mother and stepsister. It is well established in human resource literature that personal references are inadequate.
6. No criminal investigation was performed. Employers may be required to perform a criminal history check in order to comply with federal or state legislation. However, even if a criminal check was not mandated by legislation, a jury could very well decide that a greater standard of care is required of businesses employing the individuals who work with children.

THE EMPLOYEE REFERENCE

Employee references provide great value to a potential employer. Recommendations serve three significant purposes (Miller, Pitts, & Fielding, 1993; Paetzold & Wilburn, 1992; Von der Embse & Wyse, 1985). First, references verify application information provided by the prospective candidate. The solicited reference helps ensure that the itemized degree(s), certifications, and experiences are accurate. Second, the preemployment reference can reduce worker and third-party accidents. For example, it is influential for a school district to know if a candidate has a history of assaulting coworkers or children. Third, thorough employment procedures facilitate the hiring of competent, qualified individuals. Proper hiring reduces business expenses associated with employee turnover, absenteeism, recruiting, and training.

Historically, common law granted employers a qualified or conditional privilege to comment about an ex-employee. As explained by the Supreme Court of Minnesota in *Lewis v. Equitable Life Assurance Soc.* (1986, p. 889),

> The doctrine of privileged communication rests upon public policy considerations . . . the existence of a privilege results from the court's determination that statements made in particular contexts or on certain occasions should be encouraged despite the risk that the statements might be defamatory . . . . In the context of employment recommendations, the law generally recognizes a qualified privilege between former and prospective employers as long as the statements are made in good faith and for a legitimate purpose.

As noted by the *Lewis* court (1986), the qualified privilege is not absolute. Courts recognize the privilege only when employers make statements in "good faith" and for a legitimate purpose. Recommendations made as an attempt to blackmail an ex-employee, or made maliciously and with a disregard for the facts, are subject to liability (Daniloff, 1989; Martucci & Boatright, 1995).

Unfortunately, the threat of liability has curtailed the willingness of employers to provide job references. Defamation is the most frequent allegation associated with a contested employee reference, although a plaintiff's causes of action could also include "intentional infliction of emotional distress, public disclosure of private facts, and interference with contractual relations or with prospective business" (Eikleberry, 1995, p. 22). Middleton (1987) estimates that 33% of all defamation claims involve former employees suing employers alleging defamation. A study conducted by the University of Nebraska in 1992 revealed that the average, successful employee defamation award was $57,000. However, more extreme awards are not unheard of. To defend against potential liability, employers have adopted "no comment" policies or simply provide "skeletal" information including the dates during which the individual was employed, job title, and job responsibilities. As explained by Martucci and Boatright (1995, p. 120), "The rationale is that, if nothing is communicated, an employee may not claim defamation." It is estimated that 75% of prospective employers forego the practice of reference checking, as they find former employers uncooperative (Middleton, 1987).

However, a newly recognized tort, *negligent referral,* is likely to alter current "no-comment" and "neutral" reference policies (*Tarassoff v. Regents of the University System of California*, 1991). Negligent referral is a tort recognizing a past employer's responsibility to warn a prospective employer of the abusive or violent behaviors of a past employee. States have taken it upon themselves to enact legislation in an effort to insulate past employers from defamation liability for providing honest, good-faith employee references. Georgia enacted the first reference-checking statute in 1991 to legislate the concept of privilege (Leonard, 1996). As of May 1996, 14 additional states have enacted legislation limiting the liability of those providing employee references (Leonard, 1996).

The rash of workplace violence and other improprieties is not expected to end soon (Elias, 1996). Society will continue to demand that someone pay for the pain and injury resulting from insidious behaviors that could have been detected or prevented. Consequently, sport business managers should deter potential liability through aggressive employee risk management programs while providing a more risk-free environment for workers and patrons.

Sport management practices can further insulate an employer from liability or provide protection for those employers doing business in states without protective legislation. Literature identifies a number of suggestions that can assist in the preparation of a legally defensible reference (Eickleberry, 1995; Fried, 1996; Miller et al., 1993).

The following list offers some risk management techniques that can be employed to reduce the likelihood of negligent hiring or negligent retention:

- Obtain written consent from the person seeking a recommendation. A written request aids a defendant attempting to prove that the plaintiff ex-employee was cognizant of the anticipated contents and consented to the dissemination of related information. Insertion of a clause such as, "In response to your request . . . ," can provide further evidence that the letter was not written maliciously or for the purposes of revenge or retaliation.
- Seal and address the letter of reference to a particular person. Addressing a letter with the salutation, "To Whom It May Concern," provides an inference that the letter was written for multiple readers.
- Do not share letters of recommendation with other colleagues or practitioners. Personnel files should always remain locked. Open files and related sharing of information can invite legal problems.
- Only consider criminal conviction information that directly relates to the job at hand or presents the individual with an environment conducive to recidivism. It is society's intent that criminals, upon rehabilitation, be allowed to serve as contributing members of society. Similarly, arrest records should not be addressed, as they may or may not lead to a conviction. Further, research shows that minorities are arrested more frequently than nonminorities. Consequently, failure to hire may result in a claim of discrimination in violation of Title VII.

- Do not speculate about the causes for poor performance or a high rate of absenteeism. All statements should remain objective, and only verifiable facts should be reported.
- Keep all medical information regarding an ex-employee confidential. Keep an employee's medical records separate from employment records. Medical inquiries that an employer is not allowed to ask due to the Americans with Disabilities Act (ADA) should not be asked of prior employers.

The issue of providing a written reference is somewhat controversial. Written references provide documented evidence of what was and was not said. On the other hand, legal counsel dissuades the use of written references, as they provide a paper trail that can lead to more extensive litigation. If written references are provided, those providing the reference should retain a copy for use in defending potential defamatory allegations.

Providing references should be viewed by sport managers as a professional responsibility. Adherence to the above suggestions, and familiarity with existing statutory protections, can assist the sport manager in "providing a valuable, yet legally defensible letter of recommendation" (Miller et al., 1993, p. 50). A "no-weapons" policy and a zero-tolerance policy are also advocated as prudent policies to adopt in attempting to mitigate the occurrence of, and resultant liability associated with, workplace violence (Schaner, 1996).

THE JOB DESCRIPTION

The job description is one of the most basic and common human relations tools (Carrell, Kuzmits, & Elbert, 1992). It is often the first impression a potential employee has with an employer. Although a common tool, its importance and relevance has significantly escalated in the last decade as a result of government regulation and litigation. There is no standardized or required job description format. However, five general tenets of most job descriptions are (1) a job title, (2) essential job duties and responsibilities, (3) job qualifications, (4) starting date, and (5) name and address of the contact person.

The essential job duties and responsibilities need to be devised from the job analysis (discussed below). Job descriptions representing new jobs should be designed after careful thought and study regarding what a particular job will actually entail. A review of competitor job descriptions or prescribed job description forms available through self-study books and computer programs are also useful starting points. It is in this section (i.e., job duties and responsibilities) that the employer describes to the reader exactly what the job will entail. Verbs should be used to communicate to the reader the nature of the job. Common job description terms include *supervise, train, host, organize, plan, schedule, lift, carry, reach, diagram, maintain,* and *clean.* Job duties and responsibilities that are determined to be "nonessential" are subject to allegations of discrimination. Managers should also pay heed to Occupational Safety and Health Administration (OSHA) regulations requiring that job descriptions identify elements of the job "which endanger health, or are considered unsatisfactory or distasteful to the majority of the population" (Carrell et al., 1992, p. 64).

The job qualifications section of the job description is another area subject to intense scrutinization and should be constructed cautiously. This section of the job description states those minimum qualifications necessary to perform a particular job adequately. Observable skills required, necessary knowledge, abilities, and required degrees, certifications, and/or licenses should be itemized in this section of the job description. For example, a sports information director might be required to know the rules of the game, strategy, and conference tournament schedules. This individual might also be required to possess the skills to operate a fax machine, a computer, and electronic mail. Further, this individual must have the ability to write media clips detailing sporting events. Required degrees and certifications should be itemized cautiously, as the stated requirement must be essential to effective job performance and not serve as a tool to eliminate or discriminate against otherwise qualified candidates.

Benefits of the Job Description

A "good" job description can provide seven primary benefits, which are discussed below.

Assists in the Recruitment of Qualified Employees

Employee recruitment is a very timely and expensive process. Nebulous job descriptions tend to generate many responses, as the job itself and related responsibilities and qualifications are not clearly defined. Consequently, a sport business may receive numerous applications from marginally qualified individuals. The time and expense in handling and reviewing these applications can be minimized by the careful crafting of a job description that best represents the actual job.

Is Used to Standardize the Interview Process

Carefully crafted job descriptions provide the sport business manager involved in the interviewing process with a uniform slate of questions that can be asked of every candidate. For example, if one of the job qualifications is, "Supervise and train lifeguards," resultant interview questions might include the following:

- Have you ever been responsible for lifeguard supervision? If so, please elaborate.

- What type of training programs would you design for your lifeguards?
- How often would you have in-service training for your lifeguards?

Standardized questions developed prior to the interview process reduce the chance of bias, as all candidates are asked identical questions.

Defines Employee Expectations

Employees are more motivated toward a prescribed goal and tend to perform better when management expectations are clearly defined (Bell & Zempke, 1992). Job descriptions help define expectations and place management and subordinates on a level playing field. Employee confusion and potential turnover is reduced while productivity is enhanced.

Serves as Motivation, Information Regarding Job Promotions

Many sport businesses have a notebook containing all job descriptions for that particular entity. The particular notebook, in turn, remains accessible to any interested employee. Having job descriptions accessible to all employees is beneficial, as employees are able to ascertain what training and skills are needed to be promotable. This information can serve as a source of motivation for employees. Further, the additional training pursued by employees in hopes of a possible promotion at a later point in time makes for a more educated work force engaging in more prudent and productive decision making.

Facilitates Job Evaluation

The job description is a primary tool in ascertaining what criteria to use when evaluating employees. The job description benefits both the employees and management throughout the evaluation process. Employees receiving unfavorable evaluations due to evaluative criteria *unrelated* to their job description may have a cause of action against their employer. Similarly, employers taking unfavorable actions (e.g., demotions) against their employees failing to fulfill job description criteria have a legally defensible tool at their hands should their actions be legally challenged by a disgruntled employee. Further, job descriptions for individuals performing identical jobs help ensure standardization and fairness.

Serves as a Useful Tool in Comparing Jobs

Job descriptions enable managers to compare job requirements (e.g., duties and responsibilities) and pay, for example, of a particular position with other job requirements of perceived comparable jobs. Comparisons can be made with other jobs within a company as well as with comparable jobs of competitors. As espoused by motivational theories (e.g., the equity theory), employees are motivated when they feel like they are putting in comparable work effort for comparable pay at other comparable jobs (Gordon, 1991). Job descriptions can be used by sport business managers to ensure that workloads remain equitable and that similar pay is being awarded to individuals performing similar work requiring similar skills, knowledge, and abilities.

Facilitates Outplacement Efforts

Sport businesses forced to downsize may enhance public relations and better fulfill ethical responsibilities by helping employees find other work. The job description serves as a valuable tool in the identification of other jobs requiring similar qualifications. Further, the job description is useful in updating or designing an individual resume.

THE JOB ANALYSIS

A job analysis is a thorough analysis of a job's physical and mental requirements, environmental exposures, purpose of position, major responsibilities, and other special working conditions. (See Appendix 7–A.) The job analysis is an often overlooked function of management. Sport business managers fully aware of the job analysis, what it is, and its related benefits will find the job analysis a very useful tool.

A job analysis is typically begun by gathering all information pertaining to a particular job. Internal documents that might be useful include operation manuals, policy manuals, training materials, organization charts, and previous job analyses (Carrell et al., 1992). In addition, interviews with incumbent personnel and position supervisors provide valuable information. Direct observation provides additional valuable insight into jobs and related skills, knowledge, and abilities. Only the specific work behaviors of each job should be recorded (Ashe, 1980; Burchett & De Meuse, 1985; Nobile, 1991; "Uniform Guidelines," 1993; Webster, 1988). Identification of the qualifications, characteristics, and attributes of individuals currently engaged in a particular job does not constitute a job analysis. For example, simply because current employed exercise prescriptionists are all women does not mean that future exercise prescriptionists must also be women.

Benefits of the Job Analysis

Is Recommended by EEOC and Is Useful Defensive Tool in Legal Challenge

A job analysis is recommended by the EEOC in the 1978 Uniform Guidelines and is useful as a defensive tool when the employer is legally challenged ("Uniform Guidelines," 1993). The EEOC recommends the use of a job analysis for employee recruitment and selection purposes. Employers using job analyses are less likely to include unessential job functions and specify educational or certification requirements unrelated to actual job performance when designing job descriptions. Consequently, there is less probability that job descriptions will eliminate otherwise qualified, viable candidates.

Facilitates the Accurate Design of Job Descriptions

As noted above, job descriptions stipulate a position's required duties and responsibilities. This listing of duties and responsibilities is made more exact by reference to the respective job analysis.

Provides for a Communication Forum between Managers and Employees

Both managers and employees should be involved in the design or redesign of the job analysis. This process can provide valuable insight for both managers and employees. Top managers can learn first-hand exactly what, how, and why a front-line employee does what he or she does. In addition, top management is provided with opportunities to educate employees as to why certain functions are integral to the success of the entire business. Similarly, employees find management's interest in their position and the opportunity to interact with management rewarding and inspiring.

THE JOB APPLICATION

The job application provides a sport business manager with valuable information that can be used to select the most qualified individual for a particular position. However, the job application can also serve as one tool among an arsenal of complaints filed by a disgruntled employee or individual who feels he or she should have been hired. All questions asked on the application, regardless of how seemingly minor they appear, are presumed to influence any resultant employment decision. All questions should be scrutinized for potential disparate impact consequences. As a result of legislation (e.g., Title VII, ADA, Age Discrimination in Employment ACT [ADEA], the following application questions indicating any of the above ascribed characteristics or religious preferences would be illegal:

- questions asking for preferred or actual titles, such as Miss, Mrs., Ms., or asking one's maiden name
- questions about marital status prior to hiring
- questions about plans for child care and/or childbirth
- questions asking for the birthplace of the applicant, parents, grandparents, or spouse

- any inquiry that would indicate race or color (e.g., affiliation with any social sororities or fraternities)
- questions regarding proof of citizenship prior to hiring
- questions regarding whether parents or spouse are native-born
- questions about a person's date of citizenship
- questions about how foreign language skills were acquired
- request for photographs prior to actual hiring
- questions about willingness to work on religious holidays
- questions about an individual's height, weight, or physical appearance

The ADA prohibits certain questions that were at one time common to job applications. For example, the following 13 questions have been identified by the EEOC as questions that cannot be asked on application forms or in job interviews (U.S. Equal Employment Opportunity Commission [EEOC], 1992, pp. V-6–V8).

1. Have you ever had or been treated for any of the following conditions or diseases? (Followed by a checklist of various conditions and diseases)
2. Please list any conditions or diseases for which you have been treated in the past 3 years.
3. Have you ever been hospitalized? If so, for what condition?
4. Have you ever been treated by a psychiatrist or psychologist? If so, for what condition?
5. Have you ever been treated for any mental condition?
6. Is there any health-related reason you may not be able to perform the job for which you are applying?
7. Have you had a major illness in the last 5 years?
8. How many days were you absent from work because of illness last year?
9. Do you have any physical defects which preclude you from performing certain kinds of work? If yes, describe such defects and specific work limitations.
10. Do you have any disabilities or impairments which may affect your performance in the position for which you are applying?
11. Are you taking any prescribed drugs?
12. Have you ever been treated for drug addiction or alcoholism?
13. Have you ever filed for workers' compensation insurance?

The ADEA has also influenced the information that can be legally requested on a job application. As a result of the ADEA, sport business managers should refrain from asking potential candidates their age or date of birth on a job application. Regarding child labor, the application might read, "Are you younger than 18 years old?" The issue of asking about a valid driver's license could be addressed by the following, "Do you have a valid driver's license?" It becomes irrelevant to the employer if the candidate drives or has a car when the position has no driving responsibilities. Rather, the employer is only interested in knowing if the potential candidate has transportation to and from the place of employment. As mentioned earlier, the mode of transportation (e.g., car, public transportation, carpool) is irrelevant.

IMPLEMENTATION OF THE PERFORMANCE APPRAISAL PROCESS

The performance appraisal process, an often dreaded facet of the workplace by both managers and employees, has come under greater scrutiny during the 1990s. As reported by Schellhardt (1996, p. A1) in reference to a 1995 survey, "44% of 218 companies with evaluation systems had changed theirs within the previous two years and another 29% expected to do so." On the other hand, many advocate the abolishment of all written appraisal processes. As concluded by Annie Sauier, a performance management consultant, "Just blow up all the written stuff. . . . If you just concentrate on goal setting and giving feedback constantly, you'll get better performance all the time" (Schellhardt, 1996, p. A5).

Benefits of the Performance Appraisal Process

The performance appraisal process provides significant benefits to both sport business managers and employees. Four primary benefits are identified below.

Enhances Employee Motivation

The performance appraisal process can serve as a source of employee motivation. Motivated employees perform better and incur less costs associated with absenteeism, turnover, and so forth.

Enhances Communication between Sport Business Managers and Employees

Performance appraisals provide a time for a manager and the employee to discuss performance obstacles, needed resources, limited resources, objectives, competitive constraints, and the like. This open communication facilitates the understanding between both parties regarding related objectives and needs. An employee who feels that a sport business manager is a genuine advocate for his or her success is more likely to strive for optimal performance. Further, communication and the agreed-upon outcome regarding employee objectives and expectations enhance employee commitment versus the traditional top-down dictation of work performance standards.

Identifies Subpar Performance

Occasionally, employees perform at subpar levels. It is illogical for sport business managers to automatically terminate, demote, or humiliate, subpar performers as the sport business has likely made quite an investment in the recruitment of each employee. Subpar performance, once identified, often can be improved via training or assistance. The provision of training and assistance can better protect the sport business's investment in a particular employee. However, poor performers should not be retained indefinitely due to the peril of injury to a stakeholder and negligent retention lawsuits.

Provides a Legally Defensible Tool if Needed

Employees are increasingly contesting managerial decisions about hiring, firing, promoting, and training. As Eyres (1989, p. 60) states, "When memories fade or perceptions differ, the best evidence of what occurred, and why, is performance appraisal records." For example, performance appraisals serve as documentation of poor performance (as well as good performance) and opportunities provided for improvement.

Concerns Regarding the Performance Appraisal Process

Although referred to by some as a deadly disease, the benefits of a well-implemented performance appraisal process are well documented. However, attention to a variety of related issues can best provide a sport business manager with a legally defensible performance appraisal process (Miller, Fielding, & Pitts, 1993). The remainder of this chapter addresses 10 concerns of the sport manager engaged in the employee appraisal process.

Lack of Policy Enforcement

Policy manuals frequently elaborate on a performance appraisal process used by a particular sport business. For example, a policy manual may promise annual performance appraisals, due process, and/or a grievance procedure. Literature (Chargares, 1989; Harris, 1986; Witt & Goldman, 1988) notes that provisions within a policy manual may be binding regardless of a state's adherence to employment-at-will practices. A health club manager, for example, may be liable for a breach of a unilateral contract (e.g., the policy manual) by failing to adhere to the manual's contents (Eyres, 1989; Nobile, 1991; Panaro, 1988; Webster, 1988). Consider the following statement, "Each employee will be evaluated in July and December." The employee not evaluated both in July and December may allege liability via breach of a unilateral contract. The following statement exemplifies how a sport business can better transfer the responsibility, and consequent blame, back to the individual employee: "Management will *attempt* to evaluate the performance of each employee on an annual basis. Notify your immediate supervisor if you are not evaluated within the course of a year." The statement undoubtedly provides the sport manager with more latitude than the prior, more direct statement, which promises the employee an evaluation every December.

The effective use of disclaimers also aids a sport business in disputing a plaintiff's claim that the manual's contents are binding (Chagares, 1989; Panaro, 1988; Witt & Goldman, 1988). For example, Montgomery Ward used disclaimers in both their Progressive Discipline Reference Guide (PDRG) and the human resource policy manual that prevented a plaintiff's claim in 1987 (*Dell v. Montgomery Ward*, 1987). The plaintiff claimed that Montgomery Ward did not follow the discipline procedure as stated in the company literature. However, qualifying language in the discipline guide protected Montgomery Ward. The guide stated that the "procedure does not form an employment contract" (*Dell v. Montgomery Ward*, 1987). Consequently, the plaintiff's claim was not recognized. Montgomery Ward also used a disclaimer in its policy manual. The disclaimer stated that the manual's "procedures should not be interpreted as constituting an employment contract" (*Dell v. Montgomery Ward*, 1987). As illustrated above, a disclaimer using simple, unambiguous language can be effective. Unilateral policy amendments or alterations are binding only if management gives employees reasonable notice about the modification. Without proper notice, sport business managers are accountable to the old verbiage printed in prior manuals.

Failure To Conduct Routine Performance Evaluations

Annual evaluations tend to be error-prone as evaluators often can only remember the most recent events of the particular employee (either positive or negative). On the other hand, monthly or quarterly reviews, for example, provide employers and employees with better communication opportunities. Further, employee performance areas can be identified before injuries occur to the sport business (e.g., loss of profits or market share due to inefficiencies), employees (e.g., negligent retention issues, hostile work environments, or declining motivation), and/or customers (e.g., deliverance of poor product quality).

Failure To Take the Performance Appraisal Process Seriously

Often, sport business managers fail to place much weight on the performance appraisal process as issues concerning competition and accounts payable, for example, appear more pressing. As explained by Winston Connor, "Most of the time, it's just a ritual that managers go through. . . . They pull out last year's review, update it and do it quickly" (Shellhardt, 1996, p. A1). Unfortunately, a hasty process forfeits the benefits that can be derived from the performance appraisal process itself.

Improper Evaluation Criteria

The EEOC refers to the Uniform Guidelines on Employee Selection Procedures ("Uniform Guidelines," 1993) when evaluating the legality of a performance appraisal process. The Guidelines encourage the use of criterion-related, content, or construct validity studies to support criteria having an adverse impact on employment practices. Criteria with no adverse impact does not need to be validated.

Evaluative criteria should be directly related to those tasks necessary to perform a particular job. Literature encourages the use of a job analysis when selecting performance appraisal criteria (Barrett & Kernan, 1987; Huber, 1983; Shaw, 1990; "Uniform Guidelines," 1993). Courts continue to refer to the landmark decision in *Griggs v. Duke Power Co.* (1971) when deciding the legality of selection criteria. The plaintiff, Griggs, challenged the criteria for employment and job transfers. Justice Burger stated in the Supreme Court opinion that, "Under the Act, practices, procedures, or tests neutral on their face, and even neutral in terms of intent, cannot be maintained if they operate to 'freeze' the status quo of prior discriminatory employment practices" (p. 430). Evaluative criteria should remain focused on the skills, knowledge, and abilities directly related to the performance of a particular job.

Failure To Communicate Specific Strengths and Weaknesses

As reported by psychologist Harry Levinson (Schellhardt, 1996, p. A1), several factors can discourage sport business managers from giving accurate performance appraisals. These factors include guilt ("Bumstead has a family and a dog to feed"), embarrassment about praise ("real men don't say nice things about others"), taking things for granted ("isn't that what she's getting paid for?"), and not noticing ("Bumstead who?").

The sport manager should ensure that the evaluated employees receive feedback, both positive and negative, about the appraisal (Ashe, 1980; Burchett & De Meuse, 1985; Shaw, 1990). Furthermore, employers should communicate ways the employee can improve negative ratings. Failing to address deficiencies to protect the feelings of an employee can prove to be legally devastating (Ashe & McRae, 1985; Eyres, 1989; Nobile, 1991; Webster, 1988). Barrett and Kernan's research (1987, p. 496) indicates that the courts "react favorably to the use of performance counseling designed to help employees improve substandard performance."

Ashe (1980) and Metz (1988) both suggest that management provide the employee with both an oral and a written review (signed by the employee) of the completed evaluation. A court decision (*Woolery v. Brady*, 1990) also supported the employer who had employees read and sign performance evaluations. Management's liability is more difficult to prove when an employee who has read and signed a completed appraisal fails to pursue a grievance within a reasonable time span. Failure to express dissatisfaction about the performance appraisal indicates that the employee agreed to the appraisal's accuracy.

Failure To Take Punitive Action on "Nonperforming" Employees

Many sport managers procrastinate the dismissal of employees who have not performed admirably on performance appraisals or who have contributed to an adversarial, unhealthy, and/or uncomfortable work environment. Rationalizing that the retaliatory repercussions would be too great (e.g., bad attitudes, disparaging comments made by the employee about the individual manager), or that a sensitive manager hates to hurt someone's feelings or disappoint an otherwise "nice person," employees are retained for nonlegitimate purposes. The negligent retention of employees creates a great concern for all involved stakeholders. Consumers suffer as service or product quality may deteriorate, coemployees suffer as the nonperforming employee is given all the benefits of comparable colleagues, and managers fail to manage departments as effectively or efficiently as otherwise possible. Negligent retention can have traumatic and fatally injurious consequences.

Communication Leading to Alleged Defamation

Defamation by "self-publication." The performance appraisal process can lead to a claim of defamation by a disgruntled employee against a sport business and/or the sport business manager. Defamation by self-publication defies the traditional interpretation of communication. For example, communication between a health club employer and an employee does not involve a third party. However, a sport manager can be liable for comments communicated to an individual employee in a one-on-one, private confrontation. It is erroneous for sport business managers to presume that disparaging comments said to an employee behind closed doors in a heated moment cannot be later alleged as defamatory. The required defamation element of "communication to a third party" can be satisfied by the plaintiff when communicating the contents of his or her performance appraisal and the disparaging interchange to a prospective employer. Consider the following situation.

An individual applies for a job at a local health club. In the interview, the prospective employer tells the candidate that her past employer will be contacted as a reference. The candidate is fully aware that her relationship with her past employer was adversarial. In fact, the candidate vividly remembers the belittling, derogatory comments made during her annual performance appraisal review. The individual has two reasons for telling the prospective employer that a favorable recommendation may not be provided by the past employer. First, up front and honest communication allows the candidate to explain and diffuse serious allegations. Second, the candidate is being truthful. As stated by the Minnesota Supreme Court (*Lewis v. Equitable,* 1986), it is better to communicate the alleged reason for dismissal rather than to lie. "Fabrication . . . is an unacceptable alternative" (p. 888). The key issue is foreseeability. The health club manager could be liable for defamation if it is foreseeable that the employee may have reason to repeat the communicated information at a later time.

Providing information to persons who do not have reason to hear the information. Communication among managers regarding the performance of a particular employee has traditionally been given qualified immunity as the benefits derived from the flow of information outweighs any resultant harm (Duffy, 1983). For example, communication among colleagues on established search committees about employee performance is necessary when filling a higher level position. However, literature (Daniloff, 1989; Duffy, 1983; Jacobs, 1990) indicates that internal communication among sport managers can be abused when information expands beyond that necessary to achieve the sport business's objectives.

For example, a manager at General Motors elaborated on a plaintiff's "resignation" (alleged theft) to other nonsupervisory personnel to curtail the occurrence of similar behavior (*Gaines v. Cuna Mutual Insurance Society,* 1982). In the opinion of *Gaines v. Cuna* (1982), the Fifth Circuit Court of Appeals held that a manager's comments had extended beyond those who had a reason to know. As illustrated, a sport business manager should use caution when discussing with others the contents of an individual's inferior performance appraisal.

Sport managers can also be subject to defamation when failing to investigate communicated information. For example, a day manager should not merely presume that the night manager's interpretation of an incident is accurate. Sport managers should investigate the validity of all allegations that may, or may not, be truthful prior to taking punitive action or sharing information with others.

Nonexistent or Inadequate Rater Training

It is not always possible, or even desirable, for one sport manager to perform all employee performance evaluations in large sport businesses. However, it is also not prudent to have inexperienced individuals evaluating employee performance. Research (Barrett & Kernan, 1987) indicates that courts look more favorably on plaintiffs when a defendant company lacks rater training procedures. Barrett and Kernan (1987) suggest that novice raters thoroughly study employee job descriptions and engage in practice rating exercises prior to evaluating individual employees.

Longnecker (1989), on the other hand, acknowledges that a comprehensive rater training program will not eliminate all bias. As Longnecker (1989, p. 77) has stated, "Occasionally managers feel the need to manipulate ratings in the perceived best interest of their employees, their departments, and perhaps even themselves." For example, it may be more attractive for a sensitive sport business manager to intentionally inflate a particular employee's performance rating if he or she fears that a dismal, although more accurate, rating would only compound the known problems (e.g., divorce, illness) of an individual employee. This "intentional inaccuracy" should also be discussed with prospective raters (Longnecker & Ludwig, 1990).

Nonuse of Minority Raters

In *Rowe v. General Motors Corporation* (1972, p. 359), the Fifth Circuit Court of Appeals stated that minorities may have "been hindered in obtaining recommendations from their foremen since there is no familial or social association" between the all-white supervisory work force evaluating minority employees. Stacey (1976) addresses the need for minority raters who reflect the employee constituency. Sport business managers would be prudent to secure raters who are representative of the work force.

Failure To Monitor the System

The performance appraisal process cannot operate in a vacuum. In *Rowe v. General Motors Corporation* (1972, p. 259), the opinion stated that the lack of "safeguards in the procedure" insulated discriminatory effects. The implementation of a formal grievance system can provide evidence that the performance appraisal process is monitored (Ashe, 1980; Barrett & Kernan, 1987; Burchett & De Meuse, 1985; Eyres, 1989). Sport business managers should provide employees with an opportunity to file a grievance when the performance appraisal process is contested. Several complaints serve as an alarm to a sport business manager that the performance appraisal may contain flaws.

In addition to the implementation of a formal appeal system, the research performed by Barrett and Kernan (1987, p. 496) indicated that courts look favorably on an entity that has implemented a "review system by upper-level personnel to prevent individual bias." Ashe (1980) and Webster (1988) also support the use of a second rater, while other trends include the "360-degree evaluation" (i.e., employees are evaluated by multisupervisors, colleagues, self, etc., Brotherton, 1996; Gebelein, 1996). The 360-degree evaluation systems have become increasingly popular when evaluating team efforts. Sport business managers also may find a 360-degree system curtails rater bias. However, sport business managers are cautioned about providing second raters with the first rater's evaluation. As noted by the Oregon District Court, the likelihood of an objective rating is diminished when the prior rating results are known (*Loiseau v. Department of Human Resources of the State of Oregon*, 1983). The 360-degree evaluation systems are criticized, however, for the potential animosity that can be created when colleagues give each other negative evaluations (Schellhardt, 1996).

CHAPTER SUMMARY

Employees can be the greatest asset to a sport business, yet they can also be a source of contention. Sport managers, in an attempt to maximize employee-related benefits while mitigating associated problems, should put a lot of credence into the hiring, retention, training, and motivating of the work force. A variety of tools are available and proven to be effective in maximizing human resource potential. For example, the criminal check, employee reference, job description, job analysis, job application, and performance appraisal processes represent basic yet integral facets of prudent employee management.

STUDENT ASSIGNMENT

1. Identify a sport business entity to study.
2. Collect and critique the following documents from the chosen sport business:
    (a) a job description
    (b) a job analysis
    (c) a standardized form (if available) used to appraise employee performance
    (d) a job application
3. Interview the sport business manager and inquire and elaborate about the following:
    (a) tactics used to deter negligent hiring and negligent retention
    (b) the performance appraisal process (e.g., training, frequency, who appraises, use of an established grievance procedure, communication regarding the performance appraisal process stated in a policy manual)
4. Design a job description, job analysis, job application, and a performance appraisal instrument for a hypothetical sport business.

REFERENCES

Ashe, R.L. (1980). How do your performance appraisals perform? *EEO Today, 7*(3), 216–222.

Ashe, R.L., & McRae, G.S. (1985). Performance evaluations go to court in the 1980s. *Mercer Law Review, 36*(3), 887–905.

Barrett, G.V., & Kernan, M.C. (1987). Performance appraisal and termination: A review of court decisions since Brito v. Zia with implications for personnel practices. *Personnel Psychology, 40*(3), 489–503.

Bell, C.R., & Zempke, R. (1992). *Managing knock your socks off service.* New York: American Management Association.

Brotherton, P. (1996, May). Candid feedback spurs changes in culture. *HRMagazine,* pp. 47–52.

Broussard, R.D., & Brannen, D.E. (1986, June). Credential distortions: Personnel practitioners give their views. *Personnel Administrator,* pp. 129–145.

Burchett, S.R., & De Meuse, K.P. (1985). Performance and the law. *Personnel, 62*(7), 29–37.

Carrell, M.R., Kuzmits, F.E., & Elbert, N.F. (1992). *Personnel/human resource management* (4th ed.). New York: Macmillan.

Chagares, M.A. (1989). Utilization of the disclaimer as an effective means to define the employment relationship. *Hofstra Law Review, 17*(2), 365–405.

C.K. Security Systems v. Hartford Accident & Indemnity: 223 S.E.3d 453 (1976).

" 'Continuous employment' is the new buzzword for hourly employees." (1996, October 1). *The Wall Street Journal,* p. A1.

Crime Control Act of 1990, 42 U.S.C. 13041.

Daniloff, D. (1989). Employer defamation: Reasons and remedies for declining references and chilled communications in the workplace. *The Hastings Law Journal, 40*(3), 687–722.

Davidson, J. (1984). Paper tigers come in more resumes than one. *ABA Banking Journal, 76*(4), 147–148.

Dell v. Montgomery Ward, 811 F.2d 970 (6th Cir. 1987).

Doe v. British Universities North American Club, 788 F. Supp. 1286 (D. Conn. 1992).

D.T. by M.T. v. Independent School District, No. 16, 894 F.2d. 1176 (10th Cir. 1990).

Duffy, D.J. (1983). Defamation and employer privilege. *Employee Relations Law Journal, 9*(3), 444–454.

Eikleberry J.L. (1995). Job references: A legal and management paradox. *Arizona Attorney, 32*(2), 20–23, 41–42.

Elias, M. (1996, August 8). Violence in the workplace: Making jobs safe. *USA Today,* p. D1–D2.

Eyres, P.S. (1989). Legally defensible performance appraisal systems. *Personnel Journal, 68*(7), 58–62.

Fried, G. (1996). Unsportsman like contact. *American Humanics, 5*(2), 3–6.

Gaines v. Cuna Mutual Insurance Society, 681 F.2d 982 (5th Cir. 1982).

Garcia v. Duffy, 492 So. 2d 435 (Fla. App. 2 Dist. 1986)

Gebelein, S.H. (1996, January). Multi-rater feedback goes strategic. *HRFocus,* pp. 4–6.

Gordon, J.R. (1991). *Organizational behavior.* Needham Heights, MA: Allyn & Bacon.

Gregory, D.L. (1988). Reducing the risk of negligence in hiring. *Employee Relations Law Journal, 18*(2), 185–213.

Griggs, v. Duke Power Co., 401 U.S. 424 (1971).

Harris, G. (1986). Labor law-employment at will doctrine. *Rutgers Law Journal, 17*(3,4), 715–736.

Huber, V.L. (1983). An analysis of performance appraisal practices in the public sector: A review and recommendations. *Public Personnel Management Journal, 12*(3), 258–267.

Indian Child Protection and Family Violence Prevention Act, Pub. L. No. 101-630, 104 Stat. 4556 (1990).

Jacobs, R.B. (1990). Defamation and negligence in the workplace. *Labor Law Journal, 40*(9), 567–574.

Jones, D. (1996, September 13). Resume boosting can bust careers. *USA Today,* p. 2B.

Leonard, B. (1996, May). Five more states enact reference-checking laws. *HRMagazine,* p. 8.

Levin, R.L. (1995). Workplace violence: Sources of liability, warning signs, and ways to mitigate damages. *Labor Law Journal, 46*(7), 418–428.

Lewis v. Equitable Life Assurance Society, 389 N.W.2d. 876 (Minn. 1986).

Loiseau v. Department of Human Resources of the State of Oregon, 567 F. Supp. 1211 (D. Or. 1983).

Longnecker, C.O. (1989). Truth or consequences: Politics and performance appraisals. *Business Horizons, 32*(6), 76–82.

Longnecker, C.O., & Ludwig, D. (1990). Ethical dilemmas in performance appraisal revisited. *Journal of Business Ethics, 9,* 961–969.

Martucci, W.C., & Boatright, D.B. (1995). Immunity for employment references. *Employment Relations Today, 22*(2), 119–123.

Mercer, M.W. (1988, December). Turnover: Reducing the costs. *Personnel,* pp. 36–42.

Metz, E.J. (1988). Designing legally defensible performance appraisal systems. *Training and Development Journal, 42*(7), 47–51.

Middleton, M. (1987, May 4). Employers face upsurge in suits over defamation. *The National Law Journal,* pp. 1, 30.

Miller, G.D., & Fenton, J.W., Jr. (1991). Negligent hiring and criminal record information: A muddled area of employment law. *Labor Law Journal, 42*(3), 186–192.

Miller, L.K., Fielding, L.W., & Pitts, B.G. (1993). Implementation of the performance appraisal process: Concerns for the health club manager. *Journal of Legal Aspects of Sport, 3*(1), 44–50.

Miller, L.K., Pitts, B.G., & Fielding, L.W. (1993). Legal concerns in writing job recommendations. *The Physical Educator, 50*(1), 47–51.

Nobile, F.J. (1991). The law of performance appraisals. *Personnel, 68*(7), 7.

Paetzold, R.L., & Wilburn, S.L. (1992). Employer (ir)rationality and the demise of employment references. *American Business Law Journal, 30*(1), 123–142.

Panaro, G. (1988). Don't let your personnel manual become a contract. *Association Management, 38*(8), 81–83.

Pinck, C.T. (1996, July). Covering all the databases. *Security Management,* pp. 39–41.

Ponticas v. K.M.S. Investments, 331 N.W.2d 907 (Minn. 1983).

Reichheld, F.F. (1993). Loyalty-based management. *Harvard Business Review, 71*(2), 64–73.

Rovella, D.E. (1995). Laws may ease the risky business of job references. *The National Law Journal, 18*(8), B1.

Rowe v. General Motors Corporation, 457 F.2d 348 (5th Cir. 1972).

Schaner, D.J. (1996). Have gun, will carry: Concealed handgun laws, workplace violence and employer liability. *Employee Relations Law Journal, 22*(1), 83–100.

Schellhardt, T.D. (1996, November 19). It's time to evaluate your work and all involved are groaning. *The Wall Street Journal,* pp. A1, A5.

Shaw, B. (1990). Employee appraisals, discrimination cases, and objective evidence. *Business Horizons, 33*(5), 61–65.

Silver, M. (1987, May). Negligent hiring claims take off. *ABA Journal,* pp. 72–78.

Stacey, D.R. (1976). Subjective criteria in employment decisions under Title VII. *Georgia Law Review, 10*(3), 737–752.

Tarassoff v. Regents of the University System of California, 17 Cal. 3d 425 (1991).

Uniform guidelines on employee selection procedures. (1993 edition). 29 CFR Ch. XIV-7.

U.S. Equal Employment Opportunity Commission. (1992). ADA, *EEOC technical assistance manual.* Chicago: Commerce Clearing House, Inc.

Vecchio, R.P. (1984). The problem of phony resumes: How to spot a ringer among the applicants. *Personnel, 61*(2), 22–27.

Von der Embse, T.J., and Wyse, R.E. (1985, January). Those reference letters: How useful are they? *Personnel,* 42–46.

Webster, G.D. (1988). The law of employee evaluations. *Association Management, 38*(9), 118–119.

White, J.B., & Lublin, J.S. (1996, September 27). Some companies try to rebuild loyalty. *The Wall Street Journal,* p. B1.

Witt, M.R., & Goldman, S.R. (1988). Avoiding liability in employee handbooks. *Employee Relations Law Journal, 14*(1), 5–19.

Woolery v. Brady, 741 F. Supp 667 (E.D. Mich., S.D. 1990).

SAMPLE JOB ANALYSIS
Anywhere, USA, Parks Department

Job Position: _____

Purpose: _____

Mental Effort: Check the frequency of the events below using the key provided on the right.

	Never Happens	Seldom Happens	Sometimes Happens	Frequently Happens	Almost Always Happens
PLANNING					
Forecasting					
Goal Setting					
Determining Budget Expenditures					
Establishing or Revising Policies					
STAFFING					
Training and Orienting Staff					
Recruiting and Selecting Staff					
Defining Roles					
Writing Job Descriptions					
Determining Selection Criteria					
EVALUATION					
Deciding Performance Standards					
Presenting and Approving Rewards					
Preparing Performance Evaluations					
Day-to-Day Observations					
Correcting Behavior/Work Problems					
ORGANIZATION					
Describing Relationships between Jobs					
Defining Department Structure					
Establishing Priorities					
Scheduling Work for Employees					
Establishing Deadlines					
Implementing Procedures					
Determining Work Methods					
Balancing Multiple Tasks or Projects					
DIRECTING AND SUPERVISING					
Educating					
Delegating					
Coordinating					
Coaching/Developing/Training					
Motivating					
Instructing and Demonstrating					
Scheduling					
EMPLOYEE RELATIONS					
Taking Corrective Action					
Authorizing Formal Discipline					
Administering Collective Bargaining Agreements					
Investigating Grievances or Complaints					
OTHER					

Attach Organizational Chart & Job Description

continues

Anywhere, USA, Parks Department

Environmental and Physical Factors: Check the box that corresponds for each of the items below and most accurately correlates the extent to which the activity is performed by the employee.

	NA	1–2 Hours	3–4 Hours	5–6 Hours	7+ Hours
Inside					
Outside					
Humid					
Hazard					
Height					
Cold					
Hot					
Damp/Wet					
Dry					
Varying Temperature					
Dusty and/or Dirty					
Odors/Vapors/Gases					
Noisy					
Requires Standing					
Requires Sitting					
Requires Walking					

Physical Summary: Circle one description present in each of the numbered categories that best portrays this position.

1. *SEDENTARY WORK:* A. Involves mainly sitting. B. Walking and standing are minimal. C. Lifting is limited to light objects (10 lb or less).
2. *LIGHT WORK:* A. Job entails some lifting of medium objects (10–20 lb). B. Job involves standing or walking 10% to 20% of the time.
3. *MEDIUM WORK:* A. Job includes lifting heavy objects (20–40 lb). B. 20% to 40% of the job is spent standing, kneeling, squatting, or walking. C. Pushing or pulling objects may be required within the weight limits.
4. *HEAVY WORK:* A. Lifting more than 40 lb is part of the job. B. Approximately half of the time on the job will be spent walking, climbing, kneeling, standing, bending, or squatting.

Unique Working Conditions: Please outline any specific environmental, physical, or unique conditions that exist within the position.

CHAPTER 8

Funding and Budgeting for the Sport Business

A sport entrepreneur's ability to secure funds for a particular sport business represents a critical element related to the future success and solvency of the sport business itself. Funding alternatives differ depending on the sport business industry segment. For example, sources of funding differ among for-profit sport businesses, athletic arenas and stadiums, and parks and recreation departments. This chapter identifies funding alternatives available to entrepreneurs in a variety of sport industry segments.

FOR-PROFIT BUSINESSES

There are endless for-profit sport-related business ventures, including the retail or wholesale of sporting goods, health/fitness clubs, sport manufacturers, bowling alleys, miniature golf courses, tennis facilities, and more. For-profit businesses have an increasingly larger number of sources to turn to when soliciting monies for viable enterprises. The following funding sources are commonly pursued by sport business entrepreneurs.

Personal Savings or Equity Capital

Personal savings, also referred to as *equity capital,* are needed to finance any sport business venture for three common reasons. First, use of personal savings negates the often high interest rates imposed on first-time sport business owners. This is always a benefit of using equity versus debt financing. Second, banks and other lenders are leery about supporting a venture when the entrepreneur is unwilling to undertake a portion of the risk or uncertainty established by the new business. Patton, Grantham, Gerson, and Gettman (1989) state for example, that lending institutions typically require a debt/equity ratio of 60/40 for new commercial health/fitness businesses. In other words, 60% of financing is provided by creditors, and the remaining 40% is provided by the sport business owner(s). Third, sport entrepreneurs often find it difficult to secure necessary funding due to a lack of experience or inherent lending biases. Consequently, use of personal savings are often the only alternative. Although not viewed as equity capital, use of personal credit-card lending reserves has proven helpful to many who are otherwise unable to get needed monies via more traditional outlets, such as banks or loan institutions.

Family, Friends

Family and friends, referred to as *informal investors* by Ronstadt (1988), are often the most common funding alternative for small sport businesses (Ronstadt, 1988). Loans from family and friends tend to be quicker to access than the lengthy process and extensive paperwork required by formal lending institutions. Further, monies borrowed from informal sources are typically more favorable in terms of interest rates and dates of maturity.

Bank Loans

Banks are another common avenue for securing needed monies for for-profit ventures. However, one's ability to secure a bank loan is contingent on a number of factors, including the experience of management, projected product demand and related revenues, and collateral. A well-developed, comprehensive business plan facilitates the loan process while maximizing ability to borrow at reasonable interest rates. Lenders are able to access needed information from an organized portfolio. Further, the absence of the business plan raises questions regarding the degree of planning that went into the proposal and the professionalism of the potential loan candidate.

Government Loans, Programs

The Small Business Administration

Funding from the Small Business Administration (SBA) is another viable source of money potentially available to the sport business entrepreneur (Appendix 8–A). The SBA was established by Congress in 1953 to aid small business growth and development. As stated by the SBA (U.S. Small Business Administration[SBA], 1990), "Small businesses are the backbone of the American economy. They create two of every three new jobs, produce 40% of the gross national product, and invent more than half the nation's technological innovations. Our 20 million small companies provide dynamic opportunities for all Americans." As stated by Patton et al. (1989, p. 71), the SBA "granted 134 loans worth $16.1 million to health/fitness club owners" in 1985.

SBA's guaranteed loan program (U.S. SBA, 1991) is most attractive for entrepreneurs who have been turned down by a bank or other private lender. In this situation, the SBA steps in and guarantees the lender that a majority of the entire loan will be repaid. Eligibility criteria for receiving, and characteristics of, an SBA loan include the following:

- The business must be a for-profit venture.
- The average annual receipts of a service business may not exceed $3.5 million to $14.5 million, depending on the industry.
- Interest rates generally cannot exceed 2.75% over the prime rate.
- Documented evidence must be shown that the loan can be repaid from generated revenues.

The SBA, however, does much more than just serve as a vehicle to secure loans for small businesses. The SBA also offers free consultation and training on request. Three partner organizations—SCORE (Service Corps of Retired Executives), small business institutes housed at various universities, and Small Business Development Centers (over 600 centers nationwide)—facilitate the SBA in the provision of needed assistance. Additional information regarding the SBA and its partner organizations can be obtained by calling 1-800-U ASK SBA. Local SBA offices and related phone numbers should also be listed in any local telephone directory.

Other Government-, State-, or City-Assisted Programs

The ability to retain population is important to any local government. Without people, states lose needed tax dollars, Social Security monies, workers' compensation contributions, and so forth. Consequently, states have begun implementing innovative programs to facilitate small business development. For example, *The Wall Street Journal* reported on West Virginia's state funding of a $16.2 million project. As explained by Mehta (1996a, p. B2), "A new state-run retail facility in Beckley, W. Virginia, will spur small-business development and create jobs in the state . . . . The center . . . will purchase arts, crafts and food products made by West Virginia artists and home-based businesses and sell them to the public." Over 1,100 small businesses have already enrolled in the West Virginia program. Sport businesses entrepreneurs should contact the local chamber of commerce and economic development office for additional government-, state-, or city-assisted programs.

Venture Capital

Venture capital is defined by Downes and Goodman (1987, p. 463) as an "Important source of financing for start-up companies or others embarking on new or turnaround ventures that entail some risk but offer the potential for above average future profits." The increasing popularity of extreme sports, for example, in a market of limited supply and increasing demand, would appear to offer attractive sport business opportunities. Venture capitalists include, but are not limited to, individual investors; private partnerships; small business investment companies (SBICs); and subsidiaries of banks, corporations, or insurance companies (Downes & Goodman, 1987; Patton et al., 1989). Surfing the Internet can also lead to the discovery of venture capitalists who a person may otherwise have not come in contact with (Mehta, 1996b). Basically, any individual or entity with the money to invest can serve as a venture capitalist.

Venture capitalists, in exchange for their monetary investment, secure partial ownership of the entity until the loan is paid back. Sport business managers, often reluctant to relinquish ownership and managerial control, may find this source of funding unattractive for that reason. As explained by Carrol (1996, p. B1), "Venture capitalists . . . often have too little real-world experience, too short-term an outlook and too meddlesome an approach." Caution should be heeded especially if the venture capitalists, seeking managerial control, have little (if any) knowledge regarding the particular sport product or business.

Issuing Private Stock

The issuing of private stock is an attractive funding alternative for four primary reasons. First, neither the principal nor the interest has to be repaid. Second, the issuance of private stock avoids the cumbersome process of registering with the Securities and Exchange Commission (SEC) as is necessary with a public offering. Third, the exemption from registration hastens the ability to proceed with a transaction and reduces the risk of missed opportunities. Fourth, the entrepreneur avoids the underwriting expenses, agency fees, and registration fees associated with a public offering (Joy, 1980).

Public Offerings

Selling stock to the public is typically reserved for larger sport businesses, as the public is generally not interested in investing in small companies with perceived limited potential. The use of an underwriter, who guarantees the sale of the securities, is available to the sport business entrepreneur wishing to avoid the headaches that typically accompany public offerings. As mentioned above, public offerings are attractive as they generate equity capital that does not have to be repaid.

Trade Credit

Frequently, a small business looks to suppliers for financing in exchange for guaranteed business. Agreements that defer inventory payment or provide immediate, up-front financing are most beneficial in getting a sport business operative.

Factoring Companies

Factoring companies are a viable source of funding for established sport businesses with an accounts receivable figure of substance (Ellis & Norton, 1988). A factoring company can provide a sport business with a cash equivalency of the amount contained on the balance sheet in accounts receivable less a percentage for collection efforts. The relationship with a factoring company benefits the sport business as collection efforts are alleviated while up-front cash is immediately available for debt retirement, expansion, and so forth. However, sport business managers should approach factoring with caution, as some suggest that factoring can be more expensive than borrowing ("Lending Woes," 1994).

Franchising and Licensing Options

As explained by Dicke (1992, p. 2), "In a franchise system one large firm, often called the parent company, grants or sells the right to distribute its products or use its trade name and processes to a number of smaller firms. The boundaries of the relationship and the ultimate basis for control are established by contract." Sport entrepreneurs may find entry into a particular sport industry segment prohibitive due to capital requirements, existing competition, funding difficulties, and lack of experience or training. Becoming a franchisee or a licensee, however, is an attractive alternative, as the start-up expenses are significantly reduced. For example, a franchisee can receive the following benefits otherwise unavailable to a "new" sport business and its management team:

- site selection assistance
- national advertising
- management training
- immediate brand recognition, brand loyalty
- established distribution
- economies of scale
- assistance in negotiating leases
- assistance with marketing plans

Sport business entrepreneurs may find franchising a very attractive alternative. Perry (1990, p. 38) states, referring to government statistics, "A franchise is three times more likely to succeed than a new independent small business."

However, not all franchises are created equal. The following are all important considerations regarding whether or not to purchase a franchise (Montgomery Garrett, 1994):

- the amount of deviation from the original product offering
- available financial and service support

- comments and opinions from existing franchisees
- comments and opinions of franchise support personnel
- expansion plans (e.g., too fast, nonexistent)
- royalty fee requirements
- territorial agreements, restrictions
- product offering flexibility
- use and integration of technology
- the management team of the parent company
- no-compete clauses

Sport franchise opportunities are routinely listed in various publications, including *The Wall Street Journal, USA Today,* and trade magazines.

A licensee gains similar benefits as a franchisee yet at a reduced cost, as purchase prices are lower, and royalty fees are avoided. The primary benefit incurred by the licensee is brand name identity. For example, assume entrepreneur Shawn is pursuing one of two options. He could open his own health club and call it Shawn's Gym, or he could become a Powerhouse licensee. People interested in joining a health club may be more likely to pursue a Powerhouse membership due to established notoriety and goodwill. As a brand new entrepreneur, Shawn's Gym provides little, if any, immediate impression in the mind of a potential patron. Further, in comparison to the franchisee, the licensee has much more flexibility to contour his or her facility or product offering as desired. Additional benefits that licensors may provide to licensees include discounted sportswear, insurance, equipment, and supplies. Assistance in designing the floor plan, choosing a site, and establishing/installing computerized systems may also be provided (Powerhouse Gyms International, Inc., 1992).

The same flexibility afforded the licensee, however, can also serve as a disadvantage to the parent company, or licensor. Gold's Gym owner DiBiase elaborates, "My gyms had very little in common with maybe two-thirds of the other Gold's Gyms out there. . . . There was a lack of standardization and quality control that I feel may have detracted from the overall image of the chain" (McDermott, 1993, p. 30). Arnold Schwarzenegger encountered similar difficulties upon acquiring control of World's Gym in 1993. Schwarzenegger's solution was to convince existing licensees to renew their contract as a franchisee. However, those entrepreneurs successful on their own likely resisted the intrusion and the required royalty fee payment typically ranging between 7% and 15%.

ATHLETIC FACILITIES

A great deal of literature supports the economic and noneconomic benefits a city incurs when granted a professional sport franchise (Baim, 1985, 1994; Johnson, 1986; Recio, 1987; Rosentraub & Nunn, 1978; "Suddenly Everyone," 1983).

Specifically, advocates argue that a new stadium or arena (and the assumed securement of a professional franchise) can benefit a city in the following ways:

- Increased jobs enhance the area's rate of employment, providing more individuals with discretionary monies and the local government with more tax dollars.
- An increase in civic pride enhances community loyalty.
- New facilities and related activities enhance tourism.
- The new "prestige" and "status" of a city serves as a magnet for new industry.
- The stadium or arena and related events benefit the local community by providing a healthy recreational outlet.

Purcell (1991) estimated that the economic impact associated with the Georgia Dome would exceed $200 million per year. Similarly, the economic impact of the America West Arena was estimated at $294 million per year (America West Arena, 1991). Consequently, cities continually seek ways to garnish funding for sport facilities with the hope that, "if we build it, they will come." It is estimated that 4,500 full- and part-time jobs were created by the New Jersey Meadowlands Sports Complex (Shubnell, Petersen, & Harris, 1985). Similarly, it is estimated that the city of Los Angeles lost 1,300 jobs when the Raiders left town.

However, others remain convinced that sport stadiums provide no economic benefit ("Socked for Stadiums," 1996; Welch, 1996). A significant amount of literature refutes the above benefits. For example, jobs are created, but they are low paying and seasonal. Monies spent at the stadium and arena only divert dollars from other local sport or leisure businesses. Monies spent on the stadium would be better spent toward industry that provides higher paying jobs and a more educated work force. Critics view efforts to build sport-related stadiums and arenas as offensive and argue that the public money could be better spent on local police, street crime deterrent, and education. In other words, tax monies, if used for employment generation, should be used in generating those businesses that provide 12-month, skilled, salaried jobs. Regardless of critic arguments, publicly funded sport stadiums continue to abound. As explained by Welch (1996, p. B1), "Since 1990, 26 sports facilities costing $4.5 billion have been built in 22 cities. By 2000, 19 more, costing $5 billion, are planned for 11 cities. Four dollars out of every five come from public sources." The following paragraphs elaborate on funding alternatives for athletic arenas and stadiums. Appendix 8–B summarizes sources of funding used by existing stadiums and arenas (Mays et al., 1996).

Taxes

A variety of taxes can be levied to pay, in part, for new stadiums and/or arenas. The following list identifies a sampling of taxes that can be increased for the purpose of funding desired facilities.

- hotel/motel tax
- restaurant tax
- auto rental tax
- taxi tax
- "sin" taxes (e.g., liquor, tobacco)
- sales tax
- road tax
- utility tax
- property tax

The taxes viewed most favorably by the local constituencies are the hotel, restaurant, and auto rental taxes, as they are likely to be shouldered by tourists. For example, in June, Georgia levied a car-rental surcharge in an effort to raise $75 million needed to fund a new basketball arena in downtown Atlanta. Similarly, King County, Washington, implemented a 2% car-rental tax in January to generate needed monies for a baseball stadium (Lisser, 1996). As explained by Tabak (1995, p. 28), "travel-related taxes throughout the United States are rising at a faster rate than any other kind of levy."

However, continual tax increases can generate citizen discernment. In fact, New York City experienced a backlash in tourism trade amounting to an estimated loss of $94 million in tourism revenue when hotel taxes reached 21.25% for rooms over $100 per night (Tabak, 1995). Interestingly, a boycott of New York City threatened by the Professional Convention Management Association was successful in rescinding the levy 5% (Tabak, 1995). States are likely to continue the existing tax revolt. For example, in 1992, the Illinois Board of Higher Education proposed the elimination of the use of state taxes for university sport facilities (Athletic Notes, 1993).

Bonds

The issuing of bonds is the most common way for a city to generate the needed money for stadiums and arenas. A bond is defined as "An interest-bearing certificate issued by a government or corporation, promising to pay interest and to repay a sum of money (the principal) at a specified date in the future" (Samuelson & Nordhaus, 1985, p. 828). According to Howard and Crompton (1980, p. 11) a bond is simply "an interest paying IOU." Bonds issued by a government or a subdivision of a state are referred to as municipal bonds. Municipal bonds are typically exempt from federal, state, and local taxes on earned interest. Bond buyers can include individuals, organizations, institutions, or groups desiring to lend money at a predetermined interest rate. The exemption given to municipal bonds is attractive, as they can be sold at lower interest rates.

Bonds, however, are not a panacea for sport facility development for two primary reasons. First, the amount of money a state can borrow is not endless. The *debt ceiling* or *debt capacity* defines the maximum amount of money any city, county, or special district can borrow. Stadiums and arenas are more likely to attract investors when the governmental entity has few major obligations regarding competing commitments toward "schools, roadways, and water and sewer facilities" (Shubnell et al., 1985, p. 10). As reported by Simmons (1995), the actual dollar amount of bonds being issued for public facilities decreased 51% between 1993 and 1994.

Second, the tax exemption and low interest rates on bonds used for stadium construction aggravates critics. As stated by Brady and Howlett (1996, p. 14C),

> That costs taxpayers indirectly—not in taxes they pay, but in taxes the government does not receive. The way Sen. Byron L. Dorgan, D-N.D., figures it, taxpayers in his state pay an extra $6 million a year as a result. A report by the Congressional Research Service . . . says a $225 million stadium built today and fully financed by tax-exempt bonds would receive a subsidy as high as $75 million over 30 years.

General Obligation Bonds

General obligation bonds refer to bonds that are repaid with a portion of the general property taxes. As a result, these bonds are somewhat "guaranteed," as tax monies will always be available to repay the bond. Hence, from the perspective of the individual or company loaning the money, general obligation bonds are relatively risk-free, as the borrower can always levy additional taxes to get the needed monies. The low default rates of these bonds make them more attractive to a larger pool of potential investors. Philadelphia's Veterans Stadium and the Pontiac Silverdome were both constructed with monies from general obligation bonds (Howard & Crompton, 1995).

However, there are disadvantages to the issuance of a general obligation bond. First, general obligation bonds require voter approval. Local taxpayers have increasingly become resistant to an increase in taxes as discretionary income becomes smaller and smaller. Second, many taxpayers resist having to pay for facilities (e.g., a stadium or arena) that they never intend to use. Resistance is magnified as franchises become increasingly willing and able to relocate to other cities as desired. Third, the issuance of bonds increases the local debt of the issuing community and ties up monies, making the funding of future projects more difficult (e.g., schools, infrastructure).

Revenue Bonds

Revenue bonds are also an available funding source for sport arenas and stadiums. The concept of revenue bonds is similar to that of general obligation bonds.

However, the key distinction is the way in which these bonds are repaid. As noted above, the general obligation bond is repaid via property taxes. In comparison, a revenue bond is repaid using the revenues generated by the facility or its product (e.g., ticket sales, rental fees) or other designated tax sources (e.g., hotel/motel, auto rental, "sin" taxes). There are five primary attractions affiliated with a revenue bond (Howard & Crompton, 1980):

1. The revenue bond does not impose or take monies from nonfacility users.
2. Revenue bonds do not count against the debt capacity and, therefore, leave monies left for other needed capital projects.
3. In most states, revenue bonds do not require voter approval.
4. The pressure to be "profitable" often secures better management and customer service.
5. The need to distinguish between resident users and nonresident users is eliminated.

The Meadowlands and the Cowboys stadium were funded, in part, by revenue bonds.

In contrast to the general obligation bond, the revenue bond is viewed as being more risky. Changing consumer desires, competition, weather, injured players, and so forth can all have a negative impact on revenue generation.

Certificates of Participation

Certificates of participation (COPs) involve a governmental entity buying (and building) the arena or stadium. The governmental entity then leases portions of the facility to the general public. Monies generated from the leases, or COPs, are then used to pay off the facility's capital expenses.

Tax Increment Financing

Tax increment financing (TIF) is available when an urban area has been identified for renewal or redevelopment. Real estate developed with the use of TIF is attractive to stakeholders, as tax increases are not necessary. Rather, the bonds and developmental costs are repaid from the generated property taxes associated with the newly developed real estate. As mentioned above, citizens tend to favor TIF for the development of stadiums and arenas, as the TIF alternative may replace the levy of a new tax and the burden imposed on the local citizen.

However, TIF can impose burdens on stakeholders. For example, as the land develops and flourishes, citizens may desire to use the generated property tax monies toward the improvement of extant school districts. The predetermined use of property tax monies precludes the use of the generated monies, for example, to the improvement of extant school districts. In this situation, local citizens will be subject to higher tax rates or forced to accept the school district as it is for the time being. The intricacies of TIF are defined at the state (versus federal) level. Most states, however, include a definition of how long the property tax dollars can be captured, the types of development costs that can be financed with property tax revenues, and the location and size of the area subject to TIF opportunities (Michael, 1987; Regan, 1996).

Private-Sector Investment

Private-sector investment is preferred by most stakeholders as a result of declining public monies and questionable economic impact results. Regarding private-sector investment, Herbert (1991, p. 45) states,

> It is favored by local politicians and taxpayers because it avoids the commitment of tax dollars to build a sports facility at the perceived expense of other municipal needs. Developers and team owners prefer this approach because it offers greater control over the sports facility operation, such as concession pricing and luxury suite/club seating decisions, than if the facility was financed with municipal dollars.

San Francisco's Pacific Bell Park represents the first privately funded baseball park since 1962 (Hiestand, 1996b).

Private-sector investment takes on a variety of forms and degrees of contribution. The following list identifies ways in which the private sector contributes to the financing of sport arenas and stadiums:

- cash
- in-kind contributions (e.g., materials, functional expertise)
- naming rights to the stadium itself or to specific areas within the stadium
- concessionaire exclusivity
- sponsorship packages
- donations
- life insurance packages
- lease agreements
- luxury suites, preferred seating packages
- bequests and trusts
- real estate
- endowments
- securities

As noted in *USA Today,* Arlington's Ballpark which hosts the Texas Rangers received $12.7 million for the Ballpark's concessionaires (Brady & Howlett, 1996). The Ballpark in Arlington received $6 million from first-year luxury suite revenues. Also, $17.1 million was generated from preferred-seat licenses (PSLs), for which fans gave between $500 and $5,000 in return for the opportunity to buy a particular seat (Brady & Howlett, 1996). Similarly, Speedway Motorsports, Inc., in the Dallas/Ft. Worth, Texas, area plans to raise $50 million by selling 36,000 PSLs at a cost between $750 and $2,000 per seat. The money will be used to help fund the Texas International Raceway, a $110 million, 150,000-seat race track (Hiestand, 1996a).

Joint Financing between Public and Private Entities

The shared or joint financing of stadiums and arenas between public and private entities is gaining popularity. Public entities contribute via low-cost financing, access, or ownership of valuable land, other tax inducements and incentives, and control over the permit and zoning process. Private entities contribute managerial expertise and efficiency (see Baim, 1985), in addition to money securement via naming rights, lifetime seating arrangements, sponsorship agreements, donations, lease agreements, concessionaire exclusivity, and so forth. As an example of sponsorship agreements, the University of Michigan received more than $7 million from Nike; a portion of this money could be used for stadium and arena renovation ("Michigan Gets $7 Million," 1994). Further, the liability of any one entity can be reduced through strategic use of contractual language, insurance, and/or indemnification agreements. Regan (1996) identifies a number of stadiums financed jointly between the public and private sector, including the Bradley Center Arena, Coors Stadium, and the Cleveland Cavaliers Arena. However, the future of incentive provisions may be in jeopardy. Mehta (1996c, p. B2) reported that the Midwestern Legislative Conference, a unity of the Council of State Governments, convened in August 1996 to discuss the reduction of economic-development incentives "states use to lure businesses from other states."

Professional Organizations

Professional organizations also make significant contributions to the development of stadiums and arenas in various locations for various purposes. For example, the U.S. Tennis Association (USTA) spent $10 million to build the Louis Armstrong complex in New York City, housing 2 tennis stadiums, 25 outdoor courts, 9 indoor courts, "locker rooms, lounges, a pro shop, a restaurant, and administrative offices" (Howard & Crompton, 1995, p. 125). This facility is available to the city for 305 days per year. Similarly, the Atlanta Committee for the Olympic Games (ACOG) spent millions of dollars on facilities for the Atlanta Olympics in 1996. The colleges and universities surrounding downtown Atlanta received more than $116 million for construction and renovation (Schmid, 1996). Local citizens favor the influx of money from professional associations as the investment in stadiums and arenas benefits local communities long after the event has passed.

State Funds User Formula

Athletic departments of universities and public schools are often able to fund a portion of new stadiums and arenas with state monies. Prior to the 1970s, it was common practice for the state to finance the entire capital project. In the 1990s, it is more common for the state to contribute a percentage of the monies needed according to the projected amount of time the facility will be used for educational purposes. In other words, if the physical education department of ABC University will use the facility for classes 50% of the time, then the state will contribute 50% of the needed monies.

PARKS AND RECREATION

Parks and recreation facilities utilize many of the funding alternatives previously discussed above. For example, tax monies and bonds are common sources of money for parks and recreation departments. Parks and recreation departments continue to compete fiercely with police departments and schools for funding needed for renovations, maintenance, equipment, and surface upgrades. In addition to established government financing mechanisms, private sponsorships, joint venture facilities, and user fees are becoming increasingly popular funding alternatives.

Private Sponsorships

Private monies (i.e., sponsorships) represent an alternative that could provide "369 national parks, memorials, battlefields, historic sites, seashores and recreation areas" an anticipated $150 million per year. Similar to the Olympics' five-ring emblem and related marks, the national parks would register an "official" trademark or logo that corporate sponsors could use in the marketing of their own product and company. As explained by Kanamine (1996a, p. 7D), "Corporations that buy into the licensing gain public relations points, particularly among the more than 270 million people who visit the USA's beloved but beleaguered national park system every year." On the other hand, critics argue that the park-sponsorship idea "smacks of commercialization" (Kanamine, 1996a, p. 7D). However, the repairs needed at national parks exceed $4 billion. Parks needing to become more "entrepreneurial" to remain operative find sponsorships an attractive option.

Joint Venture Facilities

Joint venture facilities represent, for example, the sharing of facilities and pooled capital (Cohen, 1996). In other words, a city may provide the monies to build a particular recreation facility, while a private, for-profit health club may manage and operate the programs. In this situation, the city benefits as capital and long-term personnel costs are incurred by the private, for-profit club. The for-profit club benefits as it generates management revenues. The other option, of course, would be to have the park and recreation department build a brand new facility that competes directly with the for-profit health club. The joint venture agreements tend to diffuse hostile competition and provide for a more palatable situation to both parties.

User Fees

User fees represent another way to generate needed operating revenues. As explained by Kanamine (1996b, p. 7D), "Cash-strapped parks departments are favoring pay-to-play activities over free grassy lawns and ball fields in a shift that is likely to dot suburbs with more golf courses, batting cages and water slides." Again, critics fear that parks eventually will mirror other for-profit sport businesses whose user fees prohibit the low- and middle-class constituency from participating. As stated by Kanamine (1996b, p. 7D), "price is becoming a problem for the very people for whom public recreation was intended."

BUDGETING

Similar to other topics addressed throughout this text (e.g., human resources management, risk management), the budgeting process also remains integral to the success of a sport business. A budget (a.k.a. a pro forma income statement or a pro forma balance sheet) provides a sport business manager with acceptable, realistic estimates or forecasts of upcoming revenues and expenses. Pictorially, the budget resembles standard accounting instruments, including the income statement, balance sheet, and cashflow analysis. Accounting statements, however, represent actual data transpired from previous transactions. A budget, on the other hand, represents the best estimate of forecasted revenues and expenses. In other words, accounting statements represent what has happened, whereas the budget represents what is expected to happen.

Benefits Associated with "Good" Budgeting

Sport business managers can realize the following six benefits from the budgeting process.

Reduces Waste and Runaway Costs

Budgeting forces managers to monitor costs continually. Duplicated and unnecessary expenses can be reduced or eliminated, while escalating expenses associated with supplies or telephone usage, for example, can be investigated.

Failure to monitor costs enables a sport business to spend liberally in low-profit generating areas while leaving little working capital available for the needed development of primary activity areas, advertising, or other offensive or defensive competitive tactics.

Keeps a Sport Business Focused on Its Strategy and Mission

A budget should be a quantitative reflection of a sport business's chosen strategy. Further, decision making and resource allocation should be made in accordance with the mission and stated objectives. New ventures that would divert resources or harmfully fragment the sport business in the eyes of the consumer are better avoided via a planned budget. For example, Paul Risley (general manager of Sports World, a 32-acre amusement park) explained how management contemplated how to best use the 7 acres available for expansion. Land use considerations included the purchase of a roller coaster or the integration of games resembling laser tag or paintball. Risley would prefer to spend the monies for the roller coaster since both laser tag and paintball games have a "war-like" or violent characteristic that Risley felt conflicted with the family-oriented mission statement of Sports World (Risley, 1996).

Educates Employees Regarding Resource Limitations While Providing a Holistic View of the Organization and Interacting Subunits

Sport business managers who involve *all* employees in the budgeting process reap a variety of benefits. Individual managers or subordinates with a clear understanding of a sport business's financial status tend to have less animosity when budget monies are reduced. For example, a tennis coach is less likely to adopt a bad attitude when budgeting monies are less than expected if the coach is also able to see where expected revenues are estimated to be lower than in prior years. In addition, competition and animosity among departments or athletic areas (e.g., tennis, swimming, track) are less likely, as a good budget would convey to the individual coach that the monies were allocated equitably.

Serves as a Source of Employee Empowerment

Budgets can be initiated and developed in one of three ways: (1) "top-down," (2) "bottom-up," or (3) a combined effort between management and the employees. Top-down budget development represents a budget controlled, directed, devised, and evaluated by the key managers of a sport business entity. Bottom-up budget development represents a budget dictated to top management by employees. The combined budgeting effort represents a budget that may be initiated by top management but then reviewed by lower level managers for additional input. For example, a general manager of a large health club, intimately familiar with available resources and competitive environments, may provide initial budgetary figures based on intended company focus and overall industry knowledge. The aquatics director of the health club may then refine budgetary figures based on a more intricate knowledge of the particular industry segment: aquatics. Employee involvement benefits the sport business entity as employees become more committed to achieving forecasted revenues and keeping expenses within budgeted figures.

Infers "Good Management"

Budgeting is a basic managerial function that serves to reduce risk associated with waste, failure to remain focused, missed opportunities, and other routine setbacks. Since planning reduces risk, bank loans and other sources of credit are more easily attained if a sport business can show a creditor a comprehensive, realistic budget.

Facilitates Sport Product Pricing Decisions

Pricing strategies and decisions are influenced by a variety of factors, including the economy, competition, the strategy of the sport business, the expected consumer price threshold, and price elasticity of demand. In addition, budgeted expenses are integral to pricing so profits can be realized by a particular sport business. In other words, assume that a bowling alley plans to enhance security staff, renovate the surface of five lanes, and purchase new equipment. The bowling alley manager/owner, in order to pay off debt quicker and avoid high interest rates, may consider price increases to help cover anticipated expenses.

Additional Budget Considerations

Ensure Top Management Commitment

The support and involvement of top management remains integral to the budgeting process. Total delegation of the budgeting process sends a message of indifference to subordinates regarding the intensity with which efforts should be directed to budgeted figures.

Subdivide Budget Categories Appropriately

A budget such as the pro forma income statement can become extremely cumbersome and arduous if a sport business manager assigns an individual budget category to every expense or estimated source of revenue. For example, a sport business manager could use a budgeted line item account titled "supplies." Within this single account, the sport business manager could include items such as paper, pencils, paper clips, etc. If budgeted amounts are routinely exceeded, the sport business manager could go back and itemize each individual supply to see where the excess is occurring. However, budgets should be categorized in such a way that necessary and useful information is provided. For example, it would be erroneous for a golf club to list all generated food and beverage revenues under the line item *snack bar revenues*. Similarly, it would be erroneous for a golf club to list all generated food and beverage expenses under the line item *snack bar expenses*. Demarcation among beverages, for example, would highlight the importance of beer and alcohol sales at a particular course as well as associated expenses. Combining this information in the greater "snack bar" category would preclude a sport manager from making prudent decisions regarding those items generating the most profit and those items possibly needing to be discontinued.

Involve Employees

Budgeting was traditionally a function performed exclusively by top management. However, sport businesses and businesses in general have begun to realize the benefits of employee involvement in the budgeting process. It is not uncommon for all employees to be able to access all financial information on a company computer. Employee knowledge regarding accounting and budgetary issues provides for better educated and informed employees who possess a broad, conceptual understanding of the sport business and its resources. Further, soliciting input from employees can provide valuable insights and knowledge that management may not possess. Similarly, employee involvement is likely to ensure better commitment to the budget itself.

Allow Ample Time for the Budgeting Process

Budgeting has been referred to as the "glue" that holds an organization intact (Churchill, 1992). The budget, as explained by Churchill (1992, p. 360), "Harmonizes the enterprise's strategy with its organizational structure, its management and personnel, and the tasks that need to be done to implement strategy." Sport businesses should ensure that the budget is not performed hastily and without dedicated thought and consideration. A sport manager can facilitate the budgeting process by sending out documents including relevant historical data, competition, demographic changes, and thoughts and concerns regarding industry trends. Time should be built into the budgeting process for employees to review these documents and to supplement derived figures with their own generated research. Additional time should be allowed for managers and subordinate employees to discuss data and alter budgeted forecasts as needed.

Consider the Inclusion of a "Contingency" Account or Line Item

Businesses will often incorporate a contingency account within the larger budget. Monies within a contingency account can then be used to take advantage of opportunities or needs that develop after the budgeting is developed. For example, assume a health club would like to capitalize on the craze associated with rock climbing. Also assume that the annual budget has already been decided. It seems illogical to wait an entire year before pursuing the purchase or acquisition of a rock-climbing wall and miss out on opportunities to enhance market share, establish brand loyalty, and satisfy consumer demand. A contingency fund would provide the funds necessary to purchase the climbing wall without hindering or interrupting other program offerings.

Adopt Both an Annual and a Monthly Budget Plan

Budgets can be short term and long term in nature. Operational budgets tend to be performed in 1-year increments broken down by months or quarters. Due to the seasonal nature of sports and fluctuating demands, small sport business organizations can incur the greatest benefits via a monthly breakdown. Budget review on a quarterly or biannual basis may cause managers inadvertently to lose focus of budgetary figures and objectives. A monthly review, on the other hand, places quantified goals and objectives in front of the sport manager and/or employee on a routine basis and serves to guide more effectively daily decision making and operations. Long-term budgets (a.k.a. capital budgets), extending beyond a 1-year duration, are essential in planning for future expansions (e.g., geographic, product line), although they tend to be more flexible than the short-term operational budgets.

Use a Continuous or "Rolling" Budget

A budget that has a month or quarter "added" on is a *rolling budget*. In other words, an annual budget initially designed for July 1998 through June 1999 would extend through to July 1999 once July 1998 transpired. Similarly, the budget for August 1999 would be planned once the month of August 1998 had come and gone. In other words, sport business managers continue to budget for that 12th month on a monthly basis. In this situation, the sport business always has a 12-month plan. The budgeting process seemingly would fail to provide maximum benefits if a manager waited until June 1998 to devise a budget covering July 1998 through June 1999.

Avoid Incremental Budgeting Tactics

Incremental budgeting refers to a constant percentage at which all departments either receive increased or decreased budget monies. In other words, incremental budgeting would provide all recreational programs offered by Anywhere Parks District, U.S.A., a specified increase or decrease. The primary advantage associated with incremental budgeting is its simplicity. Sport managers practicing incremental budgeting dedicate little time toward program analysis and budget planning.

Unfortunately, three significant disadvantages are associated with incremental budgeting. First, incremental budgeting fails to distinguish between programs of merit, programs that need refinement, and programs that should be eliminated. For example, assume the popularity associated with outdoor adventure sports has significantly declined, while expenses associated with insurance, supervision, and equipment have continued to escalate. In other words, the outdoor adventure sports program offerings are far from profitable. Also assume that the popularity of the aquatic program has significantly increased, and many additional opportunities lie ahead contingent on an influx of needed monies. Incremental budgeting, regardless of demand or estimated profitability, would provide a 5% increase to *both* outdoor adventure sport programs and aquatic programs. Similarly, implementation of decremental budgeting would reduce the budget of both adventure sport programs and aquatic programs by 5%. Programs that should not be offered are continued, and viable programs in need of monies are jeopardized.

Second, incremental budgeting encourages managers to "pad" or insulate requested expenses. As explained by Viscione (1992, p. 352) in regard to decremental budgeting, "Across-the-board cuts are seldom fair, for they penalize the managers who conscientiously request the minimum necessary and they reward the managers who pad their budgets; conscientious managers quickly learn how the game is played." Falsely escalated budget requests result in inefficiency as sport business managers are required to more thoroughly scrutinize estimated expenses.

Third, incremental budgeting conveys a rather lackadaisical attitude to subordinates about management's commitment to estimated revenue generation and expense maintenance. This perceived indolence mitigates the benefits that a sport business can derive from the budgeting process (discussed above).

The opposite concept of incremental budgeting is zero-based budgeting. Zero-based budgeting requires all sport managers to defend current sport product offerings and customer demand while clearly documenting sport product needs. In other words, each year, the aerobic dance manager of a health club, for example, would be required to convince management that aerobic dance will continue to be a high-demand product generating a predicted amount of revenues and justifying a specified amount of monies for needed equipment, personnel, and so forth. Although this is an extremely time-consuming task, benefits are apparent as resources are provided only to those programs or departments that justify consumer demand or consumer potential.

Deriving Budgetary Figures

The budgetary figures used by a sport business manager can be assimilated via analysis of various data. The following suggested sources can assist a sport business manager in developing an effective and useful budget(s). The seven sources, although helpful in developing a variety of budgets (e.g., pro forma income statements, pro forma balance sheets), will be discussed in terms of the sales budget for purposes of simplicity.

Past Trends

Although it is well known that various factors influence the likelihood that history will repeat itself (e.g., weather, the economy, personnel, competition, consumer demand), historical data can still be useful as a starting point regarding budgetary planning.

Planned Promotional Campaigns

Obviously, planned promotional campaigns will influence projected expenses. However, planned promotional campaigns can also influence projected consumer demand and projected sales.

Competition

Competitive strategies and moves of the competition can greatly affect the projected sales and other financial data of a sport business. A sport business manager would be wise to engage in competitive intelligence in an effort to ascertain a competitor's planned product introductions, promotional campaigns, and other moves that would decrease or alter existing market share and competitive positioning.

The Size of a Sport Business

Small sport businesses, due to limited resources, cannot indefinitely continue to generate increased revenues without increasing prices. For example, a 25,000 sq ft health club cannot continue to increase sales without simultaneously influencing consumer congestion, satisfaction, and liability.

Changing Consumer Demographics and Psychographics

As consumer demographics and/or psychographics change, projected sales can also change. For example, it is foreseeable that sales would either decrease or increase in accordance with decreases or increases in population. Further, as consumer trends and fads change, sales may increase or decrease respectively.

Professional Associations, Trade Journals, Newspapers

Professional associations are intimately involved with the sport product. Professional sport associations, for example, routinely conduct research regarding future trends and the changing market. Professional sport trade journals report on this information on a regular basis. Further information regarding future trends can be provided by reading national newspapers (e.g., *The Wall Street Journal, USA Today*). Sport business managers also can find relevant information regarding their sport industry on the Internet.

Sport Product Suppliers and Buyers

Sport product suppliers (e.g., equipment, facilities) also keep abreast on the consumer demands, trends, and concerns. This information can be useful in predicting future consumer behavior. In addition, the consumer himself or herself can provide critical information regarding sport product likes and dislikes. This information is valuable to the sport manager attempting to develop an effective budget.

Maintaining Fiscal Accountability

Maintaining fiscal accountability is an important component of prudent fiscal and budgetary management. Fiscal accountability serves to reduce risk in the following four ways.

Monitors the Decision Making of Employees

Employee empowerment is important. However, novice employees may not have the knowledge necessary to make prudent decisions without additional input. Sport managers can adopt policies to help curb the purchase of big-dollar items without input or approval. For example, a sport business could adopt a policy requiring a cosignature by designated employees (often upper level management) on all purchases exceeding $500. Further, a bid process involving a minimum of three competitors can help ensure that a sport business is not spending more money than necessary for needed products. Communication of this policy to vendors further reduces the effect of poorly made purchases.

Limits the Number of People Who Deal with Money

A sport business can lose a portion of actual monies generated via employee theft without proper controls. For example, assume five employees are working at a concession stand at a local swimming pool. It might be tempting for a financially struggling teenager to pocket a few dollars. After all, since all five employees had easy access to the cash drawer, it would be difficult to place blame unless someone directly observed the employee pocketing the money. This risk or loss associated with this situation could be easily reduced if the pool appointed only one or two people to handle the cash. The other employees could be stationed to work drinks, hot foods, and dry foods, for example. As shifts changed, cash drawers could be counted.

Promotes Careful and Prudent Accounting and Budgetary Methods

Good accounting methods and the maintenance of appropriate accounting information informs and educates sport managers regarding the use and placement of monies, investments, and assets. Familiarity with the accounting statements provides a sport manager with the intuition and experience needed to notice unusual monetary-related deviations. Deviations can then be investigated to determine cause, and, if necessary, remedial or corrective action can be taken. Similarly, familiarity with budgets can serve to alert a sport manager to deviations that may instigate the need for further investigation.

Provides a Routine Audit

An audit of a sport business's financial documents should be performed on a routine basis by a neutral, trained individual or company. Unethical and/or incompetent employees often dictate the need for auditing. However, a sport manager should not wait until a problem emerges before implementing routine auditing practices, as auditing serves more functions than the monitoring or interception of unscrupulous acts. A formal audit serves as a valuable tool in defending taxation issues, for example. It also sends a clear message to employees that fiscal policies, responsibility, and accountability are important.

CHAPTER SUMMARY

Sport businesses cannot exist without adequate funding. This chapter identified a variety of funding alternatives available to sport business managers/owners. Careful study and analysis of various funding sources, the product, the community, the economy, and other relevant factors can enable a sport business manager/ owner to make the best decision possible in that particular circumstance. Further, funding for new ventures should be sufficient to provide the sport business with enough working capital to last 3 to 5 years while the sport business establishes brand identity and a loyal customer following and pays off high-interest–rate debt. Failure to access adequate capital results in a great deal of wasted energies and disappointment.

The budgeting process provides many benefits to the sport business manager. In particular, the budgeting process facilitates the ability of a sport business manager to make planned and prudent use of available monies. To be of use, however, budgetary figures must be carefully determined after a thorough analysis of relevant information. Last, sport business managers should insist on fiscal accountability to maintain and maximize the proper, ethical, and wise use of generated monies.

STUDENT ASSIGNMENT

1. Identify a sport business entity, and elaborate on the sources used by the sport business to provide for start-up funding requirements.
2. Interview a sport business manager regarding the budget process used. Elaborate on your findings and the information and knowledge you were able to retrieve. Questions to pursue and elaborate on should include the following:
   a. Who is responsible for the budgeting process?
   b. How often is the budget revised?
   c. Is the budget a continuous or rolling budget?
   d. Do all employees have access to budget information?
   e. Does the entity maintain a contingency budget account?
   f. Is incremental budgeting ever used? If so, when and why?
   g. Does this particular sport business manager believe in "padding" the bud213get?
   h. How are the budget figures derived?

i. What does the sport business manager you are interviewing perceive as the three most important facets associated with the budget process?
3. What types of accountability procedures does the sport business manager you interviewed in Question 2 employ? Elaborate on why the particular accountability procedure was chosen and how it is employed.

REFERENCES

America West Arena. (1991). *Skybox, (2)*3, 20.

Athletic Notes. (1993, June 9). *The Chronicle of Higher Education,* p. A30.

Baim D.V. (1985, August 19). *Comparison of privately & publicly owned sports arenas and stadiums.* Chicago: The Heartland Institute.

Baim, D.V. (1994). *The sports stadium as a municipal investment.* Westport, CT: Greenwood Press.

Brady, E., & Howlett, D. (1996, September 6). Economists, fans ask if benefits of building park outweigh costs. *USA Today,* pp. 13C–14C.

Carrol, P. (1996, April 20). More high-tech entrepreneurs turn to angels. *The Wall Street Journal,* pp. B1–B2.

Churchill, N.C. (1992). Budget choice: Planning versus control. In W.A. Sahlman & H.H. Stevenson (Eds.), *The entrepreneurial venture.* Boston: Harvard Business School Publications.

Cohen, A. (1996, October). Togetherness. *Athletic Business,* pp. 31–37.

Dicke, T.S. (1992). *Franchising in America.* Chapel Hill, NC: The University of North Carolina Press.

Downes, J., & Goodman, J.E. (1987). *Dictionary of finance and investment terms.* New York: Barron's Educational Series, Inc.

Ellis, T., & Norton, R.L. (1988). *Commercial recreation.* St. Louis, MO: Times Mirror/Mosby.

Herbert, W.B. (1991). Financing sports facilities in the nineties. *Skybox, (2)*3, 44–50.

Hiestand, M. (1996a, September 12). Seat rights. *USA Today,* p. 11C.

Hiestand, M. (1996b, September 10). Thumbs-up. *USA Today,* p. 9C.

Howard, D.R. & Crompton, J.L. (1980). *Financing, managing and marketing recreation & park resources.* Dubuque, IO: Wm. C. Brown Publishers.

Howard, D.R., & Crompton, J.L. (1995). *Financing sport.* Morgantown, WV: Fitness Information Technology, Inc.

Johnson, A.T. (1986). Economic and policy implications of hosting sports franchises. *Urban Affairs Quarterly, 21*(3), 411–433.

Joy, O.M. (1980). *Introduction to financial management.* Homewood, IL: Richard D. Irwin.

Kanamine, L. (1996a, June 11). National parks may court sponsors. *USA Today,* p. 7D.

Kanamine, L. (1996b, June 11). Squeezing extra green from public spaces. *USA Today,* p. 7D.

Lending woes stunt growth of small firms. (1994, November 16). *The Wall Street Journal,* pp. B1–B2.

Lisser, E.D. (1996, June 14). Everywhere they roam, travelers trip over taxes. *The Wall Street Journal,* pp. B1, B8.

Mays, A.L., Pino-Marina, C., Mark, M., Fitzpatrick, T., Babalolads, E., & Lister, V. (1996, September 6). The stadium binge. *USA Today,* pp. 20C–21C.

McDermott, M.J. (1993, August) Gold's upgrades requirements. *Club Industry,* pp. 30, 32–33.

Mehta, S.N. (1996a, April 21). A state "mall" in West Virginia will aid small-business development. *The Wall Street Journal,* p. B2.

Mehta, S.N. (1996b, July 2). Entrepreneurs connect with each other electronically. *The Wall Street Journal,* p. B2.

Mehta, S.N. (1996c, July 16). State lawmakers form task force to curb "incentive wars" between states. *The Wall Street Journal,* p. B2.

Michael, J. (1987, October). Tax increment financing: Local redevelopment finance after tax reform. *Government Finance Review,* pp. 17–21.

Michigan gets $7 million-plus endorsement deal with Nike. (1994, October 21). *USA Today.*

Montgomery Garrett, E. (1994, September). Up and comers: How can you tell a good deal? *Inc.,* pp. 100–105.

Patton, R.W., Grantham, W.C., Gerson, R.F., & Gettman, L.R. (1989). *Developing and managing health fitness facilities.* Chicago: Human Kinetics Books.

Perry, R. (1990, October). Site selection: Art, science or luck? *Franchising Opportunities,* pp. 38–42.

Powerhouse Gyms International, Inc. (1992). *PowerFacts* [licensee information]. Highland Park, MI: Author.

Purcell, A. (1991). The world's facility. *Skybox, 2*(3), pp. 8–11.

Recio, M.E. (1987, April 20). Build an arena now, get a team later—maybe. *Business Week,* p. 90.

Regan, T.H. (1996). Financing sport. In B.L. Parkhouse, (Ed.), *The management of sport.* St. Louis, MO: Mosby-Year Book.

Risley, P. (1996, October 30). Management principles applied to Sports World. A presentation given to a sport management class at Wichita State University.

Ronstadt, R. (1988). *Entrepreneurial finance.* Natick, MA: Lord Publishing.

Rosentraub, M.S., & Nunn, S.R. (1978). Suburban city investment in professional sports. *American Behavioral Scientist, 21*(3), 393–414.

Samuelson, P.A., & Nordhaus, W.D. (1985). *Economics.* New York: McGraw-Hill.

Schmid, S. (1996, July). Golden opportunities. *Athletic Business,* pp. 33, 34, 36.

Shubnell, L.D., Petersen, J.E., & Harris, C.B. (1985, June). The big ticket: Financing a professional sports facility. *Government Finance Review,* pp. 7–11.

Simmons, B. (1995, August). Bond for glory. *Athletic business,* pp. 37–39.

Socked for stadiums. (1996, June 28). *USA Today,* p. 12A.

Suddenly everyone wants to build a Superdome. (1983, December 5). *Business Week,* pp. 110, 112.

Tabak, L. (1995, November). Heavy lifting: How cash-strapped cities generate revenue on the backs of people just passing through. *Ambassador,* 28, 30–31.

U.S. Small Business Administration. (1990) Your business & the SBA [brochure]. Washington, DC: Author.

U.S. Small Business Administration. (1991). *Business loans & the SBA.*

Viscione, J.A. (1992). Small company budgets: Targets are key. In W.A. Sahlman & H.H. Stevenson (Eds.), *The entrepreneurial venture.* Boston: Harvard Business School Publications.

Welch, W.W. (1996, May 31). Federal taxpayers shut out of stadium payoff. *USA Today,* p. B1.

Appendix 8–A
The U.S. Small Business Administration's Business Loan Information

The U.S. Small Business Administration's (SBA) primary financial assistance activity is the bank guarantee loan program. The SBA assists small businesses by guaranteeing commercial loans made by local lenders. SBA is not in competition with commercial lenders. Each loan applicant must first contact a participating lender. The loan application must be sent to the SBA by the lender.

Loans generally can be used for equipment, fixtures, construction, leasehold improvements, inventory, debt payment, real estate, and working capital.

The following general information is provided so that you will have a better understanding of the SBA loan program. The information is general, and each loan application is reviewed individually by your bank and the SBA.

1. The SBA does not make loans: the SBA guarantees loans submitted and made by financial institutions, generally banks. The SBA does not have a grant program for starting a small business.
   - The SBA share of a guaranteed loan is limited to $750,000 (although a business may have several SBA guarantee loans). There is no maximum loan size. There is no minimum loan size.
   - The prospective borrower will be required to provide capital contributions. On new businesses, this contribution will normally be 20% to 30% of the total capitalization of the business.
   - An existing business will be required to provide financial statements showing the business is profitable, does not have delinquent taxes, and will have a satisfactory debt-to-worth ratio after the loan, or one in line with industry averages as reported by Robert Morris Associates (RMA).
   - Many confuse collateral and equity. Equity is the owner's investment or net worth in the business. Collateral is anything of value, business or personal, that may be pledged to secure the loan.

- The SBA charges the lender a one-time guaranty fee on the guaranteed portion of the loan. SBA policy allows the lender to pass this guaranty fee to the borrower.
- The SBA charges the lender a .5% annual fee on the guaranteed portion of the loan. The SBA policy does not allow the lender to pass this fee to the borrower, except through the interest rate.

2. The SBA guaranteed loan program maximum allowable "interest rates" are based on the prime rate as advertised in *The Wall Street Journal* according to the following schedule:
   - loans of less than 7 years: prime rate plus 2.25%
   - loans of 7 years or more: prime rate plus 2.75%

3. The SBA guaranteed loan maturity (length of loan) is based on the following schedule:
   - working capital loans: up to 7 years
   - fixed asset loans: up to 10 years
   - real estate and building loans: up to 25 years

Source: Reprinted from the Small Business Administration.

APPENDIX 8–B
STADIUM ARENA FACTS

Appendix 8–B Stadium Arena Facts

Stadium	Owners: State	County	City	Private	Cost ($)	Financed: Mun. bonds	Pr. invest.	Sales tax	Tax-exem. bds.	Voter-app. bds.	County bonds	Lottery	County	State	City	Seats: General	Club	Luxury	Tickets ($): General	Club/VIP	Luxury	Revenue/FYI
Anaheim Stadium Anaheim, CA, 1986			X		20m	X										70k		110	5–14		14k–27k	City & Angels split parking, conces., adver., & luxury suites revenue.
Arrowhead Pond Anaheim, CA, 1993			X		120m	X										19k	2k	84	15–150	5.5k–6.6k	69k	City & Ducks split parking, conces., adver., & luxury suites revenue.
The Ballpark in Arlington Arlington, TX, 1994			X		191m			X	X							50k		120	4–20		35k–200k	Rangers get all ticket, luxury, parking, conces., & adver., & pay city, $5.5m
Atlanta Fulton Co. Stadium Atlanta, GA, 1966			X		18.5m	X										53k	3k	30	5–25	1.8k	65k–120k	Braves owned by Ted Turner paid city $5.6m. City gets 2–3 of total.
Georgia Dome Atlanta, GA 1992	X				214m					X						72k	5.5k	183	25–41	1.8k	120k	State collects all revenue (40m) last year. Pay Falcons based on formula.
The Omni Atlanta, GA, 1972			X		17m					X						16.3k		16	10–33	1.8k	100k	TBS has lease to maintain facility. Refused to disclose information.

Facility	Marker(s)	Cost/Value	Marker(s)	Capacity	Other	Suites (#)	Price range	Premium seats	Luxury suites	Notes
Oriole Park at Camden Yards Baltimore, MD, 1992	X	205m	X X	48.2k		72	5–25		1.4k–5k	State gets 7% of ticket sales, taxes, and rent, which totaled 5 m last year.
Memorial Stadium Baltimore, MD, 1950	X	6.5m	X	65.2k			17–75			The team will keep all revenues and pay no rent, will pay gameday expenses.
Fenway Park Boston, MA, 1912	X	765k in 1912	X	34k	600	44	9–18	14k/2yrs 2 seats	NA	All income goes to Harrington (the owner of the Red Sox) and stadium.
FleetCenter Boston, MA, 1995	X	160m	X	17k–19k	2.4k	104	10–70	10k–12k	160k–250k & 40k dep.	All revenue goes to NBG Corp., a privately held subsidiary of Delaware No. Cos.
Foxboro Stadium Boston, MA, 1971	X	61m	X	61k		42	23–50		100k	Robert Kraft, owner, collects all revenues.
Marine Midland Arena Buffalo, NY, 1996	X X	122m	X X X	21k		80	10–59		55k	Sabres have rights to conces. and parking.

continues

Appendix 8–B continued

Stadium	Owners				Cost	Financed												Seating			Tickets			Revenue/FYI
	State	County	City	Private		Perm. Seat Lic.	Mun. Bonds	Pr. Invest.	Cig.&Alcoh. Tax	Tax-Exem. Bds.	Voter-App. Bds.	County Bonds	Revenue Bds.	State Bonds	County	State	City	General	Club	Luxury	General	Club/VIP	Luxury	
Rich Stadium Buffalo, NY, 1973	X				22m								X					80k		88	26–41		40k	Bills get adver., ticket, and luxury revenue. Erie Co. gets 1.4m a year from stadium.
Canadian Air. Saddledome Calagary Canada, 1983			X		176m											X	X	20k	1.5k	66	9–50	6.6k/ 5 yrs.	35–96k (Canadian)	Flames get tickets, park. conces., & adver. revenues but pay 600k in rent.
Ericsson Stadium Charlotte, NC, 1995				X	165m	X	X											73k	11k	137	19–35	3k–5.5k	40k–296k	Panthers get ticket, conces., and adver. revenue.
Charlotte Coliesum Charlotte, NC, 1988			X		52m					X								24k		12	8–170		73k–126k	City received 10.8m in gross revenue from all facility operations in 1995–1996.
Comiskey Park Chicago, IL, 1991	X				137m												X	44k	1.8k	93	4–20	NA	Up to 60k	Owner J. Reinsdorf gets all revenue, except adver. sales in excess of

Facility										Revenue arrangement
United Center Chicago, IL, 1994	X	175m	X	X 21.5k	3k	216	15–65	NA	Up to 175k	10 mil yearly. Bulls and Black-hawks get gameday revenue and split proceeds from other events.
Wrigley Field Chicago, IL, 1914	X	250k	X	38.8k		67	9–19		1.2k–2k a game	The Tribue Co. gets all revenue
Riverfront Stadium Cincinnati, OH, 1970	X	44m	X	55k–60k		20	4–14 31–43	Baseball Football	47k	Teams get tickets, adver., and con-ces., with 10% cut to local gov. City gets park.
Gund Arena Cleveland, OH, 1994	X	155m	X	X 21k		92	10–51		85k–150k	Cavaliers get revenue from vending, luxury, conces., and adver.
Jacobs Field Cleveland, OH, 1994	X	180m	X	42k	2.4k	125	6–21	2.8k	Up to 100k	Indians get most of admission & luxury revenue, & part of vending, adver., and conces.
Reunion Arena Dallas, TX, 1980	X	27m	Unidentified bonds	17.5k			5–630 14–110	Basket Hockey		Teams pay city according to formula and split park, w/ city. Keep adver. & conces.

continues

Appendix 8–B continued

Stadium	Owners: State	County	City	Private	Cost	Financed: Sales Tax Incr.	Mun. Bonds	Pr. Invest.	Meadowlands Racetrack	Tax-Exem. Bds.	Voter-App. Bds.	County Bonds	Revenue Bds.	State Bonds	County	State	City	Seating: General	Club	Luxury	Tickets: General	Club/VIP	Luxury	Revenue/FYI
Texas Stadium Dallas, TX, 1971			X		35m	Unidentified bonds												65k		380	32–46		Up to 150k	Cowboys keep revenues from stadium and pay city annual fee. Fee was 1.5m in 1995.
Mile High Stadium Denver, CO, 1948			X		1m in 1967												X	76k	71	60	20–36	200	85k	City got 6.5m last year. They got aportion of tickets, conces., adver., and parking.
Coors Field Denver, CO, 1995	X				215m	X												50k		62	1–26		105k	Rockies get conces., adver., and park., split ticket sales with city.
McNicols Arena Denver, CO, 1973			X		24m	Various gov. bonds												17k		18	9–150 10–100	Basket Hockey	105k	City got 6m last last year through ticket surcharges, conces., & park.

Facility		Cost		Capacity	Sport				Comment
Pontiac Silverdome Detroit, MI, 1975	X	48m	X	93k		102	12–45	24k–35k	City got 1m in adver. revenue and 2m in fees from Lions.
Tiger Stadium Detroit, MI, 1948	X	25m	Unidentified bonds	47k	7.3k	4	1–20	2.5k–3.5k	Tigers get all revenue from special seating and adver. City gets surcharge on tickets.
Joe Louis Arena Detroit, MI, 1979	X	34m	NA	19k		83	15–60	80k–85k	The city gets a 10% ticket surcharge, which amounted to 1.6m in 1995.
Palace at Auburn Hills Detroit, MI, 1988	X	80m	X	21.5k		180	12–45	NA	Arena Associates won't disclose revenue.
Giants Stadium East Rutherford, NJ, 1976	X	215m	X	77.7k		72	25–40	117k	Officials would not release revenue info.
Continental Airlines Arena East Rutherford, NJ, 1981	X	85m	X	20k 19k	Basket Hockey	29	18–50	140k–210k	Officials would not release revenue info.

continues

Appendix 8-B continued

Stadium	Owners				Cost	Financed												Seating			Tickets			Revenue/FYI
	State	County	City	Private		Money from Team/Organ.	Mun. Bonds	Pr. Invest.	Meadowlands Racetrack	Tax-Exem. Bds.	Voter-App. Bds.	County Bonds	Revenue Bds.	State Bonds	County	State	City	General	Club	Luxury	General	Club/VIP	Luxury	
Edmonton Coliseum Edmonton, Canada, 1974			X		57m	X												17.5k		52	15–60		Up to 125k	Oilers get virtually all revenues and pay rent to city, which represents 10% gate.
Lambeau Field Green Bay, WI, 1957			X		9.2m	X												61k	1.9k	198	28–40	85	250k	Packers get revenue from adver. and tickets, pay city 1.1m in rent, city gets conces./park.
Hartford Civic Center Hartford, CT, 1975			X		30.5m					X								14.6k	310	45	19–42	NA	33k–72k	Whalers get revenue from all events; park. & conces. are contracted out.
Astrodome Houston, TX, 1965		X			36.5m	X												54k–60k		116	4–38		Up to 57k	Astros/Oilers split adver. & tickets; Oilers get park.; conces. contracted out.

The Summit Houston, TX, 1975	X	18m	Paid with bonds	15k	X	20	11–365	70k	Rockets share adver. w/ city; conces. and park. are contracted out by city.
Market Square Arena Indianapolis, IN, 1974	X	23m	NA	16.6k		None	10–55	80–210	Pacers get all revenue but must pay co. depending on profit. So far co. got 0.
RCA Dome Indianapolis, IN, 1984	X	94.8m	NA	60.5k		99	15–32	22k–45k	Colts get ticket sales. City gets adver., park., & conces., which it contracts.
Jacksonville Municipal Jacksonville, FL, 1995	X	135m X	X	X 73k		87	15–75	Start at 45k a year	City rebuilt the 75-year-old Gator Bowl and won an NFL expansion team.
Arrowhead Stadium Kansas City, MO, 1972 (43m includes both venues)	X	43m		X	80k	80	30–41	71k	The team and co. split conces & park. Chiefs get all adver.
Kauffman Stadium Kansas City, MO, 1973	X	43m		X	41k	19	5–15	32k–44k	Team and co. split conces. & park. Royals get all adver

continues

Appendix 8–B continued

Stadium	Owners: State	County	City	Private	Cost	Financed: Money from Team/Organ.	Mun. Bonds	Pr. Invest.	Seat leases/licenses	Tax-Exem. Bds.	Tourist-tax Revenue Bonds	County Bonds	Revenue Bds.	State Bonds	County	State	City	Seating: General	Club	Luxury	Tickets: General	Club/VIP	Luxury	Revenue/FYI
Great Western Forum Los Angeles, CA, 1967				X	16m	X												17.5k 16k	Basket Hockey	NA NA	9–100 11–98		NA NA	Buss controls all revenue & does not disclose revenue information.
Sports Arena Los Angeles, CA, 1959	X	X	X		8m	X												16k		2	10–40		25k	City gets parking, taxes on tickets & con. Team/ stadium split conces. & adver.
Dodger Stadium Los Angeles, CA, 1962				X	23m	X												56k		NA	6–11	NA	NA	O'Malley gets all revenue except parking ticket, and conces. taxes, which go to city.
Pro Player Park Miami, FL, 1987				X	115m				X									75k 47.6k	Foot Base	NA	20–43 2–30		66k–180k 800-game	Revenue details were not released.
Miami Arena Miami, FL, 1988			X		53m						X						X	15.5k 14.7k	Basket Hockey	20–48 NA	NA NA	528–2k	75k–100k	Revenue details were not released.

Facility									Notes
County Stadium Milwaukee, WI, 1952	X	7.4m	X	53k		1	4–18	2,5k/game	Brewers plan to build 42k seat stadium. Miller Park (Miller Brewing Co.) will be 250m.
Bradley Center Milwaukee, WI, 1988	X	71m	X	20k		68	11–46	80–150 / 50–75k	Sports and Enter, Inc., a not-for-profit manage. co., gets conces., adver., & catering.
Hubert H. Humphrey Met. Minneapolis, MN, 1982	X	75m	X X	64k / 55k	Foot / Base	115	9–45 / 4–17	39k–78k	Conces. are split between the state sponsor Metro. Sports Co., & teams. Co. gets park.
Target Center Minneapolis, MN, 1990	X	85m	X	19k		68	10–173	50k–100k	Timberwolves get 95% of adver. signage. Gross ticket sales on all ev. was over 28m.
Molson Centre Montreal, Canada, 1996	X	230m	X	21k		135	15–105	54k–134k	Revenue details were not released.

continues

Appendix 8-B continued

Stadium	Owners: State	County	City	Private	Cost	Financed: Olympic Games	Gas/Tourist Dev. Taxes	Pr. Invest.	Hotel Tax	Tax-Exem. Bds.	Public Sources	County Bonds	Revenue Bds.	City Bonds	County	State	City	Seating: General	Club	Luxury	Tickets: General	Club/VIP	Luxury	Revenue/FYI
Olympic Stadium Montreal, Canada, 1976	X				770m	X											X	46.5k		32	7–43		40k	Would not disclose information.
Louisiana SuperDome New Orleans, LA, 1975	X				163m				X									65k		137	25–50		26k–57k	Would not disclose information.
Madison Square Garden New York City, NY, 1925				X	200m			X										19.7k	Basket	18.2k Hockey	17–115	23–100		All revenue goes to ITT, which owns the Knicks (NBA) and the Rangers (NHL).
Yankee Stadium New York City, NY, 1923			X		3.2m									X			X	57.5k		20	6–19		102k	Yankee games produced 44.7m in revenue in 1995. City received 4.5 million.
Shea Stadium New York City, NY, 1964			X		24m					Unidentified bonds								55.8k		50	6–25		NA	City gets parking parking & 10% of concessions and split special seating 50/50 w/ Mets.

Facility										Notes
Nassau Veterans' Memorial Col. New York City, NY 1972	X	31.3m	X	16.3k		32	15–80		85k–250k	Nassau Co. got got 1.8m in revenue from the arena in 1995.
Oakland-Alameda Co. Col. Oakland, CA, 1966 *25m includes both venues	X X	25m	X X	47.3k 62.5k	Base Foot	57	2–17.50 41–61	Up to 16k	34k–65k Up to 150k	Raiders and city, co. and Col. equally share conces. & park.
Oakland Coliseum Arena Oakland, CA, 1966	X X	25m	X X	15.9k			10–60			All revenue from personal seat lic., luxury suite, and club seat dep., 1.5m rent go to debt.
Orlando Arena Orlando, FL, 1989	X	100m	X	17k		26	13–200		83k	The city had 500k in net revenue in1995–96 from the Magic's use of the facility.
Corel Centre Ottawa, Canada, 1996	X	200m	X X	18.5k			24–72			Terrance Invest. keeps all revenue including 25m fee Corel software paid as sponsor.

continues

Appendix 8–B continued

Stadium	Owners	Cost	Financed	Seating General	Seating Club	Seating Luxury	Tickets General	Tickets Club/VIP	Tickets Luxury	Revenue/FYI
Veterans Stadium Philadelphia, PA, 1971	X (City)	50m	X (City)	65.8k 61.7k	Foot Base	141	23–45 5–16		75k–170k	City tax revenue included 2.3m amuse. tax, 2.3m wage tax, 500k par. tax, & 1.3m misc.
Correstates Center Philadelphia, PA, 1995	X (Private)	200m	X (Pr. Invest.); X X (State/City)	21k		126	12–54	80–160	75k–155k	Spectator, a private company, keeps all revenue.
America West Arena Phoenix, AZ, 1992	X (Private)	89m	X (City)	19k 15k	Basket Hockey	87	10–80	11k/year	60–70k	Conces./park. are split 60/40 between city & Suns. Suns get 26m over 30 yrs. from Am. W.
Sun Devil Stadium Phoenix, AZ, 1958	Arizona State U.	1m	Paid by Arizona State Univ.	73.5k		68	20–50		Up to 46k	Cardinals get all revenue but pay city 6% of the gross gate and 10% of premium seat revenue.
Three Rivers Stadium Pittsburgh, PA, 1970	X (City)	35m	X (City)	59.6k 48k	Foot Base	98	35–47 1–15		57k	City got 3.7m last year in various taxes on events. Largest 1.5m park./1.7 amus. tax.

Financed column categories: Olympic Games, Gas/Tourist Dev. Taxes, Pr. Invest., Hotel Tax, Tax-Exem. Bds., Public Sources, County Bonds, Revenue Bds., City Bonds, County, State, City

Owners column categories: State, County, City, Private

Facility			Cost			Value						Cap	Notes
Civic Arena Pittsburgh, PA, 1970	X	X	22m	X	X X	17.3k	88	74	22–50	3.6k		80k–165k	In 1995, the Arena contributed 1.7m in tax to the city of Pittsburgh.
Rose Garden Portland, OR, 1995		X	262m	X	X	21.4k	1.6k	70	NA	92–98/game		65–135k	The city gets park. receipts. Allen keeps all other revenue.
Arco Arena Sacramento, CA, 1988		X	40m	X		17.3k		30	9–145			Up to 2.5k/game	City gets sales tax of 1% of assessed val. of arena (approx. 400k). Owners get all revenue.
Trans World Dome St. Louis, MO, 1995		X	275m	X	X X	66k		120	25–45			47k–110k	Rams get all revenue from gate, conces., and luxury seating; split adver. w/ stadium 75%–25%.
Kiel Center St. Louis, MO, 1994		X	135m	X	X	18.5k	1.6k	86	30–55	Up to 3.8k		Up to 150k	Kiel Partners get conces. and adver. proceeds; luxury seat revenue is used to repay loans.

continues

Appendix 8–B continued

Stadium	Owners (State / County / City / Private)	Cost	Financed	Seating (General / Club / Luxury)	Tickets (General / Club/VIP / Luxury)	Revenue/FYI
Busch Stadium, St. Louis, MO, 1966	Private: X	22m	Gas/Tourist Dev. Taxes: X	57.6k	5–25	Gateway Partners bought the stadium from Civic Center Corp. Details were NA.
Delta Center, Salt Lake City, UT, 1991	Private: X	168m	Gas/Tourist Dev. Taxes: X	20k / / 22	9–33 / / Up to 111k/yr.	Jazz owner, Larry Miller, gets all revenue.
Alamodome, San Antonio, TX, 1993	Private: X	182m	Sales Tax Increase: X	35.3k / / 38	15–47 / 55–225 / 65k–100k	Spurs get most of game-day revenue, but pay city a portion of adver., conces., & park. as rent.
Jack Murphy Stadium, San Diego, CA, 1967	City: X	103m	Revenue Bds.: X City Bonds: X	60.8k 46.5k / Foot Base / 78	35–39 5–14 / / 32k–70k	City gets park. and splits conces. & gate with Chargers & Padres. City gets 10% of adver.
3COM Park, San Francisco, CA, 1960	City: X	56m	Pr. Invest.: X	70.2k 65k / Foot Base / 94	45 5–21 / / Up to 89k Up to 60k	Giants get all revenue but pay 200k to city/rent. City gets 4.2m from 49ers for adver., park., & luxury.

Venue		Cost			Capacity			Range	Attendance	Revenue
San Jose Arena San Jose, CA, 1993	X	162m	X		X	20k	64	18–73	Up to 125/game	San Jose Manage. Co. collects all revenue and pays city 5% of gross, plus part of park.
Kingdome Seattle, WA, 1976	X	113m	X	X		66k 59.2k	43 Foot Base	19–38 5–20	Up to 120k/yr.	Mariners get 75% of adver., & conces. & 600k from suites and ticket revenue. Seahawks got 11m total.
Key Arena Seattle, WA, 1995	X	119m	X		X	17k	58	7–100	50k–135k	City gets naming rights (15m over 15 yrs.) and park. Sonics get gate, conces, & adver.
Houlihan's Stadium Tampa, FL, 1967	X X	15m	Funding not identified			60.7k	57	23–44	Up to 92k	Bucs get all adver. revenue & split the rest with local sports authority that manages venue.
The Ice Palace Tampa, FL, 1996	X	153m X X	X			19.5k	71	12–66	65k–100k	Lightning's owner-ship group leases the arena rent-free and keeps all revenue.

continues

Appendix 8–B continued

Stadium	Owners: State	Owners: County	Owners: City	Owners: Private	Cost	Sales Tax Increase	Gas/Tourist Dev. Taxes	Pr. Invest.	Hotel Tax	Federal Grants	Luxury Seat Fees	County Bonds	Revenue Bds.	Guar. Fed. Bonds	County	State	City	Seating: General	Seating: Club	Seating: Luxury	Tickets: General	Tickets: Club/VIP	Tickets: Luxury	Revenue/FYI
Maple Leaf Gardens Toronto, Canada, 1931				X	1.5m			X										15.6k	67	16	19–65		45k–185k	Maple Leaf Gardens, which also owns the team, gets all revenue: apprx. 45m in 95.
The Sky Dome Toronto, Canada, 1989				X	570m			X			X						X	23k 51k	Basket Base	161	5–91 6–27	6k	100k–225k	The owners group splits all revenues, including 16m for luxury seat w/teams.
General Motors Palace Vancouver, Canada, 1995				X	160m			X										19.1k 18.4k	Basket Hockey	88	23–59 15–60		Up to 130k	Orca Bay gets all revenue from the arena.
Robert F. Kennedy Stadium Washington, DC, 1961	X				20m									X				57k			35–50			Stadium authority gets all park. & conces., splits adver. w/ Redskins, who get all tickets.
USAIR Arena Washington, DC, 1973				X	18m			X									X	18.1k 18.7k	Hockey Basket	77	12–45 10–40		40k–75k	Pollin collects all revenue from the arena.

Source: The capsules on the stadiums and arenas were compiled by Andrea L. Mays, Christina Pino-Marina, Mathew Mark, Tamra Fitzpatrick, Esther Babalolads, and Valerie Lister. *USA Today*, Friday, September 6, 1996. pp. 20C–21C. Chart designed by Shawn Reed.

CHAPTER 9

Site Selection

Every sport business strives to combine the elements of the marketing mix in a way that maximizes sustained market share, profitability, and customer satisfaction. Many texts address issues associated with the sport product, pricing, and promotions. Discussion and elaboration of these topics will be reserved for another course. This chapter focuses on issues associated with location or site selection decisions confronting the sport business manager operating in the service sector, as location remains one of the most important decisions a sport business manager makes (Eckert, Ryan, & Ray, 1985). Site selection, in addition to prudent strategic management, can significantly influence business success (Wilson, 1987). Mullin, Hardy, and Sutton (1993) relate site selection to market share. As stated by Mullin and colleagues (1993, p. 229),

> The choice of site will directly affect the product market; for example, 90 percent of a sport facility's customers (whether it's a court or health club, or a retail sporting goods store) can be expected to live within 20 minutes of traveling time of the facility. . . . For typical large stadium events such as a professional football game, up to 90 percent of fans typically travel less than 1 hour to the stadium.

The above quote illustrates fallacies associated with the trite statement, "If we build it, they will come." Operating a sport business in a poor location, regardless of the product quality, price, or supporting promotional mix, often fails to deliver above break-even profits.

SITE SELECTION CRITERIA FOR CONSIDERATION

Customer satisfaction extends far beyond the actual product itself. As discussed in Chapter 1, the sport industry is highly substitutable. The chosen location can

237

play an integral role in the success of any sport business venture. Fourteen site selection criteria that a sport business manager in the service sector should consider are identified below. Many site selection factors can also be identified for the sporting goods manufacturing sector or wholesale business. However, this chapter predominantly addresses site selection factors influencing the service sector. A summary of additional site selection factors are identified in Exhibit 9–1.

Visibility

Good visibility is critical for a sport business operating in a competitive environment. Good visibility can provide instant recognition and decreases required

---

Exhibit 9–1 Summary of Site Selection Considerations (Considerations and Relevance of Each Will Differ per Sport Product Offering)

1. Lot size
2. Room for expansion
3. Topography
4. Needed excavation
5. Zoning regulations
6. Visibility
7. Ingress/egress
8. Accessibility via public transportation
9. Surrounding traffic generators
10. Security
11. Weather, climate
12. Surrounding competition
13. Property taxes, costs of utilities
14. Supporting demographics, psychographics, and environmental conditions
15. Natural barriers
16. Parking
17. Growth trends, population shifts
18. Area of dominant influence (ADI), designated market area (DMA)
19. Environmental concerns
20. Incentives
21. Available work force
22. Buying power index
23. Established enterprise zones
24. Nuisance potentials
25. Hazards associated with climate (e.g., floods, hurricanes)
26. Labor costs (e.g., minimum wage rates)

advertising dollars. As explained by Kerns (1992, p. 15) and quoting Randy Marshall, the director of real estate for a sign company, "A high-visibility location allows people to get acquainted with your business long before they actually become your customers . . . . Signage is not an impulse buy . . . but if someone passes a Fastsigns store every day on his way to work, that store becomes familiar to him, and he's going to remember it when he does need a sign." A similar analogy can be made regarding a sporting goods store or a health club. A potential customer, upon seeing signage for a sporting goods store or a health club, may intuitively know where to go when he or she is in the market for a baseball bat or a health club membership.

Demographics

Demographics represent a statistical study of the population's characteristics. Demographic characteristics include age, gender, occupation, marital status, number of children, mobility, location, expenditures, education, income, one or two income earners, and race (Gray, 1995). The population referred to is defined by the potential or foreseeable target market area. It is important that the sport product be located in close proximity to those consumers with the demographic profile of either current or potential users of the sport product. For example, an upscale health club would not want to choose a site in a low-income area. Further, demographic data would be helpful in deciding whether to include child-care provisions. For example, a health club would want to include child-care provisions if locating in an area with a large number of two-income households or with a high children per household statistic.

Demographic information is typically easy to access. *Primary demographic information* can be obtained from surveys, focus groups, direct observation, or phone interviews. Advantages associated with primary data include reliability and accuracy. The main disadvantage associated with primary data is the expense. Primary data are very expensive and may be prohibitive in smaller sport businesses. *Secondary demographic data,* or information that has already been collected, exists in abundance. The *Census of Population, Simmons Market Research Bureau, Media-Mark Research, The Lifestyle Market Analysis,* and the *American Sports Analysis* are all print sources with valuable demographic information (Gray, 1995). Additional demographic information can be retrieved from professional sport associations and trade magazines, such as the *Sporting Goods Dealer, Amusement Business, Team Marketing Report, Brandweek,* and *American Demographics* (Gray, 1995). Realtors, local chambers of commerce, and city planning departments also have access to secondary demographic information. The primary advantage associated with secondary data is the ease of access. In comparison, however, secondary data may be antiquated due to rapid demographic shifts and trends.

The combined use of primary and secondary data is ideal. For example, it would be prudent for a golf course entrepreneur to exhaust secondary sources thoroughly in ascertaining the popularity of golf, city population, average income, and so forth. However, it would also be prudent for the golf course entrepreneur to probe further via consumer survey, focus groups, and/or telephone interviews, for example, how the surrounding community would feel about another golf course and, if a course is desired, what type of course (e.g., rolling hills, challenging bunkers) is preferred.

Psychographic Data

Demographic data used to be the dominant type of data collected for site selection decisions and demand forecasting. However, a sport business can still experience failure even though the demographic profile is promising. This led to the use of psychographic data, often referred to as *lifestyle data* or *lifestyle marketing*. Psychographic data move beyond statistical facts and delve into the attitudes, interests, and opinions of the consumer or targeted attitude (i.e., community receptiveness). Psychographic information includes data such as the area's political, religious, and environmental concerns. For example, entrepreneurs have concluded that regardless of supporting demographic factors, a variety of cities and towns oppose casino gambling. Similarly, Disney's America, the history theme park planned for Virginia in the early 1900s, was rebuked by those in Virginia for psychographic reasons versus demographic reasons.

As mentioned above, many communities will support new sport businesses if the particular business is viewed as a contribution to the community. In other words, communities tend to applaud businesses that provide clean, healthy fun that in turn generates needed tax dollars, provides good jobs, and so forth. It is important that the concerns of a local community be monitored and addressed prior to beginning development. Common reasons for opposition include concerns regarding environmental, social, and infrastructure problems. Andel (1993) provides some suggestions as to how the following company actions can preempt community backlash. First, become familiar with the provisions of the Clean Air and Clean Water Acts and ensure that your operation will not surpass legal requirements. Second, familiarize yourself, and comply with, storm water discharge legislation that regulates runoff water from parking lots and buildings both during and after construction. Third, plan on being a good community citizen. Although not well communicated to local citizens, Target, for example, donates 5% of all pretax income to the local communities in which it does business. Other contributions on a smaller scale can include volunteer work by the sport business managers and employees. Fourth, *listen* to community concerns. Arrogance breeds resentment, whereas a diplomatic, cooperative effort can bode community acceptance and loyalty.

Environmental Data Analysis

The *environmental analysis* refers to a study of those "forces outside an organization," including technology, government, economics, and history (Aaker, 1995, p. 27). Each of the above are described in regard to site selection considerations.

Technology

Infomercials and the ability to purchase consumer sporting goods on the computer may decrease the importance of site selection or site selection considerations, such as visibility or ease of access.

Government

State legislation may alter, for example, ticket distribution practices. Similarly, local ordinances may prohibit certain types of sporting venues from locating in certain places. Local court precedent regarding eminent domain laws may be another consideration regarding site selection considerations.

Economics

High interest rates may delay the entry into a particular sport business industry. Similarly, recessions and depressions may delay the entrance into a particular sport business due to low consumer discretionary income.

History

Many cities have excellent demographics to support a particular sport business. However, a look at the history associated with a particular sport industry often provides valuable information regarding the viability of a business and related success. For example, the city of Louisville has been the home of a number of professional team sports, including the Louisville Cats, the Shooters, and the Thunder—all of which later ceased operations. One should consider the reasons for operation cessation before introducing another professional sport franchise to the Louisville area. Similarly, EuroDisney's inattention to the prior failures of three amusement parks located in France may have contributed to its difficulty in its inaugural years.

Environmental, or external, conditions are important to a sport business manager. A sport business manager should consider how the environment and external surroundings affect(ed) a sport industry segment yesterday (i.e., the past), today, and tomorrow (i.e., the future) before committing to a particular site.

Ingress/Egress

Consumers' decisions to purchase a particular sport product is influenced by a number of factors, including convenience. For example, consumers forced to cross four lanes of death-defying traffic on a regular basis, regardless of time of day, may find a competitor's product and location more attractive. Site selection considerations should include current and future routes of ingress and egress to maximize customer satisfaction. Communication with city or county officials regarding proposed infrastructure development can prove valuable. In addition, sport businesses employing a large number of minimum wage workers or targeting an impoverished constituency may find worker selection and availability better if locating in an area accessed by public transportation.

Infrastructure

Closely related to the concept of ingress/egress is the concern regarding infrastructure. *Infrastructure* refers to interstate availability, road conditions, public transportation, lodging availability, and airport accommodations. For example, the infrastructure is of major concern to major league sport franchises or large amusement parks. Major league franchises will not likely be granted to cities where the potential patrons are expected to drive 2 hours on bad roads in order to get to a particular sport stadium or arena. Further, major league franchises are not likely to be granted to cities where airports and lodging are inadequate to meet the needs of traveling spectators, teams, and officials.

Parking

Parking creates both direct and indirect costs for patrons. First, tangible parking fees often add to already high ticket prices. Second, parking represents intangible costs associated with time spent waiting, walking, and vying for position among massive traffic congestion. As mentioned earlier, the sport business entrepreneur is attempting to provide the best product at the best price via the best promotions in the best location. Inadequate parking or parking that generates an excessive amount of tangible and intangible costs fails to maximize consumer satisfaction and customer loyalty. Signage, security, and efficient traffic flow are critical elements of a parking plan.

Proximity to Surrounding Businesses, Traffic Generators

As mentioned above, customers prefer a convenient location. It would be much easier for a patron to go to the gym, stop off at a grocery, and pick up the dry cleaning all in one trip. Similarly, miniature golf courses, bowling alleys, and roller-skating rinks may gain the acceptance of a business community due to the extended benefits accruing for surrounding restaurants and shopping centers. Surrounding businesses are often referred to as *traffic generators*. Common traffic generators include hospitals, universities, shopping malls, and shopping centers. Regarding sport products delivered through larger sporting arenas and stadiums, proximity to surrounding businesses is integral to generating community acceptance. For example, Sedwick County built a coliseum with a seating capacity for 15,000 to 20,000 people 12 miles outside of the closest city's hub of activity (e.g., restaurants, hotels). As Randy Brown explained in an editorial (1996, p. 9A),

> It's impossible to calculate the damage the Coliseum's unfortunate location has done to this community by sucking life out of its heart. The Wichita Thunder [professional soccer franchise] should be playing downtown. It is not. The Wichita Wings [professional hockey franchise] should be playing downtown. They are not. Other big indoor sports events should be downtown. They are not. Major concerts should be downtown. They are not. The Coliseum's location has stunted downtown growth while adding little to the economy elsewhere. Hotels, restaurants and other businesses that would have been attracted to a downtown arena have never been built. . . . Because of its location, the Coliseum is strictly a destination point. When people go to a Coliseum event, they don't also stroll by the river or go shopping or have dinner at a nearby bistro. People drive out, go to the event, drive home.

A facility location can be a great impact to the local community. Prudent site selection can maximize this impact while providing the patron with a "full-course" entertainment outing.

Incentives

Incentives play a very big role in site selection decisions of large sport businesses. As explained by Bergsman (1993, p. 158), "The majority of cities and states still view incentives as essential to their efforts to attract and retain industry, feeling they are at a disadvantage without a full complement of incentives . . . . Many communities may question the bottom-line effectiveness of incentives, yet companies big and small expect and demand them." Bergsman's article also refers to a comment made by a partner of the largest site selection company in the world. As stated by James Schriner, a partner of PHH Fantus Consulting, "We do 200 to 300 projects a year and in each and every case the incentives are a very important issue because they help to minimize costs" (Bergsman, 1993, p. 160). Public subsidies and incentives provided to lure professional franchises to a particular city are both frequent and substantial (Baim, 1994; Euchner, 1993). However, as noted in Chapter 8, "Funding and Budgeting for the Sport Business," the future of incentive provisions may be in jeopardy as efforts are made by committees (e.g., the Midwestern Legislative Conference) to reduce economic-development incentives (Mehta, 1996, p. B2).

Zoning Ordinances and Other Regulatory Influences

Zoning laws, including signage, type of building, height limitations, and permitted usage, can have a big impact on business operations. Further, bonding requirements may be imposed on one city or state and absent in another. Environmental legislation has also imposed additional costs on business entrepreneurs. As revealed in a 1990 survey conducted by *Site Selection* magazine (Lyne, 1990, p. 1,134),

> Over 72 percent of responding executives say that "the growing 'green movement' has affected their company's facility-location decisions" by "increasing the cost of new facilities." Another 54 percent say that building "some new facilities has taken longer" as a result. And another 10 percent say that "tough environmental regulations" have prompted their firms to pull existing operations altogether out of some areas.

Sport business managers should be sure to investigate and address all requirements at the onset as it would be illogical to invest millions of dollars into a facility only to find out 4 months later that the Environmental Protection Agency (EPA) law requires you to spend another $10 million for environmental clean-up purposes. Further, zoning ordinance changes and environmental regulations can often delay the onset of a particular sport business facility. Sport business managers will be better able to adhere to drafted time tables if the time necessitated to comply with mandated regulations is allotted.

Taxation Issues

Property taxes and service taxes are among the primary concerns regarding site selection. Sport business entrepreneurs with two equally viable sites can lower costs by choosing the site with lower taxes. Gerald Cain, a vice president for a corporate real estate company, estimates that a state's tax structure can add 10% to 15% to business costs (Lyne, 1990). States perceived as being "business friendly" impose fewer tax burdens on local businesses. Again, sport business entrepreneurs who are mobile may choose to investigate differences among a state's tax structure before committing to any particular site.

Additional site selection considerations that are self-explanatory and need no further elaboration are listed in Exhibit 9–1. Development in an enterprise zone and lease considerations are discussed below.

Development in an Enterprise Zone

Most major cities have legislation regarding a defined enterprise zone creating a "win-win" situation for the local economy, local residents, and the business itself. For example, developing in Louisville's enterprise zone offers site selection benefits including Kentucky sales tax exemption for the following (Louisville/Jefferson County Office for Economic Development, 1994; Appendix 9–1),

- purchases of new and used equipment and machinery, including office equipment, furniture, and fixtures
- motor vehicles for business use, excluding leased vehicles, noncommercial, limited to $20,000
- building materials for remodeling, rehabilitation, or new construction within the zone area
- corporate income tax credit allowed for hiring unemployed or individuals on public assistance for 90 days or more

The Louisville/Jefferson County Office for Economic Development (1994) also provides, depending on location, the following:

- a 5-year moratorium on increased property tax assessment of rehabilitated commercial and residential structures 25 years or older
- a waiver on permit fees for both new construction and additions to existing structures within the enterprise zone
- a 50% reduction in permit fees for restoration or renovation of existing structures where a permit is necessary. Buildings 25 years or older are eligible to receive a 5-year tax reassessment moratorium
- a 50% reduction on electrical, heating, and mechanical refrigeration permits on new construction, additions, and all interior renovations
- a waiver on wrecking permit fees for general contractors who use licensed subcontractors and can ensure compliance on all standards
- no fee on required certificates of occupancy
- a waiver of sign permit fees on new structures

The local communities within an enterprise zone benefit via job development, tax contributions, and an improved quality of life. Sport businesses wishing to establish programs designed to keep teens off the streets by providing viable recreational opportunities may find location in an enterprise zone to be a prudent, community-oriented business decision. Local chambers of commerce can provide additional information regarding established enterprise zones.

Topography and/or Excavation

The conditions of the land can directly influence the desirability of a particular site. For example, a golf course may seek land that has rolling hills, an abundance of trees, and flowing rivers. On the other hand, another sport business needing to excavate a large area may find the above rolling hills, trees, and water a cost deterrent.

Surrounding Businesses, Residential Areas

Surrounding businesses can influence the success of a sport business. For example, it would be illogical for a soccer facility hosting a plethora of programs for young kids to locate next to a firing range. Similarly, it would be poor judgment for a sport park (e.g., go-karts, batting cages) or other youth-oriented sport facility to locate next to a liquor sport. The proximity of residential areas also should play a role in the site selection of a sport business. Lawsuits and bad publicity can easily emanate if a ballpark, for example, has lights shining into neighboring homes during the late-evening hours. Similar problems associated with noise and trash can upset individuals in the surrounding residential areas.

THE LEASE AGREEMENT

The lease agreement is another related facet of site selection that directly influences the success and ease in which a sport business operates. Sport business managers should rarely sign a lease agreement without negotiation. As explained by Eckert et al. (1985, p. 118), "Language is malleable and is meant to be changed." Sport business managers may wish to consider the inclusion of the following 10 clauses for reasons addressed below (Eckert et al., 1985).

Escape Clauses

Escape clauses can be valuable when a sport business manager is discouraged by the lack of cleanliness of the building, surrounding vacancies, and so forth. As stated by Eckert and colleagues (1985, p. 137), a simple clause reading, "If three or more vacancies occur in the center, tenant can terminate lease" can prove beneficial for a frustrated tenant.

Option To Renew

Options to renew are important in maintaining established customer loyalty. Current customers may be tempted to patronize another establishment if your product is rather homogeneous and relocates to a less convenient location.

Transferring Your Lease; Assignment Rights

Assignment rights allow sport business managers the opportunity to sublet a facility if so desired. The inclusion of this clause at the outset of the lease provides flexibility while reducing paperwork and expense required to renegotiate the lease at a later point in time.

Cost of Living Cap

Many leases increase rates on a yearly basis in accordance with the cost of living or local rate of inflation. Prudent sport managers can protect against undesirable rent increases by stating at the outset what the maximum increase (percentage or dollar amount) can be in any given year. Eckert and colleagues (1985) suggest lessees to cap the rent increase at half the amount of the Consumer Price Index (CPI).

Percentage Lease

Consider negotiating a lease payment based on a percentage of net sales. (Negotiation based on net sales would be much more beneficial to the lessee than negotiation based on gross sales.) The advantage of a percentage lease is that rent is paid only if, and when, the tenant generates monies after expenses have been paid. On the other hand, if a tenant is very successful, that success must also be shared with the landlord. Percentage lease agreements may be most beneficial to new entrepreneurs lacking capital needed to cover start-up expenses (e.g., lease payments). Sport business managers could also cap the percentage lease at a certain amount so that the amount owed to a landlord would be capped even though the tenant's net revenues continued to escalate.

Start-up Buffers

A start-up buffer is another common facet of a lease agreement. A *start-up buffer* refers to a 3- to 6-month period in which the landlord will lease space on a "free" basis. In exchange, landlords typically like the tenant to sign an extended, long-term contract. This creates a "win-win" situation for both the landlord and the tenant.

The landlord benefits as he or she is not required to renegotiate that lease or attempt to find another lessee for a fixed time period. The tenant benefits as cash that would have gone to rent payments can be redirected to advertising, service improvements, inventory acquisition, equipment upgrades, or hiring of additional personnel.

Maintenance, Improvements of Common Areas, Leased Areas

Common areas refer to parking areas, sidewalks, entry foyers, and the like that are shared by multiple tenants. The appearance of the common areas is important in generating first-time positive impressions, maintaining customer satisfaction, and reducing risk. It should be clearly understood by both parties who is responsible for maintenance and improvements to the common areas and leased facilities. Detailed information regarding who pays for these improvements and who has responsibility for contacting the service people and ensuring performance is imperative. In addition, similar to a service agreement negotiated for equipment, a clause stating how long the improvement will take from the date of the notification can benefit a sport business lessee. For example, a sport business leasing space for Karate Instruction, Inc., will want to know that if the air conditioning goes out, it will be fixed within a reasonable time period.

Restrictive Covenants

Restrictive covenants identify a list of things the landlord cannot do. For example, a lessee of a larger building may want a restrictive covenant prohibiting the landlord from renting nearby space to a competitor.

Exit Clauses

Pacelle (1994) urges tenants to read exit clauses cautiously. As explained by Pacelle (1994, p. B1), "When tenants sign leases, real-estate lawyers say, too few pay adequate attention to 'exit clauses,' which often contain vaguely worded requirements that space be returned to its 'original condition.'" This can be a very costly undertaking, as surfaces must be torn up and replaced, atriums may need to be removed, and staircases eliminated.

Start Date for Lease Payments

Prudent landlords include in the lease the date on which payments are to begin. Close scrutinization of this date by the potential sport business lessee is important. For example, a landlord may include in the lease agreement that payments are to begin upon the date that the lessee signs the contract. This can significantly deplete the resources of the sport business manager who had not planned to move in or begin business for another 6 months. In this situation, it would be better for the sport business to demand that payments begin at the time in which the sport business occupies the particular leased premises.

The Percentage Received from Parking, Concessions, or Merchandise

Revenue generated from parking, concessions, or merchandise can be a great asset to a professional or minor league team. Sport franchise managers would be prudent to ascertain what percentage of the revenues other teams receive for these items before signing on the dotted line.

Other Contract Inclusions

Other contract considerations and/or inclusions would include language regarding the following:

- the lessee's use of the leased premises (i.e., purpose for leasing)
- the utilities that must be paid
- signage stipulations, approvals required, etc.
- required continuous operations
- payment of taxes and insurance, paid monthly versus paid annually
- agreement to abide and operate in accordance with all federal and local laws, ordinances, etc.
- ability to alter premises clause
- indemnification clause
- insurance specifications (coverage requirements and type of coverage required, such as dram shop coverage)
- notice of claim or suit clause
- assignment and subletting rights
- default and reentry rights
- control over common areas
- landlord's right of entry
- communication stipulating the nonformation of a partnership between landlord and tenant
- perceived ability to maintain a positive working relationship with landlord/tenant.

CHAPTER SUMMARY

Site selection is critical to the success of a sport business, especially in the service sector. Product substitutability, buyer power, and competition, for example, mandate that sport business entrepreneurs approach the site selection process with great prudence. The sport business manager should identify those site selection criteria that are directly related to success, and then pick the best possible site in accordance to the stipulated criteria. Valuable information and knowledge pertaining to site selection can be gained from the consumer, professional associations, and competitive intelligence. The benefits associated with development in an enterprise zone should not be overlooked nor should the lease agreement itself. As mentioned earlier, a great sport product offered at a great price is of little value to the consumer if the location of the product itself is undesirable.

STUDENT ASSIGNMENT

1. Identify a hypothetical sport business entity, and find two sites deemed most appropriate within your local area. Elaborate on why you chose the two sites.
2. Ascertain through a thorough analysis which of the two chosen sites is *best* suited for your particular (hypothetical) sport business.
3. Contact the Chamber of Commerce in your local area, and inquire about information regarding an enterprise zone (have this information mailed to you).
   a. Identify those incentives given to the entrepreneur willing and able to locate in the designated enterprise zone.
   b. What type of sport business entity (e.g., retail store, health club, gymnasium) do you feel would be appropriate (and successful) in the enterprise zone?
   c. Complete the sample site evaluation worksheet for a sport business (Appendix 9-B).
4. Interview a sport business manager and elaborate on his or her concerns and strategies regarding his or her own lease agreement.
5. Write a lease agreement for a hypothetical sport business.

Attach any additional data or information gathered that allowed you to draw your conclusions.

REFERENCES

Aaker, D.A. (1995). *Strategic market management.* New York: Wiley.

Andel, T. (1993). How to avoid rough landings. *Transportation and Distribution, 34,* 30–35.

Baim, D.V. (1994). *The sports stadium as a municipal investment.* Westport, CT: Greenwood Press.

Bergsman, S. (1993, October). Incentives, location, quality of life: All figure into the site selection equation. *National Real Estate Investor,* pp. 158, 160, 177–178.

Brown, R. (1996, May 18). Yes, if you build it . . . . *The Wichita Eagle,* p. 9A.

Eckert, L.A., Ryan, J.D., & Ray, R.J. (1985). *An entrepreneur's plan.* Orlando, FL: Harcourt Brace Jovanovich.

Euchner, C.C. (1993). *Playing the field: Why sports teams move and cities fight to keep them.* Baltimore, MD: The Johns Hopkins Press.

Gray, D. (1995). Sport marketing: A strategic approach. In Parkhouse, B.L. (Ed.), *The management of sport: Its foundation and application* (2nd ed.). St. Louis, MO: Mosby.

Kerns, C. (1992, July/August). Making the right impression. *Franchising World,* pp. 15–16.

Louisville/Jefferson County Office for Economic Development. (1994). The Enterprise Zone [Brochure]. Louisville, KY: Author.

Lyne, J. (1990, October). Service taxes, international site selection and the "green" movement dominate executives' political focus. *Site Selection,* pp. 1,134–1,138.

Mehta, S.N. (1996, July 16). State lawmakers form task force to curb "incentive wars" between states. *The Wall Street Journal,* p. B2.

Mullin, B.J., Hardy, S., & Sutton, W.A. (1993). *Sport marketing.* Champaign, IL: Human Kinetics.

Parcelle, M. (1994, July 25). Moves are often disrupted by "exit clauses" in leases. *The Wall Street Journal,* pp. B1, B3.

Schroeder, R.G. (1993). *Operations management.* New York: McGraw-Hill.

Wilson, R.C. (1987, October). Exploring the corporate site selection framework. *Industrial Development,* pp. 15–19.

APPENDIX 9–A
THE ENTERPRISE ZONE: LOUISVILLE/JEFFERSON CO. OFFICE FOR ECONOMIC DEVELOPMENT

OVER ONE BILLION DOLLARS IN CAPITAL INVESTMENT

The Louisville/Jefferson County Enterprise Zone, established to revitalize the area's industrial base and create jobs for its residents, offers special state and local tax incentives and regulatory relief to new and expanding businesses located within its boundaries. Established and administered by the Louisville/Jefferson County Office for Economic Development (OED), the Enterprise Zone consists of some of the most centrally located, prime industrial sites in the United States. The Enterprise Zone is certified through 2003 by the Kentucky Enterprise Zone Authority.

Numerous financial incentives, government services, and benefits are available to certified businesses in the enterprise zone. OED works directly with any business seeking enterprise zone certification, whether it is interested in locating in the zone or is already there.

FINANCIAL INCENTIVES

Certified companies in the Louisville Enterprise Zone receive exemption from the Commonwealth of Kentucky sales tax for the following:

- Purchases of new and used equipment and machinery, including office equipment, furniture, and fixtures.
- Motor vehicles for business use, excluding leased vehicles, noncommercial, limited to $20,000.
- Building materials for remodeling, rehabilitation, or new construction within the zone area. This exemption applies to all certified and noncertified businesses and residences.

- Corporate income tax credit allowed for hiring unemployed or individuals on public assistance for 90 days or more.

The following incentives are also available, depending upon company location:

- A 5-year moratorium on increased property tax assessment of rehabilitated commercial and residential structures 25 years or older (available to all companies located in Jefferson County).
- Within the city's portion of the zone, 5-year tax exemptions for new manufacturing establishments from city ad valorem taxes. This exemption applies to both new manufacturing establishments and for new product manufacturing by an existing company.

The following building permit incentives are available to certified businesses. Each incentive remains in effect for the duration of the enterprise zone program:

- A waiver on permit fees for both new construction and additions to existing structures in the enterprise zone. A building permit will be required to ensure Kentucky Building Code standards are met; however, no fee will be charged.
- A 50% reduction in permit fees for restoration or renovation of existing structures where a permit is necessary. Buildings 25 years old or older are eligible to receive a 5-year tax reassessment moratorium. The required $20 application fee for a tax reassessment moratorium will be waived to certified businesses or residences. The remaining $20 fee will be charged by the Property Valuation Administrator.
- A 50% reduction on electrical, heating, and mechanical refrigeration permits on new construction, additions, and all interior renovations.
- A waiver on wrecking permit fees for general contractors who use licensed subcontractors and can ensure compliance on all standards, i.e. utility cutoffs, barricades, debris removal, and timely completion of projects.
- No fee on required certificates of occupancy. Temporary occupancy certificates may be issued in special cases.
- A waiver of sign permit fees on new structures. A sign permit will be required to ensure standards are met under state and local building codes and ordinances. A 3-year inspection and fee for same will apply.

CERTIFICATION

In order to receive the complete benefits of the Enterprise Zone, businesses must be certified.

Requirements:

- The business must be located within the boundaries of the Enterprise Zone.
- At least 50% of the company's employees must perform their job duties within the zone.
- "New-to-the-zone" companies locating within the zone since its designation on May 31, 1983 must draw at least 25% of their work forces from:
  –residents of the zone,
  –individuals unemployed for 90 days or more,
  –individuals receiving public assistance benefits for 90 days or more, or
  –a combination of the above.
- "Existing" companies located and conducting business in the enterprise zone prior to its designation can be certified for new activity by making capital investments of at least 20% on net fixed assets (land, buildings, machinery, equipment, or lease hold improvements), or by increasing total number of employees by at least 20% (25% of the employees must come from the targeted work force). New activity must be completed within 18 months of the application rate.
- Subsidiaries or franchises of a new or existing business may be certified if their new site is within the zone and they maintain separate bookkeeping for business activity conducted within the zone.

APPENDIX 9–B
SAMPLE SITE EVALUATION WORKSHEET
FOR A SPORT BUSINESS

Address of Site A: _____

Address of Site B: _____

	SITE A			SITE B		
	Rank+	Weight*	Score	Rank+	Weight*	Score
Cost _____	___	___	___	___	___	___
Acreage (including room for expansion)_____	___	___	___	___	___	___
Property and/or Service Taxes_____	___	___	___	___	___	___
Necessary Excavation _____	___	___	___	___	___	___

Demographics (may want to examine data from past 5 years to establish or recognize trends or patterns)

	Rank+	Weight*	Score	Rank+	Weight*	Score
A. Population: _____	___	___	___	___	___	___
B. Average Age: _____	___	___	___	___	___	___
C. # of Households: _____	___	___	___	___	___	___
D. Avg. HH Income: _____	___	___	___	___	___	___
E. #HH Income over $ _____ :	___	___	___	___	___	___
F. Education (% over 18 w/HS ed. or more:) _____	___	___	___	___	___	___
Visibility_____	___	___	___	___	___	___
Zoning Restrictions, Limitations_____	___	___	___	___	___	___

Other Governmental and/or statutory issues (e.g. tort reform, bond requirements)

	Rank+	Weight*	Score	Rank+	Weight*	Score
_____	___	___	___	___	___	___
_____						
Surronding Competitors_____	___	___	___	___	___	___
Parking Availability_____	___	___	___	___	___	___
Access: Ingress/Egress _____	___	___	___	___	___	___
Traffic Generators_____	___	___	___	___	___	___
TOTALS	___	___	___	___	___	___
		Must =1.0	Low Score = Best Site		Must =1.0	Low Score = Best Site

* Weight - The importance of that particular factor to the success of the facility (weight remains same for each facility).
+ Rank - The rating - 1 = Best Conditions   4 = Worst Conditions
*** Your site evaluation worksheet may contain different or additional factors than those listed here (use your best judgment).

CHAPTER 10

Risk Management

The concept of *risk management* represents proactive efforts taken by a sport business to prevent loss. The term *loss* encompasses all potential losses including financial loss (e.g., lawsuit damage claims, attorney fees, equipment/property damage), entity goodwill (e.g., National Collegiate Athletic Association [NCAA] sanctions, customer complaints), and loss of market share and declining revenues. Risk management, although practiced by the nonsport industry for decades, became an increasingly essential requirement and directly related to the solvency and success of any sport business in the last two decades (van der Smissen, 1990). Risk management has recently become an integral facet of sport business management for three primary reasons. First, the recognition of governmental immunity as a viable defense has diminished over the last four decades (van der Smissen, 1990). Consequently, public entities, fraught with limited funds, became more exposed to litigation. Risk management serves as a viable way to retain costs and better manage product quality. Second, sport-related litigation continues to escalate. As reported in the *Sporting Goods Dealer,* an early survey of Sporting Goods Manufacturing Association (SGMA) members revealed that 78% had been involved in litigation (Goldman, 1976). Actual and potential litigation caused many in the sport industry to drop specific activities or products (e.g., diving boards, trampolines, skating on public ponds) or risk bankruptcy (Miller & Fielding, 1995). The plethora of sport-related litigation will continue to influence sport business into the next millennium. Third, insurance coverage became prohibitive for many sport businesses. A study by the American Law Institute (ALI) revealed a 44% increase in liability insurance costs between 1950 and 1980 (Miller & Fielding, 1995). Florio (1983) reported that some product sellers experienced premium increases of 300%, while others were unable to secure coverage at any price. Government entities, including park and recreation departments and public educational institutions, encountered extreme insurance premiums between 1980 and

1985. A report by the Department of Justice indicated a 141% increase in claims against municipalities during the early 1980s (Priest, 1987). Discussion with local sport business managers reveal that insurance concerns are still abundant (Miller, 1996).

A comprehensive risk management plan includes the following:

- administrative issues
- the identification of risks
- approaches to managing identified risks
- a continual evaluation and review of risk management practices.

The remainder of this chapter will discuss these facets of the risk management plan.

ADMINISTRATIVE ISSUES

Top Management Support

Similar to other areas of management (e.g., discrimination, quality control), the success of a risk management plan depends on top management support (McIlvaine, 1996). Top management must do more than pay lip service to risk management. In fact, it is clearly in top management's behalf to have a strong risk management plan in operation. However, the benefits associated with risk reduction are not free. Management must be willing to sacrifice daily work time for committee meetings, record maintenance, and other implementation and evaluation necessities. From a budgeting perspective, a sport manager can plan on risk management expenses approximating 5% of all operating costs (van der Smissen, 1990).

The Risk Management Committee

A risk management committee is essential to optimal risk management operations. Although support from top management remains essential to creating a culture of risk management, input from all sport business stakeholders provides a comprehensive, ongoing ability to identify and better manage risks. *Front-line employees,* for example, interact with consumers on a daily basis. They listen to complaints and concerns of patrons while often observing potential hazards waiting to happen. Front-line employees, due to their experiences, exposures, and interactions, are able to identify a number of risks that top management may overlook. *Current members or patrons* of a particular sport business also view risk and potential hazards from a different, yet important, perspective. Inclusion of a loyal patron familiar with your site and its operations provides valuable insight to risk reduction efforts. In addition, *maintenance personnel* provide valuable knowledge regarding potential losses associated with fire, security, chemical storage, and equipment upkeep. Other members of a risk management committee might include an *accountant and/or banker* familiar with financial management, the *architect*, a member of the *legal profession,* a member of the *insurance industry*, and a *fire officer or police officer.* Naturally, a member of *top management* must be represented as well.

Policy-related Issues

Established policies documented in internal documents are a starting point for proactive risk reduction. Key organizational policies for a health club, for example, might include the following four elements.

Risk Management Policy Statement

The policy statement would communicate to the reader that the particular sport business has a risk management plan and is devoted to reducing risks, enhancing product quality, and maximizing customer satisfaction. This policy statement can be communicated to stakeholders in a number of different ways. Similar to the mission statement, the risk management policy statement can be communicated to stakeholders via, for example, the policy manual, operations manual, newsletter, signage, and/or in monthly meetings.

Designated Risk Management Liaison

The risk management liaison should be a member of management serving on the risk management committee. The roles and responsibilities of this person include the continual review of the risk management plan; the updating of all relevant materials; and service as the individual who media, consumers, employees, and other stakeholders contact regarding risk management inquiries, concerns, and issues. Although risk management is the responsibility of every employee, as van der Smissen states (1990, p. 15), "Everybody's responsibility is no one's responsibility!" In other words, one person should be given the positional authority and related responsibility to ensure that the adoption and practice of the risk management plan remains a vital part of the sport business operation.

Policies Regarding Required Employee Credentials

The American College of Sports Medicine (ACSM) suggests that all health club employees, for example, maintain current first aid and cardiopulmonary resuscitation (CPR) certifications (Sol & Foster, 1992). Similarly, people teaching aerobic dance or serving as physical trainers should have proper industry credentials (*Leno v. YMCA*, 1971). Required credentials need to be reflected in current job descriptions and job analyses. All sport businesses, regardless of the sport industry segment, should ensure that employee credentials remain in accordance with industry standards and expectations, as knowledgeable and competent employees reduce the risk of loss.

Policies Regarding What Services Will Be Performed In-house and What Will Be Outsourced

A standardized policy can prevent novices from tinkering in areas in which they are not qualified. In *Massie v. Persson* (1987), a football coach modified a one-person whirlpool to accommodate more than one student at a time. A student-athlete was later electrocuted while using the whirlpool bath at the school. This tragedy would likely have been avoided if the school had a strong policy regarding who is allowed to perform, for example, electrical work on school equipment. The use of qualified independent contractors is an effective way for sport business managers to better ensure quality work while simultaneously reducing loss.

Establishment of a Risk Management Culture

Risk management is the responsibility of every employee regardless of rank within the particular sport business. The spirit of risk management should permeate every facet of the organization. A risk management culture can be established in a number of ways. Three ways a sport business manager can foster a culture of risk management are identified below.

First, employee empowerment is important to maximizing risk management efforts. Employees should be given the latitude to minimize risks or block off exposures from consumers if deemed appropriate. An illustration of a failure to empower employees highlights potential problems. For example, assume an employee of Fit-Ex Health Club sees a cable that is about to break. The employee, due to lack of empowerment, cannot work on any equipment or make a decision as to when an "out-of-order" sign should be placed on a piece of equipment. In accordance with established policies, this employee fills out a work order, places the work order in the appropriate box, and waits for maintenance to receive the work order and fix the equipment. In the meantime, a patron is injured when the cable breaks and the weight comes crashing to the floor. Obviously, the risk management system would have been much more efficient if the Fit-Ex employee had been empowered to take action.

Second, weekly or daily training sessions, documented and signed by employees in attendance, can indoctrinate risk management concepts into employees. Frequent training sessions, even if only brief, send a clear message to employees (and the courts) that the sport entity views risk management seriously. Additional risk management techniques used to create and maintain a risk-alert culture include printing risk reduction "tips" on paycheck stubs and devoting a portion of the sport business newsletter to risk reduction.

Third, the development of a risk management culture can be facilitated by leadership or "management by example." A concern for a facility's cleanliness and the safety and satisfaction of patrons and employees is contagious. As explained by an Anheuser-Busch employee regarding the company's management practices (McIlvaine, 1996), "Our plant manager has demonstrated a commitment to safety by being highly visible . . . . Seeing him reminds employees about the importance of safety and the need for them to take responsibility for it" (p. 29). If employees see managers and supervisors picking up trash, for example, they, too, will be more inclined to pick up trash. Problems emanate, and risks escalate, when the employee attitude is one of, "that is not my job!"

IDENTIFICATION OF RISKS

Every sport business contains risks. Risks can be identified in a number of ways (Exhibit 10–1). Each member of the risk management committee can contribute to the identification of risks associated with the particular sport business. "Customer complaint" boxes also serve as good sources of potential risks. In addition, outside sources are available to sport businesses often on a gratuitous basis. For example, The Occupational Safety and Health Administration (OSHA) provides consultation programs for employers on request. Similarly, valuable information can be gained from police officers, firefighters, and environmental consultants. Risks within the community or rampant among competitors' establishments also require the attention of prudent sport managers. Newspapers, visits to competitors' establishments, dialogue at professional meetings, trade magazines, and so forth

---

Exhibit 10–1 Identification of Risks: Suggestions for Sport Managers

1. communication with employees and current consumers
2. communication with, and observation of, a competitor's business
3. communication with local professionals (e.g., firefighters, police officers, OSHA consultants)
4. reading of the local newspapers, trade magazines, professional journals
5. attendance at professional meetings, conferences, trade shows
6. MBWA
7. analysis of financial statements, litigation involvement, accident incident reports, media publications

can all provide valuable information regarding potential risks. Prudent sport business managers will be expected to know what these risks are and will be required to take appropriate protective measures. "Management by wandering around" (MBWA) represents another common form of risk identification. In fact, liability via the doctrine of respondeat superior provides managers with a powerful incentive to engage in MBWA. MBWA benefits the entity in three primary ways. First, managers' exposure to the front-line operations enables them to understand operational issues and concerns better. Second, employee motivation and job satisfaction can escalate as employees sense a concern and involvement by top management. Third, management is better able to observe risk situations including "normal" risks (e.g., trip and fall hazards) as well as those often not talked about (e.g., sexual harassment; employee embezzlement). Additional ways to identify risk include an analysis of financial statements, litigation involvement, and incident reports.

Risks can be categorized in a number of different ways. One categorization scheme includes facility risks, equipment risks, personnel-related risks, contractual risks, and external environment risks. Types of risks under each category include, but are not limited to, the following.

Facility-Related Risks

- flood
- fire
- wind
- tornado, lightning
- vandalism
- layout and design improprieties
- trip/slip and fall hazards (e.g., debris, ice)
- limited parking
- inaccessible and nonaccommodating to the disabled
- exposed wiring
- faulty lighting
- improper surfaces
- improper storage of chemicals
- inadequate security, supervision
- failure to comply with legislation (e.g., OSHA, Americans with Disabilities Act [ADA], fire codes) and/or industry standards

Equipment-Related Risks

- improper or inadequate maintenance and/or service
- inadequate warnings

- improper layout of equipment
- improper selection of equipment for activity, participant
- improper supervision of equipment while in use
- improper installation

Personnel-Related Risks

- discriminatory personnel practices in violation of established legislation
- sexual harassment
- embezzlement, employee dishonesty
- disability or absence of key managerial employees
- commission of intentional torts
- acts of negligence
- statutory violations (e.g., dram shop laws)

Contract-Related Risks

- failure to use exculpatory clauses
- failure to include cogent clauses in employment contracts (e.g., indemnification, restrictive covenants, errors and omissions)
- unintentional creation of implied contracts
- failure to define assignment rights
- underinclusive contractual provisions (e.g., failure to address provision of security, postevent clean-up responsibilities, practice times)

External Risks

- recessions, depression, inflation
- limited supply
- decreased demand
- federal or state bonding requirements
- unfavorable legislation

As mentioned above, the risks identified are only a sampling of potential exposures. Sport managers need to brainstorm routinely in an attempt to identify and prevent potential risks relative to their particular facility.

APPROACHES TO MANAGING IDENTIFIED RISKS

Each of the above risks can be managed in a way to reduce the likelihood of its occurrence. Four control approaches are (1) transfer, (2) reduction, (3) retention, and (4) elimination/avoidance. These are referred to as risk *management* approaches versus *control* approaches, as it is unlikely that management will be in a position to actually control loss. Rather, the aim is to manage risk and reduce associated losses (van der Smissen, 1990).

Transfer

Transfer represents one of the most common ways managers divert risk and associated losses. This risk management approach shifts the risk and loss, or transfers risk, from the sport business to some other individual or company. There are a variety of ways to employ transfer as an approach to managing risk and loss reduction.

Insurance

Insurance is an almost universal form of risk management employed by sport managers in all industries. As described by Piskorski and Cirignani (1995, p. 8), insurance represents the purchase of "peace of mind at a (relatively) fixed cost." However, there are a few caveats associated with insurance. Insurance is not a "free" transfer of losses. First, insurance comes with a cost. The more risk within a sport business industry, the higher the premium and deductible. The employment of prudent risk management practices, however, can lower insurance premiums and provide more attractive deductibles. Second, insurance provides coverage only to the amount insured. Personal assets may still be accessible by the plaintiff, although the type of business structure chosen can absolve a plaintiff's ability to access personal assets. Further, the transfer of personal assets to a significant other (spouse, child, relative, friend) to defer access to other monies and investments is also worth considering. Third, losses emanating from lawsuits are much more than financial in nature. Even if insurance provides adequate coverage, loss of goodwill and customer loyalty can be devastating.

Independent Contractors

The use of *independent contractors* represents another way to transfer risks. Sport businesses insulate themselves from liability associated with the acts of an independent contractor so long as the sport manager hires the independent contractor in a nonnegligent fashion, performs a reasonable inspection of completed work, and keeps premises reasonably safe (van der Smissen, 1990). However, sport facility managers should ensure that individuals are able to comply with the 20-factor test used by the Internal Revenue Service (IRS) to ascertain independent contractor status. As stated by Christensen (1996), the IRS is "tormenting" industries that use independent contractors. "Between 1988 and 1994 this issue resulted in more than 11,000 audits, 483,000 reclassified workers—and a bill to businesses of $751 million in back taxes and penalties" (Christensen, 1996, p. A14).

Indemnification Clauses

An *indemnification clause* is another form of transfer commonly used in lease agreements. Lessors prefer to include an indemnification clause because it stipulates that the lessee will pay or reimburse the lessor for any damages he or she had to pay.

Exculpatory Agreements

Exculpatory agreements are contracts between the sport business and the patron in which the patron agrees not to sue for the sport business's own acts of negligence. Exculpatory agreements have proven very useful to sport businesses. However, most states provide immunity to the sport business only for acts of ordinary negligence. Exculpatory clauses do not tend to protect the sport business for acts of gross or willful, wanton negligence. On the positive side, exculpatory clauses are very useful when arguing the plaintiff assumed the risk of injury (therefore barring the cause of action) or contributed to his or her own accident or injury (therefore reducing damages via comparative negligence doctrine). As reported by Cotten (1993), there are only three states (Louisiana, Montana, and Virginia) that currently prohibit (via legislation or court precedent) the use of waivers.

Retention

Retention represents another form of risk management employed by most every sport business. The concept of retention is that the firm will absorb, in one way or another, risk and resultant losses. Acquired losses will in turn be paid for via working capital funds or reserve accounts. For example, sport businesses pay insurance deductibles through working capital or reserve accounts. Other sport businesses adopt a total retention plan, or self-insurance, due to necessity or an inability to acquire insurance. An earlier survey conducted by the Sporting Goods Representatives Association in 1976 revealed that 62% of manufacturers and field representatives were not covered by liability insurance (Goldman, 1976). However, total retention, or self-insurance, is not favorable, as deserving plaintiffs go without compensation, while a single lawsuit can force a sport business into bankruptcy (Miller & Fielding, 1995). As mentioned earlier in the chapter, sport business managers should plan to retain approximately 5% of operating expenses for risk management purposes (van der Smissen, 1990).

Reduction

Reduction has been referred to as the heart or pulse of a risk management program (van der Smissen, 1990). The concept of reduction refers to operational practices a sport business can instigate and perform on a proactive, internal basis to reduce potential loss. The operational practices available to reduce risks are

Exhibit 10–2　Risk Reduction Tactics

1. Selection of credentialed employees
2. Frequent in-service training programs, mandates
3. Communication of the risk management plan
4. Knowledge of, and adherence to, applicable legislation and industry standards
5. Documentation, and retention of, the following: lesson plans, emergency plans, evacuation plans, maintenance plans, accident incident reports, security plans, rules and regulations, job descriptions, job analyses, performance evaluations, and policy manuals
6. Content knowledge regarding the documents listed in #5 above
7. Monitoring of advertising
8. Ascertainment that participants have complete knowledge, understanding, and appreciation of the risks associated with any particular sport activity or program
9. Knowledge of the participant, activity, and environment
10. Adoption and implementation of an emergency plan
11. Adoption and implementation of a crisis management plan
12. Proper use of warnings

endless and differ depending on the particular sport business. However, 12 of the more basic modes of reduction include the following (Exhibit 10–2).

Selection of Credentialed Employees

Proper hiring eliminates a great deal of potential liability incurred by the entity as a result of the doctrine of respondeat superior. It is foreseeable that the hiring of noncredentialed employees would result in loss within any one of the five identified categories (i.e., facility, equipment, personnel, contract, external).

Frequent In-Service Training Programs

Any risk management program is only as good as the employees who are responsible for carrying out the plan. Risks can be reduced when employees are educated regarding injury prevention and care. Frequent in-service training programs and/or conferences, risk reduction reminders and tips, recognition for risk reduction efforts, attendance at risk reduction conferences, and the incorporation of risk reduction into the performance appraisal process contribute to a work force cognizant of the importance of risk reduction and related benefits.

Communication of the Risk Management Plan

As explained by van der Smissen (1990, p. 20), "The effectiveness of any risk management program is in direct proportion to the effectiveness of communications, for when communication is nonexistent, incomplete, or inadequate in any way, the program becomes inoperable and the risks, then, are not reduced as they might be." Sport businesses need to establish channels of communication that effectively reach all involved stakeholders. (See Chapter 11 "Crowd Management," for more insights here.)

Knowledge of, and Adherence to, Applicable Legislation and Industry Standards

Employees violating statutes are typically held to be negligent per se, or strictly liable. Further, it is *presumed* that reasonable prudent sport managers know of applicable legislation and industry standards. In *Marietta v. Cliffs Ridge* (1971) the plaintiff was pierced on a 1.5" thick maple sapling pole used as a gate marker on a slalom course. The plaintiff argued that a reasonable, prudent professional would have known that the use of a thinner maple pole or the use of poles constructed of a different material would reduce a skier's potential injury. The Supreme Court of Michigan held that the defendant failed to meet the standard of "reasonable prudence" for a variety of reasons. Evidence, in part, that the court considered was that the defendant subscribed to a variety of different trade magazines that illustrated the use of alternative poles. This information contained in the trade magazines should have alerted the defendant to the safer alternative. Sport business managers should subscribe, as well as read, industry trade magazines to ensure they are cognizant of new or amended legislation and industry standards.

Documentation and Retention of Important Materials, Information, and Forms

Lesson plans, emergency plans, evacuation plans, maintenance plans, accident incident reports, security plans, rules and regulations, job descriptions, performance evaluations, and policy manuals should be documented and retained. Their appropriate and timely documentation and retention become important to any legal defense. (Please note that this list of items is not necessarily all-encompassing, as, in actuality, the preservation of all written documents can be beneficial to a legal defense.) In addition to exposing actual practices and revealing facts, the documents provide evidence that the sport business is operating in a reasonable and prudent manner with the consumer's interests in the forefront.

Adherence to All Important and Relevant Documents

A sport business that adopts rules and regulations, performance appraisal documents, and the like, and then either does not enforce or adhere to them, or enforces and adheres to them intermittently, is no better off than had the documents not been enforced at all.

Monitoring of Advertising

Advertisements must accurately reflect the product being offered. Breach of express warranties, false product representations, assurances of "safety," bait-and-switch tactics, comparable value claims, and comparisons to former prices can all invite legal action (*Hauter v. Zogarts*, 1975; McGuire, 1989; Shepherdson, 1987).

Knowledge, Understanding, and Appreciation of Risks

Ensuring that participants have complete knowledge, understanding, and an appreciation of the risks of any particular activity or program is essential in the defendant-sport business's ability to argue either contributory negligence, comparative negligence, or assumption of risk. Various ways to ensure understanding, knowledge, and appreciation exist through the use of written materials; oral presentations provided by guest speakers, management, or employees; and/or the viewing of videotapes or use of related auxiliary materials.

Knowledge of the Participant, Activity, and Environment

The courts refer to the knowledge of the participant, activity, and environment when ascertaining whether a sport business provided reasonable care. Sport business employees need to know their consumer or end-user. For example, the courts require sport businesses to provide a higher standard of care for the novice participants or players with physical or mental disabilities. Similarly, sport businesses must provide a higher standard of care for football participants versus badminton participants. Regarding the environment, courts will look at things such as the weather, facility layout and design, and/or local crime or violence when ascertaining whether the sport business provided reasonable care. Knowledge of the participant or end-user can be attained via physician release forms, surveys, and observation. Knowledge of the activity can be attained through education, experience, and ongoing training opportunities. Knowledge of the environment can be attained via newspapers, television, trade magazines, and competitors.

Adoption and Implementation of an Emergency Plan

Every facility, from retail facilities to miniature golf courses, needs an emergency plan. It is important to remember that the emergency plan is not synonymous with a risk management plan. Rather, an emergency plan is an integral component of the larger risk management plan. The reader should refer to basic emergency care training offered by the American Red Cross, the American Heart Association, the National Safety Council, and the U.S. Department of Transportation's First Responder Training Program for more information regarding emergency plans.

Emergency plans tend to vary among sport businesses, although commonalities permeate them all. The plan advocated by the ACSM includes that staff be assigned four roles (Sol & Foster, 1992). First, a *first responder* assesses the situation, renders immediate care if necessary, and calls for assistance. Second, the *team leader*, typically a supervisor or member of management, is responsible for directing the general flow of the emergency plan. Third, the *communications staff person* is responsible for contacting appropriate medical service and communicating pertinent information. The communication staff person should include the following information when talking to an emergency assistant on the phone: victim description, exact location of facility, and point of entry. The person should also inquire about the estimated time of arrival. It is important that the communications staff person stay on the line until the emergency assistant hangs up. All too often, the person communicating the emergency is not understood by the receiver of the information. The communications staff person, somewhat in a state of panic, may hang up the phone before all needed information is retrieved. This can be avoided if the communications staff person is trained to remain on the phone until he or she hears the emergency assistant hang up. The fourth person is responsible for *crowd control*. It is the responsibility of this person to clear the area by removing people and equipment to make room for emergency care provisions. There are a number of other practices that are necessary to fulfill emergency responsibilities. Exhibit 10–3 identifies additional practices that need to be a part of every emergency plan.

Adoption and Implementation of a Crisis Management Plan

A crisis management plan is similar to an emergency plan in that it deals with the handling of a potential loss that can threaten the solvency of the sport organization and tends to result in injury to a stakeholder(s). Examples of crises that necessitate the implementation of an established crisis management plan include the following:

- the fatal shooting of five children at a public school
- the gang rape of high school girls at a high school football game
- poison gas emissions at a swimming pool
- a bomb explosion at a professional football game
- the implication that a health club is full of asbestos
- tangible and direct evidence of discrimination by sport business managers.

As evident, any one of these situations could eliminate future patronage. The existence of a crisis management plan can curb the hardships encountered by all stakeholders. Exhibit 10–4 includes components that a sport business manager might consider including in a crisis management plan.

Proper Use of Warnings

Warnings are another integral part of a risk management plan and are effective at reducing risk. As explained by van der Smissen (1990, p.38), "The warning is a

Exhibit 10–3 The Emergency Plan: Supplementary Considerations

1. **Emergency contact numbers are displayed on *all* phones (e.g., emergency medical service [EMS], fire department, police department).** Emergencies tend to coincide with panic. Emergency phone numbers eliminate problems associated with memory lapses.
2. **An abbreviated emergency plan is displayed on all phones with the full emergency plan displayed at a central staff location.** Problems associated with memory failure, as mentioned above, can be eliminated by displaying an abbreviated emergency plan on all phones.
3. **The full emergency plan is detailed in operation manuals and/or policy manuals.** The entire emergency plan should be accessible to all staff for purposes of orientation or review.
4. **Open access exists for all emergency personnel and their vehicles.** In the event of an injury, emergency personnel must be able to access the actual playing field or any other area where injury is foreseeable. Caution should be used when building barriers (e.g., fences) around playing fields to better manage the crowd. Some access via gate or other opening must exist so that emergency vehicles can access the playing field.
5. **First-aid kits and equipment are easily accessible and available.** First-aid kits and related equipment (i.e., backboards) need to be kept in appropriate places. For example, a lifeguard working at a water park will not be able to "reasonably" deliver emergency care when he or she has to run 200 yards to find a backboard that has been locked in the storage closet. Further, emergency kits should be routinely checked and equipment or supplies replaced as needed.
6. **Routine practicing of the emergency plan.** There is a great deal of difference between reading about an emergency plan and actually practicing the plan through simulated exercises. As alluded to earlier, "real life" emergency situations generate anxiety and panic. The practicing of an emergency plan culminates in a better response to the injured. ACSM recommends practicing the plan a minimum of two times per year (Sol & Foster, 1992). This is a minimal recommendation only, as many facilities practice their emergency plan on a weekly basis.
7. **Documentation!** Although mentioned above, documentation cannot be overemphasized. It is important that emergency drills, staff certifications, checking and restocking of medical kits, incident report forms, follow-up procedures, and so forth be documented and retained in accordance with the statute of limitations. For example, in Kentucky, the statute of limitations is 1 year. All evidence of documentation should be retained for a minimum period of 1 year. However, if dealing with children, documentation will need to be retained for a longer time period. If a child is 10, for example, and the majority age is 18 years, documentation will need to be retained for 9 years.
8. **Comply with all OSHA regulations regarding blood-borne pathogens.** OSHA significantly affects the sport industry. The aggressive nature of sport itself, coupled with environmental influences, invites injury. OSHA serves to reduce injuries while making the work environment more risk-free. A knowledge, understanding, appreciation of, and compliance with OSHA can reduce emergency situations and related losses for a sport business.

Exhibit 10–4 A Crisis Management Plan: Supplementary Considerations

1. **Designate one person as the spokesperson or liaison between all media and the entity itself.** This increases information accuracy while reducing the likelihood of conflicting stories being reported, among other things.
2. **Immediately prepare a statement.** If more investigation is needed to ascertain cause, fault, and so forth, simply report known facts. A "no comment" response should always be avoided as it tends to infer guilt. Any statement, even as nebulous as, "We're looking into the situation and will get back with you this afternoon" is better than a "no comment" remark. Stakeholders would benefit, and appreciate, sport managers who regularly issued statements to interested networks as facts develop.
3. **Never go into a news media interview unprepared.** Ensure that you have all the known facts. Anticipate likely questions, and have responses prepared. And, remember, there is no such thing as a statement made "off the record"! As explained by Yarborough (1996, p. 14), "The wrong message during a crisis can inflame and confuse the public, create doubt among employees and lead to negative media coverage."
4. **Stick to your prepared statement.** Do not veer off on a tangent, speculate, or attempt to elaborate regarding uncertainties. This only leads to trouble by callous reporters. Remember, reporters must take what information you give them.
5. **Take your time responding to questions.** You may wish to ask the reporter to repeat the question for two reasons: (1) you have more time to think about your response, and (2) you are able to ensure that you correctly understood the question. "I don't know" is always a good, honest answer.
6. **Respond immediately.** Get the facts immediately and respond. It is better to address the crisis and let the smoke die versus having the people read about the crisis in the newspaper or hear bits and pieces on the television for months on end.
7. **Avoid humor.** Efforts to "lighten" the situation can, and most often do, backfire as stakeholders view you (and the sport business) as uncaring and insensitive.
8. **Record your interview if possible.** This helps to ensure that the interview, or portions of the interview, cannot be used against you or the sport business in litigation. Further, a review of the tape at a later time can be instructive for a sport manager wishing to improve public speaking skills.
9. **Constantly monitor concerns of your stakeholders.** Be concerned about all consumer concerns regardless of how ridiculous they may appear. Customer backlash and loss of established goodwill can be devastating. Employee concerns also are heightened during a crisis. Communication regarding how the crisis affects jobs can alleviate concerns and better bond employees to the particular sport business.
10. **Cultivate the media.** The media can either help you or hurt you. Be available, accessible, respectful, and polite. Media who sense arrogance, difficulty, or callousness may be more harsh than otherwise necessary.

Exhibit 10–5 Warnings: Supplementary Considerations

1. **Warnings must communicate the risk and how the risk can be avoided.** Warnings need to specifically communicate to the observer the associated risk. As explained by van der Smissen (1990, p. 44), "A warning cannot be generalized; it must be specific to the risk or hazard so that the individual can make an informed decision. For example, the oft found sign '. . . at your own risk' has little value as a warning, since the person does not know what the risk is. A sign should indicate the risk, such as 'No diving; shallow water' or 'No trespassing; firearms range' ". As mentioned earlier, the purpose of a warning is to alter behavior. In order to be truly effective, a warning should define or explain how the danger or risk can be avoided. For example, an appropriate warning sign for a storage closet where pool chemicals are stored might read, "DANGER—FLAMMABLE LIQUIDS—NO SMOKING."

2. **Warnings must be understood by those being warned.** Warnings should not include jargon or technical language that would confuse or appear meaningless to the viewer.

3. **Warnings should be posted at what would be the average eye level of the intended viewer.** For example, warnings directed at children or wheelchair users would be posted lower than the 5–7 ft ACSM recommendation for adults (Sol & Foster, 1992). More specifically, Hall (1986) states that the warning should be 15° below or above the average sight line. A common error among sport business managers is to post the sign at the appropriate height, but in a poor location. Warning signs should not be located in places where lingering people or people waiting in line will block visibility.

4. **Warnings should avoid cultural ambiguities.** The warning language should be appropriate for the intended constituency. For example, warnings may need to be in Spanish, English, and/or additional languages in order to fully reach the intended constituency.

5. **Use symbols and photographs when possible.** The use of symbols and photographs is a universal trend. People of all nationalities and educational levels typically comprehend a sign's message when displayed pictorially. Further, pictorial warnings are more likely to be noticed and acknowledged. Warnings with excessive verbiage often go unnoticed.

6. **Warnings should be communicated in a variety of ways.** Signage is a commonly employed mode of warning intended viewers. However, sport businesses should also adopt different types of warnings. As mentioned earlier, assumption of risk and contributory/comparative defenses are only effective if the plaintiff had total knowledge, understanding, and appreciation of the risk(s). Educational research tells us that some individuals learn more effectively through videos, while others learn more effectively through literature or oral dialogue. Consequently, a sport business can build a better defense by employing various modes of warning. Brochures, signage, oral instructional warnings by individual employees, audio warnings over public announcement systems, prerecorded warnings, entry forms, videos, and/or film footage can all be used to effectively communicate a warning.

Exhibit 10–5

7. **Warnings should be posted or communicated at the point of hazard.** Consumers need to be able to view the warning at the site of the particular risk. A common error among pool facility managers is to post, for example, all the facility's warnings on one sign located at the point where the locker room exits into the pool area. Assume that the sign had some warnings regarding the diving board usage. Also assume that the individual enters the pool area and sunbathes for 40 minutes, swims laps, visits the concession stand, visits with friends, *and then decides to go diving.* One can foresee that the patron will likely have forgotten what the sign said. Warnings regarding the diving pool, for example, should be located in the diving area. Similarly, a warning given 6 months ago by a health club manager will not be remembered by the patron when the risk is encountered 6 months later.

8. **Warnings should be brief.** As stated in ACSM's *Health/Fitness Facility Standards and Guidelines* (Sol & Foster, 1992, p. 20), "As a general rule, the length of a line should not exceed 26 characters, including spaces. A single sign should include 16 words or less. No more that 50 percent of any sign face should be occupied by text, including words or numbers." Additionally, according to Hall (1986), warning signs should include no more than 10 words per line.

9. **Warnings should be an appropriate color, shape, and font.** Research has shown color to produce different psychological results. Use of the appropriate color for a sign is important to heeding the attention of the intended viewer. As identified by Hall (1986), "exciters" include the following colors: red, black, orange, and yellow. On the other hand, "relaxers" include the colors blue, green, purple, and white. As stated by Hall (1986, p. 8), "If faced with a case where only relaxers were used in the warning, it will be simple to prove the inadequacy of the warning." Hall (1986, p. 8) goes on to state, "The prudent plaintiff's attorney will use discovery to find out whether a manufacturer has in fact conducted warning label research and marketing research as relating to warnings. The manufacturer is held to the standard of an expert and is charged with constructive knowledge of research as relating to his product."

   The shape of a warning sign has also been viewed as a factor in getting the attention of the intended viewer. Sharp angles are always best at getting an individual's attention. Consequently, rectangles, triangles, squares, and hexagons are viewed as being at least moderately good, whereas circles, ovals, and other unusual shapes are categorized as "poor" (Hall, 1986). The font used on the warning sign directly influences legibility. Fancy or unusual lettering is discouraged. Bold lettering in block font is a good combination.

10. **Warnings should appropriately identify locations and situations that present physical, chemical, environmental, or behavioral hazard(s).** Warnings should be used to designate their presence and related dangers. Rooms, closets, or other designated areas in which chemicals, for example, are stored should be clearly identified with "no public access" signage. Failure to demarcate between public access and non-public access areas can leave a sport business liable when an invitee-patron is injured in a storage or equipment room that was not designed for consumer access or supervised accordingly.

preventive action to gain the assistance of the participants to prevent injuries by being aware of the condition of the equipment, facilities, and areas."

In other words, one primary purpose of a warning is to alter a sport patron's or participant's behavior. There are a number of caveats associated with the use of warnings. Exhibit 10–5 identifies key issues sport business managers should keep in mind when designing and posting warnings. A sport business manager should take warning signage seriously, as warning effectiveness can have a definite impact on the defense presented by the service industry.

EVALUATION AND REVIEW

The risk management plan should be continually reviewed by top management, the risk management liaison, and the risk management committee. Once again, risk exposures should be studied and corrected. New risks continually should be identified and monitored. A number of ways exist in which a sport business can evaluate risk exposure and loss control. Ways to evaluate risks include, but are not limited to, the monitoring of the following:

- the number and type of accident incident reports
- financial statements
- litigation involvement
- public sentiment (positive or negative)
- sales (increase or decrease)
- market share (increase or decrease)
- customer complaints (increase or decrease)
- employee turnover

To summarize, a risk management plan offers a sport business a lower cost structure. A lower cost structure offers protection against price wars and economic uncertainties (e.g., recession, inflation) while simultaneously providing opportunities for higher profit margins. Risk management plans effectively mitigate costs associated with, for example, attorney fees, court costs, poor public relations, insurance costs, and workers' compensation costs. Workers' compensation rates are based on payroll, occupation, and number of past claims. Consequently, a reduction in claims can reduce workers' compensation insurance fees. However, consumer satisfaction represents another decisive reason for the adoption and adherence to a risk management plan.

CHAPTER SUMMARY

Risk management is an encompassing task. It is essential that a sport business manager be familiar with potential risks and how to prevent the occurrence of identified risks. Risk management is a process that involves continuous learning, training, correction, and evaluation. Sport business managers should spend ample time studying this area of risk management, as it directly influences the solvency of the sport business and the safety of the stakeholders and inculcates ethical practices employed by a sport business.

STUDENT ASSIGNMENT

1. Identify a particular sport business and critique its risk management practices.
   a. Elaborate on risks identified by either the sport business entity or yourself via observation and inquiry. Be sure to identify risks within each of the five categories discussed earlier.
   b. Elaborate on ways in which the sport business entity has chosen to transfer risks.
   c. Elaborate on the types of reduction techniques employed by the particular sport business.
2. Elaborate on the following policy-related issues regarding the sport business entity's risk management plan.
   a. Does the entity have a risk management policy statement? If so, include it with your paper.
   b. Does the entity have a risk management liaison? If so, who? What are the degrees or credentials of this person? Does this person have other shared responsibilities?
   c. What type of outsourcing does the sport business engage in to reduce risk?
   d. Does a risk management culture exist within this particular sport business? Elaborate.
   e. How often is the risk management plan reviewed?
3. Critique the signage used in the sport business entity and on its premises. Strengths? Weaknesses?
4. Critique the emergency plan used by the sport business entity. Strengths? Weaknesses?
5. Critique the crisis management plan employed by the sport business. Strengths? Weaknesses? Obtain a copy of maintenance checklists, in-service training documentation, indemnification clauses used in contracts, performance appraisal forms, incident report forms, and so forth used by the particular sport business.
6. Design a risk management plan for a hypothetical sport business. Include information on administrative issues, risk identification, ways to manage the identified risks (i.e., types of reduction tactics, transfer), and evaluation techniques.

REFERENCES

Christensen, J. (1996, June 6). Self-employed under fire by the IRS. *The Wall Street Journal*, p. A14.

Cotten, D.J. (1993). Analysis of state laws governing the validity of sport-related exculpatory agreements. *Journal of Legal Aspects of Sport, 3*(2), 50–63.

Florio, J.J. (1983). Product liability, insurance, and the new federalism. *Journal of Products Law, 2*(1/2), 1–19.

Goldman, G. (1976). Panel probes liability issue at special SGMA session. *Sporting Goods Dealer, 153*(3), 50–52.

Hall, G. (1986). *The failure to warn handbook*. Columbia, MD: Hanrow Press.

Hauter v. Zogarts, 534 P.2d 377 (1975).

Leno v. YMCA, 17 Cal. App. 3d 651, 95 Cal. Rptr. 96 (1971).

Marietta v. Cliffs Ridge, 385 Mich. 364, 189 N.W.2d 208 (1971).

Massie v. Persson, 729 S.W.2d 448 (Ky. App. 1987).

McGuire, C.R. (1989). *The legal environment of business* (2nd ed.). Columbus, OH: Merrill.

McIlvaine, A. (1996). Safety patrol. *Risk & Insurance, 7*(7), 29.

Miller, L.K., & Fielding, L.W. (1995). Product liability reform from the perspective of the sporting goods manufacturer. *Journal of Legal Aspects of Sport, 5*(2), 1–33.

Miller, L.K. (Spring, 1996). Personal communications.

Piskorski, T.J., & Cirignani, W.A. (1995). Managing the risk and liability of wrongful employment practices through insurance. *Employee Relations Law Journal, 21*(2), 7–20.

Priest, G.L. (1987). The current insurance crisis and modern tort law. *The Yale Law Journal, 14*(3), 461–527.

Shepherdson, N. (1987). *Selling and the law: Pricing and discounting*. Wilmette, IL: Callaghan & Company.

Sol, N., & Foster, D. (Eds.). (1992). *ACSM's Health/fitness facility standards and guidelines*. Champaign, IL: Human Kinetics Books.

van der Smissen, B. (1990). *Legal liability and risk management for public and private entities*. Cincinnati, OH: Anderson Publishing Company.

Yarborough, M.H. (1996, February). Responding to a crisis. *HRFocus*, p. 14.

CHAPTER 11

Crowd Management

Crowd management represents a significant area of interest and concern to sport business managers as crime rates continue to escalate and litigation abounds. Litigation is only part of the problem emanating from ineffective crowd management. Crowd management directly influences customer satisfaction and the appeal of the sport itself. Crowd management influences customer loyalty, retention, profit maintenance, and business goodwill. Crowd management is an integral component of a larger risk management program. This chapter, due to the importance of crowd management to successful sport business operations, focuses on this specific aspect of risk management. Reference to past events and related mishaps (below) highlight the importance of prudent crowd management:

- Seven fans were seriously injured and approximately 70 others hurt when thousands of jubilant fans poured onto the football field following Wisconsin's 13–10 victory over Michigan ("Scores Injured," 1994).
- Twenty-five police were sent to the hospital after an altercation occurring in 1982 on the Florida State University football field (Neff, 1985).
- One individual died, 80 others were injured, 41 individuals were arrested, and over $100,000 in damages occurred after the Detroit Tigers won the 1984 World Series (Leo, 1984).
- Thirty-eight people died and another 437 people were injured in 1985 at the European Soccer Cup at Heysel Stadium in Brussels. ("Soccer Disasters," 1985).
- Eight people died and 29 others were injured in the City College stampede in New York on December 28, 1991 (McFadden, 1991).
- Twenty-two people were injured July 11, 1996, when a riot erupted in the ring of Madison Square Garden during a fight between Riddick Bowe and Andrew

Golota. The disruption lasted 35 minutes. There was no security ringside. The crowd of 11,252 was eventually ordered to evacuate the building (McShane, 1996; Schuyler, 1996).

• Eight-four people were killed and hundreds of others were injured prior to a soccer game between Guatemala and Costa Rica at Mateo Flores National Stadium on October 16, 1996. Part of the problem was attributed to the selling of too many tickets (Carrasco, 1996; "Fan Control," 1996).

Additional crowd-related incidents will be addressed throughout the remainder of the chapter. (See also Miller, 1993.)

CROWD MANAGEMENT CONSIDERATIONS

As noted by Maloy (1991), injured plaintiffs frequently place liability on those sport business managers involved with facility management. The design and implementation of sound crowd management policies assist sport businesses in the prevention of accidents and resultant losses. The remainder of this chapter addresses crowd management considerations for sport business managers.

Foreseeability

Foreseeability is a key determinant in ascertaining the liability of sport business managers. The concept of foreseeability asks the prudent professional (i.e., sport business manager) whether a particular episode was plausible or predictable under particular circumstances. As noted by van der Smissen (1990, p. 45): "The reasonable and prudent professional must be able to foresee from the circumstances a danger to the participant, a danger which presents an "unreasonable risk of harm" against which the participant must be protected."

Sport business managers are not absolute insurers of liability. Nor are they liable for intentional torts, such as a physical assault, *unless* there is foreseeability. For example, a plaintiff sued the municipality and school district when physically assaulted at a high school football game (*Gill v. Chicago Park District,* 1980). The Appellate Court of Illinois affirmed the lower court's decision. The court agreed that liability does not exist "unless there are sufficient facts to put defendants on notice that an intervening criminal act is likely to occur" (p. 673). The judgment may have been different, for example, had the school district observed prior violent acts yet failed to take remedial action. As noted by the court in *Leger v. Stockton Unified School District* (1988): "School authorities who know of threats of violence that they believe are well-founded may not refrain from taking reasonable preventive measures simply because violence has yet to occur" (p. 694).

Reference to another case, *Bishop v. Fair Lanes Georgia Bowling, Inc.* (1986), illustrates the concept of liability based on foreseeability. In the *Bishop* case, two plaintiffs were severely beaten in the parking lot of the bowling alley. The plaintiffs alleged that an altercation was foreseeable by the defendant bowling alley employees. The plaintiffs, as explained in the case, had directly informed the bowling alley employees of the heated words being exchanged between the two parties and that the dispute made them "uncomfortable" and "uneasy." The plaintiffs asked the employees to keep an eye on the alleged harassers. The plaintiffs allege that the bowling alley's failure to take action, coupled with the continued sale of beer to already intoxicated patrons, prompted the violent milieu in the parking lot. The U.S. court of appeals (11th Circuit) precluded the bowling alley's request for summary judgment.

Incidentally, parking lots represent a critical area of concern for sport managers. According to a 1994 study conducted by the U.S. Department of Justice, approximately 757,000 violent crimes, including rape, robbery, and assault, occurred in parking lots. Another study conducted by Liability Consultants, Inc., revealed that parking lots "were the most likely place for an attack resulting in a premises liability lawsuit" (Kangas, 1996).

Alcohol Availability

Alcohol availability is a critical issue for all stakeholders, including the sport business manager, the consumer, and the surrounding community members. Many sport business managers favor alcohol sales, as they generate favorable profit margins. Further, alcohol availability is often related to consumer satisfaction and can serve as an attractive product extension desired by many sport consumers. Other sport businesses, on the other hand, have concluded that the risks associated with alcohol consumption outweigh the benefits (Ammon, 1996; Berg, 1993; Oshust, 1992). Regardless, for those sport business managers serving alcohol, state dram shop acts and common law negligence place sport business managers in a perilous position.

Again, foreseeability is a key issue. Facility managers who knew, or who should have known, about an intoxicated individual may be responsible for resultant injuries. For example, an injured plaintiff sued the University of Notre Dame when knocked down by an intoxicated patron (*Bearman v. University of Notre Dame,* 1983). The Court of Appeals said the university was aware that patrons consumed alcohol before and during football games. Consequently, the university had a responsibility to take measures necessary to protect patrons from acts of the intoxicated.

On the other hand, the Georgia Court of Appeals affirmed a lower court decision in *Levangie v. Dunn* (1987). In this case, a 16-year-old suffered a catastrophic injury when knocked down by an intoxicated patron at a sports pavilion. The facility sold no alcohol on the premises. The court said neither the injury nor the intoxicated state of the individual was foreseeable. Similarly, the Michigan Appellate court stated in *Dumka v. Quaderer* (1986) that sport business employees have no responsibility to aid an intoxicated individual who has left the facility.

However, sport business managers distributing alcohol do have a responsibility constantly to monitor consumer behavior and environmental conditions. As noted by the court in *Personal Representative of Starling's Estate v. Fisherman's Pier, Inc.* (1981, p. 1,138), one cannot "simply ignore and step over an unconscious customer lying in a dangerous place upon his premises and he must take some minimal steps to safeguard any customer from extreme danger, even though the customer has allowed himself to be exposed to that danger in the first place."

Miller Brewing Company (1992, pp. 4–5) offers eight suggestions regarding alcohol distribution. It would be prudent for sport business managers to take the following suggestions into consideration:

1. Train all concession vendors, security staff, and volunteers to recognize potential problems.
2. Screen and wristband anyone who wants to drink alcohol.
3. Offer safe-ride-home and designated driver programs.
4. Identify nondrinking, designated drivers and offer free nonalcoholic beverages.
5. Display special signs to encourage responsibility.
6. Impose a two-drink-per-purchase limit and, at gatherings where the beer is free, fill only two cups at a time.
7. End beer sales or service an hour before the event is over.
8. At large events where beer is sold, prevent those attending from bringing their own alcoholic beverages, and institute security measures to ensure safety for all.

The vagueness of dram shop statutes makes the training suggested by Miller Brewing Company imperative. For example, the Kentucky statute states that persons holding liquor licenses will not be liable for the acts or injuries caused by patrons "unless a reasonable person under the same or similar circumstances should know that the person serving is already intoxicated at the time of serving" ("Limitation on Liability," 1988). The subjectiveness with who *should know* makes training essential.

Further, the ejection of an intoxicated fan is not recommended. As explained by Emmets, director of a consulting firm working with fairs and exhibitions, "Now a patron, *known* to be *intoxicated,* is going to get behind a wheel" (Berg, 1993, p. 18). An injured patron can create liability resulting from a sport manager's actual or constructive notice regarding the potentially dangerous situation (*Bishop v. Fair Lanes Georgia Bowling, Inc.,* 1986).

Type of Event Being Hosted

Crowd management measures are influenced by the type of event. For example, Lennon and Hatfield's (1980) study confirmed that greater aggression resulted when watching football versus gymnastics. Prudent sport managers employ a greater degree of security and crowd management at aggressive games like football and ice hockey than at more passive events like gymnastics and golf, *unless,* of course, altercations or related problems are foreseeable. For example, crowd management problems at tennis tournaments tend to be minor. However, venues hosting tennis tournaments had a greater standard of care after the stabbing of Monica Seles.

Surrounding Facilities and Environment

The issue of foreseeability as it relates to the immediate environment remains an important part of crowd management (Carlsen, 1991). Sport businesses located in high crime areas are more susceptible to third-party attacks. As noted by the Colorado Court of Appeals in *Lannon v. Taco Bell* (1985), an investigation into the security measures at surrounding businesses is important in checking the adequacy of an individual business's security measures. Third-party attacks at a sport business are foreseeable when surrounding businesses (both sport and non-sport related) have experienced similar attacks.

Known Rivalry among Opponents

VanderZwaag (1988) notes that intense rivalries may ignite crowd management problems. In addition, violence is foreseeable when businesses operate in districts heightened with racial tensions. Thanksgiving Day games, for example, that compete against long-standing rivals present ample opportunities for violent acts. However, the difficulty in monitoring the intensity of fan enthusiasm was succinctly explained by Mick Walker, Assistant Director of men's athletics at Iowa (Geraghty, 1994, p. A36): "It's a two-edged sword. You want to create as much enthusiasm as you can, but on the other hand, you're telling fans not to get too out of control." Regardless, the liability and social responsibility in providing a risk-free environment remains with the sport business manager.

Effective Communication

Underlying an effective emergency plan is effective communication. Antee and Swinburn (1990) believe communication is integral to effective crowd management. The use of public announcements, walkie talkies, and signage throughout an entire facility (e.g., parking lot to the activity field) enhances efforts to manage a crowd and reduce spectator injury. As explained by Ammon (1996, p. 12), "Each group (facility, medical, security, and law enforcement) must have the ability to discuss immediate problems in a quick and timely fashion." Poor communication among security personnel, ushers, and the facility staff appears to have been grossly inadequate during the Riddick Bowe versus Andrew Golota fight, which resulted in a \$4.5 million lawsuit against the arena ("More Melee," 1996). As indicated in an article appearing in *USA Today,* police were first notified of the melee by a TV viewer who called 911.

Proper Anticipation of Crowd Size and Appropriate Seating Arrangements

Accurately estimating crowd size aids in determining the number of needed security personnel, the flow of traffic, the number of usable entrances and exits, and ticket distribution. Crowding, congestion, and possible stampedes at facility entrances can be mitigated by having a number of entry sites at distances removed from the playing field and stairwells (Antee & Swinburn, 1990; Stalnaker, 1992). The use of turnstiles deters stampedes as patrons are forced to enter one at a time (Stalnaker, 1992). Similarly, an adequate number of exits and exit locations is crucial to effective crowd management.

Festival seating (a.k.a. "first come, first served" seating) should be used with caution. Festival seating often enables overcrowding and/or heightens patron anxiety as individuals aggressively compete for the "best" seats. The general seating policy within the student section of the University of Wisconsin stadium is attributed, in part, to the stampede that occurred in November 1995 (Geraghty, 1995). The probability of a stampede can be minimized via raised fences approximately 6 ft in height, well-grounded fence anchors, and changing levels. Excess publicity and inadequate consideration regarding the venue's size is alleged to have contributed to the City College of New York tragedy in which more than 5,000 people attempted to enter an arena with a seating capacity of 2,730 (McFadden, 1991; Stalnaker, 1992).

A recent trend related to general admission seating is the popularity of the mosh pits. As stated by Paul Wertheimer (owner of Crowd Management Strategies), "Moshing is dangerous, period" (Pogrebin, 1996, p. 2B). On the other hand, mosh pits exist as a result of both artist and fan demand. Facility managers should view the mosh area as it would a gymnastics room. For example, warning signs, use of exculpatory clauses on tickets, and padded barriers should exist in mosh pit areas (Herrick, 1996).

Further, a delayed opening of a particular event compounds the dangers of festival seating. For example, 11 deaths occurred at a rock concert in 1979. The plaintiffs allege the delay in opening the doors to the facility contributed, in part, to the fatalities (*Bowes v. Cincinnati Riverfront Coliseum,* 1983). McDonald (1991) suggests that facility doors open at least 90 minutes before an event's starting time. This enhances the flow of people into the facility and reduces frustration associated with traffic jams and lengthy concessions, tickets, and restroom waiting lines.

Proper Employment and Movement of Ushers and Security Personnel

Facility managers need to employ deputized personnel to handle spectator disputes. Gips (1996), in reference to the security provided at the 80,000-person capacity Georgia Dome, elaborates on the use and different roles associated with contract security, off-duty police, and proprietary officers. Special attention, however, should be given to the use of ushers. Although ushers serve valuable purposes, trouble can multiple when ushers, who have no authority to control disruptive behaviors, become injured or invoke an injury on another spectator or participant (van der Smissen, 1990).

Ushers serve two important roles. First, ushers are a vital link to a facility's communication network. Ushers can spot trouble and relay the necessary information (via walkie talkies or information technology) to appropriate parties. Second, ushers lessen patron frustration and anxiety via helpful directions about seats, restrooms, and concessions.

Sport business managers are encouraged to consider three additional facets when using ushers to assist in facility control. First, the flow of security personnel during a sporting event is important. Security personnel should move in tandem with the movement of the crowd. For example, fewer ushers are needed to patrol the entrance/lobby area as people become seated. Inside security must also be prudently planned. For example, mosh pits, although typically not common to sport events, may be apparent at larger festivals surrounding a larger sport event. In this situation, the placement of security in mosh pits can serve to better manage unruly and dangerous crowd behavior (Samms Rush, 1996).

Second, patrons should be able to identify ushers and other crowd management personnel. For example, ushers clothed in red attire will likely blend in with the crowd when a school's colors are red and white. Consequently, trouble could escalate due to the patron's delay in locating and notifying appropriate personnel. Kangas (1996) suggests that blaze orange is an appropriate color for uniforms as it remains visible regardless of the lighting intensity.

Third, providing ushers with binoculars can further enhance supervisory efforts when lights are dim and rows are lengthy (McDonald, 1991). Immediate recognition of impending or ensuing crowd-related problems provides better opportunity for prevention, or a successful resolution, of the brewing issue. As stated by Gips (1996, p. 38), ushers primarily serve as "extra sets of eyes and ears."

Proper Documentation

As in all litigation, documentation by the defendant remains an essential and valued asset. Facility maintenance, injury reports, ejection of patrons, and evaluation measures serve as important defense tools should subsequent litigation ensue. Sport business managers are advised to retain documentation until the statute of limitation expires. The installation and use of closed-circuit television (CCTV) systems is an effective way to monitor high traffic areas (area surveillance) or specific areas (point surveillance) that involve, for example, cash transactions (e.g., concession stands, ticket areas; Kangas, 1996).

Adequate Signage

Signage serves a variety of purposes, including to warn, to instruct, to inform, and to direct. These are all vital to effective crowd management. Readers should again refer to the earlier section on warnings at this time, as they are of paramount importance to sport business managers. However, benefits associated with instructional, informational, and directional signage are often overlooked. Instructional, informational, and directional signage is a way to reduce customer frustration and anxiety. As explained by Sheard (1995, p. 6), "It is the unknown which leads to anxiety in a crowd and can lead to panic." Proper signage can alleviate the "unknown" and prepare patrons for changes, for example, "in lightness and darkness, or in the width of a corridor . . ." (Sheard, 1995, p. 6). Traffic-flow signage reduces customer frustration and problems associated with congestion. Decreased congestion is important to sport business managers. As revealed by John Hof's research (Jensen, 1995), 45% of surveyed respondents indicated that crowded areas influence their decision whether or not to pursue sport-related opportunities. Similarly, knowledge regarding the location of restrooms, concessions, security, first aid, and so forth enhances customer satisfaction with the overall product. As explained by Sheard (1995, p. 6), traffic patterns should result in a "series of simple 'yes' or 'no' options." Complex decisions or confusing traffic patterns should be avoided. Sport business managers should capitalize on the benefits associated with signage. Usage inside the place of business as well as in the parking lot and on major thoroughfares enhances overall customer satisfaction. As stated by Miller, Fielding, and Pitts (1993, p. 6), "Patrons who are frustrated at various points within the service cycle (i.e., the sporting event) are more likely to become disenchanted and problematic fans."

An Evacuation Plan

An additional element of the broader risk management plan is a sport business facility's evacuation plan. Natural disasters, terrorist actions, storms, bombings, and other extenuating circumstances (e.g., collapse of an arena's roof), coupled with the severe consequences of these activities, highlight the importance of evacuation plans. Sport businesses that are able to respond in a calm, professional manner are more likely to calm customer anxieties (Antee & Swinburn, 1990). Similar to the risk management plan, the evacuation plan needs to be practiced on a routine basis. The following guidelines facilitate the successful execution of an evacuation plan (Ammon, 1996; Berlonghi, 1995):

- Anticipate potential disasters.
- Routinely practice the evacuation plan.
- Have an established chain of communication.
- Position personnel on ramps, escalators, aisles, and exits.
- Prohibit reentry of the disaster site except by qualified personnel (e.g., police officers, fire squads).
- Gather necessary information and be prepared to communicate with media and the authorities.
- Ensure that doors are open and obstructions removed.
- Have a plan of assistance established for the disabled.
- Have parking personnel and law enforcement officials assist in controlling exiting traffic.
- Ensure that emergency vehicles and crew have access to the facility at all times (post this information by all phones).
- Engage in appropriate documentation measures before, during, and after the event.

Proper Facility Layout and Design

Proper facility layout and design are essential to crowd management. Managers can make their own job easier by providing clear paths of travel, eliminating congestion, and using proper signage. Areas (e.g., chemical storage rooms, equipment storage areas, administrative offices) inaccessible to the consumer should be clearly marked with signage, and doors should always remain locked. Ample space should be allowed for spectator viewing. As mentioned earlier, congestion ignites uneasiness and frustration.

Precautions should also be taken when landscaping the outside of a particular sport facility. Bushes, trees, and statues, for example, provide convenient hiding places for those planning a surprise attack on an innocent victim. In addition, bushes, trees, and statues can serve as convenient climbing devices that can be used, again, to surprise passersby or to provide access to second- or third-floor entrances. To summarize, accidents and injuries are foreseeable when sport managers fail to design properly the internal and external components of a particular facility.

CHAPTER SUMMARY

Crowd management is another critical component contributing to the success of the sport business entity. Crowd management enhances customer satisfaction while reducing potential loss and litigation. Even in times of declining revenues, crowd management should continue to receive the utmost attention from sport business managers. (Exhibit 11–1 provides crowd management suggestions.) Although crowd management should be centrally controlled and directed to a degree, it should also be made the responsibility of every employee.

Exhibit 11–1 Crowd Management Suggestions

1. Consider the type of event and the participants involved.
2. Develop an intimate knowledge of the surrounding neighborhood.
3. Develop and implement a comprehensive emergency and evacuation plan.
4. Ensure that the event is equipped with a planned communication system.
5. Use signage (warnings, informational, instructional, and directional) appropriately.
6. Adequately maintain facility premises.
7. Avoid festival seating if possible.
8. Anticipate and plan for the expected crowd size.
9. Be sure the number of usable entrances and exits is appropriate for the crowd.
10. Reduce the congestion at points of entry.
11. Open facility doors at least 90 minutes prior to the event's starting time.
12. Ensure that emergency medical personnel have access to the facility, the crowd, and the playing field.
13. Employ deputized personnel to handle disputes.
14. Employ ushers to enhance communication and customer satisfaction.
15. Ensure that ushers are identifiable and that their attire does not "blend in with the crowd."
16. Ensure that security personnel move in tandem with the flow of the crowd.
17. Train servers of alcohol, employ appropriate alcohol-related signage, and monitor consumption.
18. Develop a comprehensive risk management plan.
19. Conduct a comprehensive analysis at the conclusion of every event.
20. Know whether your state has granted citizens, via legislation, the right to carry concealed weapons.

Source: This table is reprinted with permission from the *JOPERD, Journal of Physical Education, Recreation & Dance,* February, 1993, p. 32. *JOPERD* is a publication of the American Alliance for Health, Physical Education, Recreation and Dance, 1900 Association Drive, Reston, VA 22091-1599.

STUDENT ASSIGNMENT

1. Identify a sport business entity and critique its crowd management plan. Include all documents or materials used in your response or obtained from the sport business entity.
2. Specific questions asked of the sport business manager could address the following:
   a. inquiry regarding alcohol policies, availability, monitoring, employee training
   b. use of ushers, security, community resources
   c. communication efforts, linkages
   d. crowd management plan alterations contingent upon type of event
   e. use and availability of an evacuation plan
   f. types of documentation performed
3. Specific observations could include the following:
   a. proper and adequate use of signage
   b. imminent dangers based on observation and/or foreseeability

REFERENCES

Ammon, R.E., Jr. (1996). Facility control and security. In M.L. Walker, & D. Stotlar (Eds.), *Sport facility management.* Boston, MA: Jones and Bartlett.

Antee, A., & Swinburn, J. (1990). Crowd management: An issue of safety, security, and liability. *Public Management, 72*(1), 16–19.

Bearman v. University of Notre Dame, 453 N.E.2d 1196 (Ind. App. 3 Dist. 1983).

Berg, R. (1993, August). Safe suds. *Athletic Business,* p. 18.

Berlonghi, A. (1995, July/September). Managing a disaster. *Crowd Management,* pp. 15–17, 27–30.

Bishop v. Fair Lanes Georgia Bowling, Inc., 803 F.2d 1548 (11th Cir. 1986).

Bowes v. Cincinnati Riverfront Coliseum, 465 N.E.2d 904 (Ohio App. 1983).

Carlsen, C.J. (1991). Violence in professional sports. In G.A. Uberstine (Ed.), *Law of professional and amateur sports.* New York: Clark Boardman Callaghan.

Carrasco, S. (1996, October 17). Stampede at stadium kills 75. *The Wichita Eagle,* pp. 1A, 4A.

Dumka v. Quaderer, 390 N.W.2d 200 (Mich. App. 1986).

"Fan control." (1996, October 25). *USA Today,* p. 3C.

Geraghty, M. (1995, November 23). Protecting fans: Two tragic incidents push colleges to control spectators at football games. *USA Today,* p. A35–A36.

Gips, M.A. (1996, August). Security plays well at Georgia Dome. *Security Management,* pp. 35–42.

Gill v. Chicago Park District, 407 N.E.2d 671 (Ill. App. 1980).

Herrick, J. (1996, April/June). Planning security for concerts (and mosh pits). *Crowd Management, 2*(4), 15–18.

Jensen, C.R. (1995). *Outdoor recreation in America* (5th ed.). Champaign, IL: Human Kinetics.

Kangas, S.E. (1996, July). The fundamentals of parking lot protection. *Security Management,* pp. 44–50.

Lannon v. Taco Bell, 708 P.2d 1370 (Colo. App. 1985).

Leger v. Stockton Unified School District, 249 Cal. Rptr. 689 (Cal. App. 3 Dist. 1988).

Lennon, J.X., & Hatfield, F.C. (1980). The effects of crowding and observation of athletic events on spectator tendency toward aggressive behavior. *Journal of Sport Behavior, 3*(2), 61–68.

Leo, J. (1984, October). Take me out to the brawl game. *Sports Illustrated,* p. 87.

Levangie v. Dunn, 356 S.E.2d 88 (Ga. App. 1987).

Limitation on Liability of Licensed Sellers or Servers of Intoxicating Beverages: Liability of Intoxicated Person, KY § 413.241 (1988).

Maloy, B.P. (1991). Planning for effective risk management: A guide for stadium and arena management. *Marquette Sports Law Journal, 2*(1), 89–101.

McDonald, M. (1991, Fall). *Crowd control.* Guest lecture by a KY appellate judge, University of Louisville, Louisville, KY.

McFadden, R.D. (1991, December 30). Stampede at a game featuring rap stars called avoidable. *New York Times,* p. 1.

McShane, L. (1996, July 13). Garden riot blamed on Bowe entourage. *The Wichita Eagle,* p. 5C.

Miller Brewing Company. (1992). *Good times: A guide to responsible event planning.* Milwaukee, WI: The Miller Brewing Company.

Miller, L.K. (1993). Crowd control. *JOPERD, 64*(2), 31–32, 64–65.

Miller, L.K., Fielding, L.W., & Pitts, B.G. (1993). Prudent crowd control management: Suggestions for the facility manager. *The Journal of Sport/Fitness Risk Management, 3*(2), 3–6.

More melee aftermath. (1996, July 18). *USA Today,* p. B1.

Neff, C. (1985, June). Can it happen in the US? *Sports Illustrated,* p. 87.

Oshust, J. (1992, November). Security focus shifts: More "preparedness." *Agent & Manager,* pp. 24–26.

Personal Representative of Starling's Estate v. Fisherman's Pier, Inc., 401 S.2d 1136 (Fla. App. 1981).

Pogrebin, R. (1996, May 14). Moshing can be crippling . . . . even deadly. *The Wichita Eagle,* p. 2B.

Samms Rush, D. (1996, May 14). Coliseum, cotillion take precautions. *The Wichita Eagle,* p. 2B.

Schuyler, E. Jr. (1996, July 12). Riot erupts after Bowe-Golota fight. *The Wichita Eagle,* p. C1.

Scores injured in Wisconsin victory celebration (1994, November 31). *The Louisville Courier-Journal.*

Sheard, R. (1995, October/December). Architectural influences in crowd management in the U.K. *Crowd Management,* pp. 4–7, 26–28.

Soccer disasters. (1985, May 30). *San Francisco Chronicle,* p. 18.

Stalnaker, M. (1992, November). Security concerns at campus venues: Disaster & emergency risk control. *Agent & Manager,* p. 27.

van der Smissen, B. (1990). Legal liability and risk management for public and private entities. Cincinnati, OH: Anderson Publishing Company.

VanderZwaag, H.J. (1988). Policy development in sport management. Indianapolis, IN: Benchmark Press.

CHAPTER 12

Customer Service

Customer service represents an oftentimes trite, overused, and cliched concept to sport business managers. Unlike other managerial "quick fixes" and buzzwords that evolved in the 1980s and 1990s (e.g., *flex-time, empowerment, focus groups, just-in-time management, quality circles*), the concept of customer service is nothing new. It is a widely accepted marketing principle that managerial efforts should focus on the consumer as product demand is market driven. However, much to the surprise of many, the ability to incorporate *good* customer service into a sport business product is as difficult as effectively and efficiently maintaining any other business functional area (e.g., human resource management, budgeting, risk management). The first part of this chapter discusses the benefits a sport business manager can accrue from superior customer service delivery. The second part of the chapter presents ways in which a sport business can enhance existing customer service provisions.

BENEFITS ASSOCIATED WITH SUPERIOR CUSTOMER SERVICE

Increases Customer Retention While Reducing Costs

The literature is replete with articles and books citing the impact superior customer service has on customer retention rates. Superior customer service enhances customer retention while molding a loyal and satisfied customer base. High customer retention benefits a sport business via a lower cost structure. High customer turnover, for example, increases expenses incurred via necessary promotions, credit searches, and new account setups that a sport business must incur. Superior customer service also can reduce costs associated with the handling of grievances, irate customers, duplicated services, and sport product "freebies" provided in an effort to pacify the upset customer. For example, Wright, Duray, and Goodale

(1992) refer to the estimated $210 million a year that Merrill Lynch & Company incurred as a result of service-related errors. As stated by Mariani (1993), it costs a business six times as much money to recruit a new customer than to keep a current customer. Specifically, it costs approximately $118.00 to recruit a new customer, whereas it costs only $19.76 to retain a customer (Morgan, 1989). The approximate $100 savings per customer retained enables a sport business to gain competitive advantages as needed capital is available for expansion, product improvement, and so forth.

Decreases Switching Costs

Superior customer service decreases the propensity or temptation for an existing customer to switch service providers. For example, the literature states that 68% of all customers switch service providers because of discontentment with the way they were treated (Mariani, 1993). A Forum Corporation survey reinforces the importance of quality service to the customer constituency. As reported by this survey, 40% of survey respondents switched service providers due to poor service (Sonnenberg, 1989). Keaveny's research (1995) revealed that negative service encounter failures (i.e., interactions between employees and customers) represented the second largest reason given by customer-respondents for switching to another service provider. Service encounter failures causing discontentment included the following:

- uncaring employees
- employees ignoring the customer
- employees paying attention to people other than customers (e.g., boyfriends or girlfriends who stopped by to visit)
- rushed employees
- unfriendly employees
- lack of interest or care displayed toward the customer
- unresponsive, inflexible, and uncommunicative employees
- employees refusing to return phone calls
- uncommunicative, uninformed employees
- rude, condescending, and impatient or ill-tempered employees
- employees inexperienced, unfamiliar with the latest technology
- employees lacking confidence

The above behaviors encourage customers to switch sport service providers. However, a promising element associated with this realization is that sport business managers who incorporate the suggestions discussed later in this chapter (such as prudent hiring, routine employee training, and the incorporation of a service culture into the sport business environment) can decrease the switching costs while reducing customer dissatisfaction.

Reduces Negativity Associated with Word-of-Mouth Advertising

Word-of-mouth advertising has a powerful impact on the demand for a particular sport product. Negative word-of-mouth advertising can devastate a sport business and significantly dilute investments made in past, present, or future sport product promotions. Gerson's article in *Fitness Management* (1992b) stated the following,

- One dissatisfied customer will tell up to 10 friends about the problem.
- Of all dissatisfied customers, 13% will tell 20 people.

Similar to Gerson's article, Mariani (1993) states that one dissatisfied customer will tell a minimum of 11 others about the problem, and those 11 will each tell 5 others. Consequently, one dissatisfied customer can equate to a bad advertisement heard by 67 other people (1 + 11 + 55; Morgan, 1989). To compound the problem, employers and employees may not always hear about customer complaints and/or concerns. Gerson (1992b) states that the majority of customers do not complain. Rather, they take their business to a competitor. Mariani (1993) estimates that 96% of all patrons do not complain. "This means that for every complaint the average business receives, there are 24 silent unhappy customers" (Mariani, 1993, p. 52). These unhappy customers, in turn, represent sources of negative word-of-mouth advertising. Further, Gulbronson (1992/1993, p. 28) states that, "Psychologically speaking it takes 15 positive experiences to overcome one negative one." Superior customer service lessens the verbal negativity associated with a particular sport product.

Customer service is also important to the sport business manager operating as a monopoly or oligopoly in his or her particular sport industry segment. For example, a sport business manager who owns the only golf course in town may not perceive customer service to be of importance. However, as described by Jones and Sasser (1995), the patrons who frequent a particular golf course represent a "false" loyalty. Prior research indicates that one in four customers would switch service providers if provided a reasonable alternative (Zemke & Schaaf, 1989). In other words, these customers who receive little, if any, customer service will likely defect to a competitor if, in the future, these customers are presented with a substitute, accessible course. The substitutability of the sport product magnifies the concerns associated with false loyalty.

Represents a Source of Differentiation

As mentioned above, customer service is an often-overlooked function of a sport business's value chain. Rather, sport business managers focus efforts on the core sport product itself (i.e., the game, the equipment offered by a particular health club). Unfortunately, the sport product can be rather homogeneous in many sport industry segments (e.g., health clubs, bowling alleys, gymnastic studios). A sport business that strives to provide superior customer service can differentiate itself from other competing and substitutable sport products. In addition, customer service can further differentiate an otherwise differentiated product. Customer service can also be incorporated into the value chain of the low-cost producer. After all, smiling and delivering friendly and courteous service are seemingly no-cost activities that can add value to even the most frugally operated low-cost operations.

Increases Profitability

Customer service increases customer retention and repeat purchases while contributing to a reduced cost structure, improved word-of-mouth advertising, and sport product differentiation. As explained by Keaveney (1995, p. 71), "Continuing customers increase their spending at an increasing rate, purchase a full-margin rather than discount prices, and create operating efficiencies for service firms." Research concludes that consumers are willing to pay for quality service (Buzzell & Gale, 1987). For example, Sonnenberg (1989, p. 54) reports that companies excelling in service provisions "can charge close to 10 percent more than those rated poorly."

WAYS IN WHICH A SPORT BUSINESS CAN ENHANCE EXISTING CUSTOMER SERVICE PROVISIONS

A list of 28 customer service suggestions is shown in Exhibit 12–1. Each suggestion is discussed here.

Ensure that Top Management is Committed to the Delivery of Superior Customer Service

The delivery of superior customer service can only be accomplished with the total support of top management (Parasuraman, Zeithaml, & Berry, 1985). As defined by Albrecht (cited in Shilbury, 1994, p. 29), service management needs to represent "A total organizational approach that makes quality of service, as perceived by the customer, the number one driving force for the operation of the business." Top management support can be demonstrated by incorporating or adopting the suggestions identified throughout this chapter.

Establish a Mission Statement that Incorporates the Issue of Customer Service and Customer Satisfaction

As mentioned in an earlier chapter, the mission statement provides numerous benefits to stakeholders. A mission statement that incorporates the element of

Exhibit 12–1 Customer Service: A Summary of Suggestions

1. Ensure that top management is committed to the delivery of superior customer service.
2. Establish a mission statement that incorporates the issue of customer service and customer satisfaction.
3. Establish objectives that coincide with customer service expectations.
4. Recognize and reward customer service efforts.
5. Monitor customer service.
6. Establish a customer grievance system.
7. Listen intently to the complaining customer.
8. Attempt to isolate a highly agitated customer.
9. Apologize to the complaining customer.
10. Become familiar with current customers and what they perceive to be important service provisions.
11. Communicate customer service efforts to the patron.
12. Target the "right" customers.
13. Consider the use of sport product guarantees.
14. Engage in prudent employee selection.
15. Educate and train employees on the importance of customer service.
16. Speak to customers, smile, and call them by name.
17. Encourage employees to make extratransactional encounters on a routine basis.
18. Empower "front-line" personnel to take necessary action (within limits) in order to provide customer service.
19. Strive to maintain a loyal work force.
20. Ensure that employees wear professional attire.
21. Use technology and capitalize on its abilities to facilitate superior service delivery.
22. Deliver reliable service.
23. Avoid promising services that cannot be fulfilled.
24. Design the layout of the sport business in a "user-friendly" manner.
25. Familiarize yourself with the "moments of truth" within your sport business.
26. Encourage customers to visit your facilities.
27. Maintain an ambient environment.
28. Attempt to industrialize the sport service product when possible.

customer service highlights its importance to employees, customers, and other stakeholders.

Establish Objectives that Coincide with Customer Service Expectations

Also mentioned in an earlier chapter, objectives provide many benefits. In the context of customer service, objectives can provide guidance to employees regarding customer service expectations. As explained by Berry, Zeithaml, and Parasuraman (1990, p. 30), failure to establish service-related objectives "drains the credibility from management rhetoric about the importance of service." For example, assume that customers expect to have an employee answer a phone in a timely fashion when calling a sport business. Addressing this issue in the strategic objectives facilitates the ability of the sport business to impart the seriousness of this issue to the employee. Policy manuals, job descriptions, job analyses, and performance evaluation tools would be other appropriate places for the objectives pertaining to customer service to be addressed.

Recognize and Reward Customer Service Efforts

Customer service recognition and rewards reinforce the importance and commitment of customer service to the sport business. As explained by Zemke and Schaaf (1989) in reference to a report by the National Science Foundation in the late 1970s, "Of all the factors that help to create highly motivated and highly satisfied workers, the principal one . . . appears to be that effective performance be recognized and rewarded in whatever terms are meaningful to the individual—financial, psychological, or both" (p. 72). Similarly, as explained by Berry and colleagues (1990, p. 30), "Service standards unconnected to the performance measurement, appraisal, and reward systems . . . render the standards "toothless" while conveying management's low priority for service." Profit-sharing, prepaid trips to exciting locales, additional paid days off, and financial bonuses based on customer retention represent types of financial rewards and recognition. Psychological rewards and recognition could include new job titles, attractive jackets or other attire, lapel pins, a larger office, new office furniture, award ceremonies, plaque distributions, and the like.

Monitor Customer Service

The delivery of customer service must be monitored. Customer service can be monitored in a variety of ways. *Management by walking around* (MBWA) benefits the sport business manager's ability to monitor customer service in three ways. First, MBWA provides opportunities for a sport business manager to observe first-hand the type of encounters customers experience and their related reactions. Customer service and related satisfaction levels can be further detected via facial expressions and voice tone. Second, MBWA enables sport business managers to monitor front-line employees' ability to deliver customer satisfaction. Sport business managers then have an opportunity to address problematic situations via training or intervention before they escalate into major grievances. Third, MBWA allows the sport business manager to serve as a visible role model for other employees. For example, a sport business manager who routinely practices customer service tactics conveys a message to stakeholders regarding the importance of customer service. A manager's actions are important, as others emulate a boss's behaviors.

Establish a Customer Grievance System

Many sport business managers attribute bad headaches and untimely interruptions to the complaining customer. However, in actuality, the complaining customer represents a vital asset to the sport business manager. The Japanese refer to customer complaints as "golden nuggets" because they provide a sport business manager with an opportunity to improve current operations (Schmid, 1993). Further, they provide an opportunity for the sport business manager to address concerns internally. Unaddressed concerns often tend to become magnified; the unpleasantness of the situation becomes embellished, and the number of people exposed to the verbiage increases.

Sport business managers should make it easy for the customer to complain. Suggestion boxes, customer service telephone numbers, routine surveys, and accessible and available staff, for example, are only four of many ways that customers can express concerns. Critical to an effective grievance system is responsiveness and the commitment by the sport business manager to act quickly (Berry et al., 1990). As stated by Gerson (1992b, p. 26), "Asking for opinions and then not following up on them is worse than not asking customers for input at all." Schmid (1993) suggests a 24-hour response time. A rapid response time and an explanation regarding how the sport business plans to address or correct the problem often provide customer contentment and enhance customer loyalty. Further, a rapid response and a detailed and logical plan of action curtail the negative effects associated with embellished stories and bad publicity associated with numerous disparaging conversations.

Listen Intently to the Complaining Customer

Often, customers choose to complain in person. Listen intently as the consumer communicates the related concern(s). Wandering eyes, for example, communicate disinterest to an already agitated customer. Attempts to interject humor or "lighten" the situation tend to escalate a consumer's anger. A sport business manager should also take brief notes as the customer talks (or immediately thereafter). It is all too easy to listen to a customer complain and then get sidetracked on another issue the minute the customer walks away. Consequently, the customer complaint is never addressed. Further, when listening to a complaining customer, it is important that the sport business manager listen without interrupting or attempting to defend the customer's unsatisfactory experience. As Dale Carnegie explains, "The only way to get the best of an argument is to avoid it" (cited in Morgan, 1989, p. 15). Oftentimes, it matters little what management says as a particular individual is merely wanting to "let off steam." Regardless of whether a complaint is observed, delivered orally, or written, Gulbronson's (1992/1993, p. 30) advice is relevant: "Treat the customer like they did you a favor, because they have."

Attempt To Isolate a Highly Agitated Customer

Irritated customers wishing to discuss complaints are best dealt with in an isolated environment. Isolation benefits the sport business manager as the facts and issues can be more easily identified. Further, isolation curtails the temptation of the customer to "cause a scene" or "put on a show." Remember, the major goal of the sport business manager is to identify the problem, address the problem, and transform an agitated customer into a satisfied customer.

Apologize to the Complaining Customer

Sport business managers should apologize to the agitated consumer (Lowndes, 1996). Apologies, however, do not necessarily equate with a sport business manager admitting fault. For example, assume a customer is complaining about a treadmill that is out of order or temporarily not operative. It would be inappropriate for the health club manager to say, "Yes, I apologize for the equipment malfunction, and you are right, we do a poor job of maintaining our equipment." Rather, a more appropriate response would be, "I'm sorry for the inconvenience this has caused you. We will have the treadmill serviced and operative within the next 48 hours." Person-to-person oral communication, a sport business newsletter, and signage are three ways in which a sport business can communicate apologies as necessary.

Become Familiar with Current Customers and What They Perceive To Be Important Service Provisions

A sport business manager should become familiar with the service customers expect to receive. Research concludes that the customer's perception of service quality is determined, in part, by whether the sport business provider (for example) was able to meet the customer's expectations (Wright et al., 1992). A sport business manager may have great intentions regarding customer service, yet if he or she is not aware of what is important to the customer (i.e., customer expectations), then efforts in this area will be futile. In other words, sport business managers need to determine if customers expect, for example, a wide assortment of foods from which to choose, extended hours, a variety of aquatic-related activities, personal trainers, friendly and informative parking attendants, an interactive environment, fax machine availability, or provided soap and other sundries. Once the service expectations are determined, sport business managers should strive to meet those expectations. As explained by Barber (1992, p. 59),

> The problem with customer service is that the moment you think you have figured out the perceptions of your customers, they are apt to change their opinions, attitudes, values or beliefs. If only they would tell you in advance that they are getting tired of the relationship that you have worked so hard to establish, or what it is you can do to make them happy and keep service as your driving force.

The use of focus groups, customer surveys, and observation are three ways a sport business could ascertain a consumer's expected service provisions. Secondary data (e.g., trade journals, existing research) provide additional information to sport business managers attempting to become familiar with the consumer. A variety of customer service instruments exist, including SERVQUAL (Parasuraman, Zeithaml, & Berry, 1988), QUESC (Kim & Kim, 1995), SERVPERF (Cronin & Taylor, 1992), and the Attribute Matrix developed by Albrecht and Bradford (1990). Dominant tenents of most instruments include the identification of what is perceived as important and the measurement of how the customer perceives the service is being delivered.

Communicate Customer Service Efforts to the Patron

Communicating customer service efforts to the customer can better solidify the investment a sport business manager devotes to customer service. As explained by Parasuraman and colleagues (1985, p. 46), "Consumers who are aware that a firm is taking concrete steps to serve their best interests are likely *to perceive* a delivered service in a more favorable way." Similarly, a sport business unable to provide expected services should provide an explanation to the customer. Newsletters, oral dialogue, and signage are effective ways of communicating the sport business's commitment to short- and long-term customer service efforts.

Target the "Right" Customers

Regardless of the totality or extensiveness of the customer service provided, not all customers can be satisfied. The literature recognizes that certain target markets are not worth servicing (Jones & Sasser, 1995; Reichheld, 1993, 1996). As explained by Jones and Sasser (1995, p. 90), "The company that retains difficult-to-serve, chronically unhappy customers is making an expensive long-term mistake. Such customers will continually utilize a disproportionate amount of the company's resources, will hurt the morale of frontline employees, and will dispar-age the company to other potential customers." Similarly, as explained by Reich-held (1993, p. 66), "For various reasons, some customers don't ever stay loyal to one company, no matter what value they receive." The objective of the sport busi-ness manager is to avoid these customers and concentrate instead on customers whose loyalty can be cultivated. In other words, a sport business manager should focus on retaining customers who value the service provided, "spend more money, pay their bills more promptly, require less service, and seem to prefer stable, long-term relationships . . ." (Reichheld, 1996, p. 61).

Consider the Use of Sport Product Guarantees

Many businesses (e.g., L.L. Bean, Xerox, Federal Express, A.T. Cross) *guaran-tee* that a customer will receive "complete" satisfaction from the purchase of a par-ticular product (Kotler, 1994). Guarantees may vary, but typical guarantees enable the consumer to receive a full refund, product exchange, or additional service of-ferings (temporary and permanent). For example, a sport business could offer a money-back guarantee if the patron is not satisfied with a particular sport program or product offering (e.g., tennis clinic, yoga class). In addition, a sport business could guarantee that dissatisfied patrons will receive a related program or activity free of charge. Guarantees tend to be highly effective for new sport businesses wishing to enter a competitive market (Kotler, 1994).

Engage in Prudent Employee Selection

Not every employee is meant to work in a front-line service position. In the sport service sector, the ability to interact and communicate with people is as important as the technical competence possessed regarding the particular sport product. Berry and colleagues (1990) estimate that the ability to secure good workers will only get worse as the labor market tightens and the quality of part-time employees diminishes. Both Kevin Padrnos, a branch manager of a YMCA in Kansas, and Paul Risley, General Manager of Sports World (Wichita, Kansas), echo this con-cern (Padrnos, 1996; Risley, 1996). In separate conversations, both sport business managers stated that they attempted, first and foremost, to hire individuals with "personality." According to both Padrnos and Risley, the rest of the skills and knowledge can be learned via training.

Sport business managers should hire individuals who are experienced and de-sire to work closely with the customer. The use of multiple interviews, "structured interview guides, tests (both performance and paper-and-pencil), successful can-didate profiles, and training in interviewing skills" can better ensure that a sport business hires the most qualified individual for the particular sport position (Zemke & Schaaf, 1989, p. 60).

Educate and Train Employees on the Importance of Customer Service

The delivery of customer service is a critical responsibility of all employees, but especially front-line employees. Often, the delivery of poor customer service is not intentional but delivered due to ignorance or a lack of awareness on the part of the employee. Training should include customer interaction tips as well as a thorough understanding of the sport product. Customer interaction tips should include the needs of different consumer segments. For example, it is often difficult without education for a 17-year-old to understand the service needs of a 65-year-old. Employees' knowledge regarding the sport product is also essential to the delivery of optimal customer service (Zemke & Schaaf, 1989). For example, customer dissatisfaction can be heightened when employees respond with "I don't know," or "That is not my area or job responsibility." Video programs and role-playing incidents, for example, can be valuable educational tools. Further, verbal and nonverbal (e.g., body language, sighing in disgust, ignoring the customer) service behaviors should be discussed. Sport business managers can remind employees of their commitment to customer service via signage, electronic mail communications, verbiage printed on business cards and paychecks, and customer service evaluation standards routinely measured through the use of performance appraisals (Berry et al., 1990).

Speak to Customers, Smile, and Call Them by Name

As stated by Kotler (1994, p. 470), "Service providers must deliver '*high touch*' as well as 'high tech'" service. This is a simple, cost-effective measure to enhance customer service while reducing potential loss. The customer's impressions begin to develop the minute the customer walks through the door and encounters the first employee. Employees of sport businesses who are silent or fail to acknowledge an individual appear lazy and indifferent. The customer's immediate impression is negative. On the other hand, a friendly greeting or a simple "hello" can generate a more positive exchange. The power of a smile should never be underestimated (Gulbronson, 1992/1993). Employees should also strive to learn the names of individual customers and routinely address customers by name (Lowndes, 1996). This attention, albeit minor, can go a long way to enhance customer satisfaction. Remember, as mentioned at the beginning of the chapter, 68% of customers defect because an employee(s) was "rude, indifferent, or discourteous" (Mariani, 1993, p. 52). Further, the friendly environment created by employees who smile and call individual patrons by their names can enhance *employee* longevity and contentment while reducing costs associated with turnover, hostility, poor morale, and the like.

Encourage Employees To Make Extratransactional Encounters on a Routine Basis

Martin (1990, p. 15) suggests that employees "plan at least one extratransactional encounter with as many customers as possible." As defined by Martin (1990), an *extratransactional encounter* goes beyond the typical and expected service encounters. For example, employees at a bowling alley are expected to retrieve shoes, assign lanes, provide score sheets, and take money. The "extra" transaction occurs when, for example, an employee strolls over to a lane and asks the customers if everything is going okay or when the bowling alley attendant makes a simple "good game" comment when a patron returns his or her shoes.

Empower Front-Line Personnel To Take Necessary Action (Within Limits) in Order to Provide Customer Service

Front-line personnel refers to those personnel who interact directly with the customer. For example, the retail salesperson, the person working the front desk at a health club, and the person taking tickets at a ballgame all represent front-line employees. The empowerment of the front-line personnel to act on behalf of the customer as demanded by a particular situation is critical to ensuring prompt and efficient customer service (Carlzon, 1987). Further, employee empowerment directly influences a sport business's ability to retain quality employees. As explained by Berry and colleagues (1990, p. 33), "It does little good to recruit capable, service-minded people only to frustrate them into leaving."

For example, assume that a health club adopts a policy prohibiting the use of the sport business's phones. The policy was adopted after the club noticed patrons socializing on the line for lengthy durations during peak hours. As defined by the new policy, employees are told to have patrons wishing to make a call use the installed pay phone. Now assume a loyal patron, unfamiliar with the new policy, needs to make a phone call during the nonpeak time to check on a meeting time scheduled later in the day. Also assume that the woman did not bring her purse into the club, and she consequently has no money. She requests to make a phone call and is refused. She becomes highly agitated as she needs to know when the meeting is so she will be on time. She asks again. Again, she is refused. Should the health club employee have allowed the patron to make a brief 2- to 3-min local call? Yes, as in this situation, a lack of flexibility and strict adherence to the rules can generate a negative interaction that was easily avoidable. Gerson (1992a, p. 22) provides a similar analysis:

> If you sign up a new member and your release policy is 72 hours, and the person comes back on the fourth day and wants to cancel the membership, what should your staff person do? If you have trained them to go beyond customer service, they will immediately refund the money, and then give the person a two-week free pass to work out at the club. This way, they have both met and exceeded the expectations of the customer by returning the money and offering a free trial membership.

Negative interactions serve to reduce any existing switching costs and dilute overall customer satisfaction with the particular sport product.

Strive to Maintain a Loyal Work Force

A loyal work force is better able to deliver superior service. For example, assume a health club employee has worked with a particular customer for 10 years. This employee is familiar with the patron's fitness objectives, needs, and desires. The employee knows the sport business intimately as a result of the longevity of employment and is able to address quickly and accurately patron needs and concerns. As explained by Reichheld (1993, p. 68),

> The longer employees stay with the company, the more familiar they become with the business, the more they learn, and the more valuable they can be. Those employees who deal directly with customers day after day have a powerful effect on customer loyalty. . . . It is with employees that the customer builds a bond of trust and expectations, and when those people leave, the bond is broken.

A loyal work force, however, requires the sport business manager to be cognizant of the needs of the employee, often referred to as the *internal* customer. Employee empowerment, equitable treatment, established grievance systems, clearly defined and reasonable objectives, and a healthy work environment all contribute to the maintenance of a loyal work force.

Ensure that Employees Wear Professional Attire

Research by Bitner (1992) reports on the first impressions customers or potential customers make regarding a particular service establishment. According to Bitner (1992), the dress and professionalism of the employees contribute to the perceived quality of a particular organization. Morgan (1989) reports on a study that found that 55% of our first impressions are developed from visual cues. Professional attire "formalizes," to some degree, the work environment while communicating neatness and order (Lowndes, 1996). Professional or uniformed attire reminds young, part-time employees that they are not on the job to socialize or solidify weekend plans. Rather, they are there to serve the customer in accordance with the mission statement of the sport business. Shilbury (1994, pp. 32–33) quotes an excerpt from Solomon's work in 1986: "Like brand packaging, it is proposed that service apparel (for example uniforms) performs several vital functions for service delivery. Apparel affects the determination of how service quality is assessed, it implies consistency of service and it differentiates the service provider from its competitors." As summarized by Shilbury (1994, p. 33), "They look smart, and their work looks smart."

Use Technology and Capitalize on Its Abilities To Facilitate Superior Service Delivery

Technology can facilitate a sport business's ability to delivery quality (Zeithaml, Parasuraman, & Berry, 1990). For example, computer software programs can facilitate easy check-in procedures and limit lengthy lines and cumbersome questioning. Similarly, software programs can be used to facilitate ticket distribution practices for professional sports and other large sport and recreational events. Waiting in lengthy lines during inclimate weather during inopportune times is viewed as a costly inconvenience to many sport patrons. Computer-aided design and computer-aided manufacturing capabilities also enhance customer service via the ability to design optimal sport facility layout plans and bring to market in an efficient manner desired sport products.

Deliver Reliable Service

Berry and colleagues (1990, p. 29) identify five dominant areas that customers use to judge the quality of a business's service provisions:

1. Tangibles. The appearance of physical facilities, equipment, personnel, and communication materials.
2. Reliability. The ability to perform the promised service dependably and accurately.
3. Responsiveness. The willingness to help customers and to provide prompt service.
4. Assurance. The knowledge and courtesy of employees and their ability to convey trust and confidence.

5. Empathy. The provision of caring, individualized attention to customers.

Of the above five, studies indicate that reliability is the most important to the customer's perception of service quality. Since sport service products (i.e., the core
product) often tend to be unpredictable due to factors like weather, player injuries,
or opponent quality, it is important that sport business managers focus on providing consistent and reliable product extensions. In other words, assume a sport business manager is attempting to provide a reliable product to the sport consumer.
This sport business manager could ensure that the half-time show consistently reflects the sport organization's emphasis on family entertainment. Restrooms
should always be clean, parking lots should consistently be well lit, and the concession food should always be tasty and served at the appropriate temperature (i.e.,
not too hot or too cold).

Avoid Promising Services that Cannot Be Fulfilled

The sport business manager should use caution and avoid promising the consumer more service than what the organization is willing or able to deliver.
"Promising more than can be delivered will raise initial expectations but lower perceptions of (service) quality when the promises are not fulfilled" (Parasuraman
et al., 1985, p. 45). As explained by Sonnenberg (1989, p. 56), "Whether you make
statements to make your customers feel good about you for the moment, exagger-
ate to win business, or promise something that you can't deliver because it requires
assistance from another colleague or because you are the eternal optimist, you may
be the hero today, but you'll be a heel tomorrow." Sport business managers would
be prudent to use care when designing advertisements and other promotional materials. In addition, employees should be cautioned regarding the statements made
to current or potential customers. To summarize, a sport business should not make
promises (via personnel or promotional materials) that cannot be fulfilled.

Design the Layout of the Sport Business in a "User-friendly" Manner

As concluded by Berry and associates' research (1990), the "tangible" or physical environment significantly influences customer perceptions of quality service
provisions. Convenient and logical paths of travel facilitate the user-friendliness
and functionality of a health club, for example. A patron entering a health club
should be able to check in at the front desk (located in the front of the building's
entrance), drop off a child at the child-care room, and enter the locker room without traveling in multidirections throughout the entire club. Similarly, pro shops and
snack bars often are best placed in the front of a facility. The use of hallways and

intersections should be minimized. Signage should clearly instruct patrons regarding locations of restrooms and activity areas. Equipment should be properly placed to mitigate injury or risk while facilitating ease of use. The same type of analogy can be applied to all other sport industry segments. Input from competent and experienced sport professionals, trade journals, professional organizations, and competition can facilitate prudent sport facility layout.

Familiarize Yourself with the "Moments of Truth" Within Your Sport Business

A "moment of truth" refers to every interaction a potential or current patron has with both the core product and related product extensions (Carlzon, 1987). Sport business managers can enhance customer service by thoroughly dissecting every moment of truth to ensure that the transaction is being handled in the most efficient and effective manner. The use of a flowchart facilitates a sport business manager's ability to educate, identify, display, and communicate the moments of truth to stakeholders (e.g., employees, independent parking attendants, concessionaires; Figures 12–1 and 12–2). For example, the average patron attending a baseball game would typically encounter the following moments of truth: purchasing a ticket, parking, using the restrooms, attending the concessions, finding the seat, watching the game, and leaving the game. In other words, a customer inquiring about screened-in seating areas should be dealt with in a pleasant, patient, and thorough (yet concise) manner. Similarly, the parking experience should be as easy as possible with friendly parking attendants available for assistance and the incidence of traffic congestion reduced as much as possible. Customers should be able to give their ticket to a ticket taker and, again, receive accurate directional instructions in a friendly manner. Signage to the restrooms should be visible. The restrooms themselves should be clean. The food selection should be appropriate. Hot dogs should be hot, and soda pop should be cold. Ushers should be available to assist a patron looking for a particular seat. The game itself should be competitive and exciting to view. Patrons, upon completion of the event, should encounter a smooth experience when exiting the facility. Again, ushers should be available, signage should be visible, crowd management plans should be enforced, and steps should be taken to minimize parking and traffic congestion. Customer satisfaction with the particular sport product, and the likelihood of customer retention, represents an accumulation of these moment-of-truth outcomes. Patrons who become frustrated at various points within their consumption of the sport product are likely to become disenchanted consumers. As stated by Lowndes (1996, p. 22), "One uncaring, unkempt or rude employee can overshadow an otherwise well-run facility

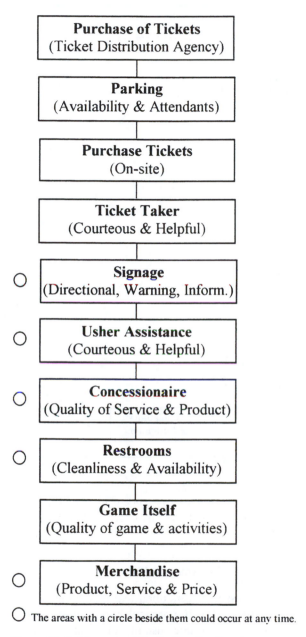

Figure 12–1 Moments of Truth: Sporting Event

Figure 12–2 Moments of Truth: Health Club

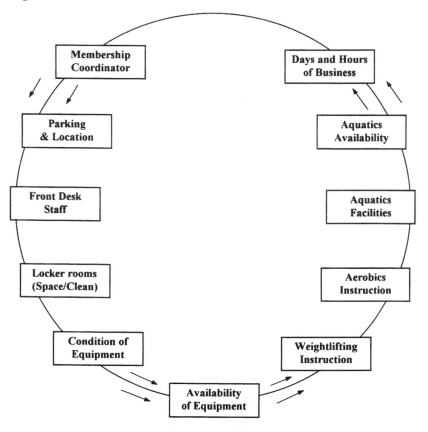

or program." The more positive the experience is in its totality, the more likely the sport business will be able to retain the customer and gain benefits associated with good customer service.

Encourage Customers to Visit Your Facilities

Although sport business managers often fear that the use of sales promotions will dilute the perceived quality of a particular sport product, they remain effective means of encouraging first-time customers to visit a sport business. A sport business confident of the value offered by its sport product should view sales promotions as an opportunity or an inducement that will get potential members through the door. Once in the door, the quality of the sport product provided and the superior customer service delivered will retain customers.

Maintain an Ambient Environment

Bitner's research (1992, p. 66) indicates that *ambient conditions,* including "temperature, lighting, noise, music, and scent" influence customer responses, service perceptions, and satisfaction. Sport business managers can enhance service perceptions via the "comfortable" maintenance of the above ambient characters.

Attempt To Industrialize the Sport Service Product When Possible

As mentioned above, many of the problems in the service industry emanate as a result of the employee. Employees are expected to be happy, smile, remain positive, display an optimistic attitude, and make superb decisions every minute they are "on the clock." Unfortunately, this is an impossible feat for any employee to achieve. Levitt (1986) suggests that the service encounter be industrialized, or mechanized, as much as possible to reduce the potential for human error associated with employee decision making. Although somewhat contradictory to the employee empowerment suggestion discussed earlier, Levitt's argument has merit. For example, computerized registers that automatically figure accumulated purchase fees reduce error and customer aggravation associated with overcharges. Similarly, timed cooking devices reduce the propensity that a concessions employee working a professional sporting event will serve customers food that is burned or undercooked. Employees' knowledge regarding specific and precalculated traffic patterns, pricing structures, emergency plans, and so forth can better provide consistent and reliable service.

CHAPTER SUMMARY

Research has shown that customer loyalty is strongest when customers are *completely* satisfied. *Complete* customer satisfaction requires sport business managers to employ superior and extensive customer service. As explained by Jones and Sasser (1995, p. 89), "There is a tremendous difference between the loyalty of merely satisfied and completely satisfied customers. . . . To put it another way, any drop from total satisfaction results in a major drop in loyalty." For example, as explained by Jones and Sasser (1995, p. 93) in reference to a study of retailing bank depositors, "completely satisfied customers were nearly 42% more likely to be loyal than merely satisfied customers." Jones and Sasser (1995, p. 99) conclude their article with a quote from Horst Schulze, president and chief executive officer (CEO) of the Ritz-Carlton Hotel Company, "Unless you have 100% customer satisfaction—and I don't mean that they are just satisfied, I mean that they are excited about what you are doing—you have to improve. . . . And if you have 100% customer satisfaction, you have to make sure that you listen just in case they change . . . so you can change with them."

A sport business that continually delivers superior service realizes numerous benefits that translate into an increased market share and higher profitability. Barber (1992, p. 10) succinctly summarizes the issue in an article in *The Journal of Park and Recreation Administration,*

> Every year hundreds of billions of dollars are spent on marketing and advertising. Yet if a customer is treated with apathy and indifference, if our recreation personnel are rude, inattentive or discourteous, and if our products don't live up to our advertising claims, then all the money in the world won't persuade these unhappy customers to return. Worst of all, dissatisfied customers talk.

Poor service quality provides opportunities for new competitors and reduces switching costs. The most successful sport business managers strive to attain superior customer service and a completely satisfied customer.

STUDENT AS.SIGNMENT

Visit a sport business and become intimately familiar with the service provisions. Apply the 28 ways to improve the delivery of customer service listed in this chapter to the particular sport business. Elaborate on each of the 28 ways individually as applied to the particular sport business (i.e., strengths, weaknesses, what you would do differently and why).

REFERENCES

Albrecht, K., & Bradford, L.J. (1990). *The service advantage: How to identify and fulfill customer needs.* Homewood, IL: Dow Jones-Irwin.

Barber, E.H. (1992, April). More than lip service. *Athletic Business,* pp. 59–62.

Barber, E.H. (1992). Customer service: The competitive edge. *Journal of Park and Recreation Administration, 7*(4), 10–20.

Berry, L.L., Zeithaml, V.A., & Parasuraman, A. (1990, Summer). Five imperatives for improving service quality. *Sloan Management Review,* pp. 29–38.

Bitner, M.J. (1992, April). Servicescapes: The impact of physical surroundings on customers and employees. *Journal of Marketing, 56,* 57–71.

Buzzell, R.D., & Gale, B.T. (1987). *The PIMS principles: Linking strategy to performance.* New York: The Free Press.

Carlzon, J. (1987). *Moments of truth.* New York: HarperCollins Publishers.

Cronin, J.J. Jr., & Taylor, S.A. (1992). Measuring service quality: A reexamination and extension. *Journal of Marketing, 56,* 55–68.

Gerson, R.F. (1992a, April). People plus service equal profits. *Fitness Management,* pp. 22–23.

Gerson, R.F. (1992b, June). Service excellence secures profitability. *Fitness Management,* pp. 25–26.

Gulbronson, C. (1992/1993). Customer service in the fitness center. *Employee Services Management, 35*(10), 28–30.

Jones, T.O., and Sasser, W.E. (1995). Why satisfied customers defect. *Harvard Business Review, 73*(6), 88–99.

Keaveney, S.M. (1995, April). Customer switching behavior in service industries. An exploratory study. *Journal of Marketing, 59,* 71–82.

Kim, D., & Kim, S.Y. (1995). QUESC: An instrument for assessing the service quality of sport centers in Korea. *Journal of Sport Management, 9*(2), 208–220.

Kotler, P. (1994). *Marketing management.* Englewood Cliffs, NJ: Prentice Hall.

Levitt, T. (1986). *The marketing imagination.* New York: The Free Press.

Lowndes, E.L. (1996, October). Rude awakenings: Don't let an employee's negative image cut into your facility's success. *Athletic Business,* p. 22.

Mariani, B. (1993, Fall). The importance of customer service. *The Professional Skier,* pp. 51–52.

Martin, C.L. (1990). The employee/customer interface: An empirical investigation of employee behaviors and customer perceptions. *Journal of Sport Management, 4*(1), 1–20.

Morgan, R.L. (1989). *Calming upset customers.* Los Altos, CA: Crisp Publications, Inc.

Padrnos, K. (1996, October 4). Branch director, East YMCA, as guest presenter in a sport management class, Wichita State University, Wichita, KS.

Parasuraman, A., Zeithaml, V.A., & Berry, L.L. (1985). A conceptual model of service quality and its implications for future research. *Journal of Marketing, 49,* 41–50.

Parasuraman, A., Zeithaml, V.A., & Berry, L.L. (1988). SERVQUAL: A multiple-item scale for measuring consumer perceptions of service quality. *Journal of Retailing, 64*(1), 12–41.

Reichheld, F.F. (1993). Loyalty-based management. *Harvard Business Review, 71*(2), 64–73.

Reichheld, F.F. (1996). Learning from customer defections. *Harvard Business Review, 74*(2), 56–69.

Risley, P. (1996, October 30). General manager, Sports World, as guest presenter in a sport management class, Wichita State University, Wichita, KS.

Schmid, S. (1993, August). Little things make the difference. *Athletic Business,* pp. 22–23.

Shilbury, D. (1994). Delivering quality service in professional sport. *Sport Marketing Quarterly, III*(1), 29–35.

Sonnenberg, F.K. (1989, September/October). Service quality: Forethought, not afterthought. *The Journal of Business Strategy,* pp. 54–57.

Wright, B.A., Duray, N., & Goodale, T.L. (1992). Assessing perceptions of recreation center service quality: An application of recent advancements in service quality research. *Journal of Park and Recreation Administration, 10*(3), 33–47.

Zeithaml, V.L., Parasuraman, A., & Berry, L.L. (1990). *Delivering quality service: Balancing customer perceptions and expectations.* New York: The Free Press.

Zemke, R., & Schaaf, D. (1989). *The service edge.* New York: Penguin Books.

Index

A000017236041